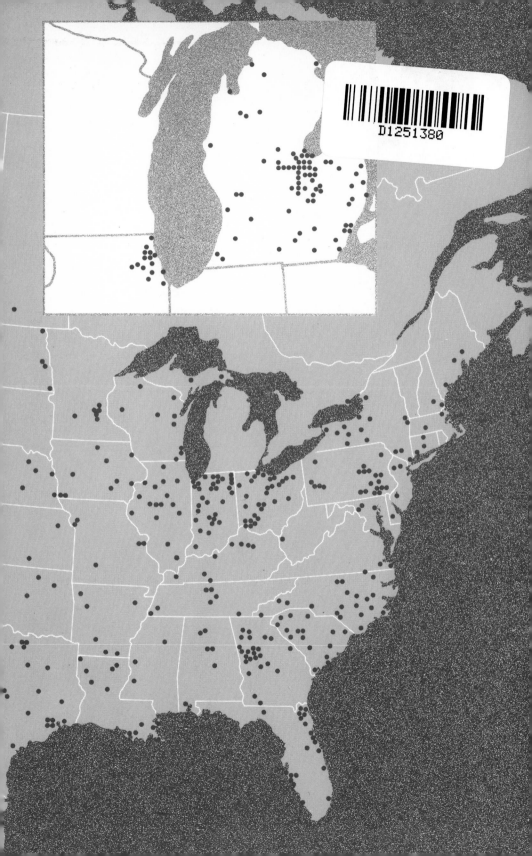

THE
WIDE
WORLD
OF
WICKES

DANIEL M. FITZ-GERALD, 1910–1975

He fashioned the Wickes Corporation out of three small companies, made it grow into a billion-dollar giant. At the height of his triumph, he was felled by cancer.

THE
WIDE
WORLD
OF
WICKES

An Unusual Story of an Unusual Growth Company

GEORGE BUSH

McGRAW-HILL BOOK COMPANY

New York   St. Louis   San Francisco   Auckland
Bogotá   Düsseldorf   Johannesburg   London
Madrid   Mexico   Montreal   New Delhi
Panama   Paris   São Paulo   Singapore
Sydney   Tokyo   Toronto

Library of Congress Cataloging in Publication Data

Bush, George, date.
  The wide world of Wickes.

  Includes index.
  1. Wickes Corporation.   2. Conglomerate corporations—United States.   I.   Title.
HD2756.U5B86   338.8′3′0973 ·   76-21799
ISBN 0-07-009279-6

1234567890   HDBP   785432109876

*The editors for this book were W. Hodson Mogan and Gretlyn Blau,
the designer was Naomi Auerbach, and the production supervisor
was Teresa F. Leaden. It was set in Electra
by University Graphics, Inc.*

Printed by Halliday Lithograph Corporation and bound by The Book Press.

For Ruth, who gave me the language to work with.

Contents

Preface

S oon after this manuscript went into production at McGraw-Hill, two seed bean companies in Idaho, M. J. Bean and Hunter Bean, were merged into The Wickes Corporation. In terms of investment, that double acquisition was no big deal by Wickes standards, but it marked yet another step in the corporation's program to stimulate the growing of beans for Wickes Agriculture to process and market around the world. The event certainly deserved coverage in the section dealing with the corporation's agricultural commodity operations; however, that part of the book already was in page proofs, and it was too late to make changes in the appropriate chapters. I did manage to include the seed bean acquisition in the final chapter, which attempts to project the future of Wickes, but other, no less significant developments have since taken place and didn't get into the book.

That's what happens when one reports on history in progress: working against the lead time inherent in book publishing, one can't be completely up to date. This is particularly true when the subject is a fast-moving organization like Wickes. Even the set-backs this corporation suffered in 1974/1975 did not make it flinch. True, it rid itself of some losing operations, but even so, in the face of adversity and gloomy economic forecasts, it continued to expand, essentially applying the same principle followed by astute investors: to buy when everybody else is dumping.

Not only in the complexity of its functions does Wickes change from day to day. The roles assigned to the corporation's executives are equally fluid. As this preface is written, some of the titles and responsibilities cited in the text are already obsolete. Moreover, in the continuing in-house game of musical chairs, an occasional player may find himself without a perch altogether, or reject the one that's offered. So don't be surprised at changes in the cast. A Wickes job is no sinecure. This statement is not intended as a criticism; in a society that accepts incompetence and honors mediocrity, it's indeed refreshing to find an organization that insists on excellence.

I don't mean to imply, here or in the text, that everybody who left Wickes—whether by voluntary or involuntary resignation—necessarily performed below par. Especially in the corporate infighting of the corporation's formative years, any number of good men found themselves in untenable positions, and had no choice but to call it quits. I am thinking particularly of Richard Wolohan, one of the key figures in the initial development of Wickes Lumber, who, I can only surmise, was squeezed out of the picture in a power play that Machiavelli might well have admired. There is no question about Wolohan's personal competence: he has since established a successful, although more geographically limited building-supplies supermarket chain of his own. Al Riedel, the crusty octogenarian ex-boss of Michigan Bean, was another early player who evidently did not reap all he was promised. He left Wickes as a rich man, but with undeniable dents in his pride; still, he shed tears at the recent death of Dan Fitz-Gerald, who had been the driving force behind The Wickes Corporation's phenomenal growth and, as such, the arch-bane of Riedel's life: in old age, the loss of one's pet adversary is no easier to bear than that of a beloved brother. Well, there's some soiled linen tucked away in every closet, and it's the chronicler's job to hang it out, discretely perhaps, but without laundering it first.

Much credit is due the Wickes leadership for understanding that a corporate history, if it is to have any meaning, can't be a puff job. Above all, I am indebted to the late Daniel M. Fitz-Gerald, who served as chairman of the board of Wickes until shortly before his death. A couple of years earlier, as a member of the board of Consumers Power Company, he had read my book about that excellent Michigan public utility, and he asked me if I would be interested in doing the Wickes story. I jumped at the chance, but set one condition: that I must have the same free access to corporate closets as any of his senior officers. To have my research restricted to dusty scrapbooks, musty minutes, best-foot-forward interviews, and publicity releases, as is often the case with such projects—that just wouldn't do. Dan agreed immediately, and from that moment on every office door and filing cabinet at Wickes was mine to open as I pleased.

E. L. McNeely, then president of the corporation and now its chairman, proved no less understanding. Perhaps he remembered one of the aborted ambitions of his youth: to become a journalist. He issued instructions to all officers and staff to be completely candid with me. So far as I can tell, most of them were.

Trying to unravel Wickes turned out to be an even more fascinating experience than I had hoped. My only sorrow is that Dan Fitz-Gerald did not live long enough to read the finished script. Soon after I started my research in late 1973, he was found to be suffering from a cancer to which he succumbed in July 1975. In the early months of his illness—in St. Joseph's Hospital in Houston, Texas, and resting at home in Saginaw, Michigan, and at his winter apartment in Boca Raton, Florida—he read chapters as they came out of my typewriter, and he caught a number of mistakes. He chuckled over the portrait I sketched of him as a lazy, rather unreliable young man, and did not bridle when he saw that I called him "ruthless" in the pursuit of his goals. He merely nodded, and said he now regretted much that he had done. But he never so much as implied that I should modify the copy. He was too big a man for that.

Like Fitz-Gerald and McNeely, the new president of Wickes, John V. Drum, then executive vice president, never tried to influence my approach. Peter W. Willox, the vice president of corporate communications, undoubtedly had occasional reservations, but being an old pro he swallowed them; he did not push his point of view. To all these gentlemen, my gratitude for their highly unusual objectivity, their patience, and their unstinting help.

And lots of help it took. Wickes is a very complex organization that engages in a wide variety of specialized activities. That's why a considerable portion of this book is devoted to annotations: the story of a diversified enterprise like Wickes must serve audiences of equally diversified orientation. The main text is intended to be of use to all who would learn about Wickes, whether they be motivated by a specific interest in the company itself or by a general curiosity about how a $12 million business can grow into a billion-dollar giant in less than 25 years. But there is much more to the Wickes story than can be told in such relatively general terms. For example, Wickes has been engaged in the mining and processing of graphite since the 1890s. Details of that operation may interest specialists in mining and metallurgy, but probably not people involved in the manufacture and retailing of furniture, which also are Wickes activities. Nor is it to be expected that someone concerned with the wholesaling or retailing of lumber and building supplies, or with the manufacture of wood products, would be greatly inclined to plow through a detailed history of Michigan's country elevators—yet that, too, is an important part of the Wickes past. Hence, the "Notes and Comments" section in the back of the book.

The fine gentleman who took it upon himself to introduce me to the workings of Wickes was Smith Bolton, ex-president of United States Graphite (one of the three original Wickes companies), who later served as the corporation's vice president of operations, i.e., chief trouble shooter. Smith, long since retired, devoted many hours to giving me the perspective on the company I had to have in order to approach my task with a sense of direction. He talked to me for hours on end, and didn't mind explaining things over and over again. He dug up old records (including some interesting papers written by Saginaw historian Ralph Stroebel, and U.S. Graphite's own Joe Edmiston), established contacts for me with Wickes people past and present, and remained in touch with me throughout, offering good advice whenever I encountered difficulties.

Smith Bolton's expert briefings covered but the first batch of nearly fifteen dozen ninety-minute tapes I ran through my Sonys. Interviews lasted anywhere from one to five hours. Often several sessions—particularly with McNeely and Drum—were necessary before I had everything straight enough to be able to shape the material.

I want to express my gratitude to all Wickes executives and staffers who so willingly gave of their time, and then didn't seem to mind my calling them back repeatedly for amplifications. I won't bother to cite their titles here; you'll find those in the text. I'll simply list everybody alphabetically: Dick Ainslie, John W. Ball, Bill Boyle, Lee Clancy, R. E. T. "Dick" Clark, Tom Cline, Don Clothier, Dick Cotton, Bob Dodge, Ed Edelstein, Jon Fish, Dick Fruechtenicht, Gene Gordon, Les Hagen, John Hekman, T. J. Hedrick, Paul Hylbert, Les Irwin, Bob Jacobs, Roland Jacobson, Clark Johnson, Harold Joiner, Don Kaufman, Tom Kennedy, Hyman Lee, Ray Mawson, Art Nasso, Roland Pretzer, Dave Primuth, Clem Putz, Ray Roeser, Tom Rulison, Tony Swies, Bob Theilen, George Valentine, Bob Welsh, Ron Woods, and Ralph Zemanek. Also still with Wickes and most cooperative at the time I did my interviewing were Ray Amberger, who has since retired, as well as Mike Absher, Leigh R. Bench, Wes Gormley, George O'Dair, Mario Randazzo, Darrell Robinson and Paul Tatz, who later resigned.

My thanks also to Art Kirchheimer, general counsel of The

Wickes Corporation, who read the script for legal implications, and finally decided (with a free-and-easy grin not at all typical of lawyers during working hours) that nothing in it compromised the interests of the company or libeled any of the *personae*.

Among my most valuable sources of such potentially tender material were former Wickes employees and others who had been associated with the corporation, its predecessor companies, and its acquisitions over the years, and I thank them all for their cooperation and often delightful companionship.

I fondly remember my first session with the aforementioned Al Riedel of Michigan Bean. A Saginaw snow storm forced me to keep him waiting, which he didn't like, this, combined with his resentments of The Wickes Corporation, didn't make for the smoothest of beginnings. But after some time Al warmed to the subject, told me many great stories, and we parted friends a few hours later. Then there was Theo van Bergeijk, the dapper industrialist son of the late Cornelis "Corky" van Bergeijk who had been instrumental in establishing Wickes as a factor in the international bean market. Theo picked me up at Amsterdam's Schiphol Airport early one morning, and drove me to his aging father's splendid villa in eastern Holland. Here I was plied with information, cookies, Dutch gin, and quantities of Amstel Export beer until Corky was too tired to continue. Theo and I then rounded out the day dining at an exquisite country restaurant and later watching the TV broadcast of that celebrated (in Holland, that is) 1974 soccer game in which the Netherlands beat Germany.

No less enjoyable was my visit to Wickes' Mexican graphite mine with Jack Splane, its former superintendent and now a prominent international mining consultant. Ralph Zemanek and Ray Amberger, of Wickes Engineered Materials, eventually joined us at our destination, and I taped everybody's interviews as we lounged on the steps of the visitors' adobe which overlooks the Moradillas Mine from a Sonora Desert hillside. After the sun had set and the scorpions emerged from their nightly hunt, we were guests at the hacienda of Pedro Adolfo Aguirre, the manager of the Moradillas and grandson of the first Aguirre who had helped the gringos from Saginaw develop the graphite claim. Pedro Adolfo's charming wife, Norma, served us the best Mexican meal I ever ate. The next morning, squatting in the ruins of the small fort that had been built to protect the original mine against raids by Indians and roving bandits, Pedro Adolfo's father, Pedro Aguirre, told about the exciting days of his boyhood, with Jack Splane translating the more complicated passages. Later, in Tucson, I learned yet more about graphite from Victor H. Verity, a mining engineer turned attorney who had rejuvenated the Wickes operation in Mexico after it had gone to seed in the 1930s.

Then, for a change of pace and subject matter, up in Columbus, Nebraska, Walt Behlen, the remarkable founder of Behlen Manufacturing, regaled me with tales of the early days of stressed-skin steel building construction. Walt and his brothers, Gib and Mike, hosted me at the unusual Holiday Inn they'd put up in their home town: the motel's vast interior court—covered of course by a Behlen roof—houses an indoor "lawn" area with swimming pool, and a pleasant alfresco-type restaurant, which incidentally serves great steaks.

My thanks also to John Ritzenthaler, founder of Ritz-Craft, who still serves as a director of The Wickes Corporation; to John McCullough, the retired Lybrand's partner who acted as a guardian of sorts to the unruly young Dan Fitz-Gerald, and without whose good offices (see text) The Wickes Corporation may never have been born; to Art Pufford, former Wickes vice president and now controller of American Forest Products in San Francisco; to Mel Zahnow, director of The Wickes Foundation; George Kelch, another Wickes alumnus, who is now a management consultant; Robert Wolohan, one of the two Wolohan brothers involved in the first Wickes acquisition and later in the corporation's first major crisis; Herman Bickel, retired chief engineer of the eventually divested Wickes Boiler Co.; Don Barnes, Boiler's former general manager, now living the easy life in Wisconsin's Door County; Jack Parker, the Saginaw advertising man who has handled Wickes accounts since World War II; Harry H. Poeling Jr., long-time independent sales representative of Lee L. Woodard Sons; and Robert P. Gerholz, the famous Flint builder, pal of U.S. presidents, ex-president of the National Association of Home Builders, and a former Wickes director.

I had but one brief meeting with H. Randall Wickes shortly before his death. By the time, unfortunately, advancing age had taken its toll. Thus, for particulars on the Wickes family, I am indebted to the late Mrs. Elizabeth Harvey, sister of Ran Wickes and widow of Albert S. Harvey, and her sons Thomas and Sarge.

Special thanks are due Peter Ferrarese, of Parker, Willox, Fairchild & Campbell, of Saginaw, and Karl Dahlem, Wickes associate director of corporate communications, whom I'd first met when he was still public relations vice president of American Airlines. Both read my script with professional expertise, and thereby no doubt made life easier for my editor at McGraw-Hill, Bill Mogan.

Mrs. Nelda Heinz, who is in charge of the reference department of Saginaw's Hoyt Library, was most helpful in providing historical sources. Miss Deloris Menthen, who had been with Dan Fitz-Gerald since his early years with Wickes, steered me to all the right people during my Saginaw research phase, made sure that I kept my appointments straight, and promptly provided all sorts of miscellaneous information which I always seemed to need in a hurry. In San Diego, E. L. McNeely's jewel of an executive secretary, Judi Sanna, also assisted in every way she could, as did the other secretaries of the corporate headquarters contingent: Doris Billingsley, Vera Ciccarelli, Donna Mehaffey, Lee Russell, and Janell McWilliams. And then there was Karl Czapor, the marvelously efficient head of Wickes office services in San Diego, who safely shepherded the shipments of countless bundles of corporate documents I used in my research.

For helping me in the preparation of the final manuscript, I particularly thank Karen Cure, a young writer of great promise. Although she was busy enough with various magazine assignments and had two books of her own deadlined at the time, she agreed to third-party edit my copy, check proofs, and even take some dictation. Others who shared in the tedious job of work of transcribing interview tapes and typing successive drafts included my faithful long-time helper Avis Powell, as well as Mary Bull, a friend dating back to the days when we both worked for *Look*, and Martha Anne Freeman, and Mrs. Jerry Silbertrust, all of Bucks County, Pennsylvania.

Lastly, my thanks to Bill Bentley, city editor of the *Atlanta Constitution*, who let me use one of the typewriters in his city room when my portable conked out in the middle of a trip, a couple of weeks after this preface was due at the publisher.

George Bush

Addendum: As pointed out above, the Wickes organizational structure is in a constant state of flux. Indeed, even as the preface was being set in type, several major changes in titles and functions were announced.

In July 1976, shortly after the corporation's divestiture of its Oregon-Pacific operation, Senior Vice President Clark A. Johnson, until then in charge of lumber and building supply wholesale activities, was reassigned to run Wickes Furniture. Arthur J. Nasso joined him as the division's vice president of administration, and Robert Thele became Furniture's vice president of operations. At the same time, Richard G. Cotton, who had been Furniture's general manager *pro tempore*, returned to San Diego headquarters and his old job of senior vice president–personnel. T. J. Hedrick, meanwhile, was promoted to senior vice president, and inherited the remaining wholesale functions (Sequoia Supply) as well as Yorktowne from Clark Johnson. Hedrick also remains in charge of Wickes Forest Industries. His general manager at Sequoia Supply is newly elected corporate vice president E. F. Warns.

Other up-dates: Roland Pretzer is once again general manager of Wickes Buildings. This division, along with Wickes Recreational Vehicles and Henry Camp's Wickes Canada (whose consistent profits used to be drowned in the red ink of Wickes Homes), now reports to Executive Vice President David Primuth, while the Wickes financial service subsidiaries—Wickes Credit Corporation and Western Diversified—report to MIS boss and vice president Ralph Pfaff.

At the time of this writing (August 1976), Wickes Agriculture has no general manager of its own. Robert G. Dodge, the group's senior vice president, has taken direct charge of that division.

THE
WIDE
WORLD
OF
WICKES

1

What's a Wickes?

I t was one of those Chicago nights when the sky hangs deep into the streets and planes get stacked high over O'Hare. Had General Lauris Norstad still been commander of NATO, with a meteorology staff at his disposal, he might have been tempted to scrub the show when the weather started looking bad. But by then it would have been too late. Norstad's guests were already on their way, flying in from every corner of the country, from California and New York, Florida and the Pacific Northwest, Texas and New England, from almost any state you'd care to name. The lucky few were those from Chicago: they merely braved pelting rain between their doors and the limousines that had been dispatched to deliver them to the Prudential Building. One exception among the locals was Paul R. Judy, president of A. G. Becker, who had intended to change into his dinner jacket at his Loop office, but since his return flight from New York was delayed, he ordered his evening clothes brought to O'Hare, and he dressed for the festivities in a men's room.

Yet the miserable weather of that Thursday, March 28, 1974, added its own touch of glamour to the gathering, not only because the Mid-America Club on the thirty-ninth floor seemed suspended in space, with Chicago's glitter drowned in the clouds that hugged the windows, but also because General Norstad's guests were proud to have made it to the party despite the difficulties and delays; if there was one characteristic they universally shared, it was their pleasure in being unstoppable when the going got tough. All were men who had made it big in their respective pursuits, a veritable cross section of American business leadership. Armstrong Cork, Borg-Warner, Owens-Corning Fiberglas, United States Gypsum, National Gypsum, the Union Bank of Los Angeles—these and other organizations of like stature were represented by their chairmen. Presidents were stumbling over each other: from the Security Pacific National Bank, Flintkote, Pioneer Plastics, Marsh & McLennan, Simmons, Federal-Mogul, the Michigan National Bank, Broyhill Furniture, Wachovia Corp., and more. Some companies, like Certain-Teed, showed up in full force, with chairman, president, vice presidents, and other brass. Distinguished firms like Coopers & Lybrand and Goldman, Sachs dispatched prides of partners. It was indeed a one-in-a-billion get-together, just as it was meant to be.

Norstad, once the country's youngest four-star general and until recently chairman of Owens-Corning, had invited these prime movers from the industrial and financial communities to celebrate the entry of The Wickes Corporation into the rarefied ranks of companies whose business volume tops $1 billion a year. Every one of the guests had no less cause to celebrate this attainment than Wickes itself, for in a sense they were all partners in the enterprise. Their companies had sold Wickes goods and raw materials in ever-increasing measure; they had provided financing through security issues and bank loans, shipped Wickes products, handled Wickes auditing, underwritten Wickes risks, advised Wickes on its policies. With its phenomenal expansion, Wickes had become one of their most important customers.

As befits joyous festivities, there was backslapping, buffoonery, and brouhaha in abundance. The formal handshake line, staffed by General Norstad and E. L. McNeely, then president of Wickes, rapidly dissolved into cocktail-party camaraderie. Top executives, who'd heard each others' names for years but had never met, swapped golf jokes and munched peanuts together like old poker partners. The beef Wellington went down fast, and the speeches, mercifully enough, even faster. There were companionable catcalls when Norstad, still every inch of his slim six feet a general, allowed as how he might be talking too much. It was that kind of shindig.[1]

For the Wickes people it was a real high. They had hoped to hit the billion-dollar mark in fiscal 1975, and here they were a year ahead of schedule. But, much as they relished the compliments and congratulations, they knew that all was not as it should have been. The architect of their success, the gala's intended guest of honor, Daniel M. Fitz-Gerald, was missing. That very evening he lay in St. Joseph's Hospital in Houston, where specialists had diagnosed a spreading cancer in his face and were about to operate. Some Wickes executives had wanted to cancel the dinner, but Fitz-Gerald nixed that notion. Gregarious, always ready for a party, he intended to be there regardless of what the doctors said, and he insisted that a place be set for him.

This doggedness was typical of Fitz-Gerald, although it hadn't always been. He'd launched his life as a lazybones, and it had taken him some years to discover that he was made to be a leader. Not until he was well into his thirties did he define his purpose, namely, to prod, shove, and finagle Wickes into the big time. He pushed Wickes's sales from about $10 million in 1947 to $248 million in 1965. Then fifty-five years old, he might well have rested on his laurels, having achieved more than anyone would have expected. But that's when the growth bug really bit him.

"You know," he told McNeely, who'd been with the company only a few months and wasn't yet a senior officer, "I've got ten years to go, and I sure would like to see us crack a

billion before they boot me out." The two men were just
shooting the bull in the company's office in Saginaw, Michigan, and Fitz-Gerald himself seemed appalled at his audacity.
"Hey, wait," said McNeely, "why not?"

And then it all happened. Within four years, by 1969,
Wickes's volume jumped to nearly $376 million, with a net
income after taxes of more than $11 million. Now on January
26, 1974, the company had closed out the latest fiscal year with
more than $1.1 billion in volume and a record-setting bottom
line to match—more than $21 million. The Wickes people still
could scarcely believe it. Sure, the economy had been just
right, and a couple of recent acquisitions had given them that
final boost over the billion-dollar barrier, and here they were in
the *Fortune 500*, and all dressed up in unaccustomed tuxes,
black ties, and cummerbunds. There wasn't one in the bunch
who had been born to power; most had been country boys,
more at home on farms and mainstreets than in boardrooms,
and had worked their way up from low-paying jobs as men do
in the story books. They appreciated General Norstad's closing
statement, a veiled warning not to catch the businessman's
equivalent of a politician's Potomac ego fever: "We must honor
the country that makes this kind of achievement possible." Not
that they were likely to forget their humble origins.

Here, in their circle of associates, jovially gathered around
intimate tables, everyone knew them and knew what Wickes
was all about. But out in the world, *The Wall Street Journal*
and assorted trade publications notwithstanding, these men
usually got a politely blank stare when they said they were with
Wickes. Here and there, somebody might remark, "Oh yeah, I
picked up some shingles at your place the other day," or,
"That's a nice vacation cottage you people build," or, "My
wife's been thinking about one of your bedroom sets." An old-
timer in the machinery business might crack a nostalgic smile:
"We used to have one of those big Wickes lathes in our shop. It
must have been at least thirty years old when I retired, and it
was still working." Or an engineer in the steel industry might
comment: "That Mexaloy of yours sure makes a great hot

topping," and the embarrassed Wickes executive would reply, "Glad to hear it. Incidentally, what's a hot topping? I hope you'll excuse me, but I'm in beans." And it has also happened that a fellow passenger on a jet remarked after an across-the-armrest introduction, "You people make candle wicks? I suppose that must be a pretty good business now with everybody worried about power failures."

Even *Fortune* doesn't quite know how to categorize Wickes. The magazine lists the corporation as the nation's thirty-first largest retailer, but only because the editors can't figure out where else to fit it in, and, in any case, retailing is Wickes's major activity, though not its only one by far. In all the confusion about what Wickes really does, there's at least this certainty: It doesn't manufacture candle wicks—but you never can tell, one of these days it might, just to add to the puzzlement.

Nobody knows better than McNeely that Wickes, despite all its evident successes, remains one of the country's most widely unknown companies to this day—so unknown, in fact, that Peter W. Willox, the corporate vice president of communications, felt compelled to produce a slide-and-sound presentation entitled "What's a Wickes?"

What indeed is Wickes? How can you explain the diversity of guests at the Wickes Billion-Dollar Dinner?

For one thing, that old machinist was absolutely right. Wickes makes lathes. In fact, it's the world's biggest manufacturer of crankshaft lathes. Yet lathes usually constitute less than 1 percent of the corporation's business. It is also the world's biggest marketer of beans, especially navy beans. But, even combined with Wickes's other sizable agricultural commodity operations, that's only about 10 percent of its volume in an average year. The Behlen Division of Wickes produces unique stressed-skin steel buildings that enclose huge spaces without interior roof supports; this division also is by far the leading maker of grain and corn storage and grain-conditioning equipment, as well as a big producer of galvanized steel fencing, farm gates, hydraulic presses, and even power steering for farm tractors. And yet all this usually amounts to only about 6 percent of the company's business.

Beyond that—and here we come to the hub of the enterprise—Wickes is the world's largest retailer of lumber and building supplies, with 268 outlets in the United States and 17 in Europe.[2] It is also establishing itself as a major retailer of furniture, and now has twenty-two warehouse-showrooms in twelve states, with more stores to be added in 1976 and the years to follow. To round things out, Wickes harvests lumber on leased lands, manufactures particleboard, wholesales wood and wood products, distributes building supplies through a nationwide chain of warehouses, produces roof trusses and other structural shelter components, builds and markets vacation cottages and garages, makes kitchen cabinets and top-of-the-line wrought iron furniture, constructs wood-frame farm and utility buildings. And as if all that weren't enough, Wickes provides credit and insurance services to its wholesale and retail customers; manufactures die-casting machinery, powder metallurgy presses, and precision tools needed to make automatic transmissions; builds recreational vehicles; mines graphite in Mexico; provides special graphitic mixtures for the production of carbon steel and pig iron; makes precision parts from exotic metal powders for use in a variety of equipment, large and small, ranging from jet aircraft, atomic submarines, and space rockets to lawn mowers.

For Wickes to have achieved such astounding growth and diversification evidently would have been all but impossible except by the acquisition route. When the present corporation was chartered in 1947, it merged three local companies controlled by the Wickes family of Saginaw. The Wickes ancestors' original business, dating back to 1854, had been the manufacture of gang saws and other machinery for the mills that were then devouring the white pine forests of the Wolverine State and turning them into houses for the settlement of the Midwest. By the time of the merger, Michigan's lumber boom was long past, and the Wickes companies were engaged in such diverse activities as graphite mining, the manufacture of indus-

THE CRADLE OF THE WICKES CORPORATION

When this aerial was taken in the early 1960s, Wickes Boiler was still part of the company (see inscription on powerhouse chimney at right). Wickes Machine Tool occupies the buildings along the Saginaw River to this day. The modern office building (left) is now three stories taller, and it houses the headquarters of Wickes Lumber.

trial boilers, and the making of machine tools. As it happened, the unlikely union of these operations, which had been arranged merely for the sake of saving on taxes, resulted quite by accident in what may well have been the country's first true conglomerate: a corporate agglutination of unrelated profit centers.

Since then, conglomerates have shot up like mushrooms after a spring rain. They had their rousing heyday, enjoyed a Wall Street vogue, and then declined, temporarily discredited. The image many of them left behind was that of blue-sky operators who parlayed a minimum investment into control of assorted enterprises, and who then employed the assets of these companies to finance further acquisitions, until they finally overextended themselves and encountered grievous trouble, usually at their shareholders' expense. But The Wickes Corporation was no lollipop that melted away after a

7

few hearty licks. Along with some other soundly diversified operations, it was to prove, especially in the inflation-recession crunch that hit the country in 1974 and 1975, that the pursuit of several mutually countercyclical operations can lend a company great viability. As with everything else, the success of diversification depends on how well it's planned and managed.

True, after its first amazing triumphs, Wickes occasionally plunged into ventures that were at best ill-advised. There was, for example, a premature effort to gain a foothold in manufactured housing, a move prompted to a large degree by the exhortations of George Romney, then Secretary of Housing and Urban Development. After two years this Wickes project had to be abandoned, but the potential to reenter this field at a moment's notice is still there, and that moment is bound to come sooner or later, even if the industry-produced unitized housing of tomorrow takes a different form from that envisioned in the 1960s.

Wickes's false start in modular construction cost the corporation a small bundle but it didn't hurt. That's one of the beauties of size. To a person with a go-for-broke temperament, it would seem that the opposite were true, that the bigger a company, the bigger the risks it must take in order to show real growth. But this is not so. As a corporation increases in size, it can afford to release a whole bunch of little trial balloons it couldn't launch before. Some of these will fizzle, but a lot of them are bound to fly, and once they fly you can enlarge them and make them carry an ever-increasing payload.

"That's the kind of a company we are," says McNeely. "We do take chances. If a risk looks reasonable to us, we'll take a shot at it. We're at the opposite end from plodding and restricted management, and we have rejected and will continue to reject the fellow who wants to think something over for five years before committing himself, or keeps on revising his plan of action a dozen times. There has to be some intuitive aspect to planning. Of course, it's concomitant that you've got to have some kind of financial controls, and we do have those. And you've got to know what's going on in the world, and we

E. L. McNEELY

Lured to Wickes by Fitz-Gerald in 1964, he soon showed his mettle. By 1969, he was the corporation's president. Now Fitz-Gerald's successor as chairman of the board, McNeely is working on Wickes's second billion. (Portrait by Karsh, Ottawa)

do know that at least some of the time. One thing you can be sure of, we'd never have won the race for a billion if we'd snowplowed all the way down the hill."

When Fitz-Gerald and McNeely, back in 1965, first talked about aiming for the big time, there were still a number of people in the company who would have much preferred to snowplow than to schuss. Not that Fitz-Gerald and McNeely walked out of the office arm in arm, grinning as if they'd had hashish in their pipes and telling everybody that they were headed for a billion dollars. They weren't that dreamy. Nor was their plan really all that well defined. What they did recognize, however, was the importance of setting an ambitious goal that would impose its own discipline and really pull the company together. From now on, all actions and decisions would have to further that cause.

The first job was to sell the snowplow set. This took a while, of course. Nobody spoke up against the concept, but then few people are likely to argue with their boss. Still, big ideas take time to sink in. Equally important was planning, of which Wickes had done very little until then. Successes had come the corporation's way by good fortune, as it were, and that good fortune had been in most part due to Fitz-Gerald's almost infallible instinct as to what would work and what wouldn't. Such instinct now would be no less important, but it had to be supplemented by a concerted effort to search for every available growth opportunity that made sense. In effect, Dan Fitz-Gerald, and later McNeely, who was soon to become the president, gave everybody a sort of blank check to proceed in all directions that promised to enhance the corporation's worth. No effort was ever restricted except in terms of likely return on investment. The standard was 9 percent after taxes. Less than that could get by if it was felt that future yields, say after five years, would meet this minimum or exceed it. Raising money presented no special difficulties in those years. Says McNeely: "We backed everybody all the way to accomplish more than the norm."

Working at Wickes suddenly became more exciting than

ever before. A whole new entrepreneurial spirit infected almost everyone in the company. Those who were immune departed, usually voluntarily. Indeed, the whole idea of the billion-dollar goal became a fine screen that filtered out psyches of more prosaic bent. By the same token, Wickes was clearly not the place for executives of infinite patience—the kind it takes to nurse the development of precision machinery, for example. Some of that mold tried and failed. Conversely, however, Wickes was wide open to anyone of an adventurous mind. It became a company where the youngest junior executive could freely tell the wheels at the top that they were wrong, that something else should be done. The bosses always listened, and often agreed. If there was any problem with the free spirits attracted by Wickes's elbow-room philosophy, it was that many of them felt that structured planning would impose a burden. There was the fear that such planning might stifle the growth it was supposed to promote. Not until 1968 did McNeely succeed in introducing a formalized planning process, and after that it still took some time for many to realize that astute planning was an adventure in itself.

There is no doubt that in the meanwhile some mistakes were made, though the damage they wrought was kept in check. But with the planning, Wickes gained a clearer understanding of its purposes. Like a gourmand who turns gourmet after considering the flab around his waist, the corporation became increasingly selective in its acquisition diet, and is far trimmer today as a result. The new streamlining, however, is still somewhat obscured by the complex folds of the corporation's vestment. What on earth could be the connection between beans, graphite, machine tools, and powder metal shapes on the one hand, and lumber, building supplies, and the retailing of furniture on the other? Obviously there isn't any, except as a circumstance of history. As we shall see, it was the bean business—of all surprising things—that led Wickes into the shelter field.

Today that's where the corporation's major effort is directed—toward an ever-increasing participation in this vast market: the shelter shell as well as its contents, wholesale as well as retail, vertical as well as horizontal, agricultural and industrial as well as residential, and with financing and insurance services supplementing the merchandising. All else, despite its seeming prominence, is merely supportive. The bean operation, always a respectable moneymaker, proved itself a most precious property in 1973 and 1974 as skyrocketing commodity prices compensated for pinched profits elsewhere, notably those in recreational vehicles (due to the oil embargo followed by the higher cost of gasoline) and mobile homes (due to the mortgage drought). In the fiscal year that ended in January 1975, Wickes's sales of beans and, to a lesser degree, other crops provided 28.6 percent of the corporation's pretax profits. But even apart from the luck of being big in a basic commodity in an era of shortages, a great deal of cushioning is built right into the corporation's shelter-related enterprises, so that, although Wickes is no more depression-proof than any other business, it is recession-repellent, at least to a degree.

When housing starts are down and big-ticket money is tight, lumber and building supply sales to contractors fall off, but the do-it-yourself home improvement volume picks up. By the same token, when the breadwinner is temporarily laid off but has a modicum of savings and is collecting unemployment benefits, that's the time when many home owners take advantage of their enforced vacation by making long-needed repairs or renovations around the house. A similar built-in buffer protects the corporation's relatively new furniture division. When a family feels it can't afford to take its annual trip (and the camper and motor home business gets hit as a result), whatever discretionary funds may be available are often invested in a new chair or sofa. To top off the Wickes array of compensatory balances, there's this fact about times when agricultural commodities are scarce: even as high food prices crimp consumer spending, farmers are more prosperous than in the days of surplus and low prices, and they are then more able to invest in agricultural equipment—corn bins, grain driers, fencing, and the like—produced by the Wickes-owned

Behlen Manufacturing Company. In fiscal 1975, this division accounted for nearly another quarter of the corporation's pre-tax profits. Combined with the healthy proceeds of the bean sales, the Behlen activity was enough to make up for much of the bottom-line reduction some of the other divisions had to live with as a result of the general economy.[3]

Meanwhile, Wickes is all set for the inevitable resurgence of housing starts. With the hard-core demand estimated at 2.5 million per year, and with about 13 million new units (including around 3 million mobile homes) built between early 1969 and late 1975, the deficit in 1976 appears to be around 2 million. This statistic, however, is somewhat deceptive: you don't see people sleeping in the streets. More realistic seems to be the somewhat less exuberant projection of Don Clothier, a Wickes senior research analyst, that the housing demand left unsatisfied in early 1976 will total about one million units. This pent-up need will of course have to be added to the new demand arising in 1976. Clothier easily foresees about 1.4 million single-dwelling starts for that year. Regardless of which estimate of the backlog proves closer to reality, there is little doubt that once the economy really rolls again, there will be a rush for new shelter and the furniture that goes with it.

Oregon-Pacific Industries, which Wickes acquired in 1972, wholesales lumber and plywood to retail yards (like Wickes's own), which in turn serve building contractors. So does the Steel City Lumber Company, now married to Oregon-Pacific in the new Wickes Wholesale operation. Sequoia Supply distributes building materials through thirty-four warehouses in twenty-two states. Wickes Forest Industries, headquartered in Dinuba, California, harvests and mills timber, and manufactures particleboard, window frames, moldings, and assorted other wood products.

The one-time automated modular-housing plant at Mason, Michigan, now makes structural building components like roof trusses, as do ten other smaller installations attached to various Wickes lumber and building supply centers. Moreover, almost every one of the centers was planned with enough spare real estate to allow the setting up of such facilities for component and other modular production. At the same time, every Wickes lumber and building supply center is in an area where demand for additional housing exists. The Yorktowne Division builds kitchen cabinets. Behlen's stressed-steel shelter system, so far used only in commercial and civic structures, may yet find itself applied to multiunit residential housing. Says John V. Drum, who succeeded McNeely as president when the latter became chairman of the board in 1975: "We're in the business of selling building materials in whatever form they are wanted, from lumber to the finished product or any part of it. That's our big thrust."

2

Green Gold

On the Dow Jones ticker, The Wickes Corporation's symbol is WIX, making it one of the few stocks that can be recognized easily even by a neophyte.[1] Wickes is lucky that way. Not many names lend themselves so readily to phonetic abbreviation.[2] More than a century ago, when most of Michigan was still wilderness and the vast majority of its inhabitants were but semiliterate, the same angular capital letters made their debut as log marks on timber that floated down the Saginaw River and its skein of tributaries.

Not that some early sawmill developed quite logically into the Wickes lumber business of today. History is rarely that simple. To the contrary, Wickes Lumber's lineage is rooted in the farm economy that sprang up only after the Saginaw River Basin had been denuded of its trees and its fertile soil laid bare. Indeed, the drama arises from the fact that here we have an enterprise that was born on the forest frontier, and once the white pine was all cut, grew in other directions, only to find itself back at its font—driven by fate, as it were—much like the peripatetic son of so many ancient legends. How this happened, how Wickes came full circle from playing an important role in providing shelter for a newly opened continent to once again participating prominently in the production of housing, this time for a society that burgeoned beyond all expectations: that is the subject of later chapters. Here we are concerned with the beginning.

Henry Dunn Wickes was just twenty-one years old in 1854 when he arrived at Flint, Michigan, then known as the Village of Grand Traverse, after journeying from the town of Auburn in the long-settled State of New York. Like so many others, he had caught the "Michigania fever" as word spread through the East of the great opportunities to be found in the new country between the Great Lakes. Henry was by no means the first to succumb to this emigration epidemic. In fact, the Michigan land rush was about to peak. In 1830, seven years before the Michigan Territory's admission to the Union, the total population was estimated to be only about 31,000. But that year Congress passed the "Squatter Act," which enabled settlers to buy one or two parcels of 80 acres each. The price was $1.25 per acre, and they could pay off their claims in two years' time.

This legislation put an end to the disheartening real estate auctions that had been held under the Land Act of 1820 and that had cost many settlers their hard-won homes. It hadn't mattered then how much you'd sweated cutting down trees, building your cabin, and clearing the land. If you couldn't scare off the city slickers and speculators who had never set foot in the wilderness but brought fat wallets to the auctions, they'd outbid you, and the land you'd slaved over for many months was theirs. But the Squatter Act changed all that. Now you could be sure to keep your claim. As a result, land sales in the Michigan Territory jumped to 447,780 acres in 1833, more than quadruple what they had been in 1829, and by 1836 they exceeded 4 million acres, more than the government sold that year in any other state or territory. Michigan's population increased nearly tenfold in a decade, to 212,267 by 1840. The head count more than doubled again by 1855, and although the biggest growth was still to come, never again would be it be nearly so dramatic.

Yet Henry D. Wickes was anything but a latecomer. Most of Michigan's immigrants had pushed westward along the Territorial Road, whose course roughly followed that of today's Interstate 94. The gently rolling land here was ideal for farming, a rich earth of many varied soils that had been deposited by the glaciers of four ice ages. Between shady stands of hardwood there were "oak openings" aplenty, ready to be cultivated but for getting rid of some brush. Moreover, the Potawatomi Indians of this area, one of the Algonquin tribes, were friendly. Not a shot nor an arrow had been dispatched here in anger since Governor Lewis Cass had purchased the lands south of the Grand River at a treaty *powwow* in 1821. Towns grew up along the Territorial Road in a hurry, clear over to St. Joseph on Lake Michigan: Ann Arbor, Jackson, Battle Creek, Kalamazoo. From there, the settlers branched north to build Grand Rapids and Muskegon.

But such was not the situation around Michigan's "thumb," where Henry Dunn Wickes had chosen to make his fortune. To the north and east of Flint, swamps and dense forests discouraged farming, and while the Potawatomis of central and western Michigan derived their sustenance mostly from growing corn, the Chippewas of the Saginaw River Basin depended for their survival on the hunt. Lewis Cass had also managed to talk this warlike nation into a treaty, back in 1819, which gave the Chippewas 50,000 acres for their reservation and deeded them perpetual hunting and fishing rights in the entire Saginaw Valley region. But a few early adventurers soon violated this treaty, not caring that a society without written contracts knows no greater crime than the breach of one's word. Morover, to the Chippewas, all this was holy ground. Not surprisingly, they did not treat intruders too kindly, and for many years the few settlers who dared to approach their domain played it safe and stuck close to the tiny frontier outposts along the trail from Detroit to Saginaw. Not until the mid-1830s did a few especially hardy types again venture into the Chippewa hunting preserve west of the trail, and even when Henry Dunn Wickes arrived, that region was still only sparsely settled.

No one knows why he picked Flint. He was a mechanic by trade, and it would seem that the bigger, more prosperous communities of western Michigan would have offered him greater opportunities, for the machinery business of that time was largely concerned with the making of plowshares and other rather primitive equipment that could be used in farming. Henry had been born on a farm at Starkey, New York, near Seneca Lake, on August 19, 1833. About five years later his family left the maternal homestead for some obscure reason and moved to Reading Center, slightly north of Watkins Glen. There Henry obtained the meager free schooling offered at that time, until, at the age of nineteen, he became apprenticed to a foundry at Penn Yan, a small town at the northern tip of Keuka Lake. For a short period after that, he was a machinist in Auburn, New York, before emigrating to Michigan.

As it turned out, a person of his talents couldn't have picked a better base than Flint. A stampede akin to California's Gold Rush was about to engulf Michigan's forests, which began just north of this community, and Henry's mechanical aptitude was precisely what that new state's first major industry required.

Sawmills had been a profitable business in Michigan ever since its settlement began. But until the 1850s these mills had largely provided sawed lumber to meet local demand. They were cutting mostly hardwood and only very little pine. But now the timber barons of the East, with their old stands in New England all but depleted, began to realize that a broad belt of softwoods stretched all the way across the northern Great Lakes region, through Michigan, Wisconsin, and Minnesota. Of these states, Michigan was the closest and most strategically located. Its lumber could be shipped west from ports along Lake Michigan and east from ports along Lake Huron. Not only was the Saginaw River Basin both an ideal location for the latter purpose and the most easily accessible of all Michigan's forest regions, but also it had a network of streams on which the logs could be floated to sawmills prior to loading them on ships. Thus, the Saginaw area was the first to feel the bite of the big saw.

When the stagecoach dropped Henry Wickes off in Flint, several other travelers kept right on going. They were bigger and stronger than the bearded young mechanic who, although far from frail, was hardly a rugged outdoor type. But the other men were. They had to be for their business. They were "timber cruisers"—men knowledgeable of wood, capable of spending weeks on their own in the wilderness, adept at shinnying up a tall tree to use it as an observation platform—and they were heading up to Saginaw, and from there into the forests to select stands for cutting. The cruisers scouted for the big operators, who were now getting in on the Michigan land rush, buying up the state's choicest pine forests, still paying the bargain price of only $1.25 an acre. There was a fortune in "green gold" waiting here, which topped California's wealth of yellow gold by more than $1 billion.[3] Early surveyors had estimated Michigan's pine stand at 150 billion board feet. They were amazingly close. By 1897, 160 billion board feet had been cut: enough to build about ten million six-room houses. Of this total, 31 billion board feet came from the Saginaw Valley Basin and the northern part of the thumb—more than from the entire Upper Peninsula, and nearly as much as was taken from the forests around the fabled Au Sable River.

The family of Henry Dunn Wickes was to get into timber only in a modest way, just enough to warrant their own log mark, the hammered imprint on both ends of a log that identifies its ownership. The part Henry Dunn Wickes was to play proved to be far more significant. Without his engineering skill and entrepreneurial spirit, it probably would have been impossible to process so much timber so quickly, but he developed and marketed the Wickes gang saw, a steam-powered giant up to 6 feet wide whose parallel blades could rip two or three logs into boards at the same time. By 1887, some 300 of these tree-gobbling monsters were in use,[4] and before Michi-

gan's white pine was exhausted, nearly every mill in the state was equipped with at least one of them.

Conservationists may argue that the gang saw was anything but a great contribution. True enough, when the timber barons were done with their ruthless cutting, much of Michigan lay in desolation. Its beautiful white pine was gone. Its land was bare, littered with the slashings of great trees and the smashed corpses of trees too small to cut. The litter fueled forest fires that sometimes razed whole settlements. Rivers were in bad shape too. The logs had buffeted and torn their banks, and the level of the streams fell, for, with the forests gone, the climate changed and there was less rain. The fact that the timber barons cheated themselves, or at least their heirs, by not reforesting to provide crops for the future, is hardly a counter-argument to the conservationists' position. But what must not be forgotten is that the country's future breadbasket, the Great Plains, didn't have any trees. Without the exploitation of the northwoods, that area couldn't have been settled and developed when it was, and our society would not have become affluent enough to allow its members the luxury of being conservationists. In any case, in the seven decades since this ravage ended, Michigan's forests have been nurtured to rise again. Any cutting today is provident of the future. Indeed, for

Henry Dunn Wickes (left).
Edward Noyes Wickes (right).

the past several years more timber has been planted in the United States than cut.

Henry Wickes didn't develop his famous gang saw immediately. At first he ran a general foundry and machine shop, which engaged principally in repair work and the making of odd castings for whatever equipment was required in those days by a frontier settlement. He worked in partnership with a younger brother, Edward Noyes Wickes, two years his junior, who joined Henry in 1856.[5] Together with a gentleman by the name of H. W. Wood, they established a firm called the Genesee Iron Works and did a fine business in Flint for several years. Soon it became apparent, however, that Saginaw was yet a better place to be.[6] All the pig iron used in the Wickes foundry came to Saginaw by sailing ship and then had to be hauled cross-country on wagons and sleighs to Flint. Conversely, the growing amount of sawmill equipment that Henry and Edward manufactured at their works had to be transported back to the river on whose banks the mills were of course located. This back-and-forth did not strike the two brothers as particularly efficient.

Moreover, Saginaw was really booming. It had grown up around a Louis Campeau trading post a short distance downstream from the confluence of five rivers: the Tittabawassee

SAGINAW RIVER SAWMILL

At the height of the Michigan timber boom, seventy-four mills were in operation along that 28-mile-long waterway.

and the Shiawassee, the Cass, the Flint, and the Bad. In turn, the Tittabawassee was fed by the Pine, Chippewa, Tobacco and Molasses rivers, and all these direct and indirect tributary streams of the Saginaw River flowed out of timberlands, providing some 860 miles of winding waterways made to order for "driving" logs down to Lake Huron. In 1854, there had been twenty-nine sawmills along the 28 short but mighty miles of the Saginaw between Green Point and Bay City. By 1870, there were to be seventy-four along that stretch, plus another thirty-six in Bay City itself and a couple more in Bay City's tiny sawmill satellite of Bangor, which had been named, with optimistic abandon, after Bangor, Maine, focal point of an earlier timber stampede. These Saginaw and Bay City mills sawed not only the logs harvested along the Saginaw River's feeder streams, but also those that had been cut along other rivers that emptied into Lake Huron nearby: the Rifle, the Au Gres, and the Kawkawlin. What's more, an entirely new and differ-

22

ent industry had developed as a result of the sawmill operations. The swamps around Saginaw were rich with salt, and the
tons upon tons of sawdust and wood scrap left over from the
sawing yielded cheap fuel to evaporate the brine, making salt
production on a large scale very profitable. This synergy, as it
would be called in modern corporate jargon, resulted in Michigan's providing nearly half the nation's salt during this lumber
era. Indeed, when the Genesee Iron Works were transplanted
to Saginaw in 1860, the town was on the threshold of its most
dynamic years.

Money flowed as if the world were coming to an end. The
city still sported wooden sidewalks (white pine, of course) so
that pedestrians didn't have to wade in its muddy streets, but
the newly built Bancroft House, erected in 1859, was one of
Michigan's most elegant hotels, four stories high, topped by an
ornate cupola, and boasting a fine chef especially imported
from Paris.[7] While the Bancroft served the tycoons and frontier dandies in rococo splendor, lumberjacks spent their hard-
won wages on Water Street, which soon earned the sobriquet
of "Hell's Half Mile." Eventually there were to be more than
200 saloons, as well as numerous bawdy houses, whose existence, no doubt, helped guard the "decent ladies" of Saginaw
against being molested. Long lines formed outside these establishments when the 'jacks arrived after their long winter in the
woods, and when there weren't enough girls to go around, Ma
Smith, one of the leading madams around town, was not above
donning a tight corset and "baking a batch of rolls" herself, as
she called it. The 'jacks strutted around with dollar bills tucked
in their buttonholes, daring anyone they met to fight them for
the loot. The "river hogs," who drove the logs down the
streams after the spring melt and into the summer, were no less
boisterous. Saginaw was rich and rowdy all year long.

The city soon gained fame not only for its "Saginaw pine"
and its wide-open life style. George Lavigne, the "Saginaw
Kid," was to reign as the world's lightweight champion in the
Gay Nineties. Lelia Koerber, a plump little girl who had
attended Hoyt Grade School, left Saginaw for the stage and

later the movies, where she gained fame as Marie Dressler. Charlie Harris, a bellhop at the Bancroft, wrote the classic hit "After the Ball." Henry H. Crapo, who had brought with him some of the capital amassed by his shipbuilding family in New Bedford, Massachusetts, multiplied his fortune in Saginaw and Flint, became governor of Michigan, and saw his grandson, William Crapo Durant, found General Motors.

Living in Saginaw wasn't all roses, however. Mr. Wood, the partner of Henry and Edward Wickes, finally couldn't stand its swamp-bred mosquitoes any longer. He sold out in 1864, and the firm's name was changed to Wickes Bros. Iron Works.[8] The new factory, which had been erected on two lots of land on the East Saginaw bank of the river and fronting on Water Street, employed around forty men in the beginning, and grew to have more than a hundred workers by 1887. Its offspring, the Machine Tool Division of The Wickes Corporation, is still headquartered in the same location, behind the modern (1962) office building that now serves as the national nerve center of Wickes Lumber.

Wickes Bros. manufactured gang saws right from the first, but did not produce its revolutionary model until about 1869.[9] The basic improvement has been credited to Frank E. Kirby of Detroit, who later became a noted marine engineer. Apparently the then twenty-two-year-old inventor sold Wickes Bros. a design that gave an oscillating motion to the saw frame, causing all the teeth of the parallel saws to cut evenly and smoothly. This innovation overcame the problem of only the lower teeth of the saws doing all the cutting, as had been the process until then. Other improvements of the new gang saw were developed by Henry and Edward before long.[10] The speed of the saw was increased, and blades of a thinner gauge were used to reduce the kerf, thus augmenting capacity while cutting down on waste. This was a highly important advance, since conventional circular saws wobbled a great deal and often produced nearly as much sawdust as they did lumber. With its built-in advantage, the Wickes gang saw soon paid for

THE BIGGEST GANG SAW OF THEM ALL

The Wickes No. 1 model, reproduced here from an undated sales catalog, usually measured 3 to 5 feet in width, and was designed for cuts from 16 to 25 inches deep. But yet bigger versions "of any size that may be required" could be special-ordered.

itself as an investment. The little firm was besieged by orders from all over, and even when there was no more timber to be cut in Michigan, Wickes produced gang saws for sawmills in Wisconsin, Minnesota, and the Pacific Northwest.

Saginaw's lumber days reached their climax in 1882 with a local production of nearly 1 billion board feet and some 300 million shingles in a single season.[11] The city's population then stood at about 30,000, and while this growth momentum carried on until shortly before the turn of the century, the time of glory was over. No longer did Saginaw's sawmills operate six days a week on twelve-hour shifts. No longer did the Genesee Avenue drawbridge, connecting East Saginaw with the city of Saginaw, open nearly fifty times a day to let the lake ships pass that came to pick up boards and shingles from the mills.[12] No longer did lumberjacks cut a "round forty," a term which meant logging not only the legally owned acreage but poaching hastily in all directions beyond the tract's boundaries. Now they were lucky to find 40 acres that still had trees on them. At the peak of the cutting, giant 16-foot-wide sleighs, carrying up to 60,000 pounds of timber to the nearest stream, were dragged by teams of horses on log roads that were watered down every night in winter to provide a slick surface. Now 8-foot-wide sleighs, such as had been used in less productive New England, came back into use, and finally there were no sleighs at all. The Tittabawassee Boom Company, organized in 1856 as a cooperative venture of logging firms, closed down in 1893. There was no longer any timber to be driven down the rivers, no longer those huge floats of sawed-off tree trunks confined by booms of chained-together logs. The logging firms and sawmill operators tried to stay in business for a while by cutting and processing Canadian wood from around Georgian Bay on the Ontario side of Lake Huron, but then Canada slapped a tax on its timber, and this operation became unprofitable. The sawmills closed down one after another, followed first by the whorehouses and finally by the saloons, demonstrating that desperation is more cheaply cured by drink than sex. For the first time

. . . AND THE SMALLEST

Catalog picture (right)
shows that even the relatively small
Wickes No. 5 was far bigger than
it appeared in action (above)
when only the top part of the
machinery protruded through the
work floor. This saw came in two
sizes, 26 and 32 inches wide, both
for an 8-inch depth of cut. Its chief
use was sawing pine into flooring
strips.

in its history, Saginaw lost population. The head count dropped from 46,322 to 42,345, or about 10 percent, between 1890 and 1900.[13] Railroad tracks had linked Saginaw with Flint and Detroit since 1863, and with Ludington since 1870, and now the trains were fuller pulling out than coming in.[14]

There is no doubt that the business of Wickes Bros. declined as well. The company's thrust, quite naturally, had been pointed at the lumber business during all those years. In addition to the gang saw, Wickes supplied steam engines, although on a lesser scale. As early as 1858, Henry had designed and patented an engine, equipped with rocking valves, which was to be the forerunner of the later-dominant Corliss product.[15] How many of Henry's steam engines were sold is not a matter of record, but the volume couldn't have been great. The old Wickes Bros. operation just wasn't big enough to go in for the mass production of heavy machinery.

TOUGH SLEDDING

Sleighs up to 16 feet wide brought the lumber to the sawmills. Horses pulled sleighs, but the 'jacks had to load them.

There was no such thing as an assembly line. Every item manufactured was built as an individual unit. This was only to be expected when it came to unusual one-time orders like the huge steel prow of an icebreaker that one of the Wickes engineers, Edward Heyde, designed for the Russian government in 1888. Or the steel tubes for the railroad tunnel that was built under the St. Clair River between Port Huron, Michigan, and Sarnia, Ontario, in the years 1889 and 1890. But even the gang saws were usually produced one at a time. In retrospect, this turned out to be a blessing. Had Wickes Bros. been geared to mass production even as it existed before the turn of the century, the company would have been in far worse straits when its sawmill market dried up.

Another drawback that eventually worked out to the company's advantage was that it was forced to make its own

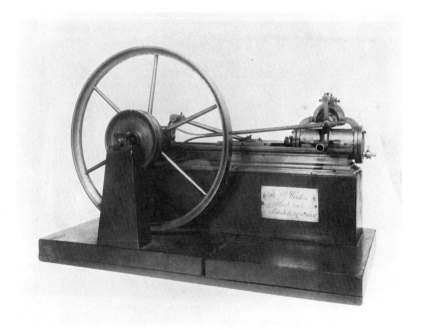

WICKES ROCKING VALVE ENGINE

Original company manufactured all kinds of machinery, including this steam engine designed in 1858.

machine tools: as yet, no manufacturer of such equipment was established in the Middle West. Among the tools required in the company's own production were lathes, and so Wickes Bros. built them for itself, which involved considerable time and effort. For example, no available planer was large enough to level and channel a 48-inch lathe bed. Wickes workmen had to chip and file the ways, using a straightedge and hand tools. Sweating over such projects, no one had any idea that the expertise developed in the process would someday pay off in making Wickes Bros. the world's leading manufacturer of crankshaft lathes, with almost every major automobile maker among its customers.

But that was still some years in the future. Meanwhile, Wickes Bros. had to swim with the tide to stay afloat. One natural diversification was to buy up the equipment of sawmills that were shutting down, and, after reconditioning it, to sell it in other parts of the country. Another logical course was to

NOT SO GAY IN THE NINETIES

There wasn't a smile in the bunch when these Wickes Bros. foundry machinists posed for their group picture shortly before the turn of the century. By that time, the bloom was off the timber boom, and gang saws were not selling too well.

expand this repair and resale business to all kinds of machinery. And this, indeed, Wickes Bros. did. The company advertised for used machinery in just about every state, made the required repairs, and then sold the rebuilt items out of warehouses in Jersey City and Chicago. The company even overhauled electrical equipment. One Wickes Bros. advertisement of unknown vintage—but very likely published in the 1890s—announced the availability of three dynamos ("Arc Lighting Machines Cheap"), each "perfectly serviceable . . . tested before shipping . . . complete with rheostat and regulator."[16]

Among the secondhand devices that seemed to be most frequently for sale were industrial boilers, and it wasn't long before they became a big part of the business. Wickes Bros. had built a few boilers around 1887, and since no plate bending rolls were commercially available at that time, had made its own from rough sketches drawn up by one of its engineers. Here, too, the homegrown know-how came in very handy, and when it turned out that the demand for boilers was far greater than the supply, Henry and Edward predictably decided to develop their own line. As time went on, this part of the operation assumed such an important role in its own right that

WICKES RELIC

This gang saw of unknown vintage was found recently in a mill of Willamette Industries in Oregon. (Photo by Palmer's, Dallas, Oregon)

it became a separate enterprise, known as the Wickes Boiler Company, after Henry's two sons had taken over the family business.[17]

Meanwhile, the transition from gang saws to other product lines could not have been easy, and the Nineties must have been anything but gay for the two original Wickes brothers, even though they were hardly down at the heels. There was always enough profit to allow wintering in Mexico, which may have been a luxury for Henry but was prescribed for Edward, who suffered from tuberculosis. While Edward rested up in Guadalajara, Henry frequently went off on hunting trips into the interior with friends and associates from Saginaw. As we shall see, one of these expeditions led to yet a third Wickes business, the United States Graphite Company, today the Wickes Engineered Materials Division.

By 1901, the year Henry and Edward died within five weeks of each other, the direction of the Wickes interests had been charted for the next half-century.[18] For all practical purposes, the enterprise was now divorced from lumber and would not return to it until 1952. Michigan's "green gold" was gone, and "black gold" from Mexico took its place.

3

Black Gold

It is only a forty-five-minute jet flight on Aeroméxico today from Tucson, Arizona, to Hermosillo, the modern capital of the Mexican state of Sonora. But drive a few miles out of Hermosillo, with its high-rise hotels, its splendid villas set in voluptuous gardens, its young ladies uniformed in the plaid skirts of the local private school; get away from these urban refinements, and you'll soon know that this is still tenuous frontier. Out of the concrete ribbon of Route 15, which points south toward Guaymas on the Sea of Cortés, another highway, only recently paved, veers off to the east. In a year of drought, such as 1974, the carcasses of cattle line the road, some freshly bloated, others desiccated by the sun and gutted by buzzards, stiff legs sticking up like those of tumbled grand pianos. When it does rain in this merciless wasteland, the sky gushes, and the dry washes, the arroyos, turn to torrents. That eastbound highway to La Colorada and Tecoripa now crosses the Sonora River on a new bridge, but until recently it simply forded the stream bed, a bumpy traverse at best, and impassable after downpours.

The stream was raging when Henry and Edward Wickes arrived on horseback at the Sonora's western bank in late 1890. They'd heard in Hermosillo that up in the desert mountains below La Colorada, there was a mine with fabulous riches of graphite. Back in 1867 a prospector had noticed a dark streak on the wall of the canyon, and, digging into it for a few feet, had found a workable vein of ore of about 85 percent purity and the rest soft clay that would not be detrimental to the amorphous graphite's extraction. Nothing much had been done about the find, however. A few tons were carried out on the backs of mules and sent to Germany by sailing vessel out of Guaymas. And that's where the venture ended because of the prohibitive cost of transportation. Now the discovery was up for grabs. That's all the Wickes brothers knew, except to watch out for rattlers and Yaqui Indians, and to shake the scorpions out of their clothing and boots before getting dressed in the morning.

Graphite is the softest mineral in nature. Almost any solid will scratch it, and it smears on everything else. Like diamonds, coal, and coke, it is a form of carbon. It is light, inert to chemical reaction, and friable. Because of its smearing quality, it has been used since the time of the Greeks for recording human history. Because of its stubborn stability, it has served as a refractory in the making of crucibles for molten metal since the early days of the Spaniards. Soft as it is, graphite is practically impossible to destroy.[1]

More than likely, the Wickes brothers were unaware of the special qualities that make graphite so useful and valuable. But Henry and Edward were entrepreneurs, and their life on the Michigan forest frontier had convinced them that anyone was a fool who did not take advantage of any chance that circumstance and nature offered. They waited for the river to subside, then splashed through it on their horses and rode toward the blue mountains that rose above the horizon. It took them nearly three days to cover the 60-odd miles of barely discerni-

OLD MAN OF THE MINE

The late Salvador Aguirre, godfather of the original Santa María graphite claim, was in his nineties when he posed for this snapshot with son Pedro several years ago. The more recently developed Moradillas mine is now owned and managed by Salvador's grandson, Pedro Adolfo.

ble trail, past La Colorada, an adobe village where a few
adventurous Britishers were mining gold, then up into the hills
where scrub oaks and manzanitas were green again after the
rain. At the Los Positos Ranch, part of a vast former Spanish
land grant in the wilderness, a muscular, barefoot sixteen-year-
old met them, his high cheekbones and bronze skin testifying
to his partly Indian ancestry. His name was Salvador Aguirre.
The interpreter-guide the Wickes brothers had hired in Hermosillo could barely keep up with the young man's machine-
gun bursts of speech.

Yes, Salvador Aguirre said, there was a mine. Yes, the
gringos could buy it if they wished. But they must be careful of
the Yaquis, he said. The Yaquis came around every so often.
The secret was to stay on good terms with them. They were
hungry and just wanted to be fed. Of course, if you didn't feed
them—and Salvador Aguirre made the age-old gesture of cutting his throat. Would Salvadore Aguirre be willing to help out,
recruit labor, and run the mining camp? Yes, with great pleasure. Salvadore Aguirre's mother then feasted the visitors,
waiting on the table while the men ate, even as the beautiful,
college-educated young wife of Pedro Adolfo Aguirre, Salvador's grandson, does today when executives show up from
Saginaw.

And so the first exploratory contact ended. Henry and
Edward returned to Saginaw, not sure what to do with the
graphite or, for that matter, how to get it up to Michigan, but
convinced that here was an opportunity they mustn't miss.
They passed the information on to Henry's sons, Harry Tuthill
Wickes and William Jarvis Wickes, who, together with several
of their business associates, incorporated The United States
Graphite Company just a few months later on April 30, 1891.[2]

Luckily, the Ferrocarril Sud Pacífico de México was just
then building the rail line that extends down from Nogales,
Arizona, through Hermosillo and Guaymas to Guadalajara
(now known as the Ferrocarril del Pacífico). Graphite could be
carried by mules from the mine to La Colorada, a distance of
about 30 miles, then shipped another 13 miles on the narrow-

gauge railway of the La Colorada gold mine to Torres, where it was loaded on Southern Pacific cars and sent to Saginaw. The mine, named Santa María, was quickly equipped with a small stone fort whose thick walls would, with luck, keep out bandits and Yaquis. As soon as it was completed, a primitive shaft was sunk into the graphite vein.

Up in Saginaw, in the meanwhile, a shed on a railroad siding, abandoned by an unsuccessful tool manufacturer, was rented. A corner was partitioned off for use as an office, and a Wickes-made boiler and engine, plus some grinding, mixing, and bolting machinery, all secondhand, were installed. This, in the words of Harry C. Woodruff, who became assistant general manager of the company in 1896, and from 1926 to 1930 served as its president, "was quite an undertaking for young men who until a few months before did not even know that the terms graphite, plumbago, and black lead were synonymous."[3] Indeed, when the first carload arrived, these young men were not too sure what to do with it. But, if nothing else, the stuff certainly was black, as anyone who came even in the slightest contact with it could attest. Once powdered, it permeated everything. It invaded your pores, your nose, and your throat.[4] Its most promising use was evidently as coloring matter, and the company's first efforts were directed toward such sales. After being ground and sifted, much as flour is, the graphite was marketed to manufacturers of paint, stove polish (which was also used on the front of steam locomotives to make them nice and shiny), and of course to companies that made pencils. Soon the material's slick softness led to its use in axle grease and other lubricants. The United States Graphite Company was on its way.

As always, necessity soon had to be the mother of invention. With the burgeoning use of illuminating gas, the old-fashioned kitchen ranges and base burners that burned wood and coal were supplanted by gas stoves, and the demand for stove polish fell off. Likewise, the advent of the automobile and the motor-driven farm tractor put the skids on the use of axle grease. Just about the only outlet left was the pencil industry. As fortune would have it, the Mexican graphite was of such fine quality that for a number of years after the turn of the century the Saginaw company supplied the "lead," as it is mistakenly called, for at least 90 percent of the world's pencils.[5] Boxcar after boxcar of processed graphite pulled out of Saginaw on the first leg of the long trip to Germany, France, Belgium, Italy, Russia, Japan, and even China. If it hadn't been for this sustained foreign demand, United States Graphite might well have folded under the pressure of the Pancho Villa revolution, especially since the Santa María mine was about to give out.

Pancho Villa never attacked the mine. He wasn't interested in graphite. He wanted gold, and struck La Colorada instead. Several days later, the sole survivor of the raid dragged himself up to the Los Positos hacienda. He had saved himself by jumping into the cesspool of an outhouse. All the others who hadn't been shot or had their throats cut were strung up and left to dangle.[6]

Had Villa decided to attack the Santa María, there is little doubt that its crew would have suffered a similar fate. The fortification might have held out for a little while, but not for long. It appeared fairly formidable with its observation tower and gun ports, and when you stand in its ruins today, you can see that it had good fields of fire in all directions. But the truth is that only two men were stationed there full time—the rest were usually busy in the mine shaft. Such token defense had been enough to hold off war parties of the Yaqui Indians, who were hungry and bent on vengeance after the Mexican government encouraged settlers to oust the Indians from their rich farmlands in the Yaqui Valley beyond the Bacatete mountains 25 miles to the south. With the womenfolk in the Santa María fort loading rifles, the two guards were able to put on a pretty good show of firepower by running from one port to another, and the naked Yaquis, still equipped mostly with lances and bows and arrows, were soon scared off. Pancho Villa, however, would have presented a different problem. His marauding army was at least as well equipped as the forces of the Mexican government. By 1915, Villa posed such a threat to communities along the United States border that General Pershing was sent with a sizable expeditionary force to fight a brush-fire war that was to go down in the annals of combat as the last to involve a massed charge of the U.S. horse cavalry and the first in which the Army's "air force"—then one flimsy scout plane—saw action.

Yet, in the long run, the Yaquis were actually more of a threat to the continued operation of the graphite mine. While Pancho Villa's raid on La Colorada stopped the Santa María's ore shipments for several weeks, the Yaqui harassment of central Sonora lasted for more than thirty years, from about 1890 to 1926. The mining camp was never sacked, but it wasn't safe to venture far afield. Three men were killed just a half-mile away while they dug out samples of what appeared to be another graphite vein, and the Los Positos hacienda, home of the Aguirre family since 1835, was burned down twice.

Ironically, what finally saved the Aguirres from repeated trouble almost cost them their lives. Salvador was working in his fields one day when he suddenly found himself surrounded by about a dozen Yaquis. They told him they were going to kill him. Trying to postpone the inevitable, he kept talking, and somehow they grew a little friendlier, and he invited them to the hacienda for coffee. The Indians were on foot, but they allowed him to mount his horse, and as soon as he was a little bit ahead of them, he took off. By the time the Yaquis reached the hacienda, all the Aguirres were cradling repeaters in a show of force that made a considerable impression on the Indians, especially since they were invited to eat anyway. They gulped the food that was offered and by that time were feeling so good that they promised never to attack the Aguirres again, nor to steal any of their cattle. In return, Salvador promised them not to tell the soldiers that Yaquis had been around. He kept his word. Not that it would have made any difference if he hadn't: knowing where the Indians had been one day didn't help you figure out where they'd be the next. The Mexican army, however, didn't see it that way. Colonel Lazaro Cardenas, who was later to become Mexico's president, rode up with some of his garrison from La Misa, 45 miles down the line, accused the Aguirres of harboring Indians, gave them one week to leave the ranch, and threatened to hang them if they didn't. The Aguirres took their chances and stayed on, and, as it turned out, they had gauged Cardenas correctly. He found more important things to do, and never came back to the ranch.

Only two Americans were stationed at the mine at the time. One of them was Carl Kellogg, a tall, rough-and-ready frontier type from Saginaw, who as a little boy had tagged along with Henry and Edward Wickes on fishing trips, carrying the rods and making himself otherwise useful. Young Kellogg had proved himself a talented mechanic, and the Wickes brothers had trained him and originally sent him to Mexico to repair the mine machinery that was getting in bad shape. Later, as manager of the operation, Kellogg developed a new and far more extensive deposit in a nearby canyon, also on the Aguirres' 55,000-acre property. The rights to this mine, called the San José de Moradillas, were bought for $36,000 at a time when the peso was worth 50 cents, a remarkable bargain, considering that the Moradillas is still in operation today. Since its first graphite was hauled out in 1918, a shaft has been sunk that now goes down about 1,000 feet, with a maze of galleries, some of which are more than a mile long. Over the years, the mine's annual output rose from 3,000 tons in the beginning to about 30,000 tons in World War II, and it now averages about 18,000 tons.[7]

As the output increased, so did the need for transport. The Villa raid on La Colorada had put an end to the narrow-gauge railway to Torres, and a new loading point had to be developed. Kellogg picked a railroad siding at Moreno, southwest of Torres on the way to Guaymas, and only about 22 miles from the mine. The ore packs on the backs of mules soon yielded to wagons running on steel-rimmed wheels and each carrying 5 tons; the wagons were drawn by teams of sixteen of these stubborn creatures, which were immensely strong and sturdy despite their deceptively small size—no bigger than large St. Bernards. A wagon trail was carved that climbed laboriously out of the canyons of the mining area. The rugged mountains on all sides were covered with kapoc trees, palo verde, and ironwood, good for building fires. Down in the narrow desert valleys there were also a few ironwoods, but most had already been cut. Left were organ pipes, saguaros, and mesquite, and small groves of green-barked twisted trees, a landscape of peculiar desolation, yellow and dusty green, inhabited by jackrabbits and Gila monsters and dotted here and there by high, jagged rocks resembling the eroded cones of ancient volcanoes. It was rough country, and the ore transports had a hard time of it. But once they were out of the mountains, the going was easier. The flats of a vast plain opened up toward Moreno, and here the mule teams could move at a good clip, provided they were willing. But at best the trip took twenty hours, and eventually tractors were purchased to pull the wagons.

The production facilities in Saginaw also had to change to accommodate the increased flow of graphite. And so did the markets. Pencils were still a good business, front-end luster for steam locomotives still sold, and there was still a pretty good volume in stove polish and axle grease. But, as time passed, the company pushed its sales effort more and more in the direction of marketing what was then known as "boiler graphite." This development was rather logical since the Wickes people were, after all, involved in the manufacture of boilers. Boiler graphite was highly refined ore that was used to clean the scale out of steam boilers before the introduction of water softeners. The graphite, added at the rate of about 1 pound per 100 gallons of feed water, was so fine that it entered the tiny crevices of the scale, worked its way between the scale and the boiler plate, and eventually stripped the scale off, obviating the necessity of shutting down the boiler for cleaning.[8] That part of the business alone absorbed some 3,000 tons of graphite a year in the 1920s.

Yet more interesting from a business point of view were the inquiries that kept coming in for graphite brushes for use in electric motors and generators. In addition to its other qualities, graphite is unctuous, self-lubricating, and endowed with the ability to conduct electricity. It therefore makes a fine commutating carbon. The people at U.S. Graphite had tested the value of this product in a most antique manner. "We made it a habit to toss interesting samples into a drawer," wrote Harry C. Woodruff, the early assistant general manager. "One day in the year 1915, I think, several pieces of brush graphite [shaped for use in electric motors] were selected from this drawer and quotations what they might sell for obtained. Imagine our surprise to find, when these samples were placed on a balance scale over in the laboratory, that their price in silver coins outbalanced said samples even though the materials in their production were quite inexpensive. This indicated a substantial spread between cost of raw materials and the selling price—a difference ample to cover (1) labor and overhead and (2) profit. As the labor item could not be large once a reasonable level of production was achieved, it was deduced that the profit should be quite satisfactory."[9]

By the time U.S. Graphite (or USG, as it was called by its staff) started flirting with the manufacture of brush carbons, the company had moved from its original shed to a new installation on Holland Avenue in Saginaw, which is still the location of its descendant, Wickes Engineered Materials. In the old factory, the ore had been processed by means of extremely primitive techniques. They used burrstones, formed like mortar and pestle, that ground the ore by rotating action. A fan mounted behind the burrstone blew the powdered graphite into a series of rooms, separated from each other by partitions that reached only part-way to the ceiling. The coarser graphite settled in the first room, the finer graphite in the next, and so on to the fourth, where the finest stock accumulated. What would have been the best grade, of course, went out into the atmosphere—the whole area was covered with black dust.

In the new plant, the burrstones were replaced by more modern tube mills in which 6-inch steel balls smashed the graphite into powder. This powder was then graded in big cyclonic separators that, by centrifugal force, fractionated the particles through screens of various fineness. The output was much greater, as it had to be, since the business was now shipping carloads of boiler graphite. It was in this new factory, during World War I and the early 1920s, that USG's graphite brushes were developed by Charles Field III, a former faculty member of the Massachusetts Institute of Technology. By 1923—and just in time, since the boiler graphite business was to run out within the decade—the brush department outgrew its first modest quarters in the back of the plant, and a special addition was built for the manufacture of this product.

U.S. Graphite never became a leader in the brush field, but remained merely one of several major suppliers. But, as we shall see in the next chapter, this first step to actually make something out of graphite rather than simply sell it in bulk marked the beginning of an entirely new and different era, which saw the company emerge as a pioneer in powder metallurgy; that is, in the compression of powdered metals and metal alloys, of graphite and other carbons, into a variety of sophisticated materials vital to many industries. There is no modern use for natural amorphous graphite that was not originated by U.S. Graphite's engineers.

Meanwhile, however, as the staff in Saginaw increasingly concentrated on expanding the manufacturing operations, less and less attention was paid to the mine. The deliveries of graphite continued more or less on schedule, and when there were delays or shortages, it was easy enough to shrug them off as part of the *mañana* syndrome. Albert Sargent Harvey, Harry T. Wickes's son-in-law, the jovial and kindly man who took over the company's presidency from Woodruff in 1930, seemed to regard his periodic visits to the Moradillas more as adventurous outings than inspections. He had come down to the mine ever since his youth, accompanying his father, Thomas A. Harvey, one of the graphite company's founders, and much of each stay was always devoted to hunting mountain lions and other big game. More than anything else, Albert Harvey's competence lay in his ability to generally surround himself with good people, which he did up in Saginaw, and it's a good thing that most of them were talented, since he was extremely loyal and would never believe anything but the best about his associates. Thus, with the Moradillas mine in the hands of Kellogg, that trusted family retainer, Harvey felt no cause to be concerned, and for some time did not catch on that there was something radically wrong down there, namely that Kellogg, while a top-notch, hard-working mechanic, was anything but a manager. One big trouble, of course, was that neither Harvey nor anyone else in Saginaw knew anything about mining, so even as they began to sense that all was not well at the Moradillas and that maybe *mañana* wasn't all to blame, they couldn't quite put their fingers on what might be wrong.

As it happened, the leaders of the maturing Mexican government, no longer inclined to let United States business run their country as an economic colony, were beginning to make legal difficulties for USG's Mexican subsidiary, the Companía Minera de San José. The trouble came mostly in the form of ever more burdensome and often disproportionate taxation.

ALBERT S. HARVEY

Harry T. Wickes's son-in-law and president of U.S. Graphite, Al Harvey enjoyed hunting more than mining, and making friends more than firing people who had been working for him for years.

To help out with these problems, Harvey hired an attorney from Tucson, Arizona, by the name of Victor H. Verity. Whether it was Harvey's good luck or innate astuteness is hard to tell, but Verity, then thirty-three years old, was not only a lawyer but a trained mining engineer who had done considerable work south of the border.[10] Verity spotted the trouble immediately the first time he went down to the Moradillas, on New Year's Day of 1937, in the company of Laurence Field, Graphite's secretary-treasurer. It was quite simply that the Moradillas was a mess from the word go. The old wooden head frame from which winches lowered and raised the cage in the mine shaft had never been replaced, and it now leaned over at a dangerous angle that no professional mine superintendent would ever have condoned. But Kellogg, who was one of those old-fashioned empirical people who could put any piece of machinery back together with spit and chewing gum, didn't pay any attention to equipment so long as it worked. Transport of the ore from the mine to Moreno was equally makeshift. Kellogg had replaced the tractor-drawn wagon trains with some antiquated trucks. The problem was that these trucks ran on solid tires that had a very short life span on rough roads. Every time one of these tires needed repair, it had to be shipped all the way to Tucson, since the frugal Kellogg kept no spares on hand. Not surprisingly, there were no records of where prospecting shafts had been sunk or tunnels dug, or what grade of ore one could expect to encounter in the different veins. Field had no choice but to let Kellogg go.

His successor was John A. McDonald, an experienced Spanish-speaking miner who was recommended to Verity by Grover Marsteller, the mine company's Nogales, Arizona, accountant. McDonald immediately anchored the old head frame to the hillside with a cable—frayed and rusty it was, but the only one to be found on the property—while a new steel head frame was being shipped down from the States. The hard-rubber tires were quickly replaced by pneumatics that could be changed on the spot. Verity himself prepared a plot of the mine and set up a plan of development. Within a few months the mine's output increased dramatically.

At the same time, Verity managed to keep legal relations with the Mexican government on a fairly even keel, partly because of his efforts to improve the workers' lot. There was no other source of employment between Hermosillo and the Moradillas, but this was no reason to let the 350 miners and their families live in shacktown squalor, even if they expected no better. It was difficult anyway to get people to work in those tunnels, where temperatures, despite forced-air ventilation, hovered around 100 degrees,[11] and where, after a few minutes of sweaty labor, workers were so thickly covered with graphite they looked as if they were made of shiny black metal. Considering such conditions, it was evident that not only had the wages to be raised—the pay was then something like $1.50 a day—but that provisions must be made for better housing, an infirmary, and a real school. "It was very interesting to watch over the years how conditions changed," says Vic Verity, now seventy-two years old and semiretired. "When I first went down there, these people were really poor. The clothes on their backs were all they had, and they wore sandals made from pieces of old automobile tires and leather thongs. But after a while, first you'd hear a little radio here and there, and then you'd hear that so-and-so had bought his wife a sewing machine, then finally one or two automobiles cropped up and when somebody got sick you didn't have to drive him to Hermosillo any more, banging him around for 60 miles on a dirt road, like they used to do between the once-a-month visits of the doctor."

The hospital, for which a physician was brought in from Mexico City, came in handy for victims of mine injuries and of the stabbings that occasionally occurred at fiesta time, but it was slow to attract people when they were sick. Typhoid and dysentery were common, and even though a hospital was available, the miners' wives still clung to witches' brews. Mothers would not bring their children to the hospital until they were just about goners. Sick babies were sometimes so dehydrated that the soft part of their heads had caved in. Often, indeed, medical care came too late.

If anything, better living conditions actually brought more discontent. Eric Hoffer once wrote that without expectation there is no rebellion: nobody fights for something that seems completely out of reach. As the mineworkers got more, they quite naturally wanted even more, and much that they wanted could not be provided overnight. United States Graphite, by itself, could not modernize a whole region that until 1975, in fact, had no telephone service and still has no electric power network. The discontent that smoldered below the surface was fired up more than once by agitators, who were preaching revolution.[12]

Such difficulties aside, relations with the Mexican government became ever more difficult. With increasing frequency officials levied peremptory taxes, and it took considerable finesse on the part of Fausto R. Miranda, a prominent Mexico City attorney retained by Verity, to keep the imposts low enough to make it worthwhile to continue operating the mine.[13] It wasn't even a matter of profitability. For many years, the Moradillas had been mined not so much for producing actual revenue—as had been the goal in the days of boiler graphite—as for assuring the Saginaw company a steady supply of certain grades of ore for its powder metallurgy needs. Beyond a certain point, of course, it would have been cheaper to buy these ores on the open market than to dig them out. Thus, not surprisingly, when the "Mexicanization" Law was passed in 1961, it was anything but unwelcome. The law stipulated that 51 percent of the stock in all foreign mining companies had to be sold into Mexican ownership within twenty-five years. Once this was accomplished, a company was entitled to substantial relief in production and export taxes.[14] Mexicanization, in effect, solved the Moradillas dilemma. Nothing was more logical than to sell control in the mine to Pedro Aguirre, Salvador's middle-aged son, who was raising Brahma bulls and Charolais cattle on the old family ranch. With the resultant tax relief, the graphite sales in the United States would provide a sufficient income for the Aguirres to slowly pay for the mine; at the same time, Wickes Engineered

SAN JOSÉ DE MORADILLAS

Scorpion-infested canyon (above) is site of the Wickes graphite mine in Mexico's Sonora desert. In early days, mules carried out the graphite. Now trucks do the job, but it's still a struggle.

Materials had its pick of the amorphous graphite crop without paying exorbitant prices for it.

The name of the company was changed to Cía. Minera Moraguirre, a combination of the name of the mining camp and that of the Aguirre family, and a charter for the new corporation was issued November 22, 1967. Pedro Aguirre, still robust in his early sixties and without doubt one of the handsomest men of the Hermosillo establishment, has since turned the new Casa Grande over to his thirty-three-year-old son Pedro Adolfo, who now manages the Moradillas and is its legal owner.

Saginaw still keeps its hand in. Jack Splane, who succeeded

SHOWER, ANYONE?

Prime movers at the Moradillas since World War II have included (left to right, in 1954 picture at right) John A. McDonald, former superintendent, and Ralph A. Zemanek, veteran U.S. Graphite executive, now Wickes's senior vice president of the corporation's industrial manufacturing divisions. Shown below (left to right) are Carlos Tapia, foreman; John L. Splane, another former superintendent; and Smith Bolton, who was in charge of U.S. Graphite sales when this picture was taken in 1948. (Photos by Victor H. Verity)

McDonald as superintendent from 1948 to 1954, returns periodically to the comfortable hillside hacienda he built as the superintendent's residence during his tenure. The vast underground complex that exists today, as well as the modern housing now provided for the miners, were largely Splane's design, and he still serves the Moradillas as a consultant.[15] Another frequent guest at the hacienda, which is reserved for visiting brass, has been Ralph J. Zemanek, who worked his way up from metallurgist at U.S. Graphite to his present position as senior vice president in charge of all Wickes industrial manufacturing divisions as well as general manager of Wickes Engineered Materials.

Zemanek and his right-hand man, Ray Amberger, another USG alumnus, recently discovered that things haven't changed very much over the many years they've been coming down to the Moradillas. Traveling through Sonora remains an adventure. On a trip in late 1974, the company station wagon Zemanek usually keeps parked in Hermosillo was blocked by a flash flood deep in the desert between La Misa and the mine after a typical Sonora downpour. When Zemanek tried to push the wagon out of the mire, he slipped and got soaked to the skin. So he stripped down to his shorts and hung his pants out the car window to let them dry in the sun. Suddenly he found himself staring into the barrel of a .45 Colt.

It wasn't a bandit's gun, though. The station wagon, with its mysterious brown paper bags in the back, a bare-chested man behind the wheel, and trousers flapping in the breeze, had aroused the suspicion of Mexican police. The cops thought they'd nailed a couple of hippie smugglers, albeit middle-aged, but when the *Federalistas* dug into the bags they found neither marijuana nor peyote, but only supermarket groceries for the Moradillas hacienda, and they apologized profusely and sent Zemanek and Amberger on their way.[16]

4

Legacy

Henry Dunn Wickes's bent and training had made him an outstanding practical mechanic. Coupled with his sense of opportunity, this just about guaranteed him success in that era of great industrial growth, when the ability to apply simple principles to problems at hand, and the willingness to take a gamble on such semi-improvised know-how, gave rise to the first generation of technological entrepreneurs. Not surprisingly, he was interested chiefly in building what one might call primary machinery, i.e., implements required to help create final products. There had to be intermediaries between his gang saw and a finished house, between his lathe and a completed piece of production machinery, between his graphite and a pencil. Almost everything he manufactured and sold served an indirect or collective function. This was typical of industry before the introduction of the assembly line, when the marketing of items designed to appeal to individual consumers was hardly a worthwhile pursuit. It certainly wasn't in the realm of any enterprise that aspired to be big business.

Now that sales and services constitute the heftier half of the gross national product (GNP), and with The Wickes Corporation's major efforts pointed in these directions, it only stands to reason that Henry Dunn Wickes's original manufacturing ventures and their linear descendants add up to pretty small potatoes in terms of the company's total volume. Out of projected sales of close to $1.3 billion in fiscal 1976, they will account for only about $37 million, or something like 3 percent. Even Wickes Furniture, the relatively new warehouse-showroom retail operation, is expected to gross more than double, and net one-third more operating income than the industrial divisions whose predecessors gave birth to today's corporation and nourished it in its infancy. And that despite the preeminence of those divisions in their respective fields.

Wickes Machine Tool, descendant of the old Wickes Bros., is the world's leading manufacturer of automotive crankshaft lathes. Wickes Engineered Materials, the offspring of United States Graphite, manufactures seals and bearings used in every U.S. atomic submarine, in most nuclear power plants, in the engines of jet aircraft, and on NASA rockets that have roared into orbit and outer space. Wickes Boiler, before it was sold to Combustion Engineering in 1966 for reasons that shall be explained later, was a leader in the heating and industrial boiler business, and had been a major supplier of power plants for Liberty ships and destroyer escorts in World War II.

But build an enterprise that really succeeds, and it's sure to outgrow your original concept and antiquate your original approach. This was already apparent when Henry Dunn Wickes died. The ability merely to make machinery was then no longer enough. Marketing became the key. With increasing technological sophistication, engineers could be hired to devise products according to demand. The challenge was to pin down the demand and meet it. This required market-oriented businessmen rather than product-oriented mechanics to run the show. Indeed, Henry's sons, Harry Tuthill Wickes and William Jarvis Wickes, although apprenticed in the family machine shop as kids, were trained primarily to be managers and sales-

THE SECOND GENERATION

Harry T. Wickes.   *William J. Wickes.*

men. And so was Harry's son-in-law, Albert S. Harvey, whom we already encountered at United States Graphite in the previous chapter. There was other evidence as well that times were changing. The penny-pinching frugality of the pioneer generation was no longer the order of the day. Business dealings now often involved lavish, sometimes not altogether sedate, parties on a series of private yachts. And while the three men undoubtedly worked hard, William Jarvis Wickes, at least, played harder. He tossed money around with utter abandon, and when he died in 1925 his estate was bankrupt.

No matter how lax he was about his personal finances, however, William Jarvis Wickes proved himself extremely astute when it came to business.[1] In 1907, he took over Wickes Boiler when it was separated from Wickes Bros. and became a corporate entity. That split, which W.J. had instigated, was in itself a most provident move. Within the framework of Wickes Bros. the key boiler people like E. C. Fisher, who ran that part of the operation, had to be content with being middle management. But once on their own, they could be promoted to corporate positions, with attendant prestige and other benefits, including the right to buy shares in the company. This practice was not yet widespread in industry but it was one in which William Jarvis Wickes, as well as his brother, firmly believed.

As previously recorded, the first buyers of Wickes Bros. boilers had been the sawmills of Michigan's timber stampede. In those days before central power stations, every mill had to have its own steam installation to run the machinery. When no more sawmills were built, Wickes started making ships' boilers for F. W. Wheeler & Company of Bay City, for the Chicago Shipbuilding Company, and for Alexander McDougall, who was constructing whaleback steamers. Although the Scotch marine boilers manufactured by Wickes continued to be featured until 1900 in elaborate hardbound books used as sales promotion literature, the ship business was actually not much more than a prestige line—the profits were too small. What finally propelled Wickes to the forefront in the steam-plant and institutional heating business was the company's development of straight-tube vertical boilers that lasted a long time and could be easily cleaned even before the discovery of graphite as a boiler-scale detergent. [2]

The Wickes Vertical Safety Boilers were phenomenally successful. They sold by the hundreds to factories and institutions. For a while they couldn't be produced as quickly as the orders came in. But once again we have a case of a great accomplishment guaranteeing its own obsolescence. When something sells like wildfire, the people who created the product rarely see the need for further improvements, and by the time they make them, it's often too late. Herman Bickel, one of Wickes Boiler's oldest living veterans and its chief engineer until his retirement in 1964, recalls the great reluctance in the plant to try something that might be an improvement on the vertical boiler. [3] E. C. Fisher, who had shepherded the straight-tube model, swore by it and wouldn't hear of anything else, even though it had one obvious drawback: it was not adaptable to larger sizes. At best, it could produce only about 45,000 pounds of steam per hour. Not until Wickes nearly lost all its boiler business to competitors in the early 1920s did Louis Baker, the shop super-

BOILERS TO THE RESCUE

Branching out into the boiler business helped Wickes survive the lean years after the lumber bubble burst and before lathe production became important. Railroad spur on Saginaw's Tilden Street serviced both Wickes companies. (Photo by Bradford-LaRiviere, Inc.)

intendent, consent to the experimental construction and testing of the bent-tube boiler, a type that lends itself more readily to manufacture in giant sizes. And even then Baker went halfway behind Fisher's back.

The funny thing is, E. C. Fisher might have been partly right. There was indeed a demand for more powerful boilers, but when Wickes got around to producing them, they made a great impression but very little money. Of course, during the Great Depression the boiler business went to pot everywhere. Only beer tanks, which are manufactured by the same method, sold to the new post-Prohibition breweries in any quantity. By the same token, there was no way for any manufacturing company to go broke in World War II. With the excess profits tax you couldn't make a fortune, but comfortable survival was assured. The U.S. Maritime Commission purchased some 360 Wickes 1,000-horsepower units for Liberty ships, and other boilers were made for small Navy vessels. The company upped its working force to 500, established a production line, went on three shifts, and was rewarded with the Maritime Commission's "M" Award of Merit in January 1944 "for outstanding achievement."

After the war, Wickes engineers brought the bent-tube boiler all the way up to 350,000 pounds of steam per hour, and the company's representatives in Detroit, Milwaukee, New York, Chicago, and Tulsa sold them to factories, refineries, hospitals, schools, and municipal utilities with great success.[4] Wickes Boiler, then under Divisional Vice President and General Manager Robert J. Stormont, even obtained a $1,350,000 government contract to build three mammoth boilers for the atomic energy plant at Oak Ridge, Tennessee. Of course, a

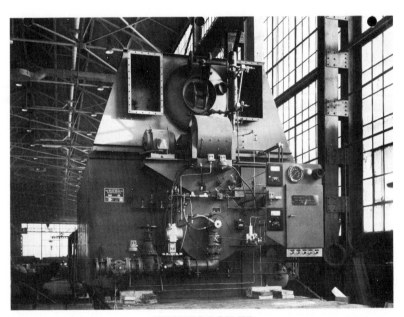

WICKES BOILER

A typical Wickes A-type industrial boiler, which was equipped with a combination oil and gas burner, and came completely piped and wired.

seven-digit deal like that is peanuts in heavy industry, especially when it comes to supplying Uncle Sam, but anything to do with atomic energy made the headlines in those days. Ten years later, there was more national publicity when Wickes fabricated a giant boiler, weighing 185,000 pounds, for the United States Navy base at Guantanamo, Cuba. This boiler was to be used to desalinate seawater when Fidel Castro shut the tap on the base's fresh water supply. There was publicity, too, when Wickes made mobile boilers, which could be shifted from one dock to another, to supply steam power for atomic submarines while they were in port with their nuclear engines down. Indeed, Wickes Boiler maintained a profit margin better than that of the industry as a whole, but it was a mighty slim margin, and not enough to make up for the risks that boilers always entailed.

Boilers—even "safety" boilers—have a way of blowing up, and it's difficult, if not impossible, to pinpoint the exact trouble. Nobody cares if it's not the boiler itself that causes the accident. Luckily, no one was ever seriously hurt in explosions that involved Wickes boilers. But in the late 1950s and early 1960s, damage suits against the company totaled in the millions of dollars. One explosion at Muscatine, Iowa, in a plant that processed exotic fuels for jet bombers, wrecked much of the installation. A suit by the Borden Chemical Company demanded damages in the neighborhood of $20 million for a malfunction in a plant at Geismar, Louisiana, that kept on causing the bent tubes inside the boilers to blow up. Altogether, it was a mighty expensive proposition, considering that in 1959 the division's volume was $6.2 million, of which only 2.3 percent, or $138,000, went to the pretax bottom line.[5] The Wickes Corporation was in no mood to continue such risks. By that time every resource was directed toward expanding the highly profitable Lumber Division, and there was no point in carrying on with any potentially costly activity that barely produced a profit even in its best years. Fortunately, it so happened that Combustion Engineering, which was well established in the big utilities field, wanted also to get into smaller industrial boilers. And so the division was sold, and Wickes got out from under.[6]

Under Combustion Engineering's ownership, the old Wickes Boiler plant remains right where it had always been, on that quarter-mile stretch of Wickes industrial properties between the Saginaw River and North Washington Avenue. Wickes Machine Tool also is still located here, and to this day flourishes under the Wickes banner. More than anything else, the tool operation's endurance can be credited to its eventual specialization in crankshaft lathes—a development that, despite its obvious benefits, entails some built-in drawbacks, however. If the day ever comes that the automotive industry switches to engines like the turbine and the rotary, which don't require crankshafts, Wickes Machine Tool will have to do some mighty fancy footwork to stay in the running.

Like Wickes Boiler, Wickes Bros. had stumbled along some-what haphazardly during the first half of the century. Under the tutelage of William J.'s brother, Harry Tuthill Wickes,[7] and the latter's heir and successor, Harvey Randall Wickes, it profited hugely some years and barely broke even or plunged

WICKES LATHE

One of the earlier 20-inch lathes designed for turning crankshaft line bearings.

GEORGE A. KENDALL

*A self-taught engineer, he made
a major contribution to the
design and manufacture of
Wickes crankshaft lathes.*

into the red the rest of the time. Wherever a buck was to be made in the machinery business, Wickes Bros. tried to get its foot in the door. In Chapter 2, you read about the days when Wickes still made gang saws but supplemented this shrinking source of revenue by selling reconditioned machinery. That scattered effort went on for years. The product line eventually included such diverse capital equipment as gang saws, plate bending rolls, punches, shears, flanging clamps, radial drills, engine lathes, die-casting machines, and plastic-injection molding machines. Tom Rulison, one of the Wickes old-timers we shall meet in a later chapter, who is now vice president of operations of the Lumber Division, remembers the time— not very long ago—when Wickes Bros., then under Vice President Carl Bintz, even built blueprint apparatus and was unsuccessfully trying to establish itself in the white-print line, the predecessor of today's duplicating processes.

It wasn't until well after World War II that Wickes Bros.

really found its niche in the scheme of things by concentrating on crankshaft lathes. This thrust was largely due to adversity. Because of intense competition, both domestic and foreign, the business in standard lathes had fallen off dramatically, and something had to be done. The man responsible for the resurgence, which made Wickes Bros. even more important than it had been in its gang saw days, was George A. Kendall, an exceptionally competent engineer who was totally self-taught. After a year at Tri-State University and a brief stint with the Consumers Power Company, Kendall had joined Wickes as a draftsman in the 1930s, and then moved into sales. But his professional love was engineering, and he bought all the books and learned the whole business while married and rearing children. By 1948, he was chief engineer at Wickes Machine Tool, the descendant of Wickes Bros., and he personally worked out much of the crankshaft lathe design. Made general manager in 1952, he pushed ever harder in this direction, and within ten years his factory was the undisputed leader in the field. [8]

Wickes Machine Tool's list of customers soon began to read like a *Who's Who* of the automotive industry. Just about any company that manufactured cars or trucks bought its crankshaft lathes here—General Motors, Ford, Chrysler, International Harvester, Caterpillar Tractor, John Deere, Volkswagen of Germany, Fiat of Italy, Rolls Royce, and Perkins of England. Before long Wickes had about 65 percent of the world market and more than 70 percent of the domestic market.

One of the product lines Wickes Machine Tool had been trying to get into without much luck was die-casting machinery that shaped zinc and aluminum into die-cast parts. The prime mover in that direction was Joe Oeming, who managed the plant for several years after World War II. Machine Tool built and sold a number of such machines, but somehow never managed to really crack the market. Then, in 1963, one of those rare chances arose. The Kux family of Chicago, whose firm had been making such equipment for forty-five years, wanted to cash out of the business. Its founders, the brothers Albert and George Kux, were both dead. Albert Kux's nephew, James J. Kux, was running the operation, but the ownership was vested mainly in two elderly ladies, a sister of the founders and the widow of George, neither of whom was interested in remaining in business.[9] It was the kind of situation that creates the most favorable climate for an acquisition: the original owners want their capital gains, and some prospective buyer wants the property. There's no need then to raid the stock of a flourishing company in the hope of gaining control by buying up enough of its shares on the open market to force it into a subsidiary position. Wickes had just started its expansion by means of acquisitions, and up to this point had merged only two companies into its corporate fold. Both had been head-quartered right in Wickes home territory in Saginaw. Kux was to be the first venture beyond the boundaries of this domain.

Not that Kux was the buy of a lifetime. Unlike Wickes Machine Tool, it didn't have a corner on any market. Any number of companies made die-casting machinery, so the price of the Kux products was limited by market factors and could not be based on the uniqueness of the product. As a result, the Kux profit margin was fairly low, usually less than 10 percent pretax, and on a rather small volume at that. But the company was available at the bargain price of about $1 million—not bad for a business that was hitting about $2.2 million in sales that year. Moreover, nearly half the purchase price was covered by inventory, work in progress, and raw materials. For a good name like Kux and the plant's machinery, the remaining $600,000 wasn't too much to pay, and Kendall, by then vice president (and later senior vice president) in charge of Wickes industrial operations, went along with Oeming's desire to get into die-casting machinery and endorsed the acquisition.

Apparently it was Kendall's original intention to move the Kux operations eventually to Saginaw, and put them under one roof with Wickes Machine Tool, for the Kux plant was not part of the deal. It was merely leased for two years. But then Machine Tool got ever more busy making crankshaft lathes; at the same time the Kux volume picked up, and the move to Saginaw was never made. Instead, a new 56,000-square-foot plant was built for the Kux Machine Division on South Wolf Road in Des Plaines, just outside of Chicago. Kux now has about 110 employees and its annual sales have risen to more than $5 million.

Since 1969, R. J. Jacobs, a longtime mechanical engineer-turned-executive, has been the vice president and general manager of the Wickes Machinery Group, as the indirect offspring of Wickes Bros. is now called. Jacobs, who gives the deceptive appearance of being easygoing, is that rarity among present-day technocrats, a contemplative, studious man of catholic interests, a specialist in his field but able to converse knowledgeably and sensitively on most any subject. If he

BUNDLES FOR RUSSIA

Wickes crankshaft lathes slated for export to the Soviet Union crammed the Saginaw production line when this photo was taken in 1943 at the height of World War II.

weren't constituted that way, he would have a hard time surviving at The Wickes Corporation of today, where the big wheels are well versed and vitally interested in almost everything under the sun with the notable exception of machine technology. Anyone who was less of a liberal arts type than Jacobs would be a fish out of water.

The Machinery Group, as now constituted, includes yet a third manufacturing facility which was purchased a little over a year before Jacobs arrived on the scene. This is the Saginaw Machine and Tool Company, which was merged into The Wickes Corporation as a subsidiary in 1968. Like that of the Wickes Machine Tool operation, Saginaw Machine Tool's fate was then totally linked to the fortunes of the automotive industry. Its specialty was the making of multiple-spindle vertical boring and grinding machinery of the high precision required for the manufacture of automatic transmissions.[10] At the time of the acquisition, this Saginaw-born, then nearly fifty-year-old company had a substantial portion of that specialty market sewed up. It had two customers—General Motors and Ford—but they were enough to produce about 3 million dollars worth of business a year. And again, as at Wickes Machine Tool, the profit margin proved to be substantial: the products of both companies were unique.

But if Jacobs had known what he was walking into, there's a pretty good possibility he wouldn't have accepted the job. He had kicked around big industry for the better part of twenty years since his graduation from the City College of New York, and had advanced from product engineering through sales and marketing to general management in a succession of positions in the aviation, paper machinery, and injection-molding areas. He certainly knew enough to look up the Wickes operations in the *Thomas Register*, but he was never given a chance even to see the plants before he came aboard.[11] "George Kendall gave me some insight," Jacobs says, "but he was also the kind of fellow that figured you should find out for yourself, and he didn't want to have you prejudge the situation." No wonder. What Kendall didn't divulge, after a Chicago headhunter deliv-

ROBERT J. JACOBS

*He didn't know the troubles
he'd see when he took over
the machinery divisions.*

ered Jacobs to the Wickes doorstep, was that Wickes Machine
Tool had been leaderless for some time. Joe Oeming had been
let go some five months earlier, one of a number of people we
shall encounter in this narrative who fell victim to The Wickes
Corporation's growth. The point isn't whether they couldn't
adjust to the expansion that was to take the company out of the
parameters of their vision, or whether the top management
lacked the psychological perception to fit its old-timers into the
new scheme of things. What matters is that, regardless of its
causes, here was a loggerhead situation. As a result, Oeming
was out despite his considerable talents, and now there was no
real leadership. Another thing that Jacobs wasn't told, because
nobody knew it at the time, was that Oeming was about to go
into competition with Wickes Machine Tool. After recruiting
three of the Wickes key men, Oeming had started a Saginaw
firm, the C. M. Systems Company, which picked up the sales
agency for the Crankshaft Machine Company of Jackson,
Michigan. With a major order in his pocket from the start,

64

Oeming seemed determined to knock Wickes off its crankshaft pedestal.

"When I heard about Oeming going into competition with us, it was a real shocker," recalls Bob Jacobs. "This created a big threat to us. We warded it off through a very strong sales effort, through careful pricing, and through a tremendous amount of personal contact at all levels. But it did knock the pins right out from under the profit margins for two years in a period when business was very poor. We were able to survive only because of our international crankshaft sales. One thing good about it: It pushed us into doing some redesigning that was perhaps long overdue."

With engineering improvements and the increased sales effort, especially in Europe, Jacobs was able to keep the Oeming enterprise at bay.[12] In the meanwhile, of course, it also became important to enlarge the scope of Saginaw Machine and Tool so it wouldn't be completely at the mercy of the cyclical nature of the automotive industry. Similarly, it was necessary to expand the product line at Kux with special

F. A. SIMMONS

He cracked the European market for Wickes Machine Tool. (Photo by Bosch) emphasis on bigger die-casting machines, which are far more profitable than the smaller ones that had been this division's traditional stock-in-trade. Kux also got back into the business of making powder metal presses, a line that had been originally developed by James Kux in earlier years but had been allowed to lie dormant for some time. The impetus in this direction was in no small part due to the fact that Kux was now a Wickes company. Wickes Engineered Materials, the old United States Graphite, had grown to become a leader in the powder metallurgy field, and was itself a customer for such equipment.

Meanwhile, Saginaw Machine and Tool's product line was extended to cover more than automatic transmissions. The Allison Division of General Motors now uses machines made in that Wickes-owned plant for the manufacture of pistons and sleeves for aircraft engines. General Electric and Frigidaire also became major customers. What's more, the whole marketing approach was changed. Even in the automotive field, Saginaw Machine and Tool now mainly makes automated equipment rather than the traditional boring and grinding models that required manual loading and unloading and human inspection. A machine that used to cost $60,000 now demands $200,000 for its sophistications, the difference being returned to the buyer in labor savings. Saginaw Machine and Tool is up in the $6-million-a-year category from a nadir of less than $1 million, to which it had plummeted shortly after its acquisition by Wickes. The general manager at Saginaw Machine and Tool is F. A. ("Art") Simmons, who had been largely responsible for building up the European export business at Wickes Machine Tool.

At Kux, the emphasis is now on 800-ton rather than 200-ton presses, and on providing all manner of auxiliary equipment for die-casting machines, which Kux customers otherwise would have to buy elsewhere. By selling such packages rather than just presses, the sales here were similarly increased, bringing this division also to an annual volume of close to $6 million from a low of about $1.2 million the year Jacobs took over.

At Wickes Machine Tool, the direct lineal descendant of

Wickes Bros., Jacobs found himself pretty much locked in. Its heavy machinery was unsuitable for operations other than the manufacture of crankshaft lathes, and being an old plant, its adaptability to new product lines was extremely limited. But meanwhile the rotary engine has not caught on to the degree it was once feared, the automotive industry is still using crankshafts, and the Russian government recently placed a $2.5-million order with Wickes for lathes for the Kama River Truck Plant.[13] In any case, with all these innovations plus a quota of good luck, the Machine Tool Group made more money in the Wickes fiscal year that ended in January 1975 than it had ever before, and it was still carrying a considerable backlog of orders into fiscal 1976, despite the downturn in the economy.[14]

At the top of all the Wickes industrial manufacturing divisions today sits Senior Vice President Ralph J. Zemanek, sixty-two, the impish but hot-tempered general manager of Wickes Engineered Materials, whom we first met in the previous chapter as he crossed the Sonora desert stripped to his underwear after falling into a king-size puddle. Zemanek, percolating with energy like a college-age youngster, is a rarity among Wickes executives. He came with Wickes in 1935, and he's still there. When Zemanek joined United States Graphite with a brand-new engineering degree, Albert S. Harvey was still president of that company, but increasingly the decisions that mattered were devolving upon Smith Bolton, one of Harvey's young protégés. It's a good thing that this was the case, for Graphite had been slipping steadily for quite a spell. The company's only true loss year, 1938, was yet to come, but if Bolton hadn't been able to take the initiative at just about that time, and hadn't built a team that ever more prominently included Ralph Zemanek, USG might well have drowned in its own puddle of red ink, and there wouldn't have been the wherewithal to give The Wickes Corporation a sound start.

Just why Graphite stumbled is impossible to fully diagnose in retrospect. Of course, there was the Depression, but the company's troubles predated that national disaster. We do know that the Moradillas mine had been left to the makeshift devices of a well-intentioned and hardworking but otherwise totally unqualified handyman type from Saginaw (see the previous chapter). We also know that while USG did become a major supplier in the carbon-brush field, it hadn't gotten its foot in the door early enough to assume real leadership in the development of electrical carbons. Moreover, it is readily apparent that neither Harvey, nor his predecessor Harry C. Woodruff, despite their innate Midwestern conservatism, were given to trimming off excess organizational fat. Both of these fine gentlemen, and particularly Al Harvey, were far too loyal to their longtime employees ever to consider making out pink slips when the going got tough. There's also some indication that United States Graphite may have taken itself just a mite too seriously, considering its rather modest volume, which hardly ever exceeded $500,000 a year before Bolton stepped into the picture. The temptation certainly was there: what other little company was there in Saginaw that could lay claim to mining the bowels of remote Mexico for raw material, and then shipping its products to every corner of the world? So Graphite played it big. It maintained amply staffed sales offices, complete with personable secretaries, in New York City, Philadelphia, Atlanta, Pittsburgh, Cleveland, Cincinnati, Detroit, Chicago, Denver, and San Francisco, as well as in Berlin, way over there in Prussia where the Kaiser used to hang out, plus a host of graphite drummers who beat the bushes around Boston, Buffalo, St. Louis, Minneapolis, and Kansas City. Tightly run the organization was not. As *The Greaser*, USG's internal house organ, reported plaintively in its September 1925 issue, "We have heard nothing from our Berlin, Germany, sales manager Mr. E. H. Warmber, since July." Perhaps a homey bit of go-and-get-'em philosophy also published in that magazine should have been taken more seriously by everyone: "Don't have your wishbone where your backbone ought to be."[15]

Among USG's 200 or so employees at that time, there was, however, one category that never got those bones confused: the people in the company's metallurgy lab.[16] Their first major breakthrough, which came in the late 1920s, was the revolutionary development of oilless bearings, made from mixtures of graphite and powdered metals, mostly copper and copper alloys at that time. The mixtures were compacted under great pressure into the shapes required—cylindrical, flanged, and self-aligning sleeve bearings, whose creamy graphite content made external lubrication unnecessary. The company trade-marked such metal-graphite blends as Gramix in 1926, and the first Gramix best-seller, of which hundreds of thousands were produced, was a bearing for electric car-heater motors. Gramix was soon followed by Graphitar, another compressed powder mixture that, however, contained no metals but was a blend of graphite and other carbons.[17] Graphitar was to prove itself yet more efficient than Gramix as the constituent material in self-lubricating seals and bearings, and eventually it became one of USG's leading products as the formula was improved.

Smith Bolton, under whose leadership the company finally learned to take full commercial advantage of its remarkable scientific know-how, went to work for Al Harvey in 1934, the year before Zemanek came aboard. Bolton was then thirty-two years old, a very worldly young man, tall and blue-eyed, with the gentlemanly manner of reserved cordiality that's the brand of an Eastern prep-school education. His mother's family had been in the sawmill business on the Saginaw River. His step-father had owned a large automobile dealership, which Smith Bolton ran after he graduated from the University of Michigan.[18] He was definitely a member of the Saginaw Establishment. Al Harvey, although considerably older, had been friends with him for some time. Harvey no doubt sensed Bolton's potential, but there was no way to persuade the young man to come to work for him until Bolton's stepfather died and the Bolton Auto Company fell victim to the Depression. Bolton, happy to get a job even if it paid only $185 a month, which was quite a comedown from the car agency's better days before the Crash, learned about graphite from the ground up. He started out in the plant, worked his way through the order department into the sales department, and soon discovered that United States Graphite didn't have anywhere near its potential market share in any product line. The excuse of USG's salesmen had always been that their competitors bribed their way into the big accounts, like General Electric. Bolton went over to Schenectady and learned that this just wasn't so: the salesmen of the competition simply worked harder at selling. Graphite's district sales managers, most of whom had been with the company for around twenty-five years, seemed to possess very little knowledge of the company's products, and were more inclined to run impressive branch offices and to socialize over long and comfortable lunches than to go out into the cold and dig up new business.[19]

But recognizing shortcomings isn't the same as fixing them, and as a newcomer Bolton had to bide his time, proving himself first. Promoted to assistant sales manager in the 1938 doldrums, he prepared a projection that USG needed $1.2 million in annual sales to show a satisfactory profit, and he proceeded systematically to build up the volume. First he went after General Electric, and managed to bring in a big chunk of that corporation's business, including not only electrical carbons, i.e., brushes for electric motors, but also mechanical carbons, as pressed-graphite products like self-lubricating bearings are called. Then he snared Ford, Chevrolet, Oldsmobile, and a host of other customers in an impressive tour de force, each for about $100,000 to $150,000 worth of business a year. He soon crossed the $1.2 million line, and, not surprisingly, Al Harvey promoted him to sales manager in 1940. Bolton's first action was to discontinue the district sales offices, forcing the sales staff to go calling on clients instead of waiting for phone calls. Not only did this move bring in yet more business immediately, but it also saved $100,000 a year in overhead, a gain that translated directly to the bottom line.

With World War II, the United States Graphite Company finally burst into full bloom. Lest any reader of this book be inclined to prejudge industry as just a bunch of nasty war profiteers rolling in money while the soldiers rolled in mud, let it be on record that the profits, slimmed down by the wartime excess profits tax, were minimal; moreover, most government contracts were cost-plus, and they contained a provision for refunds to Uncle Sam in the event a company made more on an order than it had expected to when it quoted the price. No, USG's blossoming was of a far richer texture than the temporary gloss of immediate profits could ever be: the company burgeoned in technical accomplishment. USG became the world's largest manufacturer of carbon packing rings for steam turbines, turning out as many as 10,000 a month of all sizes, and there was not a ship in the United States Navy whose engine room was not equipped with this Graphitar product. Eventually, the company's contributions to the war effort were recognized with an Army-Navy "E" Award (for "excellence in production") in 1945.

But one contribution that was not mentioned at the ceremonies, which took place when the war was still going on, was that United States Graphite had provided the shielding for the first atomic pile, used by Dr. Enrico Fermi to prove the feasibility of a nuclear chain reaction. For this purpose, after a highly secret visit by a gentleman who carried a letter from President Franklin D. Roosevelt, USG manufactured two or three carloads of $2 \times 4 \times 8$ inch bricks whose purpose was concealed even from the company's employees. These bricks were made of a special Graphitar whose impurities had been volatilized by means of a graphitizing process developed by the Dow Chemical Company. This shielding then went around Fermi's experimental uranium pile at the University of Chicago's football field—and the Manhattan Project, with its incalculable consequences, was on its way.

Since Smith Bolton had been instrumental in getting the United States Graphite Company on its feet financially after the 1938 loss year, and since during the war he had carried the major burden of the company's relations with the War Production Board, it only stands to reason that he must have been in line to become general manager. That's what Bolton believed too, but it was not to be. After Harvey's death in 1941, H.

Randall Wickes, the scion of the Wickes family, had assumed the presidency of the company, and Laurence Field had become general manager. Field then also passed away, but Ran Wickes, shortly after the merger of all the family's interests into The Wickes Corporation in 1947, appointed Harold Ward, a cost-accounting specialist, to run Graphite.[20] This turned out to be a big mistake, since Ward didn't have the training to cope with the responsibilities he suddenly faced. But it could have turned out to be an even bigger mistake if Bolton had quit in his disappointment, as indeed he was inclined to do. He stuck around only because he knew that Ward couldn't last long, which in fact he didn't, and Bolton finally got the job in late 1948. The only reason that this intramural shuffling deserves mention here is that it had a direct bearing on the future of The Wickes Corporation. Had Bolton resigned when he was bypassed, he wouldn't have been part of the legacy on which the new corporation built its foundation, and as we shall see, this could have had some dire consequences, for Bolton was to be instrumental in later years in helping the corporation overcome one of its gravest crises. Having proven his mettle by deblundering United States Graphite, he was then called upon to clean up the Lumber Division, whose blunders, in turn, were threatening to wreck the still-adolescent corporation.

But when Bolton took the helm of USG, that crisis was still more than a dozen years into the unknown future. Meanwhile, he took hold of Graphite with his accustomed acumen. He had built the operation into the biggest moneymaker of the three Wickes predecessor companies when he was its sales manager; now he expanded on that base. He revitalized the Moradillas mine by giving his full support to those who knew mining best—specialists like Victor H. Verity and John S. Splane. He pushed engineering research and development, then under Harold Mitchel. Bolton also enlarged and modernized the factory on Holland Street, and he upped production to the point where USG never had fewer than 500 employees, and in some peak periods as many as 800. And he even won a naval battle against Admiral Hyman Rickover. This crusty sailor-scientist, father of the nuclear submarine, had insisted—but without success, for Bolton proved himself no less stubborn—that the Navy be given the formula of Graphitar manufacture so that other suppliers could produce that magic compound in the event the cold war turned hot and USG met with atomic demise.

For Graphite's contributions to the national purpose had only just begun with the steam-turbine packing rings of World War II. The Navy's Bureau of Ships determined that no other material was as appropriate for the manufacture of seals and bearings for atomic submarines as was Graphitar, and the voyage of the U.S. submarine *Nautilus* under the polar ice cap had backed up this laboratory finding. Since then, Graphitar seals and bearings have been used in nuclear power plants of every kind, mobile and stationary; they are integral parts of jet aircraft engines; and they've been aboard many U.S. space rockets.

The emphasis on research and development continued under Ralph Zemanek, who succeeded Bolton in the leadership of Graphite in 1961 when the latter was called on to serve as senior vice president in charge of all Wickes Corporation operations. Zemanek, a metallurgy graduate of the Michigan Technological University at Houghton (then called the Michigan College of Mining), had started his career at Graphite as a product engineer—the technical specialist who could talk to, and understand the talk of, engineers employed by customers and potential customers. It was Zemanek's job to find out what these customers needed, and then to see that Graphite could produce it to their satisfaction. Zemanek later became Bolton's sales manager and right-hand man, but he never lost track of the fact that the basis of all sales by an outfit like Graphite lay not in soft talk but in hard technology. So metallurgical research continued to progress at a great pace. In the Gramix line, means were found to increasingly replace expensive copper and tin with cheaper iron, and to turn out equally sound

RUNNING ON GRAPHITAR BEARINGS

Admiral Rickover's nuclear submarine Nautilus *sails off on its historic voyage under polar icecap. Graphitar components, manufactured by Wickes Engineered Materials, have been essential to operation of atomic reactors, both mobile and stationary, ever since.*

machinery components, most of which now contain no graphite whatsoever. Hence the far more descriptive name, Wickes Engineered Materials, which this division bears today. Indeed, these pressed metal-powder components, in terms of volume, are now the division's most important product.

New uses for graphite were also found, however. In World War II, Zemanek discovered that every ton of graphite could save 25 tons of pig iron, which was then extremely scarce. Pig iron, with its carbon content, had been essential in steel production, but Zemanek developed a system whereby graphite could be added to scrap steel in an open-hearth furnace, and the same quality of new steel achieved as when pig iron was used. Zemanek spent the war years visiting practically every steel plant in the United States and Canada to teach the

RALPH J. ZEMANEK

*Expert metallurgist
and incisive
executive, he
proved himself
no less stubborn than
U.S. Navy's Hyman
Rickover.*

procedure. Besides helping the war effort, this activity vastly increased USG's business. Sales of the Moradillas graphite for use in steelmaking doubled, and by 1945 reached 10,000 tons per year, enough for about 1 million tons of steel. Later Zemanek saved more pig iron by developing Mexite Briquettes, in which graphite is compacted with a special cement as binder into brick-size blocks. These blocks proved invaluable in making cast iron, since loose graphite charged into a cupola

75

(a vertical melting furnace) would be blown out by the surge of heat. But the graphite in briquette form stayed in the cupola, so that now scrap and graphite also could be used as a substitute for pig iron in the production of cast iron. During the Korean conflict, when once again pig iron was at a premium, USG sold more than $1 million worth of Mexite Briquettes in nine months, and at one point had a backlog of orders for 130 carloads.

Zemanek also revived and modernized one of graphite's most ancient uses—as a refractory. He developed Mexaloy, a graphitic ingredient for coating the gigantic crucibles employed in modern steelmaking. Mexaloy mixtures will not crack despite their exposure to molten metal; they remain stable despite the intense heat, and they possess enough natural lubricity so that the steel won't crust in the crucible. And there's Mexatop, a composition of graphite and clay (not very different from the innards of a pencil), which is used as a so-called "hot topping," i.e., as insulating material to cover molten ingots.[21]

After some relatively low-profit years, mostly due to increased costs as the inflated 1960s turned into the still more inflated 1970s, Zemanek proved himself no less of a money manager than he was an engineer-salesman: he managed to turn the operation around.[22] With the help of Ray Amberger,[23] Zemanek's sidekick as Zemanek was once Bolton's, Wickes Engineered Materials will gross over $18 million in fiscal 1976, with an amazing return on assets of 33 percent, or nearly double that of the corporation's overall 17.7 percent return.

As pointed out earlier, in terms of actual cash this may not seem like a whole lot for a big-budget business, such as Wickes is today. But that's only comparative. By the same token, neither the old USG, nor Wickes Tool and its adopted siblings, Saginaw Machine and Tool and Kux, appear quite at home in the new Wickes scheme. But again that's misleading. Capital-intensive and operating on assets that have for the most part long been paid for, these divisions have considerable profit leverage. Although accounting for only about 3 percent of the corporation's total sales volume, they were responsible for nearly 6 percent of the corporation's 1975 profits. And that ain't hay, even if it isn't quite as bulky as beans, which were to be The Wickes Corporation's first venture outside the realm of technology.

Thus the puzzle of Wickes—its deceptive appearance as a conglomerate. Despite what many people think, namely that the corporation's industrial manufacturing divisions are digressions, they are actually its base. The corporation has since grown in other directions, but like anyone blessed with affluent ancestors, it is more than happy with the regular stipends of its inheritance.

5

A Matter
of Embezzlement

W inston Churchill once wrote that "the longer one lives the more one realizes that everything depends on chance." To back up this not altogether astounding statement, he evoked battle. A soldier discovers that he's forgotten his matches. He turns back to get them. Before he has walked a hundred yards, a shell arrives from 10 miles away and explodes exactly where he stood when he found himself without a light. Proving, if nothing else, that in this chancy world even smoking can be good for one's health.[1] Had Churchill been an industrialist rather than a warrior-statesman, he might well instead have used the origins of The Wickes Corporation as a corporate entity for his illustration of fate as the "omnipotent factor in human affairs."[2] Take the chance ingredients of this amazing story:

Item—The William J. Wickes estate, as we already know, is bankrupt. Stock in the U.S. Graphite Company must be sold to satisfy W.J.'s creditors.

Item—Watling, Lerchen and Hayes, a prominent Detroit stock brokerage house, happens to be charged with this secondary offering. Watling, Lerchen and Hayes also happens to think highly of Lybrand, Ross Bros. & Montgomery, a national firm of public accountants with a branch office in Detroit.

Item—A Saginaw lady of good will and civic virtue, a trusted employee of the U.S. Graphite Company for many years, has learned how to keep duplicate sets of books with one hand, while her other is in the till.

Item—An ambitious young accountant—so ambitious that he has worked his way through night school in both accounting and law—can't stand his glory-grabbing boss in the New York headquarters of Lybrand, Ross Bros. & Montgomery.

Item—Absentee landlordism by assorted friends of Winston Churchill's paternal ancestors had made life miserable for the Irish under the British Crown. When the potato famine struck in the 1850s, it left its scars for decades after. One of these scars was still clearly visible on the lung x-rays of the Lybrand partner who managed the Detroit office. This handsome black-haired Gael from County Cork dies in 1933 at the early age of forty-eight, leaving what looks like a ne'er-do-well son.

Thus the stage is set, and any promising playwright walking into the darkened theatre should be able to project more or less what is about to happen. Except for the surprise fillip at the end of the first act.

The ambitious young man was John McCullough, who had been born in Philadelphia in January 1904, the fourth child in a family that ultimately consisted of twelve children. Even under ordinary circumstances, this family situation probably would have been enough in those days to instill the work ethic in a kid, but John had more going for him, and as a result matured very early. His father worked for the Metropolitan Life Insurance Company, selling small policies to people in whichever neighborhood he lived, and there were many of these neighborhoods, since he was burdened by what were then referred to as "personality problems," which caused him to be transferred any number of times between New York City, Philadelphia, and New Brunswick, New Jersey.

Needless to say, there was no money to send young John to

college. When he graduated from Townsend Harris, a preparatory school for the City College of New York, with prizes in
French and Latin in his pocket, John McCullough went to
work in the accounting department of the Manhattan Life
Insurance Company, and five evenings a week for eight years
trundled over to night classes, first at City College and then at
New York University, to earn his B.S. in business administration. At the same time, he qualified as a certified public
accountant (CPA), and in 1929 joined Lybrand, Ross Bros. &
Montgomery as a junior accountant.[3]

His boss, Hermon Bell, a Lybrand's partner, was a brilliant,
broad-gauged man who went beyond the basics of accounting
and interested himself in income tax matters and management
accounting, neither of which was a subject widely pursued at
that time. This experience stood McCullough in good stead,
but Bell was so imperious and hard to take as a boss that the
men who worked for him were nicknamed "bellboys." After a
couple of years, McCullough had had enough, feeling that he
wouldn't be permitted to fully develop his talents. Meanwhile,
however, having become interested in income taxes through
his association with Bell, McCullough had taken up the study
of law, also in night school, and when in 1933 he let it be
known that he was thinking of moving on to another job,
Walter Staub, the managing partner of the New York office,
suggested to McCullough that a position in the firm's Detroit
office might bring him great opportunities for advancement.
McCullough accepted the offer, being promoted to senior
accountant in the process.

Before he left for his new assignment, McCullough was
summoned for an unexpectedly personal talk with Thomas B.
J. Henderson, the senior partner in charge of the Detroit and
Chicago branches. "Let me tell you a little bit about what's
going on in the Detroit office," Henderson said, and proceeded
to do so: Richard Fitz-Gerald, the big, jovial Irishman who had
built up the Detroit office from scratch, had died a few months
earlier, in July, after a long and terrible illness. He had suffered
a series of ever more serious strokes, and in the end pneumonia

overpowered his tuberculous lung. Moreover, just before Fitz-Gerald's illness, three of his ablest aides had left the organization to found their own firm, taking a lot of brokerage auditing business with them. From being one of Lybrand's leading branches, Detroit was suddenly limping, and in the midst of the Depression at that.

"I wish that were all," Henderson said to the barrel-chested, stubby young man, who was staring back at him so earnestly. Henderson must have had his second thoughts for a moment. McCullough looked more like a middleweight boxer than the scholar that he was. But there was the vaguest hint of a sensitive smile, not of amusement but of anticipation, in McCullough's square face, and if his firm chin testified to his determination, so did the bemused, questioning smile bespeak his tact.

Indeed, diplomacy was needed. "The real trouble is," Henderson continued, "that the man who is now in charge of the Detroit office doesn't know what he's doing. Fine fellow, but incompetent. I can't understand how Fitz-Gerald ever hired him, but so long as he was around it didn't matter. Now it does. I want you to go up there and backstop that fellow. Keep all the business he might be losing for us. And get more. We need every bit of it."

McCullough understood. He was to keep an unofficial eye on the whole Detroit operation. His specific assignment, meanwhile, was to concentrate on the branch office's tax department. Which suited him just fine. He had learned under Bell that taxes were rapidly becoming the key determinant in accounting, which was no longer a matter of merely keeping and auditing books but of advising management to make the right kind of accounting decisions. That's why he had taken up the study of law: he wanted to know everything that was possible under the Internal Revenue Code, and at the same time enjoy the peace of mind that would come with the certainty of always operating within the code. Ingenuity could almost always devise a legal way, but ignorance decreed eventual disaster.

"There is something else I'd like you to do for me," Henderson said. "You probably know that Fitz-Gerald and I were great friends. Well, his son—Dan is his name—didn't turn out exactly as Dick might have hoped. He put the boy to work in his office a couple, maybe three, years ago, tried to make an accountant out of him, but Dan can't keep his mind on his work. Keeps flunking his CPA exam, too. Good-looking fellow, just like his old man was, and he's a hell-raiser. I'd like you to try and straighten him out."

McCullough consented readily enough. With so many younger siblings, he was used to older-brother responsibilities. And so, in his new capacities of troubleshooter and nursemaid, he boarded the New York Central's *Wolverine* and discreetly invaded Detroit.

Not that the client situation in Detroit was quite as bleak as Henderson had painted it. The three men who had left the office to set up their own firm[4] may have taken a lot of business with them, but Lybrand's still had many faithful clients, among them the Ford Motor Co. Like most of the others, Ford had been brought into the stable by the indomitable Richard Fitz-Gerald, who had simply arranged to go on a trip to Europe on the same ship as Charles Sorenson, then in charge of Ford's factory operations. Somehow, Richard Fitz-Gerald had been convincing enough to sell Sorenson, who in turn sold Henry Ford, a job that couldn't have been easy since Ford was congenitally opposed to lawyers, bookkeepers, systems, and accountants. In any event, Fitz-Gerald was instrumental in obtaining a tax refund in connection with Ford's reincorporation in Delaware, and if anything breeds a reputation in a close-knit industrial community like that of Detroit's automotive world, such an accomplishment will do it.

McCullough was quick to pick up where Richard Fitz-Gerald had left off. Under the "supervision" of the head of the tax department, he took over Ford Motor's tax affairs, and it wasn't long until, as a result of this work, he was introduced to Charles S. Mott, the largest single stockholder in General Motors. Not surprisingly, McCullough's roster of new business kept growing.[5]

McCullough's other assignment—keeping an eye on boisterous Dan Fitz-Gerald—was in many ways probably more challenging. It's interesting how recollections vary. "We got along very well together right from the start," says McCullough, now retired as a Lybrand's senior partner. "I could have killed the s.o.b.," recalled Dan Fitz-Gerald shortly before his death. "He was after me all the time."

In the years when Dan Fitz-Gerald ran The Wickes Corporation first as president and then as chairman of the board, he grew fond of the kind of self-deprecating humor that prompts many a chief executive to refer to himself as being "only the office boy around here." Not that Fitz-Gerald ever stooped to that cliché. His favorite line was that he had been born in the Bronx, across the street from Fordham University, and that his father always said "the shadow of the university never took." Dan was born on February 6, 1910, seven years after his father had emigrated to the United States from Ireland at the age of seventeen to make his fortune.[6] By the time Dan was born, Richard Fitz-Gerald, although only twenty-four, already had his own accounting firm in New York City and did a lot of European business. His family commuted regularly between the United States and Ireland, where they rented a house near Cork, while the elder Fitz-Gerald did business on the Continent, Ireland, and in New York City. He was in Germany when the First World War broke out, and when they threw him off a train in Berlin to load troops, he walked and bummed rides to Amsterdam where he finally managed to board a ship to London. Meanwhile, his wife, with Dan and a younger sister in tow,[7] were crossing the submarine-infested Atlantic in a blacked-out ship, and they had no sooner debarked in New York than it was sunk by sabotage. With all that excitement in his early years, it may not be surprising that Dan was to develop a preference for action rather than study.

He was ten years old when the Fitz-Gerald family moved once more, now to Detroit, where his father established the branch office for Lybrand's. This was the Detroit of the Roaring Twenties, of the Purple Gang, Detroit River rumrunners, and Ty Cobb's Tigers, all of which made for more excitement while Dan lurched through the University of Detroit High School and a little more than a year of Wayne University. At that point, shortly after the stock market crash of 1929, he figured he'd had all the schooling he needed. He had grown 6 feet tall, wide of shoulder, and narrow of hip, handsome black-Irish like his father, with light-blue sentimental eyes. Books took too much time away from what life for a young man like that was all about: hitting golf balls, chatting up girls, swapping blarney with buddies, and watching baseball games from the Tigers' dugout. So he went to work. As he told it, "My father sent me down to Lybrand's to see if the boys had anything for me to do. He being my father, they found something for me to do—every dirty job they could think of: office boy, telephone operator, file clerk."[8]

After about a year of this, Dan realized with some reluctance that he had better get a degree after all. "Dad," he said, "you'll be happy to hear that I've decided to go back to school." Said the elder Fitz-Gerald, "Dan, I think that's great. Now I hope you can afford it."[9] So Dan registered for night classes at Wayne, where he majored in mathematics and English, and more night classes at the Walsh Institute for Accountants, but he was still the same old Dan, who felt that hitting the books was like being in prison and that promotion to "junior accountant" at the office was a bore. Whatever work he did was barely enough to get by.

The way John McCullough went about remedying this situation was mostly through ridicule—in private, of course, for an embarrassed Dan might have slugged McCullough. Anyway, demeaning a person in front of others was not Mc-Cullough's style. He could tell Dan had a brilliant mind, and it was just a matter of getting the young fellow on track and moving. So McCullough, in his firm but quiet manner, would take the sloppy, improvised reports that Dan gave him, politely put them in the wastebasket, and tell him that they weren't worth looking at. Would Dan be kind enough to give the matter some more thought and submit something that perhaps could be filed away for posterity? On one occasion, while out on a job for Fisher & Co.,[10] McCullough threatened to send Dan back to the Lybrand's office if he didn't perk up and start to make a contribution. When Dan did turn in a creditable performance, on the other hand, McCullough praised him lavishly, and somehow this combination of irony, stick, and carrot seemed to work. Eventually Dan even passed his CPA test after flunking it four times.

Despite their relationship of tormenting mentor and frequently obstreperous pupil, however, the two men soon became close buddies outside office hours, for, when the day's work was done, McCullough was no less prone than Dan to go out for a night on the town. Since accountants, by and large, are a rather conservative lot, this recreation isolated John and Dan from the more staid members of the firm and served to draw them yet closer together. It is no wonder, then, that as Dan's professional competence improved, McCullough took him along on more and more jobs, including an audit of U.S. Graphite that came up in 1935.

Right at the outset, Al Harvey, the president of Graphite, made it very clear that he had no intention of retaining Lybrand's on a permanent basis. Graphite had its own public accountant, a Mr. Faulkner, and only in this particular instance were Lybrand's services required since, in order to file a stock registration with the Securities and Exchange Commission, it was necessary to have the books certified by a national accounting firm.[11] But when the brokerage house of Watling, Lerchen & Hayes brought this piece of one-time business to Lybrand's, explaining the necessity for making a market for Graphite stock on the New York Curb Exchange in order to salvage W. J. Wickes's estate, Henderson's orders were explicit: "Go up to Saginaw, do a good job, get paid, and keep the account." Neither McCullough nor Fitz-Gerald had the vaguest idea of how to persuade Harvey to drop Faulkner in favor of Lybrand's. Even at their first interview with Harvey, they could tell that here was a man who could not be budged in his loyalties. Still, it was a job to be done, and the two young men moved into Saginaw's Bancroft Hotel for the duration.

In any audit, there are five basic ingredients: cash, accounts receivables, inventories, fixed assets, and liabilities. Cash and liabilities are relatively easy to determine. The cash is in the bank or you can take it out of the safe and count it. For the liabilities, you've got bills from the payees. Valuations of inventories and fixed assets may involve considerable interpretation, depending on how they are carried on the books. Checking up on accounts receivable requires mailing letters that request confirmation of the balances.

McCullough and Fitz-Gerald sent out these letters, and while waiting for the replies, proceeded with the other aspects of the audit. All seemed in very good shape. In fact, the books were so orderly, and the bookkeeper, a fussy maiden lady in her late forties, was so precise in her answers to McCullough's questions, that one day he complimented her, and as was his custom kidded her a little bit in his dry, ironic way. "Now," he told her, "you just be sure to always give me good answers like this, and we'll never have any trouble."

The next morning and on the days that followed, work progressed at a somewhat slower pace. The lady bookkeeper, unfortunately, had taken ill, and wasn't around to help. Then, as the accounts receivable confirmations started coming in, it became evident that something was wrong somewhere. Right off the bat, Chrysler Corporation reported that, according to its records, the outstanding balance was considerably less than shown on Graphite's books. Similar discrepancies showed up in other confirmations.[12] Soon there was no doubt that more than a bookkeeping mistake was involved.

McCullough and Fitz-Gerald first broached the bad news to Laurence Field, then Graphite's treasurer. It was difficult enough to convince him, but at least he had some knowledge of accounting and could follow the presentation of the two Lybrand's men. But with Harvey it was a different matter. He was no accountant, and there was no point in going through the intricacies with him.

Dan Fitz-Gerald thought Harvey was going to hit Mc-Cullough when the latter first mentioned the definite possibility of embezzlement. "Look," McCullough bluntly told Harvey, "all I know is that we've got letters that tell us that a number of your customers don't owe you as much as you think they do. There is only one person who could possibly know about this, and she's not around anymore. They tell me she's sick."

Harvey flushed and jumped up from his desk. "Young man," he said, barely controlling his voice, "you'd better be able to prove what you're saying. Because if you can't, we're going to have you in deep trouble." And then he started to tell how many years this fine lady had been with Graphite, and how much everybody thought of her, and what a great job she'd been doing. McCullough countered, "That's probably half the trouble, Mr. Harvey. It's never somebody that's just come in. It's always somebody that's been with the company for a long time and is well trusted. Those are the only people who can do it. Anyway, Chrysler has agreed to give us copies of all their checks. We'll soon find out."

"Just bear in mind what I told you," Harvey said, shaking with anger. "Don't you dare show yourself in this office again until you've come to apologize or have absolute proof."

The investigation took longer than Fitz-Gerald had expected—or, more likely, than he had hoped it would. Even though now a full-fledged professional CPA, he was still impatient with the finicky details of accounting, as indeed he always would be. For nearly three months, McCullough and Fitz-Gerald checked and rechecked payments against deposits. Painstakingly they reconstructed what must have happened: the lady bookkeeper, who conveniently remained home with her stubborn cold while all this detective work was going on, had started her profitable second career about twenty-five years earlier by "lapping" the cash expense accounts of Graphite's salesmen. When a salesman sent back the unused balance of his cash advance, she'd pocket the money instead of crediting the salesman's account with the $100 to $150 that might be involved. Then, when the next salesman returned the cash he had left, she used it to close out the first salesman's account, and so on ad infinitum. Along the way, while staying ahead of the game by jockeying the accounts of the company's thirty-some salesmen, she kept on withholding more and more cash until her withdrawals could no longer be covered by the advances. It took her about five years to reach this point, and that's when she started to dip into the accounts receivable, which were naturally much larger. Chrysler Corporation, for instance, had sent checks to Graphite for as much as $15,000, of which only $10,000 was credited. She'd convert the check to a cash deposit, only part of which she'd funnel into the salesmen's account kitty, leaving her lots of room for indiscretion. Soon she was not only lapping the salesmen's accounts but also the accounts receivable, which was not too difficult in those days before banks kept photostatic records of receipts. But even so, there was only one reason why she could continue her lapping for so many years, running up her take to somewhere around $50,000. The reason was simply that Graphite's accountant had only audited the company's books, which she had always managed to balance, but he had never bothered to confirm the accounts receivable.

When McCullough and Fitz-Gerald went in to see Harvey again after that hot and heavy summer, they carried the proof he had demanded. Just to make absolutely sure, Lybrand's attorneys had gone over the material, and had agreed that there was enough evidence to take the case to court. Harvey sat there behind the desk, not saying anything, just listening, and suddenly he started to cry, and the tears were dripping down on his Mexican shirt. After a while he said, "If she needed money, she only had to tell me. I would have given it to her." Then he asked McCullough and Fitz-Gerald to leave his office. He wanted to be alone.

So far as the two men from Lybrand's were concerned, the case was closed, the future obvious. Detectives from the Burns Agency visited the bookkeeper at her house, and she readily surrendered the duplicate set of books she kept there: a complete record of her machinations. Now it was just a matter of turning the case over to the bonding company. The latter would make up the loss under its obligations, thus putting the

Graphite balance sheet in order for the secondary offering. And the lady would go to jail.

Indeed, the bonding company, after examining the facts, agreed to its liability and demanded all the records so it could take the bookkeeper to court. This, they felt, had to be done, for letting one embezzler off the hook sets a dangerous precedent for others. But the bonding company hadn't reckoned with Al Harvey. "No," he told them, "we're not going to do that. You keep your money, but she's not going to be prosecuted. We're going to adjust the balance sheet and absorb the loss." And so the lady did not go to jail. The whole affair was hushed up.

Now for the promised twist:

The bookkeeper, a mousy woman of such nondescript appearance that few people noticed her even when she was in the same room, never kept a dime of her ill-gotten fortune for herself. She had been puffing up her ego not only by proving that she was smarter than U.S. Graphite, but by playing Robin Hood. All the money she stole she gave to others—to the sick who couldn't afford their sickness, the families who couldn't buy coal to heat their homes or meet their mortgage payments. She had cheated to be loved.[13]

All else that now happens is predictable:

Graphite has its stock listed. The estate of W. J. Wickes is bailed out. Faulkner loses the Graphite account to Lybrand's, another feather in the cap for McCullough, who is soon destined to be appointed Detroit manager, then regional manager and partner.[14] Meanwhile, Al Harvey and McCullough become good friends. Harvey introduces McCullough to H. Randall Wickes, the scion of the family.[15] They also become good friends. In 1941, when Ran Wickes becomes president of Wickes Brothers, Wickes Boiler, and U.S. Graphite, he asks McCullough to come to work for him. McCullough declines. He says he can do just as much, if not more, from where he sits over at Lybrand's. He has discovered that a talented accountant in a key spot with a national firm can be one of the most important factors on the business scene—a behind-the-scenes matchmaker, the guy who first pulls the strings. Instead, Mc-Cullough recommends that Ran Wickes hire Dan Fitz-Gerald, for McCullough knows that his young friend will never be happy shuffling ledgers but that he has the makings of a hot executive; that he is a man not frightened but pleasured when big decisions are to be made; and that he is endowed with an instinct for coming down on the right side of these decisions.

Back in 1934, when Dan was barely twenty-four years old and still something of a sleeper, he had already shown his talent as a decision maker. As executor of his father's crash-crunched estate (totaling something in the neighborhood of $30,000, and that mostly life insurance), he had decided to invest all that was left in common stocks. It just wasn't in his nature to see the country as having gone to hell permanently. Dan's intuition, if not yet wisdom, proved him right. He could not have picked a more propitious time to gamble on America's vitality. "More than anything else," McCullough says, "that's what impressed me with the brilliance of Dan's mind. You've got to remember that he was still only a young fellow when he was faced with the awesome problem of having to manage his family's nest egg. He sought the advice of everyone who was supposed to know about such things, and the overwhelming advice, including that of Mr. Henderson, who was a trustee of the estate, was to buy bonds. Dan's decision to buy stocks in the face of all this contrary advice, and then his refusal to look back and chew over his decision, and his ultimate silence about his success—all this showed executive ability of the highest order. I've never forgotten it."

This, then, was the man to whom Ran Wickes turned, on McCullough's advice, after several years during which Lybrand's had handled the annual Graphite audit. "I'm getting a little tired of paying Lybrand's for your time," Wickes said to Fitz-Gerald. "I think it would be a lot cheaper if you were on the payroll."

"Fine," Fitz-Gerald responded in his rich Bronx-Irish baritone that, in his later years, made him sound like the successful son of a New York cop. "I'll be glad to come to work for you, Mr. Wickes, but I don't know what I'll be able to do for you."

It didn't take him very long to find out.

Proving that being embezzled is sometimes the best thing that can happen to a company.

6

The Monkey and
the Giraffe

May 1, 1942, was one of those hot, steaming days, all the
sweatier for arriving without a prelude, that often over-
power Michigan in spring. On that day, Ran Wickes ushered
Dan Fitz-Gerald into the barren room that was to be the
latter's office at Wickes Bros. The air in the room was stale and
stifling. When Fitz-Gerald opened his rickety window, it fell
out into the parking lot. Frustrated, he crumpled into his tilt-
back chair. When he roused himself and sat up, the chair
stayed tilted back. Fitz-Gerald leaned on his desk, and felt grit
under his fingers. Always a meticulous dresser, he dusted off
his sleeves, and wondered how he had ever landed in this rat
trap. But there was no turning back. All he could do was
hunker down to a job which led he knew not where.

One of the first things he found out, thanks to a firm request
by the Internal Revenue Service for back taxes from the estates
of William J. and Harry T. Wickes, was that these two men had
dipped their hands into the till even more deeply than the
embezzling lady over at United States Graphite. Of course,

they had every right to; the companies, in effect, were theirs. But their approach was highly unorthodox. For years neither of the second-generation Wickeses—W.J. at Wickes Boiler and Harry T. at Wickes Brothers—had bothered with anything so mundane as a salary. Any time they needed cash in addition to the sizable dividends they collected from Graphite, they'd take an "advance." At other times, they simply forwarded their bills to the Wickes companies for payment, including those for the rather expensive upkeep of H.T.'s luxurious 125-foot steam yacht, the *Capitola*, with a crew of eight under a Norwegian skipper, which was docked in the Saginaw River right behind the boiler works. At least this ship, which was primarily used by H.T. for partying with his friends on trips to the Grand Hotel on Mackinac Island, was legally listed as a company asset until a strong wind for some reason blew practically all the water out of the river and up into Lake Huron one day. When the water rushed back up the river, it swamped the stranded vessel, and Wickes Boiler collected insurance on it.[1] So that slate was clean, but aside from such "company expenses," the brothers' personal withdrawals had built up to something like $300,000 apiece. That was a lot of money in those days—being equivalent in purchasing power to perhaps $1 million today—but it didn't really add up to an overly generous compensation for the bosses of fairly prosperous enterprises when divided over a period of perhaps ten years. In any event, the day of reckoning had come. The IRS insisted on its share, claiming that W.J.'s and H.T.'s borrowings actually were dividends paid to them by their companies.[2]

As we have already learned, W.J.'s estate was bankrupt. With the latitude permitted those financially defunct, it got away with paying back to the company something like 10 cents on the dollar, and this part of the case was closed. The estate of Harry Tuttle Wickes, however, proved solvent, and it looked like his estate would have to pay back his advances in full. McCullough was instrumental in the negotiations that got the estates off the hook without having to pay either back taxes or nonpayment penalties, and it only stands to reason that Ran

THE LIFE AND DEATH OF THE CAPITOLA

*Proudly afloat (above) and capsized in the Saginaw River (below), Harry
T. Wickes's steam yacht all but symbolized the fortunes of the second
Wickes generation.*

Wickes must have been mightily impressed with the two young men from Lybrand's, one of whom he'd had the good fortune to hire as the comptroller of his companies.

Not that Ran Wickes was much given to handing out compliments. Then in his fifties, he was a quiet, reserved, almost diminutive man in rimless spectacles, who tended to keep his own counsel and never said very much either in praise or in criticism. As a young man he had liked to hunt, and in his middle years he became fond of fishing. The trophies of both sports, along with a cozy Franklin stove, dozens of photographs, and an immense clutter of dust-collecting souvenirs, adorned his pine-paneled office. Yet one could not help feeling that Ran Wickes liked hunting not so much for the sake of the hunt, nor fishing for the sake of fishing, nor his almost daily card-playing sessions at the Saginaw Club for the thrills of the game, but rather, because hunting, fishing, and playing cards were activities that brought him friendships with the kind of men he admired and felt a kinship to: virile, outgoing types with lots of machismo. He himself was only about 5 feet 6 inches tall, with tiny, tender hands, a kind, gentle face, and thinning hair, and he must have known that he hardly cut an imposing figure. His strengths—a computer brain backed by firm fibers of will—were all on the inside. He could be an important mover in any enterprise but could not play it out from center stage, and he had the good sense not to crave the limelight: that didn't mean anything to him. "I don't think," said Dan Fitz-Gerald in retrospect, "that I could have worked for anybody other than a type like Ran Wickes. He had to put up with a hell of a lot from me. I'm just wondering if anybody else would have been able to swallow it. If he'd wanted to be the guy to run the show, we'd definitely have had a break."[3]

But when the chips were down, Ran Wickes had a way of grabbing the reins despite his apparent frailty. One day, during a strike at Boiler, for which the union had imported out-of-town goons, the picketers threw the main switch that controlled the flow of power not only to Wickes Boiler Company but also to Wickes Machine Tool. So, although Machine Tool

THIRD GENERATION

Ran Wickes in his souvenir-cluttered office (right) at about the time he recruited Dan Fitz-Gerald in the 1940s. Formal portrait of the same period (left). (American Photo, New York)

was not on strike, it was also out of business. About fifty picketers, not in a pleasant mood, were crowded around the switch box when Ran Wickes suddenly strode out of the building and headed straight for the trouble spot.

"Hey, Ran, what are you doing? You're going to get clobbered!" shouted Fitz-Gerald, who had dashed after him.

"I'm going to put that switch back on," Ran said calmly, without breaking his step. He walked right through the strikers, threw the switch back on, then turned around to the men. "Now, boys," he said, and there wasn't a quaver in his voice. "It's perfectly okay for you to go on strike, and nobody's complaining about that. But don't touch that switch anymore because that will put other men out of work." And he pushed his way out of the crowd, and nobody touched him, so surprised were all at his audacity.

Ran Wickes was cool, all right—as any absent-minded person better be, especially a sloppy pipe smoker. Time and again he would forget to put out his matches, tossing them away while they were still burning. Some thirty years later, Fitz-Gerald still remembered one morning when he passed Ran's office and smelled smoke. He rushed in. Ran was reading a newspaper, and the wastebasket at his feet was burning. "Your wastebasket's on fire," Fitz-Gerald yelled. Ran casually glanced at the basket, nodded, and said, "Yeah, so it is," then turned back to his paper, leaving the job of putting out the fire to Fitz-Gerald.

Indeed, Ran Wickes increasingly left matters in Fitz-Gerald's hands, and not only when it came to dousing wastebaskets. Although Fitz-Gerald had not yet even been named vice president and wouldn't be for several years, he was charged with putting out just about every fire in the Wickes companies. He became, in effect, Ran Wickes's surrogate, as if he were the scion of the family being groomed to inherit the throne. There is little doubt that Ran, whose only child was an adopted daughter, came to look on the boisterous young Irishman as a son. And like any old-fashioned father, Ran had no intention of spoiling his brat with fast promotions or, for that matter, with too generous a purse.

Interestingly enough, as time went on Ran Wickes seemed to develop something of a dislike for John McCullough. It was probably a kind of jealousy. Fitz-Gerald and McCullough still spent a lot of time together, as they would for their whole careers, and especially in those early years hardly a day went by when Dan didn't pick up the phone to call his buddy in Detroit about some problem, counting on his keenly analytical mind for sound advice. That may well have been what McCullough, even if only instinctively and subconsciously, had intended all along. With Fitz-Gerald pivotal at Wickes, McCullough now had his own man in Saginaw. Like the coach of a football team, he could devise his power plays with the comfortable feeling that his featured player was a guy who could really carry the ball. Conversely, of course, Fitz-Gerald had a pipeline right to the top of Lybrand's, a circumstance that, as we shall see, soon accrued to the advantage of all concerned.

To start with, it was through Fitz-Gerald that McCullough saved the Wickes family a considerable sum of money while firmly entrenching Ran Wickes as Saginaw's leading philanthropic benefactor. Ran Wickes had always been very charity-minded, handing out money right and left whenever he felt, often impetuously, a cause to be worthwhile. As a result of such diffuse giving, much of his money was wasted on projects that were not what they seemed at first, and the community rarely gave him the credit he deserved as a generous donor. Moreover, he frequently failed to keep track of his contributions, so that he couldn't even take appropriate deductions from his taxable income. With the war years and the defense contracts they entailed, this income was considerable, as were the taxes he had to pay. So John McCullough came up with the concept of a Harvey Randall Wickes Foundation as the vehicle through which Ran Wickes could channel all his donations with the assurance that they would be properly used.

Thanks to Fitz-Gerald, the Foundation immediately got off

to an extremely profitable start. At that time, early in 1945, the government was issuing certain bonds that could be purchased only by individuals. Fitz-Gerald was convinced that these obligations, which carried a favorable interest rate, would rapidly increase in value, since the original buyers were permitted to resell them to businesses and banks, all eager to outbid each other. It was arranged with the Michigan National Bank that Ran Wickes, his wife, and his three sisters would each borrow $200,000 to buy such bonds. As soon as the bonds rose in price, they were to be given to the Foundation. Sure enough, within a few weeks the bonds were worth $1.25 million on the open market. At this point the gifts were made as planned, allowing each of the five donors a deduction of $50,000 on his or her tax return. Not long after that, the value of the bonds jumped to $1.4 million, and were then sold by the Foundation, which, cash in hand, paid off the million-dollar bank loan and had about $400,000 left over to start its community service operations, plus its original capital of $10,000 contributed by Ran Wickes and $100 from John McCullough, who had insisted on making the very first donation.

But the really big idea of those years was Dan Fitz-Gerald's dream of a consolidated Wickes Corporation. This concept, rather vague at first and without much of an inkling of what such a fusion could accomplish, had crept into the back of his mind even before he'd left Lybrand's. It had occurred to him then, as he checked through the books of the three Wickes-controlled companies, that the family would have been much farther ahead financially if these companies had been merged instead of being operated as separate entities. When he mentioned this to McCullough, his friend said, "Could be, but first you had better take a real good look."

Poring over ledgers was no less painful for Fitz-Gerald after he had joined Wickes than it had been when he was still an accountant with Lybrand's. But the thought of a consolidation kept gnawing at him, and he finally prepared a schedule that went all the way back to 1913, the year the federal income tax had been enacted. The figures he came up with dumbfounded him. If United States Graphite, Wickes Brothers, and Wickes Boiler had been one company, the tax savings over these years would have totaled somewhere in the vicinity of $5 million!

The reason, quite simply, was that, as separate companies, their profits and losses could not be consolidated. If, in any given year, two of the companies made money and one showed a loss, full taxes had to be paid on the earnings of the profitable enterprises, while the losses of the third had to be incurred as complete losses—they couldn't be used to offset part of the profits of the other two. Nor, as the law read in those days, could these losses be written off against past or future income. Thus, whatever losses the Wickes interests had anywhere in their domain they had to take in full. United States Graphite, of which the Wickes family owned 40 percent, had been a consistent moneymaker except for 1938, the company's only year in the red. Wickes Boiler and Wickes Brothers, in which the family held about 95 percent of the shares, had their ups and downs but in the aggregate, there had always been a profit, if not nearly as much as the tax bill showed.

Fitz-Gerald had told Ran Wickes about his idea right from the first. At the beginning, Ran wouldn't listen at all. Later, after Fitz-Gerald had gone to work for him, he'd say things like, "Great work, Dan, but forget it." Finally, when Fitz-Gerald had all his facts and figures neatly tabulated and shoved them under Ran's nose, several hours of convincing argument netted Fitz-Gerald nothing but a chuckle and a twinkle and the pronouncement: "It's ridiculous. It just wouldn't work. You know what you're trying to do? You're trying to marry a monkey to a giraffe."

Of course, from a production standpoint Ran Wickes was perfectly right. There was no way to marry either the making of lathes or the building of boilers to the mining and marketing of graphite. But the boiler and machine tool works had proven their compatibility when they'd been part of the same company before 1907. The accounting of all three certainly could be combined, and so could the cash operations of the various businesses. In fact, after the death of Frank Payne, the treasurer of the Boiler Company, Charles G. Morrell, had become secretary-treasurer of both Wickes companies, and he held this dual position at that very moment. Fitz-Gerald himself served both companies, as did Eugene J. ("Dean") Bierlein, the traffic manager. Functions could be combined or shared or left separate—it really did not matter one way or the other. What counted was that if you remarried the monkey to the giraffe and both of them to the Mexican donkey, you'd have a financial *ménage à trois* that was something to be reckoned with, a multimillion-dollar empire that could spin off some mighty attractive profits.

It took Dan Fitz-Gerald more than three years to convince Ran Wickes that he was just "tossing money down the sewer" by keeping his operations separate. If nothing else, Ran's holding out for so long against consolidation proved that, despite his apparent frailty, he was a mighty stubborn man, for Fitz-Gerald was blessed with great persuasive charm even in his youth. What in the end seems to have clinched Fitz-Gerald's argument was that neither Wickes Brothers nor Wickes Boiler were listed securities, but if they could be merged with Graphite there'd be a listed stock for all three companies, a possible source of substantial capital gains. For the time being, however, no public sale of the stock was planned.

The consolidated Wickes Corporation, once it materialized, was to have an authorized capitalization of $10 million, consisting of 2 million shares of $5 par value. Of this issue, 770,000 shares were required for the exchange of stock with the companies to be absorbed, leaving 1,230,000 shares in the corporation's treasury. Already, Fitz-Gerald could envision a far more constructive use for this extra stock than its mere conversion into cash: it could be tendered in the purchase of yet other manufacturing companies. What these might be, Fitz-Gerald had as yet no idea, but the concept of growth by acquisition had taken hold of him as soon as he had realized that if the existing diversification was possible under one corporate umbrella, then there was practically no limit to bringing other operations into the fold.

Ran Wickes, still hesitant, consented to the plan on one

condition. He insisted that the 40 percent of United States Graphite shares owned by the Wickes family would not vote for the merger until the remaining 60 percent had overwhelmingly approved it. As stated in the proxy material, he required an 80 percent favorable response for the shares outside his control. That way he could be sure that the Wickes family vote would not tip the scales.

He need not have had any reservations on that score. Graphite's other stockholders were almost unanimously in favor of the merger. The vote was 85.15 percent, as if somehow Graphite's owners had sensed the phenomenal growth that was to come about as the result of the consolidation. Since then, the Wickes Corporation common[4] has been split four to one, thus giving the stockholders twelve shares for each one of their old company. At the time of the merger, Graphite stock was selling for around $17 to $18, so that at the top of the 1960s bull market, with Wickes Corporation stock at $58, their shares had multiplied nearly 40 times in value. Even in the bear market of 1974, when Wickes stock tumbled below $8, Graphite's owners were still nearly 450 percent ahead. Moreover, they were receiving $12 in dividends for each of their old Graphite shares, and had been for a number of years. This was an annual return of more than 68 percent on their investment in the consolidated enterprise.[5]

The Wickes Corporation had been born, for the moment only on paper, on October 3, 1947. By December 14 of that year, all the votes were in and the corporation became a fact of life. The three companies were transformed into divisions, each with its vice president/general manager, and Ran Wickes assumed the office of president of the corporation. One would suppose that he rewarded Dan Fitz-Gerald with a promotion. Not so. Fitz-Gerald remained comptroller for another two years, and then was advanced only to treasurer.[6] This wasn't ingratitude on Ran's part, nor a failure to appreciate Dan's talents. Always a cautious man who wanted to be liked by his fellows, Ran Wickes did not wish to antagonize any of his old associates by passing them over. He knew that things would soon sort themselves out.

7

Up the Country Elevator

Anything to do with farming strikes today's city folk as a rather dull, if often healthfully relaxing way to make a living. They couldn't be more wrong. The raising of crops and their marketing is one of the most exciting business ventures anyone would ever want to undertake. Only professional gamblers and in-and-out traders of securities live in similar day-to-day suspense. When nature is too bountiful, prices drop so low you can't make a profit. If the harvest goes bad, prices may be high, but then chances are you won't bring in enough of a crop to cover expenses. A single rainstorm can bankrupt you. A year's gain or loss may hinge on a guess and a gamble. Take the lettuce brokers around King City and Salinas, California, who commit themselves to the growers for a certain price, and then send refrigerator cars filled with salad across the country. Say the lettuce market collapses in Chicago. The broker diverts his shipment to Philadelphia. The market collapses in Philadelphia. He sends the cars on to Atlanta. The market collapses in Atlanta, but by that time the lettuce has turned brown and must be dumped at a huge loss along the tracks. Conversely, the broker might have made a fortune. To an even more exemplary extent, that sort of educated crapshooting is what trading on the commodity exchanges is all about—anticipating weather, projecting crop levels, outguessing consumer demand some months in the future.

With grains and beans, the physical part of the business transaction starts at the country elevators where farmers deliver their crops for processing (i.e., sorting, cleaning, drying) and storage prior to shipment. You've seen such structures all over the Midwest, nearly always next to railroad sidings. Some elevators, in or near little towns, are quite small, maybe only two or three stories high, with a conveyor belt leading to an intake up top. Others, tall as skyscrapers, are clusters of king-size silos or huge, boxlike buildings divided into evident compartments; these giants loom as distant landmarks in the states of the big sky, and they are more prevalent today since farming has become increasingly big business. As a rule, these enormous facilities are called "terminals" to differentiate them from their country cousins.

But not too long ago, in the heyday of family farming, the small country elevator was the hub of rural commerce and the center of social life during the harvest season. As recently as forty years ago, before tractors became common, farmers with their horse-drawn wagons waited in lines, sometimes as long as a mile, for their crops to be unloaded. While the men waited, they chatted and maybe wandered off for a little shopping at the local drug store and a refreshing drink. In Michigan's bean country, the farmers' wives meanwhile worked in the elevators, sorting the beans by hand, getting paid piece-labor rates while holding their annual gossip sessions. Given this situation, it is not surprising that some of the more astute elevator operators soon figured out how to make money out of the farmers both coming and going. They began stocking fertilizer and salt blocks, feed for livestock and chickens, lumber for fencing and construction, and while the farmers were often in too much of a hurry to bother loading their wagons with merchandise for the return trip, they saw what was available, talked prices, placed orders, and came back when all the crops were gathered and disposed of.

In lower Michigan, particularly in the Saginaw Valley and the Michigan thumb, where the major crops included corn, wheat, barley, alfalfa, hay, sheep wool, and, ever more prominently, navy beans, the Wolohan family was one of the first to spot the all-around potential of country elevators as farm stores. Charles Wolohan, who died in 1943 at the age of seventy-seven, had started in the business in 1895 with an elevator at Birch Run, where at first he only bought and sold hay. In the early days, this was perhaps the most important commodity, just as petroleum is today, for almost everything was horse-powered, and the horses needed to be fueled. Wolohan soon became the leading hay shipper in Michigan, and he then branched out into grains and beans. His firm was incorporated in 1920, and by the time of the Second World War, the Wolohans had seven country elevators in the Saginaw Valley area—in Birch Run, Davison, Freeland, Gera, Gladwin, Hemlock, and Merrill—all but one of which were, in effect, agricultural shopping centers in miniature, with lumber and coal yards, small millwork operations that could handle windows and doors, and retail stores that sold feed as well as a limited line of other farm supplies. There was also a separate Wolohan feed store in Saginaw itself. Not that these retail sidelines netted the Wolohans a fortune. In fact, most of the company's elevator managers considered such sales more trouble than they were worth. It was indeed still a chicken-feed business.

Looking back, it is difficult to assess whether the elder Wolohan, or even his sons—Thomas, Robert, and Richard—who by that time had taken over the reins of the family firm, had any real idea of what this tiny retail chain operation could possibly grow into. A seed had been planted, but its eventual blossoms were still a mystery to the men who tended it and watched it sprout. Nor did Dan Fitz-Gerald of The Wickes Corporation yet recognize that the Wolohans' pioneering of lumber and millwork sales to farmers would eventually make him the boss of the world's largest retail operation in building supplies. What intrigued Dan about country elevators in the first years of his association with Wickes was something else entirely, namely that elevators were hardly more sophisticated in their market approach than proverbial mom-and-pop stores. Here, in the very heart of the navy bean country, not one single elevator operator had achieved a truly solid grip on the worldwide market for this basic commodity.

The biggest outfits in the bean business were Frutchey Bean, Michigan Bean, Wallace & Morley, Bad Axe Grain, and Charles Wolohan, Inc. Of these, only Frutchey had more than two dozen elevators. Wallace & Morley, with sixteen, was second to Frutchey with its chain of twenty-eight. Michigan Bean came next with fifteen, and Bad Axe owned ten.[1] Worse yet, the capacity of the existing elevators was minimal in relation to the size of the bean crop, and in most cases they handled other crops as well. Wolohan, for example, could store only about 150,000 bushels at one time, and Michigan Bean only 365,000. Meanwhile, the region's bean harvest, although measured in hundredweights, corresponded in volume to roughly six million bushels in the average postwar year.[2] Thus, the country elevator business was not only ludicrously fractionated but nearly always short of storage space— two crucial circumstances that impaired the efficiency of the marketplace and therefore proved highly detrimental to the profitability for growers as well as elevator operators (or "processors," as they are often called). Time and again, with local elevators being filled to capacity, both grains and beans had to be shipped off in a hurry to Toledo and Buffalo, the nearest major storage points. The bean business of Saginaw, Bay, and Tuscola Counties especially was handicapped in that regard. With most other crops being harvested first, there was often hardly any room to accommodate beans when they finally came in, let alone hold them in anticipation of top prices.

Fitz-Gerald had first noticed this rural anachronism, relic of a more leisurely, less centralized economy, when he was still an accountant with Lybrand's, which handled the books for nearly all the major bean processors. Fitz-Gerald himself had worked on the Wallace & Morley and Bad Axe Grain accounts, and it had occurred to him then that either client would have been considerably better off with double or triple its number of elevators. But Fitz-Gerald did not puzzle deeply about how he himself might become a major factor in the Michigan bean business until some time after he had joined Wickes and had precipitated the incorporation of its interests.

A successful inventor is one who discovers an unsatisfied need in the scheme of things and then manages to produce a device that fulfills it. So also the successful entrepreneur whose hallmark is not so much his competence at running a business as his ability to spot an opening in the marketplace. Fitz-Gerald, as the restless promulgator of growth in a fairly prosperous but still somewhat somnolent small-town company, was filled with ambitions that were far from clearly defined. He knew only that he had to move, and that at this juncture the bean business presented a promising avenue.

Never a man to think small, Fitz-Gerald's first notion—half-baked though it turned out to be—was to somehow arrange a supermerger involving just about everybody who owned more than a half-dozen elevators.[3] All the rational arguments were on his side, including the inescapable fact that the market was changing rapidly. Where at one time there had been some 400 canners and countless groceries that dealt in bulk beans, mergers had reduced the canners' ranks to barely a handful, and the old-fashioned, sweet-smelling grocery store was being replaced by supermarkets selling prepackaged foods. It only made sense that since there were fewer customers, the number of suppliers should be similarly reduced, lest the bottom fall out of the market because of excessive competition. Fitz-Gerald's neighbor on Saginaw's Benton Road, whose name was Albert L. Riedel and who happened to be president of Michigan Bean, agreed in principle. Riedel himself was merger-minded, and had over the years steadily expanded his company by means of small but shrewdly planned acquisitions. But that's as far as it went. While Riedel was perfectly happy to grow by merging other organizations into his own, he had no desire to turn his business over to anyone else to run. As we shall shortly see, Al Riedel was perhaps the proudest, most outspoken, most stalwart businessman on the Saginaw Valley scene, the kind of mule-stubborn fellow who wouldn't give you a fraction of an inch if he felt it was rightfully his—even if it didn't cost him anything to give it to you. But it wasn't just Riedel's own singular individualism that resisted the idea of becoming a cog in a big corporate machine. The other processors were equally reluctant.[4] They were all small-town entrepreneurs of the homegrown variety, cussedly independent, who disdained nothing so much as impersonal, professional management. For all practical purposes they were a clique of cronies, cousins, and in-laws; they cut each others' throats unmercifully and formed and dissolved partnerships and small corporations with great regularity, but in their continuous rounds of musical chairs, it was always the same fellows who got to sit down, never an outsider.

The only likely merger prospect out of the whole group was Charles Wolohan, Inc., which seemed to be in temporary difficulty, having invested quite heavily in a chicken-raising operation and then seen most of the chicks wiped out overnight by disease. If Wolohan could be brought into the Wickes stable, there'd be at least a modest foothold in that new, and to Fitz-Gerald still mysterious, arena. But he knew that more leverage than mere ownership of a few country elevators was required. Availability of extensive storage was the key. "If we had the space," he told Ran Wickes in the latter's memento-cluttered office one day, "we'd have some influence right off."

And so, as merger negotiations with the Wolohans progressed slowly through 1949, Fitz-Gerald set about to obtain that space: a giant new elevator that could hold more than a million bushels—1,057,000, to be precise. The structure, on the Carrollton bank of the Saginaw River near the Sixth Street bridge, remains one of Michigan's biggest grain terminals to this day.[5] It has since been expanded so that its capacity now exceeds 2¼ million bushels, but even its vital statistics at birth

BIG BIN

Saginaw Grain Terminal was Fitz-Gerald's first venture into a new business. Structure's scale may be gauged from picture above, taken when new silos were added to the 1950 giant. See workmen (arrows) in lower right. (Photos by Dale Wieck)

were impressive. There were twenty-four silo-type bins, each 25 feet in diameter and standing 110 feet tall, about the height of an eleven-story building. Two railroad spurs, one along each of the property's 1,035-foot frontages, were designed to accommodate a total of forty-four hopper cars for loading and unloading. At the northern end of the quadruple bank of storage bins, a 189-foot-high "workhouse" was constructed. Here the crops are still weighed, dried, and cleaned; the workhouse's two conveyor mechanisms, known as "legs," can each empty a carload of grain in ten minutes. Needless to say, such a project constituted an immense investment for a relatively small company like The Wickes Corporation of the late 1940s. The estimated cost was $750,000, and, as is the contrary nature of cost estimates, turned out to be short of reality. By the time the terminal was completed, the construction had gobbled up close to a million dollars.

Either figure was more than Ran Wickes was willing to part with, at least at that moment, for going into a business with which his firm had no identification—an important consideration in the parochial commodities game. The problem, however, lent itself to a most logical solution, one that would have the practical effect of a merger without depriving any of the participants of autonomy, while at the same time introducing the Wickes name to the agricultural community under sound auspices: the formation of an entirely new enterprise, the Saginaw Grain Company. Dan Fitz-Gerald proposed that this organization be owned in equal 25 percent shares by Wickes, Wolohan, Frutchey Bean, and Michigan Bean.[6]

So it was to be—but not for long. Work on the terminal was begun in April 1950. Despite the rush to get it ready in time for that year's harvest, the construction was still in its early stages when the merger of Wolohan with Wickes was approved by the stockholders of both firms on June 9 of that year. One immediate result of the acquisition was, of course, that Wickes now owned half the immense, still unfinished storage facility. And this was only the beginning. When, within a few weeks of the merger, Frutchey Bean backed away from putting up the additional $100,000 required to pay for its share of the terminal's rising construction costs, Wickes, whose $9,497,000 in assets included a $4,238,000 hoard of working capital, was easily able to buy out Frutchey for the latter's original investment. Thus, even before the Saginaw Grain Terminal received its somewhat belated inaugural crop, the winter wheat of 1950, Wickes found itself in 75 percent control of Michigan's then biggest elevator operation.

Unbelievable as it may seem, a quirk of personality now played further into Fitz-Gerald's hands—the aforementioned Al Riedel's stubborn pride. A self-made man who had spent most of his life building a $100,000 company into a two-million-dollar property, acquiring a healthy chunk of it in the process, Riedel was in no mood to play second fiddle to anyone, even in a joint venture and no matter how profitable it might turn out to be. Nearly eighty-three years old at the time of this writing, with his powerful frame barely bent by the burden of time, he says he still gets "madder than hell" when he remembers the Saginaw Grain Company deal.

What had happened, according to Riedel, was that he'd agreed to participate in the company on the automatic assumption that he'd become its president. After all, he had been the first processor Dan Fitz-Gerald had approached; in fact, they'd picked out the terminal site together. Then Riedel had gone off on a long out-of-touch vacation in Mexico, during which time the project rapidly matured. When he got back, he found that the presidency of Saginaw Grain Company had been promised to A. D. McIntyre, the president of Frutchey Bean, in order to make the deal more attractive to him. In the vice-presidential slot was Riedel's own subordinate, William J. Orr, vice president and treasurer of Michigan Bean. Robert E. Wolohan, who ran the newly merged Wolohan firm, was going to be secretary, and Dan Fitz-Gerald the new company's treasurer. Riedel, not even slated for a directorship, felt that he'd been left out in the cold.[7]

"I came in with Michigan Bean anyway," he grumbles. "There isn't any question, it was the right thing to do. But when Frutchey sold out, McIntyre left the company of course, and what happened is that Bob Wolohan was made president. It was a thing I couldn't swallow very damn easily. It kept on gnawing at me until I couldn't stand it anymore. Well, you know, Dan was a fellow that I always liked, and I respected him. I think he was like all the other people; as they develop maturity, they kind of level off and become Christians usually before they die. But in those days he was a ruthless fellow, very aggressive, and he had just one thing in mind. He was going to be president of Wickes, and it was going to be a damn big company, you could be sure of that. Well, maybe I did the wrong thing, not that it made any difference in the long run, but I finally went to Dan a few months later, in 1951, and told him to buy us out too."

Which is precisely what Fitz-Gerald did. Or rather, being still only treasurer of Wickes (since 1949), what he persuaded Ran Wickes to do. The result was that The Wickes Corporation now owned all of Saginaw Grain, and was well on the way to becoming a power in the agricultural business exactly as Fitz-Gerald had planned.

Had he foreseen that events would take this course? Not exactly. True, he was no flower child, dreaming that a new world could be built on a foundation of porridge. He was aggressive, perhaps even a bit ruthless. As the *Saginaw News* commented in a feature story about him, "In another time he might have been a buccaneer." But Dan was never a Machiavelli. His style was to ride roughshod over business adversaries, to pressure them into submission if he could not charm them, but never to knife them in the back. Thus, he probably counted on eventual complete control of Saginaw Grain, figuring that some circumstance or other would sooner or later place him in the proper position for leverage, but he certainly couldn't have expected Frutchey to sell out so promptly; nor did he plot to withhold Saginaw Grain's presidency from Al Riedel with the intention of thereby also eliminating Michigan Bean. Quite the contrary. Dan's long-range design called for an even closer association with Riedel's company.

8

The Legend
of Al Riedel

Y ou'd think that after the Saginaw Grain Terminal misunderstanding, Al Riedel would have learned his lesson and given the "ruthless" Dan Fitz-Gerald wide berth except maybe socially in their neighborhood, or at the Saginaw Club they both belonged to, as did most men of the city's business elite. But, as already pointed out, Al Riedel was as tenacious as they come, and even having made what he considered a blunder in his first deal with Fitz-Gerald, he simply refused to believe that the next time around he wouldn't be in the driver's seat.[1]

Riedel's perseverance is not surprising when you consider his background. The grandson of a German immigrant, he hailed from Forestville, on the Michigan shore of Lake Huron. He was nine years old when his family's small elevator burned down in 1901, and the Riedels moved to Minden City to build a new one in partnership with a couple of other processors.[2] On the then-fashionable advice of a local businessman that "nobody needs an education beyond the eighth grade"— advice that Riedel says he has regretted accepting ever since—

he quit school when he was thirteen and went to work in the Minden City elevator, getting his start unloading gondola cars and firing the steam boiler. A few years later, having been promoted to a desk job, though certainly not because of nepotistic considerations, and having proved his talent for keeping accounts, he was asked to become junior partner in the Producers Elevator Company, which was at that time being organized in Port Huron by one Alfred Chamberlain. A Minden City banker lent young Riedel $2,000 to buy in, and the First National Bank of Port Huron arranged a $20,000 credit line for operations. Soon this proved far from enough.

It's in the nature of the business that elevator operators must rely heavily on credit. They pay farmers on the spot for "cash crops," but then have to hang on and wait for checks from canners and other wholesalers. Riedel quickly learned that the more valuable a processor's inventory and the brighter his prospects, the gloomier immediate reality can be. Overextended as a result of heavy purchasing, Producers Elevator was about to go down the drain when it was bailed out by one of the big wheels in the Michigan commodities business, William J. Orr, Sr. That gentleman had just sold his interest in the Wallace & Orr Company, which was later to become the aforementioned Wallace & Morley Co. and which still exists today as a division of Blount Inc.[3] Now it so happened that Chamberlain's mother had helped bring up Orr when he was a boy. Close relationships like this were not uncommon in the tight little world of Michigan elevator operators. On the basis of this quasi-family relationship, Chamberlain approached Orr for help, and with Orr's fortuitous sale of his share in the Wallace enterprise, he had the wherewithal to rescue Producers Elevator and make it part of a new outfit, the Michigan Bean Company, which was thus born on December 1, 1915.

To start with, Riedel held 2 percent of the new $100,000 corporation—exactly his original $2,000 worth. Most of the stock, of course, was Orr's, and it was a lucky break for Riedel suddenly to find himself working for such a keen businessman and, moreover, holding a piece of the action.[4] Under Orr, all the debts inherited from Producers Elevator were cleaned up the first year, and Michigan Bean even paid a 10-cent dividend, a $200 windfall for Riedel, who was making $100 a month as the number four man in the outfit. He was its secretary, head accountant, and a director of the company. Then Chamberlain made a mistake in overpricing the inventory, had a falling out with Orr, and found himself a couple of new partners who helped him buy back the Port Huron elevator. Riedel, although he liked Chamberlain personally, made the right choice and stayed with Orr's Michigan Bean, which now had elevators in Croswell, Harbor Beach, Vestaburg, and Owendale.[5] It was the right choice if for no other reason than that Chamberlain's new venture failed within four years, while Michigan Bean kept growing.

By 1917, the company showed assets of $244,542, an increase of nearly 150 percent from its original worth. Orr tried practically anything to make a buck, although sometimes not successfully. One time, while Michigan Bean still had the Port Huron elevator, some extra storage space was available there, and Orr (who had been in the salt fish business as part of the Wallace & Orr operation) suggested that this space might be used for fish. So Michigan Bean bought great quantities of herring, then plentiful in the Great Lakes, and Orr sent Riedel to Pennsylvania and points east to sell them. "Don't come back," he said, "until they're all gone." Riedel didn't know anything about fish, of course, except that you couldn't keep them from one season to the next, even pickled in brine. The trouble was, the herring market seemed to have no bottom, and the prices offered to Riedel were way below those Orr had told him to get. So, almost every night, from Pittsburgh, Wilkes-Barre, Scranton, wherever there were brokers, Riedel telegraphed to Orr "Wire instructions," and the only answer he ever received was "Sell fish." Which is precisely what Riedel did, squeezing for every penny he could get, but even so his sales added up to about $8,000 less than the investment, and when he finally returned he was very apologetic. Orr waved him off. "Listen," he said, "you did a lot better than I could have done. I might have lost twice that much. You know why? I knew before you left that the fish market had gone to hell. But you didn't, and that's why I sent you. Nobody can sell anything if he knows that it isn't worth a damn."

Orr, only in his late fifties, died in 1921, but not before having bestowed upon hero-worshipping young Riedel some of his own irascibility as well as his disdain for fancy euphemisms when four-letter words were more to the point. Orr had also taught Riedel a good deal about the business. For instance, commodity prices don't necessarily keep on rising—something that a youngster getting in on the World War I boom might easily have assumed.[6] Moreover, Orr lent Riedel $2,000 so he could buy into Orr's other elevator operation, the Orr Bean & Grain Co. of Midland, Michigan, and this purchase in turn helped increase Riedel's holdings in Michigan Bean when it absorbed Orr Bean & Grain in 1927.

Meanwhile, Riedel kept buying a little Michigan Bean stock here and there whenever he had some spare cash. Upon Orr's death, the company's next-largest shareholder, Frank W. Merrick, formerly its vice president, had been named president,[7] and Riedel promoted to treasurer and general manager at a salary of $3,000 a year, which was then quite a respectable sum and which allowed him to make occasional investments. Not that these were fat years. As Orr had predicted, grains and beans took a tumble after the Germans capitulated, and the commodities business didn't really pull out of its tailspin, except for minor upswings, until the late 1930s when Hitler— much to his later chagrin, one would suppose—provoked the United States to shake off its Depression doldrums. In the intervening years, Michigan Bean was riding high when it could show a $30,000 net, but getting steady raises and increasingly larger bonuses, frugal Riedel kept on building his equity. By 1930 he owned 1,250 shares of the 12,400 then outstanding, and the dismal economic picture did not discourage him from looking for more. Nor did Michigan Bean succumb to the shock of the Big Crash. In fact, the Thirties turned out to be fat years for the company—not in bottom-line earnings, of course, but in its positioning for the future.

In a stock deal in 1929, it had absorbed the Cass City Grain Co., which had ten country elevators, thereby increasing

Michigan Bean's book value to $440,000, and before that otherwise sad year was over, Michigan Bean had also acquired the Saginaw Milling Co. in a similar arrangement, adding six more facilities. Not all these "plants," as elevators are called in the commodities jargon, remained with Michigan Bean. In the intricate intramural merry-go-round of the elevator fraternity, Frutchey Bean Co. (which we remember from the last chapter as one of the short-lived partners in the Saginaw Grain Terminal deal) emerged as an independent entity from Michigan Bean in 1932. The Frutchey brothers, who had been involved with Michigan Bean, decided to go out on their own, and bought nine of the Michigan Bean elevators for $81,000.[8] A couple of other elevators were also sold along the way. In turn, yet others were bought or built, including the predecessor of the present Michigan Bean Terminal on North Niagara Street in Saginaw, which was purchased along with some other properties from C. K. Eddy & Sons in 1943.[9]

Good times for farmers and commodity marketeers—if not for draftees—had come with the war years. But Riedel, who had succeeded Merrick as president of Michigan Bean upon the latter's death in 1938, still couldn't quite buy the brave new world of agricultural prosperity. The C. K. Eddy Company wanted $85,000 for its Saginaw bean elevator, and Riedel, cautious as ever, insisted on a contract that would allow him to pay off the balance in fifteen years after a $10,000 down payment. And Riedel still couldn't believe his company's good fortune when, instead of taking fifteen years, Michigan Bean was able to pay that debt off in less than three. Indeed, the business was booming, and not only in beans and grain. The company also handled feed, seed, coal, fertilizer, wool, building materials, and a number of miscellaneous items.[10] By 1945, Riedel was paid $11,000 in salary, plus a $6,000 bonus. Five years later when the Saginaw Grain deal with Wickes was on, his base salary had risen to $17,000, and his bonus to $12,000. His income from Michigan Bean stock, of which he now owned close to 14 percent, or around 13,000 shares, came to another $13,250 (at $1 per share, plus a special dividend of 25 cents that year). In short, he had worked his way up to become a big man in the bean business as well as on his way to the bank.[11] No wonder that he considered himself on at least equal footing with Dan Fitz-Gerald, who hadn't known from beans until only very recently.

So, perhaps even more keenly than Fitz-Gerald, Al Riedel was aware that the agricultural business was changing drastically—that it was now a big-money game and that in the mechanized future, only big operators could survive. Where in 1920 there had been about 3.5 million farms of 10 to 99 acres in the United States, by the mid-1950s there were only about 2.5 million such farms, and their number was declining at an increasingly rapid rate. And while in 1920 the country had counted only 67,000 farms of 1,000 acres or more, there were now more than 131,000 farms in this giant class, accounting for nearly half the acreage being farmed. Meanwhile, on the marketing side, the number of major canners had dropped to eight, and these were doing more than 75 percent of the business. The small processor's day, just like the family farmer's day, was over. True, Michigan Bean had made quite a name for itself. It had pioneered compulsory grading and grade labeling of beans. It had been among the first firms in Michigan to whom open terms—that is, sales without prepegged prices—were granted by country shippers. Its "Jack Rabbit" bean package was widely known, and the product served as a quality standard for comparison. The company had developed a waterproof bag, first used in World War II for throwing food overboard from fast ships where dock facilities were not available or had just been blown up; the equipment for filling these bags had since been duplicated and was in common use throughout the country for packing free-flowing dry products including flour. In short, Michigan Bean was hardly a backwoods firm. Nor was it small by the standards of that day, but, look at it as you will, the company did not have the dimensions to cope with the demands of tomorrow.[12]

Riedel knew well that to remain a going concern, Michigan Bean had to expand, and the kind of expansion he had in mind went far beyond his company's resources. Meanwhile, however, there was now Wickes, which had successfully estab-

MR. MICHIGAN BEAN

The irascible Al Riedel
fought Fitz-Gerald
tooth and nail
over the years,
but he was
an affectionate adversary:
there were tears
in his eyes
at DMF's funeral.
(Photo by Bosch)

lished itself in the agricultural business, thanks to its Saginaw Grain Terminal and its nucleus of country elevators.[13] Moreover, Wickes, with its substantial assets and cash flow was in a far more favorable position to raise capital than relatively small Michigan Bean. And with The Wickes Corporation's resources backing up Michigan Bean, there would not only be capital for expansion but also that credit cushion inevitably required by any agricultural operation for borrowings during harvest time. No company, regardless of its resources, can have enough cash on hand to directly finance such a high-investment, small-margin operation.

Thus it came about that in 1955 Riedel allowed his realism to override his rancor, and when Dan Fitz-Gerald approached him about merging Michigan Bean with Wickes, Riedel went along with the proposition. Not that he made it easy. The negotiations involved property worth some $2 million, but true to form he made every penny count. After having come to a general agreement with Fitz-Gerald, mostly in brief after-lunch talks at the Saginaw Club, and in a few remarks passed here and there when they happened to bump into each other, Riedel asked Dan over to his office at the Michigan Bean Terminal one evening. "We're going to stay here until we get this settled even if we have to stay here all night," Al Riedel said, and they pretty nearly did. After hours of horse-trading, they were finally down to $\frac{1}{32}$ of a share. "Why in the hell don't you give in?" Riedel challenged. Fitz-Gerald countered, "Why in the hell don't you give in?" But Riedel had one final indisputable argument in his arsenal. "Because I am older than you are," he said. Fitz-Gerald couldn't help laughing, and that's when he cracked.

The merger terms they arrived at were an exchange of 1$\frac{5}{64}$ shares of Wickes Corporation for each Bean Company share. With 93,380 shares of Michigan Bean outstanding at that time, this involved 100,676 shares of Wickes stock, which was then worth around $16 a share.[14] Thus Fitz-Gerald acquired Michigan Bean for slightly in excess of $1.6 million, or about $400,-000 less than the Bean Company's book value. This was of course a hypothetical price, since acquisitions by means of an exchange of shares are generally predicated on the numbers of shares to be exchanged, not on their respective market values (unless specifically stated in the contract, something that is done only on rare occasions). Since Wickes was making good money at the time, and Michigan Bean stock was traded over the counter where it often sold far below book, Riedel was satisfied with the arrangement. He expected Wickes stock to go up, making the original Michigan Bean holdings that much more valuable as time went on—and indeed, this happened.[15] The merger was approved by the stockholders of the two companies on December 30, 1955, and Michigan Bean was now part of Wickes.

Not surprisingly, Riedel was soon "madder than hell" once again. As he recalls it, he had been promised not only the titles of president and divisional general manager of what was to be called the Michigan Bean Company Division of Wickes, but also a directorship of the corporation. He got to be divisional president, all right, but not a director—and he almost didn't get the divisional presidency either.

What happened was that, within a few days of the Michigan Bean acquisition, all the corporation's division heads were told to resign their directorships. True to form, Riedel stormed into the office of Melvin J. Zahnow, then the secretary of The Wickes Corporation.

"What the hell is this performance?" Riedel growled. "I got news for you. I was promised that I could retain the title of president and general manager of this division and by God I'm going to retain it. It's something that I've earned over a hell of a lot of years and I'm not about to give it up. I don't give a damn what the rest of them do."

Zahnow tried to placate Riedel by telling him that this move had been prompted by the corporation's attorneys as a necessary legal step. But that wasn't good enough for Riedel. "I'm going to tell you something," he yelled at Zahnow. "There are no two damn attorneys that agree on anything, and you just keep talking to attorneys until you find one that says it's all right because this is the way it's going to be as far as I'm concerned."

The confrontation ended in a trade-off. Riedel remained

ROBERT G. DODGE

*Al Riedel's erstwhile protégé
is now a senior vice president
of Wickes.*

president of Michigan Bean which, according to the records,
was actually more than he had been promised, but he was not
elected to the Wickes board of directors, which indeed he had
been promised.[16] And as a result of this first Riedel revolution,
all the other division heads got their resignations back—
although they had to relinquish their directorships—and
moreover they were promoted from the status of divisional vice
presidents to that of division presidents, certainly a compensatory jump in prestige.[17] Moneywise, however, Riedel had nothing to complain about. After making $25,000 plus a $5,000
bonus in 1955, he was now making $20,000 salary plus $25,000
bonus, like all the other Wickes division heads, and more, in
fact, than Dan Fitz-Gerald, whose combined income at that
point was $35,000.

But Riedel's war with Wickes was far from over. His *casus
belli*, besides the festering resentment that he hadn't gotten on
the board of directors, was his understanding—or at least his
assumption—that he wouldn't have to leave his post until he

was seventy-three years old. "I had no damn notion of retiring until I had put in fifty years, and there, one day after a board of directors' meeting, they said to me, 'Al, we should tell you that we just passed a bylaw resolution that retirement will be compulsory at age seventy.' And I said, 'We were a going concern when you took us over, and I'm a going man, so to hell with that damn notion as far as I'm concerned.'"

Riedel's cussing didn't do him a whole lot of good against all the heavy corporate artillery, but a very promising young man got caught in the cross fire, and it was his good luck that he had been born with a wry and sly humor that helped him ward off the slings and arrows of an outraged Riedel.

That young man was Robert G. Dodge, today a senior vice president of Wickes. He had been born on a farm near Ithaca, Michigan, the son of an agronomist for the Borden Milk Company. By virtue of his rural birth and choice of bride—her father, Bart Pomeroy, owned five country elevators—he was a natural for the commodities business. After an early career whose desultory miscellany included the Navy, Dow Chemical, and the Michigan Farm Bureau, he had applied for a job with the Frutchey Bean Company, then declined it when he found that one of the men he'd have to work with displayed a fondness for grain that went far beyond its storage in solid form. Driving down the street after his Frutchey interview, Dodge saw the Michigan Bean sign and decided to try his luck there. At first, Al Riedel was suspicious and more than slightly intimidating. He looked like a teutonic version of Telly Savalas, except of course that nobody had dreamed up Kojak yet. Did Bob Dodge want to learn the business so that he could later go to work for his father-in-law? No, Bob said, he didn't believe in working for relatives, especially in-laws. In the end, Riedel's doubts were allayed, quite possibly because young Dodge appeared eager to give his all for just 90 cents an hour. And so the slim, crew-cut youngster (since then not quite so trim, and now fashionably sideburned and more gray than blond) learned the agricultural business from the ground up, which in his case was the dusty floor of a country elevator at Merrill, Michigan, owned by Michigan Bean. After a few years in a variety of functions, he finally got his big chance in 1950—to be a bean trader.

Trading is the key job in the commodities business. It's the trader who keeps abreast of the market, who hedges against adversity by buying long and selling short on the commodity exchanges, who deals in crops before their first tender shoots have even poked through the topsoil, who calls Campbell Soup, H. J. Heinz, Stokely-Van Camp, and A&P, and dickers with them over nickels and pennies and even penny fractions that, when translated into bulk shipments, account for thousands upon thousands of dollars. Not that Dodge was given the responsibility for trading with the select handful of big-time canners. Al Riedel predictably reserved those accounts for himself. But the first day on the job, which Dodge had fallen into only because his predecessor had exceeded his authority by selling some futures short, another prerogative that was strictly Riedel's, Dodge did happen to be charged with selling five carloads of beans, and if possible to Campbell Soup. The only problem was that Riedel hadn t bothered to instruct Dodge on the price range he could trade in. Who knows, perhaps Riedel half-remembered the late W. J. Orr's strategy when the latter had sent Riedel on the road to sell fish. Anyway, Dodge phoned Howard Hirth at Campbell Soup and asked him how much he'd pay for those five carloads. Hirth's reply ("and I'll never forget it," says Dodge, "because it was the best thing that ever happened to me") was: "Listen, young man, if you have beans to sell you put your price on them. If I want to buy them I will, and if I don't I won't. But if you call me looking for information, you've got the wrong damn number, and you're wasting my time." And Hirth slammed down the receiver.

This brusque advice marked the beginning of a long and friendly association. Dodge and Hirth remained in almost daily contact for many years as Riedel's company, under the auspices of Wickes, ended up as the world's largest processor of beans. Not the whole pie, of course, but a substantial slice—so substantial, in fact, that Wickes exports beans even to coun-

A TOWER FOR CROSWELL

This facility, built in Croswell by Michigan Bean in 1964, is typical of the twenty-six country elevators of Wickes Agriculture. (Photo by Bradford-LaRiviere, Inc.)

tries like Mexico, where beans are considered a staple of the native diet.

In the United States, the states that lead in bean production are Michigan, California, Idaho, and Colorado. Next in line are Nebraska and the Minnesota–North Dakota area. Michigan, whose specialty is navy beans, alone produces as much as California, Idaho, and Colorado together. Not that Wickes handles all the Michigan bean crop. There are and always will be many other processors. But by buying and selling between 40 and 50 percent of Michigan's beans, Wickes, as a single company, has achieved a volume that exceeds the total bean harvest of the state of California.[18]

It is only reasonable to suppose that it wasn't just Dodge's innate intelligence and talent for the business that catapulted him into the number two spot at Michigan Bean, and eventually earned him the title of assistant general manager. Equally important—perhaps even more important—was the fact that Bob Dodge stood his ground whenever Riedel lost his temper. Like most strong personalities, Riedel couldn't help but breed his coterie of yes-men: face to face with a bulldozer, the average person scrambles for safety. Bob Dodge was one of those who didn't, and Riedel respected that. After all, he'd never been a shrinking violet himself.

It wasn't long before Riedel started taking Dodge along to conventions, and pretty soon the young man became a favorite guest at the Riedel home. Dodge, as tenacious in his subtle way as Riedel was in his bluster, even managed to modify the latter's life style. Riedel was a great believer in working hard and playing hard. At canners' conventions it was his routine to roust Dodge out of bed for a 7 A.M. breakfast devoted to a discussion of that day's strategy. This was followed by a long day of making calls on potential customers, and then in the evenings there were open-house cocktail parties where Dodge, if not Riedel, was likely to hang on half the night. So Dodge, who treasured his sack time, slyly recruited the help of the only boss Riedel ever recognized—his wife. One evening at the Riedel house, Dodge remarked to Mrs. Riedel, "You know there's only one thing that bothers me about your husband, and that's that he can't sleep in the morning. I think it's ridiculous to have breakfast at seven." She said, in the quietly imperious way wives used to have before liberation deprived them of their superiority, "Albert, I really don't see any reason why you should get your people up that early." And from then on Dodge was allowed to nurse his hangovers in private.

When the time came for Riedel to retire, it was a foregone conclusion that Dodge would take his place.[19] Although Riedel had been born on April 21, 1892, and he would thus be older than seventy for the last two months of his tenure, the date of his departure was set for June 30, then the end of the Wickes fiscal year. (It has since been changed, and is now the last Saturday in January, the traditional year-end of retailers, since that's the best time to take inventories.) In any case, June 30, 1962, came and went, and suddenly it was July 1, and Bob Dodge was now general manager of Michigan Bean, and he walked into the daily 8 A.M. meeting, where everybody always talked about the weather, not small talk as in other places but because weather is crucial in this business, and—lo and behold—there was Al Riedel, ready to get down to work as always.

To be readable, a writer must dramatize his material. He cannot falsify, but he lives with the constant temptation to emphasize that which amuses and to play down the dull. What follows here is a case in point. I have three tape transcriptions, each different in its details. Here are their summaries, all paraphrased in part, and with potentially libelous material deleted. Which version would you choose?

AL RIEDEL: On June 12, Ran Wickes and Dan Fitz-Gerald asked me over to the Saginaw Club for lunch, and told me they just wanted to remind me that it was soon time for me to go. I told them I didn't like it and still didn't agree, but that I needed more than a couple of weeks to wind up my affairs and clean out my desk. I figured it might take four to six weeks. Sure I showed up at that meeting on July 1. I had to keep the staff informed on last-minute business.

DAN FITZ-GERALD: Al asked me if he could continue to use his office over at the Michigan Bean Elevator. I made the mistake of saying, 'Of course you can.' We put Bob Dodge in charge of the operation. One day Bob called me and said, 'Do you want me to run this operation?', and I told him I did. He said, 'Well, you're going to have to come over here and tell that to Al because he's having meetings with the staff and running the company just as he always has.' It was a very unpleasant day when I had to go over and ask Al to give up his office. I think we've become friends again, but at the time it was rough. I hope that Al has forgiven me, but you never know.

BOB DODGE: At that morning meeting, Al immediately announced that although I was now the general manager, 'things aren't going to be any different.' Then the meeting proceeded as per usual. Afterwards I found a message from Dan Fitz-Gerald, asking me to come over to his office [at the corporate headquarters building on North Washington]. When I arrived, Dan complimented me on my taking over and calling a meeting immediately. 'But I didn't call the meeting,' I said. 'Al did.' I could see Dan tightening up and all he said was, 'I'll meet you at your office.' In fact, he got there before I did. Together we walked in on Al Riedel. 'Hi, Al,' Dan said. 'I'm surprised to see you here. I thought you'd retired.' Al said, 'Well, I did, damn it. I don't have any choice.' And Al got madder by the minute, pounding the desk. He yelled that I'd undermined him and worked behind his back to get his job, all sorts of things. Dan tried to assure him that this wasn't true. Al finally gave in. He agreed that he'd move out that very night, and he did, lock, stock and barrel, except for his beautiful old desk. But for weeks after that he still tried to keep track of what was going on.

So there you have it. To what degree Al Riedel attempted to cling to his beloved Michigan Bean no one will ever know for sure. But even if he did, you couldn't blame him. He knew more about that business than anybody else in sight, and he had invested all his life in it. One of the tragedies of modern existence is seeing people put out to pasture when they still have all it takes to lead the team. And you surely can't blame anyone in such a position for resenting it.

SAGINAW LANDMARK

Michigan Bean elevator, largest of its kind, is visible for miles. Jack Rabbit trademark, outlined in neon, has been bounding across city's skyline for years. (Photo by Bradford-LaRiviere, Inc.)

Says Bob Dodge, "It was really sad because I loved Al and I still think he's the greatest. I would have had no objection to sharing information with him, but he cut me out of his life, wouldn't even say hello to me on the street or at the Saginaw Club. I guess he really thought I'd done him in."

This went on for months. Then, in early December, there was a food brokers' convention in New York City where Riedel—now an independent consultant and honorary president of the National Dry Bean Council—was giving a speech. As chance would have it, he and Bob Dodge found themselves waiting for the same elevator at the Park Sheraton Hotel. Suddenly Bill McCormick, a prominent commodities trader from San Francisco, a big hulking fellow, came up to them, threw his long arms around their shoulders, pulled them together, and said, "I've known you fellows too long. Let's cut out all this nonsense, and stop being mad at each other."

Dodge said, "I'm not mad at Al, and I've never done a damn thing to him. He put me where I am and I've learned everything from him." Al grumbled around a little bit and then he said, "I guess you're right, Bill. Life's too short, anyway." And from that time on they slowly became friends again.

Maybe Riedel really believed that Dodge had done a little

131

politicking on the side, something which, after all, is not unknown in the corporate world or any other. But being a man of unshakable loyalties, Riedel eventually wiped the whole thing from his mind. Ask him about Bob Dodge today and he'll tell you proudly that Dodge was the best thing that ever happened to Michigan Bean: "I brought him into it, I trained him, and look what he did. He built one hell of an organization."

In fact, Al still contributed to Michigan Bean's growth even after his retirement. In 1967, when Frutchey Bean ran into financial difficulties, he was called in by the courts to act as receiver, and despite his resentments against The Wickes Corporation, some of which were not entirely without cause, he settled the bankruptcy by selling seven Frutchey elevator properties[20] to Michigan Bean, thus entrenching his creation even more firmly as one of the undisputed leaders in the commodities business. There is indeed little doubt that if it hadn't been for Riedel, The Wickes Corporation wouldn't be where it is today. It takes all kinds to build for the future, including irascible one-of-a-kinds like the unforgettable Al Riedel.

9

Full of Beans

One day in the spring of 1950—and a fateful day it turned out to be in the history of the young Wickes Corporation—Dan Fitz-Gerald and John McCullough paid a call at downtown Detroit's Hotel Fort Shelby, then one of the city's leading establishments for business travelers. An impressively handsome Hollander with slicked-down graying hair, medium-long in the traditional European style, opened the door. He vigorously shook the hands of the two younger men, and when McCullough introduced him to Fitz-Gerald as Cornelis van Bergeijk (pronounced bear-hike), said expansively, "Just call me Corky. In England they call me Corny, but that wouldn't do here at all." His speech was graciously continental, with hardly the trace of an accent.

Here, indeed, was a man of the world, and there was no chance for Dan Fitz-Gerald to forget it as they sat in over-stuffed chairs and discussed the international bean business while the phone kept on jingling with calls from Paris, Amsterdam, Madrid, and Bucharest, and as Mr. van Bergeijk, no less busy placing long-distance calls himself during the conversation, explained to the flustered Fort Shelby operator, "No, my dear, I mean Moscow, Russia; not Moscow, Idaho."

At first, Fitz-Gerald thought the Dutchman a fraud. But nothing could have been farther from the truth. Mr. van Bergeijk was one of the big operators on the international commodities scene, a buyer, seller, and shipper of agricultural crops from one curve of the globe to the other, and if, with his bluff good humor, elegant attire, and Hotel Meurice manners, he somehow appeared a confidence man, so much the better; you'd hardly trust someone in cheap slacks and white socks to instantly convert Bulgarian leva into Swiss francs in his head. The purpose of the meeting, which of course had been arranged by John McCullough, was to gain Wickes a direct pipeline to canners all over the world. Foreign markets were vitally important and highly profitable. Great Britain, for example, consumed then, and consumes today, more navy beans per capita than any other country. Moreover, in those postwar years, the economies of Europe, especially of Eastern Europe, had not yet found their equilibrium. The United States, still recognized and respected as the savior of the world, was everybody's banker and breadbasket.

That's why Corky van Bergeijk had come to the United States in the first place. Back home in Rotterdam, after serving as a sailor in World War I, he had launched himself into the commodities business aboard a bicycle, cruising the surrounding farm country in search of beans, peas, seed, and grain, which he then peddled on the Rotterdam Corn Exchange. By 1925, at the age of thirty-two, he was general manager of Graanhandel, an export-import firm that paid him a share of profits in addition to his salary. But that wasn't good enough. Seven years later, in notorious 1932, he managed to obtain a $100,000 credit line for farm product purchases, and went on his own. He bought beans from Hungary, Romania, and Bulgaria, sold them in Britain, Belgium, and France. He also dealt in poppy and caraway seeds from Czechoslovakia and Poland, much of which he shipped to San Francisco. But mostly he

CORKY VAN BERGEIJK

*For once, going Dutch paid
dividends. (Photo by
Abelardo, 1961)*

bought beans of every kind and wherever they could be
obtained, for the world's appetite for them seemed insatiable.
Soon Corky became a legend even in the highly sophisticated
Dutch fraternity of international traders.

To understand the immensity of the business involved in
feeding people, one illustration will suffice. In 1935, a New
York speculator who fancied the title "King of Garbanzos" but
was about as worldly as the legendary emperor without clothes,
had bought 5,000 tons of those Mexican chick-peas in Sonora.
Unable to find a market for them in Central America, he
loaded them on a freighter in Mazatlán and sent them off to
Europe on a gamble. It wasn't until the ship had touched port
in Liverpool, London, and Antwerp that the "King of Garbanzos" discovered that most Europeans didn't even know what
chick peas were. Close to desperation when the ship next
docked in Rotterdam, he raced to the chamber of commerce to
look at the list of local importers. As luck would have it, van
Bergeijk's name was at the top of the roster since it started with
a B, so that's where the garbanzo man went. Now it so happened that van Bergeijk had a contact in Bilbao, in Spain, the

only country in Europe other than Italy where chick-peas were popular. What's more, as one telephone call revealed, the garbanzo crop in Spain had gone to hell that year. A couple more calls, and Corky had all the garbanzos sold. The profit came to $400,000, and Corky's cut to $80,000. Not bad for an afternoon's work during the Depression.

By the time Hitler invaded the Low Countries in 1940, the van Bergeijks were millionaires many times over. Five years later, when the Allies chased the Nazis out of Holland, the van Bergeijks were paupers, except for a truck without tires, a bombed-out factory building, and some vintage wines buried in the garden.[1] But soon Corky was back on top of the world again, with his dapper son, Theo, who had been born in 1929, now helping him in the business. And once again Corky shopped for beans in Eastern Europe, which was now behind the Iron Curtain. Once again he bought seeds and peas, and always more and more beans, now also from Africa, from Tanganyika, Angola, and Zambia—and hungry Europe still hollered for more.[2] Only one country had a bean surplus: the United States, and it was all in Michigan.

As we already know, during the war the United States government had asked farmers to increase the bean crop (as all other crops), and the farmers had responded with such efficiency that soon there was an immense surplus. Washington had set up the Commodity Credit Corporation, a government agency that advanced funds to the farmers for their production, and if the farmers couldn't sell all they grew on the open market, the CCC bought it and stored it. Uncle Sam, in effect, had become the world's largest processor of beans—and these beans were warehoused all over Michigan, wherever storage space could be found, with the government paying generous rent for that space. Among the bean warehouses were several old factory buildings on the Bay City waterfront that had originally been used for the manufacture of wooden radio cabinets; these buildings later had been bought by the Eddy Shipbuilding Co., which built air rescue boats during the war and then went out of business. The property was taken over by

Uncle Sam's Reconstruction Finance Corporation, from which it was eventually purchased by Wickes and leased back to the government for the storage of surplus beans. This is mentioned here not merely as an example of how the Commodity Credit Corp. scrambled for every available cubic foot of potential storage space, but also because the old shipyard was destined to be one of the key locales in the history of Wickes: it was here that the corporation was to launch its lumber retail operations several years later.

Meanwhile, however, the beans stored at the old Eddy complex were slowly moldering, just as they were in all the other surplus facilities. Beans, if properly stored at low humidity, can last for many years, but time does eventually take its toll and it did. By the late 1940s, with typical bureaucratic paternalism, the United States government considered those beans unfit for domestic consumption, but could see no reason for not selling them abroad, presumably on the assumption that foreigners had less sensitive stomachs. Actually, once these beans were polished—i.e., the mold rubbed off—they were perfectly edible, if not of the most appetizing appearance. The postwar world, still largely in shambles, clamored for proteins: damn the cosmetics, full feed ahead.

Which brings us back to Corky van Bergeijk's expeditions to America. He had heard of all those beans stacked ceiling-high in Michigan warehouses and wanted to buy them, or at least as much of them as he could finance. Whereupon he ran into another one of those governmental inconsistencies: the beans, although for sale only to other countries, could be sold only through a United States firm. To start with, Corky went to see Al Riedel at Michigan Bean, then still an independent company, and tried to set up a joint venture with him.

Now, any reader who has waded through the last chapter can easily imagine that a clash of personalities between these two men was inevitable. On the one hand, you have Corky: suave, elegant, rich, a continental bon vivant then in his mid-fifties, an age much appreciated by young ladies of discernment, especially when it is accompanied by worldly manners and a bulging wallet. Moreover, like most Europeans, Corky considered tax laws not as a means to raise public revenues but as an obstacle thoughtfully provided by government to train businessmen in the art of survival. On the other hand, you've got Al Riedel: as American as apple pie, the kind who'd put his hat over his heart at the sound of the national anthem even when nobody was looking, shrewd in business but staunchly moral—in short, the epitome of Midwestern solidity. A Harry Truman type, if you will (though of course a Republican). Needless to say, there was just no way for these two prototypes to get together, especially since Corky wanted to make money in the United States but not to pay U.S. taxes.

It so happened, however, that Riedel at that time was a Lybrand's client. He introduced Corky to John McCullough, who managed to convince the artful Dutchman that, while paying United States taxes was unavoidable, he would have the right to operate in the United States if he set up a family partnership in this country. Thus the Agricultural Products Company, owned by van Bergeijk and his sons, was born, and thereupon engaged in joint ventures with the Charles Wolohan, Inc., Division of The Wickes Corporation—a result of the aforementioned meeting at the Fort Shelby Hotel.[3]

It didn't take Dan Fitz-Gerald long to find out that Corky was anything but a fraud. Those long-distance calls paid off every time. "Corky was a tremendous salesman," McCullough recalls. "I think he could sell anything to anybody anywhere at any hour of the day." Said Dan Fitz-Gerald, "Well, this guy was from heaven. He was Mr. Bean of Europe. He's traveling back and forth on the *Queen Mary* and it's quite a deal. You go down to see him off and he's practically taken over the boat before it leaves the harbor. He knows everybody on the boat, knows the captain, he's got champagne in his stateroom, and gin and whiskey and vodka from the various officers for a welcome aboard. Of course he's a big shipper and everybody is trying to be nice to him, including me. Sure, I did his bidding. He was a prima donna. If we were going to be worth a damn, we had to have big export outlets. I can't think of anybody else who could have done it for us."

Soon all Michigan's surplus beans were cleaned out, and Wickes had to start buying beans from shippers everywhere to keep up with Corky's sales abroad. The financial arrangement was simple enough. Wickes financed the purchasing, Corky did the selling, and Corky and Wickes split the profits down the middle. Not that there were always profits. As in any business, the partners didn't come up smelling like roses every time. In fact, in the early days they had a mishap of such proportions that it wiped out the bottom line for a couple of years. At that time there was still a shortage of transport, and practically any ship would do, including dilapidated Greek tramps. It was on such an ocean hobo that 5,000 tons of beans were loaded at Bay City, consigned for England. This freighter, the S.S. *Taxiarhis*, long since gone from Lloyd's Register, first rammed a bridge and then collided with another ship before she even got out into the Atlantic. The Greek tramp didn't sink, but took on enough water to soak the beans in her holds. When she finally arrived in the United Kingdom, the ship smelled like an old garbage pit. The beans had decayed and couldn't be canned. There was some problem about the way the shipment had been insured, and The Wickes Corporation and the Agricultural Products Company had to swallow the loss between them—something like $300,000 apiece.

But that's the sort of adversity you have to take in your stride, and it certainly discouraged neither Corky nor Dan. Corky, who had never had any formal schooling but was fluent in six languages just the same, had built his business from scratch twice, once as a young man, and again after World War II. He was a man of extreme vitality, so inexhaustibly energetic that he would be drinking with Dan Fitz-Gerald and John McCullough until three o'clock in the morning, leaving his American pals, who weren't exactly slouches either, in a state that approached suspended animation. But he himself would be up three hours later, talking to Europe on the phone, his voice as clear as a bell. No, anybody who could make $80,000 in an afternoon without batting an eye could take a $300,000 kick in the pants without getting desperate about it. Nor did the setback discourage Dan Fitz-Gerald in the slightest. To be sure, his boss, Ran Wickes, did have some reservations. In fact, he didn't like van Bergeijk at all. But again, as with Mc-Cullough, this may well have been because of a sort of paternal jealousy. Dan, despite his ambitions to succeed Ran, was not the kowtowing type. Although respectful, he used his own judgment and pursued his own course, which took him ever deeper into the agricultural business.

The Saginaw Grain Co. was now a subsidiary of Wickes. Charles Wolohan, Inc., had become a division of the corporation. The association with Cornelis van Bergeijk had opened the door to world markets. It was with this momentum that Fitz-Gerald pursued the merger with Al Riedel's Michigan Bean, and, as the years went on, he kept buying, expanding, and building new bean and grain elevators all over the rich farm areas of Michigan. Wickes now sold not only to H. J. Heinz of Pittsburgh, but even more to Heinz England; not only to Campbell Soup and Stokely-Van Camp, but also to Crosse & Blackwell of London. Wickes beans, under a variety of labels, were and still are being marketed in Britain, Ireland, France, Italy, you name it—indeed, in just about every country under the sun.

Since 1961, the $500,000 Wickes Marine Terminal, constructed on the site of the old Eddy Shipbuilding Co., where all those beans had been stored in the surplus years, has handled most of the corporation's traffic through the St. Lawrence Seaway into the Atlantic. The first vessel to dock there was the German M. V. *Erika Schulte* out of Hamburg. Interestingly enough, this motorship, one of the first of the new postwar breed that ran on diesels rather than on boilers, not only picked up 1,250 tons of navy beans but also 100 tons of graphite from the U.S. Graphite Division of The Wickes Corporation. Bean shipments were the main purpose of the new facility, but slowly the pieces of Wickes were beginning to fit together, just as, in later years, Fitz-Gerald's association with Corky van Bergeijk was to pay off in a wealth of contacts when Wickes Lumber started to branch out into the Common Market countries. As might have been expected, the first Wickes stores in

Europe were to be in Holland. It is this sort of interplay that makes history not only fascinating but useful. As Shakespeare said in *The Tempest*, "What's past is prologue."

Corky van Bergeijk is part of the past—of future's prologue. He was in his eighties when he died in November 1975 after a long illness. By then, his Agricultural Products Co. had gone out of business long ago, as had his Dutch firm, Van Bergeijk N.V.[4] The Michigan Bean Company, as Al Riedel knew it, is also of the past. In fact, even its old name is now gone. In early 1975, Michigan Bean became the Michigan Division of a new corporate group, called Wickes Agriculture. And although the Wickes Marine Terminal at Bay City is still in operation and processes some St. Lawrence Seaway traffic, far bigger shipments, packed in mammoth containers, are now trucked to Montreal, Quebec City, Baltimore, and other harbors for overseas sales.[5] But thanks to this colorful past, no other exporter of beans anywhere equals The Wickes Corporation's volume, which on the average ranges between 25 and 33 percent of all beans sent abroad. Nor does any other single processor handle as large a share of the domestic bean business.[6]

Although navy beans remain at the hub of the corporation's agricultural activities, other commodities do not lag far behind. In terms of volume, if not in share of market, Wickes actually handles far greater quantities of grains. In an average year, about three million bushels of beans pass through the corporation's twenty-six country elevators,[7] its Michigan Bean Elevator in Saginaw (at 300,000-bushel capacity, the largest specialized and fully automated bean processing plant in the world), and the other Wickes processing and storage facilities, including the 2,250,000-bushel Saginaw Grain Terminal, roughly a fifth of which is now equipped to handle beans.[8] But the real bulk is in grains: some 15 million bushels a year of corn, white wheat, soybeans, and oats, of which 10 million bushels are bought through Wickes's own elevators,[9] and the rest purchased from other sources. In periods of rising commodity prices, this can produce a respectable bundle of revenue.

One of Wickes's latest and most successful acquisitions is a

JOIN THE NAVIES . . . .

Wickes Marine Terminal in Bay City was a major navy bean export center in the 1960s after Cornelis van Bergeijk established Wickes in Europe.

case in point. In October 1973, just before the real inflation in food costs started, Wickes bought the Gormley Bean Company of Greeley, Colorado, which in its very first year under the Wickes umbrella came up with a pretax bottom line that just about covered the $3 million cost of the acquisition.[10] The results for fiscal 1975 were even more impressive—$5 million in pretax earnings, constituting a return on net assets of a whopping 225 percent.

This amazing operation had been launched in 1964 by two brothers then in their mid-thirties, Wesley and Richard Gormley, who believed, and rightly so, that pinto beans could be grown successfully in the Great Plains of mid-America. The Gormleys started out with a 30-acre demonstration farm near Grand Forks, North Dakota, and soon convinced growers in that state as well as in the Red River Valley of Minnesota that pintos were a promising crop indeed. By 1974, nearly 200,000

. . . .AND SEE THE WORLD

Freighters from all over called at the facility to fill their holds. Today, truck transport to ocean ports is more practical. (Photos by Dale Wieck)

acres in North Dakota and Minnesota were in pintos, and all were shipped through Gormley Bean. Half that year's crop, in fact, was exported to Mexico, where a severe drought had wrecked the native harvest. Gormley Bean has since branched out into Nebraska to handle great northerns as well, and is a fully integrated part of Wickes Agriculture.[11]

Boss of the newly formed Wickes Agriculture group is Vice President Roland Pretzer, a tall, professorial-looking fellow in his late forties, who has come full circle since he joined the Charles Wolohan Division of Wickes in 1951 as manager of the Bay City Bean Terminal. In those twenty-four years, Pretzer participated in the birth and growth of the Lumber Division, and until recently ran Wickes Buildings as that division's general manager. Among the executives reporting to him is Clemens O. Putz, who had succeeded Bob Dodge as Bean's general manager, and held that position until the formation of

UP-TO-DATE BEAN CARE

Cultivating beans for Wickes Agriculture. (Photo by Bradford-LaRiviere, Inc.)

Wickes Agriculture. Since then he has had a special project on his hands. Putz, a compact 165-pounder with an engaging smile and an impressive mane of wavy white hair, runs Agriculture's interesting retail operation, which is right up his alley.

Putz, then thirty-two years old, had joined Riedel's outfit back in 1950 after service as a first lieutenant in the Army Quartermaster Corps.[12] His sister, Irma Cannan, was Al's secretary, and Putz went to see Riedel not for a job but for a recommendation, hoping to find a position with some hardware firm in the Pacific Northwest. Instead, Riedel offered him a job, and Clem Putz, who really had no clear-cut idea of what he was going to do with his life, accepted. Clem's last assignment in the Army had been to get rid of surplus property, so maybe Riedel thought that here was a man who could market surplus beans. Be that as it may, Clem's first function with Michigan Bean was that of manager of retail operations.

144

You may remember from a couple of chapters ago that elevator operators not only bought crops from farmers but sold them supplies as well. You'll also recall that Charles Wolohan, Inc., had been one of the pioneers in that retail area, a fact that was to contribute mightily, if indirectly, to Wickes eventually becoming a billion-dollar operation. Riedel's old firm was in the retail business too, although to a much lesser degree, so that Clem's first job couldn't have been all that important despite its impressive title. But Al Riedel must have thought a lot of young Clem because he kept on telling him off. As Riedel once explained to Putz, "So long as I'm giving you hell, that means I still think there's something good about you. When I quit giving you hell, you're on your way out, because I feel there's no point in trying to correct you." Difficult as Riedel

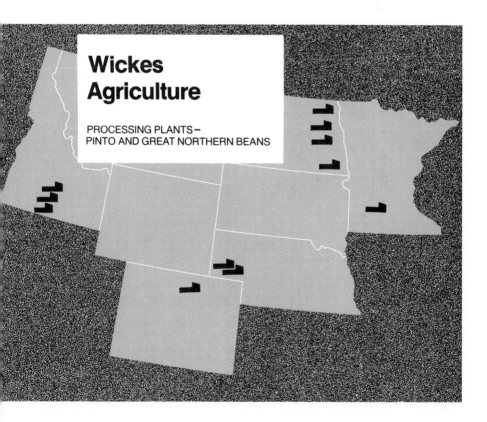

**Wickes
Agriculture**

PROCESSING PLANTS—
PINTO AND GREAT NORTHERN BEANS

Wickes Agriculture

ELEVATORS

TERMINALS

BIG ACRE

NAVY BEAN
GROWING AREAS

COLORED BEAN
GROWING AREAS

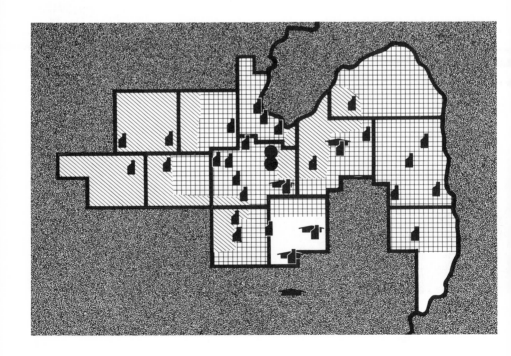

FROM BEANS TO BOARDS
AND BACK TO BEANS

Wickes Vice President Roland A. Pretzer, who started twenty-five years ago as manager of the Bay City Bean Terminal. (Photo by Bosch)

CLEM PUTZ
He tills the Big Acres.

must have been to work for—and it certainly must have been hard for Clem Putz, for Riedel was a clean-desk man and Putz is not—young Clem stuck it out. And, apart from all other considerations, it's a good thing he did, because it was Putz who put Michigan Bean into its highly profitably sideline of operating what are now called the Big Acre Stores.

While the Wolohans had expanded their elevator retail operations in the direction of building supplies, Riedel had stuck pretty close to what farmers needed. The Michigan Bean country elevators primarily carried feeders and water fountains for farmers who raised chickens, and stock tanks and fencing for breeders of cattle. The company's big breakthrough into retailing didn't come about until Michigan Bean established a proprietary line of seeds. Where all the other elevator operators simply sold seeds in plain bags without brand names, Clem

SUBURBAN SUCCESSOR OF THE COUNTRY STORE
Big Acre store in Caro, Michigan, is typical of its kind—simple but attractive on the outside, crammed with hobby, farming, and gardening merchandise on the inside.

Putz got together with the Northrup King people of Minneapolis and arranged for Michigan Bean to become an outlet for their famous field seeds: alfalfa, clover, timothy, and the like. From there, Putz expanded into fertilizer, which Michigan Bean started to sell under its own brand name. Al Riedel himself didn't concern himself much with these sidelines, but after Michigan Bean had merged with Wickes, and the Wolohan and Michigan Bean elevators became, in effect, part of the same business, feed and fertilizer sales really took off.

The two best retail locations at that time were the old Wolohan elevators at Birch Run in Saginaw County and at Davison in Genesee County, and Putz prevailed on their managers to take on a broadened line of farm supplies. At both elevators the original dingy retail stores were remodeled, and new shelving was installed so that the merchandise could be properly displayed. Dale Ott, the manager at Davison, proved especially receptive. With Flint's suburban sprawl encroaching on farm lands, his corn and bean business had shrunk to almost nothing, and Ott was eager to find new ways to make money. Before long, he established a regular retail store next door to the now almost dormant Davison elevator, and he stocked everything that a suburban hobbyist with a few acres might possibly be interested in, from chicken and horse feed to fancy saddles and snowmobiles.

This was the beginning of the Big Acre Stores. Now there are five of them in Michigan (in Davison, Birch Run, Fenton, Caro, and Brighton), and one in Rockford, Illinois. Together with the feed and seed retail business of Wickes Agriculture's country elevators, the Big Acre Stores generate about $2.5 million a year in sales.[13] That may not seem a whole lot when considered as part of a billion-dollar corporation, or even just as part of the division which, in the fiscal year ending January 25, 1975, had total sales of about $157 million. But remember that, in the handling of commodities, the profit margin is usually small in relation to the required working capital, while in retail sales, the markup traditionally hovers around 30 to 40 percent. Also, profits in the elevator business are limited by nature: you can sell no more than has been grown in the particular area, and in a bad year that can be very little. But the retail business, at least theoretically, is limited only by your ability to compete: here you can sell as much as the customer is willing to buy at your price. Thus, in years of relatively stable (and until fairly recently) low commodity prices, Michigan Bean's comparatively modest retail operations can produce as much as 25 percent of the division's profits. And here's what is so neat about that: just as The Wickes Corporation's agricultural activities serve as a handy cushion for that now basically retail-oriented giant, so do the Big Acre Stores and the feed and seed sales at the Michigan country elevators[14] provide a similar buffer within the corporation's commodity diversification.[15]

Of course it isn't likely that the Big Acre Stores will ever generate anywhere near the kind of cash flow and earnings that Wickes has achieved with its lumber and building supply centers. Current plans call for opening four new Big Acre stores in fiscal 1976, and six stores each year thereafter until 1980, by which time Clem Putz hopes to hit a sales volume of $22 million. In the light of the astronomical figures that get kicked around in the billion-dollar Wickes Corporation, this may not seem a whole lot. But every dollar counts—and with inflation, ironically counts ever more as it counts less.

10

McMullin's Baby

To face one's board of directors is no small matter even for most top officers of a corporation, let alone middle management. Here is this forbidding body of successful men. They may smile at you, joke with you, ask about your family, say all kinds of pleasant things, but the next day you can find yourself out of a job. Luckily, Joseph S. McMullin, a country elevator man from way back, wasn't average. He was a pugnacious, cigar-chomping little guy who refused to be intimidated by anybody. In business, he was brusque to the point of rudeness. When somebody on the phone offered him a deal he didn't like he simply hung up. Not another word, no polite noises, nothing. With the people he worked for he wasn't quite that boorish, but he let it be known loud and clear that he considered himself as good as they were any day.

So here Joe McMullin came to his big bosses, the Wickes board of directors, with an idea that was way out—and on top of that required a front-end investment of somewhere between $10,000 and $15,000. Which only goes to show how small-time

Wickes still was in those days, back in 1952, for so trifling an outlay to demand the attention of the corporation's leadership. What Joe wanted was to take a corner of the Bay City Bean Terminal—the former Eddy shipyards we remember from the preceding chapter—and turn it into a new type of retail outlet for building supplies. Thanks to Corky van Bergeijk's acumen, the two-story shed McMullin had his eye on stood there empty and unproductive. The surplus beans that had been stored there for so many years had all been sold. In this vacant building and around it, McMullin wanted to stock dimensional lumber, plywood, doors, and assorted other basic construction materials for cash sale to small contractors who would then load up their trucks on the spot and take with them what they paid for.

He reasoned that such an operation would be in a position to offer extremely attractive prices. For one thing, the cash transaction would eliminate a lot of bookkeeping. For another, that inevitable percentage of bad debts wouldn't have to be factored into the overhead. On top of that, there would be no delivery costs. And in any case, the property was just sitting there, going to waste. Not that this involved a great loss to The Wickes Corporation, which had purchased the shipyard with its 143,000 square feet of floor space for the ridiculously low price of something like 50 cents a square foot. "We really didn't know what we were going to do with the building at the time," Fitz-Gerald once said, "but it was so cheap, it was kind of like when gals go bargain hunting—we couldn't resist it." But bargain or not, there was no point in letting any of the space remain idle. All factors considered, Joe McMullin figured he could undercut competitors by 25 to 40 percent.

What did he need the ten grand for? Well, down payments on inventory to start with, although he intended to hold his stocks to a minimum, replacing the merchandise as it was sold. More important, some structural alterations were necessary, and above all he needed to fence the area so that the lumber wouldn't be carried off by cashless shoppers after everybody went home from work.

JOSEPH S. McMULLIN

Long retired, the man who started the Cash Ways is now back in Hemlock, where he once ran a country elevator.

Only one member of the Wickes board of directors, Dan Fitz-Gerald, was the kind inclined to take a gamble—an ironic circumstance since, as the corporation's treasurer, he was its money watcher. And only one other man on the board knew anything at all about lumber, and that was Richard V. Wolohan, one of Charles Wolohan's sons, whose country elevators—by now a division of Wickes—sold building supplies to farmers.[1] Everyone else on the board was not only very conservative when it came to expenditures, but just about totally ignorant about selling 2 × 4s. It's a good thing that Dan Fitz-Gerald carried a lot of weight. Having proved his mettle with money by prompting the consolidation of the Wickes interests, and his ability to pinpoint potentially profitable areas by maneuvering Wickes into the bean and grain business, he was in the enviable position of being rarely squelched by Ran Wickes. Dan supported the McMullin proposal, as did Dick Wolohan and his brother Bob, who, as general manager of the Saginaw Grain subsidiary, was also on the board. When at last Ran Wickes nodded his agreement, all the other directors climbed on the bandwagon.[2]

"I'm sure glad you see it my way," Joe drawled dryly around his cigar. "I kind of figured you would. So I went ahead and spent the money. I'll open up the place in a couple of weeks."

Nobody else in the organization, with the possible exception of Dan Fitz-Gerald, could have gotten away with such effrontery, committing funds before they were appropriated, and then talking about it to the board of directors without even cracking a conciliatory smile. But Joe McMullin was not so much an employee as an institution. He'd gone to work for Charles Wolohan in Birch Run as a boy, then moved to Hemlock when old Wolohan bought that elevator in 1915. The Wolohan firm, like similar businesses elsewhere, was based on family relationships, neighborhood friendships, intermarriage, and community loyalty. Conflicts rarely arose over incompetence but usually came as a result of personal squabbles. Thus McMullin was a member of that closely knit fraternity of Wolohan old-timers, a group that in later years came to be referred to in some Wickes circles as "Hemlock U." Unlike some other graduates of that grass-roots institution, however, McMullin was extraordinarily gifted: he possessed an almost infallible instinct for judging markets, calling crops, predicting price swings, and turning a buck.[3]

At the time he jumped the gun by buying some $6,000 worth of cyclone fencing for the as-yet unauthorized cash-and-carry lumber yard at the Bay City Bean Terminal, he was director of lumber purchasing and marketing of the Charles Wolohan, Inc., Division. Actually, that impressive title didn't mean very much as yet, since retail operations at the country elevators were still rather limited, and to run them wasn't even a full-time job. McMullin's prime responsibility was still the supervision of the Hemlock elevator, which, under his hard-nosed management, was the biggest moneymaker among the original Wolohan properties. But the possibility of expanding lumber sales beyond the country elevator level had long been on McMullin's mind. Roland Pretzer, today vice president in charge of Wickes Agriculture, who had also come into the corporation with the Wolohan acquisition, recalls that Joe had already been dreaming out loud about a "lumber supermarket" several years prior to the Wolohan merger of June 1950. It was evident, however, that country elevators didn't lend themselves to enterprises of that scope.

To run a supermarket, you've got to have a lot of customers, and if it's a building supply supermarket, your major customers have to be contractors. This in turn demands a high level of home building activity in your market area. Hence there is an innate conflict of purposes: once a rural neighborhood gets built up enough to warrant a lumber supermarket, the local country elevator languishes for lack of arable land from which to obtain crops.

But the Bay City Bean Terminal was no country elevator. It sat in the heart of an industrial and trading center, had all the space you could possibly want for the storage of bulky lumber and plywood, and was equipped with railroad trackage that made it easy to bring in supplies. So now Joe had his big chance to translate his dream into action, and he grabbed it. He was sure he would succeed. However, the powers at Wickes were not yet convinced, although they had approved the appropriation. Looking back, it's interesting to note that they shied away from endowing the new venture with the Wickes (or even Wolohan) name, a caution undreamed of in modern corporate public relations. McMullin's baby was baptized "Bay City Cash Way Company," and there were few people who knew that it was a sibling of Wickes Brothers, Wickes Boiler, United States Graphite, Saginaw Grain, and Charles Wolohan, Inc. If it went sour, its failure would not rub off on the reputation of the corporation. Indeed, The Wickes Corporation's annual reports did not even mention Cash Way until 1954, by which time it had proven itself so successful that a second lumber supermarket had been built in Kalamazoo, at the other end of lower Michigan, far from the traditional stamping ground of the Wickes operations, and it wasn't until the 1955 *Report to Stockholders* that a Cash Way photo made corporate print. Little did even Dan Fitz-Gerald realize that in backing the $10,000 Bay City lumberyard appropriation, he had taken the first big step in building a billion-dollar business.

You've seen motion pictures of space launches. It seems at first that the rocket will never take off. It lifts ever so slowly, hovers a few feet above its pad, then gradually gains speed, and suddenly it's out of sight. This, essentially, is what happened with the Cash Ways, except for the lack of smoke and thunder.

To fully understand how McMullin's concept changed the lumber business and in effect helped make Wickes what it is today, you have to set your mind back a quarter-century. World War II was over, and the ten million young men who had served in it came home, eager to forget their life in barracks, squad tents, foxholes, and ship bunks. Every one of them wanted his own little nest, a wife, and children. To be single in those days was almost nonconformist. Naturally there was a tremendous housing shortage. Yet, surprisingly, the large merchant builder—the developer of huge tracts—had not yet emerged in most parts of the country, and apartments were all but unknown except in the biggest cities. Homes were still custom-built by small contractor-builders, and "custom-built" didn't mean then what it does today: it didn't carry the inference of special quality. Just about every house, whether cheap or expensive, was put up one at a time. When it was finished and sold, the builder moved on to the next one. He bought his materials piecemeal instead of all at once, a truckload of lumber today, another of roofing some weeks later. And just as the building business was antiquated in terms of society's needs at that time, so was the building supply business.

Lumber was still sold by small independent dealers, as it had always been ever since the days when Michigan was stripped of its pine, and its timber shipped out to build the farm communities of the Great Plains. The people who sold this lumber built sheds along railroad tracks—that's why they were called "line yards"—and all the business was transacted right there, from unloading to sale. There were probably close to 50,000 such little lumberyards all over the country, mostly one-person operations that didn't advertise, didn't merchandise, but simply sat there and waited for buyers to show up. More often than not, customers couldn't get what they wanted, for the small yards were generally understocked. Needless to say, being virtual monopolies in their own trading areas, they were also overpriced. Just about everything was marked up 50 percent. If the dealer bought lumber, say, for $80 per 1,000 board feet delivered, he sold it for $120. That's thirty-three points of margin—a stupendous markup, even allowing for the fact that much of the business was done on credit. The bigger yards, and there were some of those too, were equally overpriced, though often not much better stocked. They did provide some services, such as help with blueprints and taking care of deliveries, which was convenient but in most cases not really necessary. Still, such amenities added to the overhead, and the customer had to pay for them whether he needed them or not.

Thus any lumber operation that went in for organized purchasing, instead of merely hoping for the right materials to be dropped off a freight train, was a boon to small builders, remodeling contractors, and do-it-yourselfers. The latter, particularly, presented a vast, as yet untapped market. Wages in the building trades were just beginning to rise out of proportion to other incomes, and under the new system the do-it-yourselfer could obtain the wide range of materials that had not been readily available at traditional lumberyards.

Here was an astounding opportunity. All you had to do was to stock the right merchandise, take advantage of the savings inherent in quantity purchasing and cash-and-carry selling, and be willing to live with a small markup—and you had it made. Wickes was about to overhaul a whole industry.

When Joe McMullin launched the Bay City Cash Way, he sent out direct-mail advertising to builders in the area, pointing out how much money they could save by doing their purchasing there. The results were truly stunning. When the yard opened its doors on a cloudy April day in 1952, a fair number of builder-contractors showed up—some of them from as far away as 60 miles—but most of them came in cars, not trucks. They just couldn't believe that desirable materials could be offered at the low prices advertised, and they wanted to check out the situation first. All they needed was one look, and they drove off again, returning as soon as they could with their pickups. Before the end of the second week, the original inventory had been turned over.[4] Joe's plywood, especially, was in demand. He bought it directly from a mill, marked it up about 20 percent, and set it out in piles as it came in, regardless of quality. This made a big hit with the contractors. They could buy a mixed batch for a price that would have been low for even the cheapest grade in the pile. By sorting it themselves they had plywood for every conceivable use from shelving to roofing.

Soon, owners of independent lumberyards showed up too. They found they could do better at Cash Way than buying through wholesalers. Then do-it-yourselfers started walking in from the street. By the end of that summer, the sales volume swelled to such a point that Corky van Bergeijk had to work overtime cleaning out the remaining surplus beans in the Bay City Terminal to make room for lumber. Daily sales averaged about $8,000, and on a busy Saturday could run to $15,000. The Bay City Cash Way alone was turning over almost as much lumber as all the Wolohan country elevators combined.[5]

You might well ask why no one else got the message and started competing with Cash Way, especially after the Kalamazoo outlet was opened in 1953. By that time the advance mailing was considerably more consumer-oriented, so that word must have gotten around all over the place. The answer, as Roland Pretzer sees it, was that competitors simply couldn't believe the bargains Wickes offered. They knew what the costs were but were unable to relate them to the selling prices. "They must have felt that either we had special deals with the mills or else were bound to go broke very fast," Pretzer says, "and so they sat back and watched us instead of getting on the bandwagon." What the potential rivals apparently didn't understand was Joe McMullin's philosophy of operating on unprecedentedly small margins—as low as sixteen points. "So long as we don't get greedy," he used to say, "and so long as we hold labor costs down, we can keep our volume going and make money." This was the "secret" no one outside Wickes seemed able to fathom.

And they still didn't catch on when, in February of 1955, yet another Cash Way, this one at Milan, Michigan, about 12

miles south of Ann Arbor, was opened. True, it split its customer territory with the earlier establishment at Kalamazoo,
but by now buyers came long distances, attracted by the
savings. Some even drove all the way from Michigan's upper
peninsula to pick up truckloads of plywood and doors—and
you've got to remember that this was in the days before the
Mackinac Bridge, and they had to pay for ferry transportation
across the Straits. Cash Way pricing made long, expensive trips
worthwhile.

Roland Pretzer, now Wickes Agriculture's boss, was in on
that historic moment when McMullin's Cash Way rocket
started zooming out of sight. Pretzer had been manager of the
Bay City Bean Terminal for about a year when he was reassigned to help out at the first Cash Way and to learn about the
lumber business from the ground up. When the Milan yard
opened, he became its assistant manager and he continued to

This Cash Way cash-and-carry center in what is now Rootstown, Ohio, racked up $8 million in business in 1957, a record that remains unbroken to this day.

prove himself so competent that he was McMullin's choice when Cash Way took its leap across the Michigan state line into Ohio in January 1956.[6]

That lumberyard was in Rootstown, then called New Milford, 18 miles east of Akron on Route 18 (and now just south of Interstate 80). Mailings were made to contractors in about an 80-mile radius, and the response was overwhelming. Almost the whole inventory, some $300,000-worth, was cleaned out in less than one month. Already on opening day, the yard was swamped with customers, who were so eager that they wrestled the merchandise right off the railroad freight cars parked next to the 408 × 60 foot warehouse. It was a windy, cold day, the kind of Midwestern winter day when sensible people stay at home, but that was no deterrent. The customers didn't even have to be sold. Indeed, there were no salesmen—another of the money-saving tricks of the early Cash Ways. Only Pretzer

161

and his assistant manager really knew anything about the business. The yard's six other employees merely had to know how to tally invoices.[7]

Pretzer's volume had been impressive enough when he was just dealing with contractors. But when spring finally came, he sent out his first consumer mailing, and do-it-yourselfers flooded in from all over the eastern third of Ohio, right down to West Virginia, and even from parts of Pennsylvania.

There wasn't anything fancy about those pioneer Wickes lumber centers like Pretzer's in Rootstown: just some long, barnlike storage structures on 20 to 30 acres of fenced land in rural areas near growing population centers. The merchandise was equally basic: lumber, plywood, insulation, doors, and windows; that sort of stuff. Plumbing, heating and electrical supplies were not added until later. Amazing as it may seem in retrospect, they were sold by a separate division for a couple of years before these two obviously meshing functions were combined.

Customers would line up in the early dawn, long before the yard opened at 7:30. Then they'd get a number and, while waiting for their turn, look over the merchandise. When their number came up, they'd show one of the "yard men" what was wanted, and he wrote it up and helped with loading it on the trucks. Ten-foot-high piles of plywood, huge stacks of dimensional lumber, sheds full of insulation, mountains of roofing, would be gone before you could blink an eye. Pretzer would call McMullin in Hemlock, who still handled the purchasing, and order "two carloads of this and three carloads of that, and they thought I was out of my mind. They told me the stuff will be sitting here until next fall, but after they began to see some of the receipts they became believers." By July of that year, just six months later, Rootstown alone had done a little over $4 million worth of business,[8] or just about as much as the total working capital of The Wickes Corporation a few years earlier when it had acquired Wolohan. Now, that's an impressive enough statistic. But to really visualize what it means, think of it in terms of $3 doors and 25-cent 2 × 4s, and you begin to see the magnitude of this new business.

Pretzer's big year came in 1957 when sales at his Rootstown yard jumped to $8 million, a record for any individual Wickes lumberyard and, indeed, for the whole building supply retail industry—and one that has been approached but never equaled since. By that time, in addition to the outlets at the Wolohan country elevators, Wickes had six lumber centers whose sales totaled $26,225,610, a nearly fivefold increase from two years earlier when Cash Way had started its first operations in Bay City, Kalamazoo, and Milan.

The reason Rootstown's 1957 record was never broken is inherent in the nature of our free enterprise system. Other people in the building supply business finally caught on that Joe McMullin had led Wickes into a veritable gold mine, and they were opening similar outlets that started cutting into Wickes sales. Not that this competition seriously hurt Wickes, but it did reduce the volume of the individual Wickes outlets and presented the corporation with a crucial choice that any successful and therefore widely imitated enterprise eventually must face.

The choice was this: Wickes could either surrender much of its market share to competitors—or it could compete with itself. In short, instead of letting others encroach upon its existing building supply markets, Wickes could open additional outlets of its own within these markets. The individual lumber center might thus do less business, but most of the business it lost would go to another Wickes store, not to a competitor. And that's precisely what Wickes opted for.

Within the next few years, for instance, Wickes lumber centers were opened at Saegertown, Pennsylvania, and at Norwalk and Newcomerstown, both in Ohio. All were in the territory from which Rootstown had drawn its customers. In fact, the locations for these new yards were chosen by Roland Pretzer himself, who by then was at headquarters in Saginaw, having been promoted to regional manager. Needless to say, those three new yards took a lot of trade away from Rootstown, whose annual sales volume today runs around $4 million, and in good years maybe a little over that.[9] But the decision to slice up the Rootstown territory was certainly appropriate. If it hadn't been done, the Carter Lumber Company, which started its own cash-and-carry system in nearby Akron, Ohio, might have succeeded in driving Wickes clear out of that highly important area south of Lake Erie.[10]

Of course, Wickes also expanded into new territories. By 1962—now no longer called Cash Way but at last operating under the name of Wickes Lumber Company—it had forty-one building supply centers not only in Michigan, Ohio, and Pennsylvania, but also in Indiana, Illinois, Wisconsin, Minnesota, and Kentucky in the Midwest; and even as far away as Virginia, Maryland, New York State, New Jersey, and Connecticut along the Eastern Seaboard, Texas in the Southwest, and California on the Pacific Coast.[11] Their sales for the year totaled $66,343,532. This one division alone was now responsible for more than half the business of the whole corporation. "The growth was almost in spite of us," said Dan Fitz-Gerald, "and the profits were fantastic. The whole thing was absolutely unbelievable."

And it still is. Even Joe McMullin had not envisioned how his Bay City baby would spurt into gawky adolescence almost overnight. But like all youngsters, especially precocious ones, Wickes Lumber had its problems, and its biggest problem was its rapid growth. Its corporate family—strangers to the new world of mass merchandising—could no longer cope with the vitality of this unexpected mammoth child. No plans had been made, no educational system set up, to help it reach a healthy maturity. Even after Rootstown's explosive success, Saginaw still couldn't believe that the lumber centers were more than little stores which just happened to do a lot of business. When the Wickes yard at Elkhorn, Wisconsin, was opened one Friday in October 1958, its manager frantically phoned Saginaw. "The banks just closed," he said with a shaky voice. "I've got two shoeboxes with $95,000 in them. What do I do?" The best answer anyone could give him was to take the money home and sleep with it under his pillow.

By 1963 Wickes had a potential runaway on its hands: the Lumber Division now did just about two-thirds of all the corporation's business[12] and was flailing in every direction, seemingly out of control. A tough tutor was needed—not necessarily a subject-matter specialist, but someone who could pinpoint faults and enforce the disciplines to correct them. Luckily, such a taskmaster was at hand in the Wickes hierarchy. This was Smith Bolton, a soft-spoken man, meticulously polite and somewhat aloof as was the manner in those days of Eastern prep-school graduates. But his gentle voice could turn frigid in mid-sentence, and his blue eyes punch holes in you even as he smiled. Tough but never harsh, and unfailingly fair, he was one of those rare personalities that could be liked and feared at the same Time. Dan Fitz-Gerald, who had been named executive vice president in October 1956, made the right choice in picking him to hammer the out-of-kilter Wickes corporate framework back into shape. Smith Bolton, who had made his mark by putting United States Graphite solidly in the black, was the man for this season.

11

A Chronicle
of Crises

S mith Bolton was fortunate to be alive. Anyone is who has
been chauffeured by a Soviet tank commander on a U.S.
highway. In World War II, when Bolton was still running old
Graphite, his division sold quantities of that rich black dust to
the U.S.S.R. to lubricate delicate components of the Russian
arsenal. One of the purchasing agents was a young Red Army
captain from an armored division, on detached duty with the
official Amtorg Trading Corp. because he could speak fairly
decent English. Once, on a sightseeing ride around the Saginaw countryside, this Russian officer insisted on doing the
driving. Bolton, being a good host, had little choice but to let
him. Unfortunately, so far as the Russian was concerned, an
automobile was equipped with only two controls. One was the
gas pedal, the other the brake, and one or the other always had
to be flush with the floor. The gung-ho captain usually had his
hands off the wheel and was turned around in his seat, animat-
edly talking to Bolton in the back of the car. But as gut-
wrenching as the ride proved to be with its numerous near-

collisions, it wasn't as shocking by half as Bolton's experience when he inquired how the Wickes Lumber Division came up with its choices for locations.

Bolton had been whisked from U.S. Graphite by Dan Fitz-Gerald in late November 1961 to assume the newly established office of corporate vice president in charge of operations. The activities of all the Wickes divisions were thus under his command, from his old familiar Graphite to building materials and beans.[1] When he first took office, Bolton didn't know enough about lumber to drive a nail straight, and the cash-and-carry yards hardly seemed anything to worry about. After all, they were phenomenally successful, making more money with each passing day. But when a report filtered through to Bolton in the spring of 1962 that this division had invested some $150,000 to build a yard in Grapevine, a small town in Texas he'd never heard of, he began to wonder, and dug out a map.

At first glance, the location looked pretty good. Grapevine sat between Dallas and Fort Worth, in a rural area of cheap real estate that had every earmark of eventually being overcome by suburban sprawl from both directions. Yet, Grapevine's choice was puzzling. At that time it was still in the middle of nowhere, and the fact that ten years later the world's showpiece airport would be built nearby wasn't yet even dreamed of by the airlines. Why put a Wickes center in Grapevine, and not, say, Keller or Lewisville or Midlothian? These little towns were also in the same general area.

So Bolton asked for the file on how Grapevine had been picked. For several weeks he got the type of polite runaround reserved for top executives. When, after much prompting, he finally received the manila folder on Grapevine, it felt amazingly slim. He opened it, and found a road map of the kind that gas stations used to hand out for free, plus a sheet of yellow foolscap with a scribbled note that said something to the effect, "We drove down Route 21 and there was this railroad, and vacant land was available for sale, and I think we ought to buy it." That was all. And on the basis of this report, Wickes was in Grapevine, Texas.

Bolton had never been poor. In fact, he came from a pretty well-fixed family. But, having been born in 1902, his initial career as the owner of an inherited automobile dealership had come to an end with the Great Depression. An investment of $150,000 was no small matter to him, and the precipitous plunge into Grapevine gave him the willies. Apprehensively he began looking into the rationales for the other lumberyard sites during that first period of explosive expansion: nearly all of them, except those in Wickes's home territory around the Great Lakes, had been picked for similarly flimsy reasons. Nowhere had anybody conducted a real market analysis. Nor even bothered to inquire whether the established local lumber dealer might be the brother-in-law of the local banker—a question that could seem esoteric to the average person but would immediately occur to any astute entrepreneur trying to move in on a new territory. Moreover, expensive commitments had been made to buy real estate for lumberyards in the heart of the Deep South—in Alabama, Louisiana, and Mississippi—an area where at that time no Damn Yankee had the chance of a snowball on a mint-julep day of establishing a successful business.

The more Smith Bolton looked into the lumber operation the less he liked what he saw. There was nothing wrong with the concept of collective purchasing to obtain lower prices, but this surely didn't mean that the inventory had to be the same in every lumber center—or, for that matter, that it should be. Different parts of the country had different building codes and different tastes in architecture, and they used different materials. The five new yards in Texas, for example, were stocked to the rafters with beautiful western pine—desirable everywhere else, but Texas grew its own yellow pine that could be bought at the local mills much more cheaply than the shipped-in lumber. Also, there were stacks of unsold garage doors at those Texas outlets. Why? The answer should have been apparent to anyone who has ever visited that part of the country: in those days few people down there bothered to build garages; almost everybody used car ports.

Altogether it was an incredible situation. While Mc-

TWICE TO THE RESCUE

*Saginaw's Smith Bolton,
a firm disciplinarian,
first revitalized U.S.
Graphite, then helped
Wickes Lumber grow up.*

Mullin's idea was a natural winner, its very success now served as a virtual invitation to disaster. The Lumber Division's bottom-line triumphs were dangerously deceiving. Practically all the profits came from the centers in Michigan and neighboring states. The new yards elsewhere were nearly unproductive, and in some cases actually lost money. If the division, with its sudden financial force, continued on its helter-skelter course, it could pull down the whole corporation before anyone even knew what was happening. "If we had kept on investing hundreds of thousands of dollars in properties like Grapevine," Bolton says, "we would have been sunk."

It wasn't that the people in the Lumber Division didn't know what they were doing. But their concept of doing business did not tally with that of the new Wickes Corporation now beginning to take shape. If anything, the expansion into other parts of the country had been foisted on them, and they didn't like it. Most of them were still thinking Hemlock when Dan Fitz-Gerald had long been dreaming hemisphere.

The division, as we know, had grown out of the acquisition of the Charles Wolohan country elevators, and the men who ran it were nearly unbeatable on their own home grounds.

There they knew almost everybody they bought from and sold to, and they knew whose word was worth a damn and whose wasn't. But forced out of their own environment by Dan Fitz-Gerald's indomitable drive for growth, most of them felt lost. Texans and Californians, let alone New Englanders and New Yorkers, were strange creatures, and the methods of mass merchandising required to meet a nationwide market were stranger still. No longer could these grass rooters rely on the instincts that had rarely failed them in home territory. No longer, indeed, could they take a man's word for granted. When Smith Bolton asked one of the division's purchasing agents how he knew he was getting the best price on shingles, the man answered that his supplier had assured him he couldn't do better anywhere else. That supplier had seemed like such a nice down-to-earth guy over dinner and drinks in Chicago, and my, the fella sure took him to a fancy place, and insisted on picking up the tab. Competitive bidding? Who ever heard of such high-hat nonsense![2]

Bolton's troubleshooting did not go unnoticed. The pressure was definitely on. Dick Wolohan, Wickes Lumber's handsome, clean-cut divisional president, was the first to feel it. An executive echelon had been shoved in between him and Dan Fitz-Gerald: Dick Wolohan now reported to Smith Bolton. When something like that happens, you know you are on shaky ground. Always deeply religious, Dick Wolohan in earlier years had never smoked or touched a drink. He even walked out of a room when somebody told an off-color story. He was no less high-principled now, but the stresses around him were building up to such a degree that he indulged in an occasional before-dinner cocktail—something that seemed totally out of character to everyone who had known him for a while.[3] He was, quite obviously, a thoroughly unhappy man, and nobody could blame him. Rather, he was so well liked and respected that everybody sympathized, including Dan Fitz-Gerald, although it was he who had precipitated the crisis.

From the ne'er-do-well who kept flunking his CPA exam, Fitz-Gerald had turned into the prototype of a rising corporate executive. His personal ambition had become linked to that of the corporation. He wasn't a job shopper as are so many others (though rarely the truly successful ones) who try to achieve the pinnacle of their own success by hopping from rung to rung on different corporate ladders. Wickes had become Dan Fitz-Gerald's life and the corporation's growth his purpose. Such a single-minded stance is never without risk, and this was particularly true of the Lumber Division situation.

Remember that Charles Wolohan, Inc., had been acquired through a merger that gave the Wolohan family a considerable chunk of The Wickes Corporation's ownership, and two Wolohans were then divisional presidents—with Dick's brother Bob not only running the important Saginaw Grain subsidiary but also serving on the board of directors.[4] When Dan Fitz-Gerald had first gone to Ran Wickes to suggest placing Bolton above Dick Wolohan, and thus in effect making Wolohan impotent and probably squeezing him out of the picture, Ran Wickes pointed out to Fitz-Gerald that the Wolohans owned half a million shares of Wickes stock. "Instead of you letting Dick go," Ran warned him, "it's just possible that the Wolohans might let you go." Dan said he'd be willing to take that risk and would proceed if Ran agreed in principle. Ran's answer was, "Well, go ahead, but if the Wolohans start a fight, I will not be able to protect you."

Of course by then corporate infighting was nothing new to Dan. As the strongest contender for the corporation's leadership, he had been targeted before and would be, as we shall see, again. But it turned out that in the Wolohan case at least, there was little cause for anxiety. In later years, Fitz-Gerald liked to boast that he learned long ago not to worry about anything. Be that as it may, it's doubtful that he had already reached that state of pragmatic fatalism back then, in 1963, when he was still one official notch short of attaining the Wickes presidency. But whether he did or did not worry about the outcome of the Bolton maneuver really didn't matter. Indeed, that's what may have taught Fitz-Gerald not to fret. For out of the blue, one late afternoon, Dick Wolohan appeared in Smith Bolton's office and asked him as a friend if Smith thought he should resign. "I have the feeling," Wolohan said, "that I'm not handling this thing the way you people think it should be done. If that's the case, maybe I'd better quit."[5]

Bolton did not answer Wolohan immediately. This was too important a step to make a snap decision on. But Wolohan's own apparent willingness to leave provided the opportunity Fitz-Gerald had been hoping for: he could now reorganize the Lumber Division without a destructive showdown. Within a few days he asked Wolohan point-blank for the latter's resignation and received it on the spot without objection. The problem was solved—or so it seemed at the moment. In point of fact, however, Dick Wolohan's departure provoked a crisis that was, if anything, more serious than the one that had just been sidestepped.

Smith Bolton immediately assumed direct command of Wickes Lumber, which now encompassed also electrical, heating and plumbing, and which was called the Wickes Lumber and Building Supply Division. Bolton's first smart move was to promote Roland Pretzer, whose Rootstown operation had been the first to bear the Wickes name instead of being called a Cash Way, and had done the name proud. Pretzer, already in Saginaw as regional manager, was now placed in charge of the division's merchandising and advertising. But Bolton didn't get the chance to do much more than that as he prepared, in that fall and winter of 1963, to shift the division's people into slots for which they seemed most qualified. He didn't get that chance because no sooner had Dick Wolohan handed in his resignation than other resignations started trickling in. Every week two or three of the old-timers quit until almost forty were gone, depleting the division of practically all its key people.

What happened was that Dick Wolohan had decided to go into direct competition with Wickes. Not that he intended to challenge Wickes on a nationwide basis. He figured a couple of dozen or so yards would be enough to handle, and he would spot these in the central Great Lakes area, starting with the original Wickes-Wolohan home territory, the still semirural regions of lower Michigan.[6] This area was of course where the old Wolohan staffers were able to function most effectively, and so it's not surprising that they were happy to leave Wickes, whose horizons they were loath to grasp, and join an organization that would allow them to operate on familiar grounds, for a boss they really liked, under rules they understood and appreciated, and within parameters they considered realistic.

On the face of it, this exodus of people who couldn't see things the Wickes way might not have been such a bad thing from the Wickes point of view. But the problem, which neither Dan Fitz-Gerald nor Smith Bolton had envisioned, was that they were now left with an organization that had no muscle and hardly even a skeleton. Several building supply centers had recently opened. Others were under construction. Still others were planned and committed on paper. But there was barely enough qualified field staff to operate the existing facilities, let alone make a success of new ones. Worse yet, at Bolton's Saginaw headquarters, there were Pretzer and perhaps a tiny handful of others who felt at all at home in the building supply business. Wickes had succeeded in taming its wild offspring, but now the poor kid had no sap.

Yet this was the time to get the show really on the road. The Lumber Division now had momentum. Articles in the trade press talked up the Wickes system of selling building supplies. Other lumber retailers were becoming interested in pursuing the same course. An upsurge of competitive enterprises was inevitable.

It was evident that Wickes could proceed on the basis of its own pattern; that is, it could study the areas where its existing building supply centers were especially successful, chart their common properties, and select future sites on the basis of these criteria. But who was going to do the analyzing? Who was to go out into the field and investigate a multitude of localities in detail to spot those that fit the pattern? Who, for that matter, would be competent to judge potential competition? In some locations the one or two existing lumberyards might fold up almost immediately. In others, they might stick it out for a while, just long enough to hurt the initial Wickes business. In yet other locations, the owners of existing building supply outlets might be smart enough to learn a thing or two and end up as serious rivals. And what about the aforementioned possibility that existing lumberyards might be closely tied to the local banks and local building and loan associations that would only lend to contractors who bought from the existing yards? All this investigative spadework required personnel—and highly qualified personnel at that.

Then what about the actual breaking into a new market? If Wickes yards were indeed to be building supply supermarkets, they had to be run like supermarkets. Their prices had to average out below those charged by the independent competition—the lumber "corner groceries." Yet the Wickes prices on some items would have to be no lower, just so long as heavily advertised sales leaders, dramatically marked down below the local price structure, pulled in the traffic.[7] Apparently, this had never been fully understood by many of the early managers of the Lumber Division. They had maintained a standard markdown on almost all items regardless of local conditions, and had thus sold some merchandise far too cheaply, reducing the profitability of the operation. But to handle such competitive pricing intelligently requires professional merchandising talent. Who was going to do that important job?

What's more, it might turn out—as indeed was to be the case—that in many, perhaps even most, areas, Wickes would be better off to go the acquisition route than to build its own stores from the ground up. Any number of small lumberyard chains might be open to merger or purchase; their facilities could then be restyled, their marketing system revamped, and their merchandising coordinated with that of the rest of the Wickes division. But who was to investigate the potential candidates for acquisition? Who was going to provide the information that enabled a sound decision on whether to build or buy?

The fact that the Wickes system worked best in areas where the family housing market was dominated by small builders who put up three or four homes a year was obvious. Mass builders who constructed 500 homes at a crack in metropolitan centers could do better dealing directly with wholesalers. But this still left one heck of a lot of country to investigate—in fact, most of it. Again this required highly qualified people.

And there were hardly any around.

As the Lumber Division's key staffers left one after another to join the new Wolohan organization in that fateful spring of 1964, there was a frantic shifting of Wickes bodies. Assistant managers, even if they had very little experience, were promoted overnight to be in charge of their centers. Anyone who seemed to show promise was transferred to Saginaw to help with site selections, purchasing, and all the other problems that the headquarters of a growing retail chain must cope with. The whole organization was in a mess. Something had to be done—and fast.

12

New Players

P opular history is a chronology of the obvious. In 1976 we celebrate the Bicentennial of the Declaration of Independence, but in 1963 only a few people were aware that it was the two-hundredth anniversary of Patrick Henry's Parsons' Cause arguments, which had molded public opinion against British colonial policy. Everybody knows about the Bolshevik Revolution of 1917, but the year Karl Marx published his first volume of *Das Kapital*—1867—remains an esoteric detail for scholars. Completion of the oil pipeline from Prudhoe Bay to Valdez will be hailed as a momentous occasion—as indeed it should be—but the purchase of Alaska was dismissed as "Seward's Folly" at the time.

A crucial but virtually unnoticed year in the history of The Wickes Corporation was 1952, when Joe McMullin launched the Bay City Cash Way. Another, no less portentous, turned out to be 1964, when the Wolohan exodus and the personnel crisis that followed propelled the corporation from the past into the present. Only one event of that year seemed deserving of public notice at the time, and that was Dan Fitz-Gerald's succession, in October, to the company's presidency. But, as important a milestone as this was, it really was not much more than the recognition of a fait accompli: for all practical purposes, Fitz-Gerald had been running the show, albeit at Ran Wickes's sufferance, as executive vice president for the past eight years. The basic changes wrought prior to 1964 were far more profound.

Dan Fitz-Gerald had risen to the top in the dog-eat-dog world of a provincial conglomerate that at times seemed to be profitable almost despite itself. He had prompted its formation, had pushed its growth in the face of consistent opposition by his peers, had expanded its horizons to both coasts and to Europe, had outmaneuvered his adversaries in the play for power. Even so, the corporation's management was still saddled with much inherited incompetence. For many years— though by the 1960s this had finally been stopped—it had almost been a company tradition for liquor bottles to emerge from desk drawers as five o'clock approached. Several executives were out-and-out alcoholics in the true clinical sense; indeed, this disease had been so rampant in the top echelons of the Graphite Company that at the time Smith Bolton was put in charge of that division, Charles Morrell, then the treasurer of Wickes, had entertained his friends at the Saginaw Club with the prediction that Bolton now would also take to drink. Office parties were a disaster area. Not one Christmas passed without sequels that starred tearful secretaries and irate secretaries' husbands. Intramural fisticuffs were common. At one festive gathering, Ran Wickes himself was knocked down when he accidentally stepped into the path of a punch aimed at another celebrant in the course of a fight for the favors of a typist.

Fitz-Gerald's effort to change the life style of this corporate Peyton Place was hardly popular. Nor were his evident ability and promise. Not unexpectedly, he was the prime target in the free-for-all for the top position. There had been the time, for example, when Robert J. Stormont, who then ran the Boiler

October 16, 1961, was the date when The Wickes Corporation was admitted "to list and dealings" on the Big Board. It probably was also the last occasion that found most of the Wickes leaders of the 1950s together in front of a camera. Shown with New York Stock Exchange President Keith Funston (just

Division, tried to get rid of Fitz-Gerald by having all the major Boiler people sign a petition, tendering their resignations unless Fitz-Gerald was fired. But Stormont had underestimated Ran Wickes's capacity to call a bluff. Ran Wickes told Stormont and his cohorts that their resignations were accepted. When Stormont, dumbfounded, pointed out that Boiler couldn't operate with all its management gone, Ran Wickes told him, "Well, Bob, you've resigned, and I see no necessity of discussing the company with you any further." There was nothing for the Stormont clique to do except get up and leave. Of course, everything was forgiven the next day: who indeed would run the Boiler Division without its experienced cadre? Not that this ploy endeared Stormont to Ran Wickes. Instead of cutting Dan Fitz-Gerald's throat, Stormont had cut his own.

Such amateurish machinations and other fraternal entertainment may strike today's reader as so primitive as to be almost fiction. But the fact is that the practices and relationships at Wickes were much like those at many other companies, whether big or small, young or old, which stumbled through that no-man's-land of the free enterprise system that separates the eras of entrepreneurship and of the modern, highly structured corporation. In a sense, The Wickes Corporation of that time, along with other companies of the same genre, was not much different from the inbred microcosm of

178

THE BIG TOWN

left of center in horn-rimmed glasses) are from left: James Shackleton, George Kendall, Mel Zahnow, Corky van Bergeijk, R. Preston Davis, Herbert Russell, Dan Fitz-Gerald, Smith Bolton, Al Riedel, Elbert Rounds, Richard Wolohan, and Robert Wolohan. (Photo by Wagner-International)

the country elevator world. What, from the outside, appeared to be a chess game was frequently not much more than a brawl.

Fitz-Gerald had chosen Smith Bolton to straighten out the Wickes operations because hard-nosed old Smith, with his no-nonsense approach to U.S. Graphite, had proved that "he was the one guy we had who could bat the ball out of the park." Now, with the middle-management ranks depleted as the result of the Wolohan split, it became painfully apparent that one single batter can't clinch the World Series when the bases aren't covered and there's no backup in the dugout. To win the game, Fitz-Gerald first had to build a team, and it is to his everlasting credit that he recognized that here was a new game that required a new kind of player.

Let's pause for a moment to examine Fitz-Gerald's management philosophy, for it is central to the development of The Wickes Corporation as it progressed from this point forward, and helps to explain why in this account you often find a name in a pivotal position and then never see it again. The Peter Principle that everyone ends up a notch above one's competence doesn't apply at Wickes: if you can't cut the mustard, you step back down or you're out. "As a company grows up," Dan Fitz-Gerald used to say, "it becomes a different animal altogether. It is constantly changing, and the people who are running it are constantly having to be changed. I think that's

179

the greatest mistake made in business today—the assumption that individuals can continue indefinitely to be successful. They can't. The very company they're building catches up and passes them, and as soon as that starts to happen they stifle its growth. We make our contribution, and then we become a drag, and it's time to step aside. That applies to everybody. It applies to me. And some day it will apply to Mac."

The "Mac" referred to here is E. L. McNeely, now the corporation's chairman of the board and chief executive officer, who succeeded the ailing Dan Fitz-Gerald on the latter's retirement in May 1975. But back then, in 1964, McNeely was one of the new players Fitz-Gerald and Bolton were looking for so desperately—the people who were to change the whole nature of the company, enabling it to live with the growth Fitz-Gerald had fostered. It may be somewhat of an irony that the man charged with the search for this new type of managerial talent required by bigness was the fellow who had clobbered Ran Wickes at that Christmas party; ironic, because T. E. ("Tom") Rulison's rough-and-ready appearance and down-to-earth demeanor seemed to epitomize the corporation's traditional style. But appearances can be deceiving, and so can happenings. Despite the incident of the misplaced punch, or quite possibly because of it, Tom Rulison had become the company's one-man morals squad. Nominated by Fitz-Gerald as vice president of personnel, he had effectively stopped the drinking on the premises, both in the offices and in the field. It didn't take much more than a few words to the wise from that hard-muscled, quick-tempered troubleshooter for people to understand that he meant business. When Rulison said to get rid of those bottles, they went. Not surprisingly, Rulison also was the logical choice to represent the company in union elections and labor negotiations. But to recruit the corporation's future leaders was an assignment that required more tact, if no less finesse: as a man who had gone to work right out of high school, Tom Rulison knew he lacked the basic credentials now required for admission to the room at the top. Anyone he interviewed might end up to be his boss—as indeed it happened with McNeely, and within the short span of two years at that.[1]

Now, in McNeely's case, appearances are not deceiving. If anyone ever looked like a 1970s executive straight out of Irving Wallace or Harold Robbins, it's he. As the old saying goes, Central Casting couldn't have done better. With blondish hair now turning a distinguished gray and just long enough to show that he's with it but not so long that he's out of it, perpetually tanned, athletically trim, lithe of movement, always immaculately dressed and impeccably groomed, he seems to have been polished to a fine gloss with a chamois. His penetrating blue eyes never waver when you talk with him, he smiles easily but never grins, and he is blessed with a radio announcer's vocal cords. People who underestimate what it takes today to be a big businessman would be amazed at his erudition. McNeely reads all the time, everything from the minutest departmental memos to works on sociology, and it's all immediately computerized: press the appropriate memory button and it's there in whatever context is required. He writes his own speeches; in fact, at one time he considered becoming a journalist, then thought the better of it. He is outspoken, but always polite. Four-letter words have no place in his vocabulary, he disdains off-color stories and allusions, and if he drinks one watered-down Scotch before dinner, that's a lot. No Riedel, he, nor a Dan Fitz-Gerald.

Besides native intelligence, about the only thing McNeely has in common with the old Wickes crowd is his lack of inhibition about being pragmatic. Competition is his driving force. This is manifest even on the golf course, the favorite playground of Wickes executives. Once, when his golf ball landed in a parking lot, he demanded that all the cars be moved out of his way.[2] He refuses to lose, even to the softer self that must be tucked away somewhere inside of him. He always rises at about 5:30 in the morning, regardless of the time zone he happens to find himself in, and when he's off on a trip, which he usually is, dawn finds him jogging hard at the nearest deserted shopping center.

In later years, as McNeely rapidly advanced at Wickes, associates sometimes complained to Dan Fitz-Gerald about McNeely's indomitable ambition and drive. Invariably, Fitz-Gerald answered, "Why the hell do you think I made him president?" But, speaking to McNeely in private, he often cautioned the younger man: "Like it or not, power follows you. You're lucky, Mac, to have me around to tell you when you're wrong." Of course, since Fitz-Gerald handed the chairmanship over to McNeely, the latter has been on his own, and it's interesting to note that, despite McNeely's evident qualifications, Fitz-Gerald hesitated until almost the last moment before he committed himself on his successor. What in the end clinched it for McNeely was that, despite his aggressiveness, he doesn't mistake human beings for cogs in a machine.

"You'll probably think I'm just a sentimental Irishman," Fitz-Gerald liked to tell his executives, "but in the end it's the people that count, and their feelings." He himself, admittedly, had not always lived by the Golden Rule. Only in later years had he allowed himself to become sensitive to the sensitivity of others. "When you fire somebody or demote him, you've got to make him understand why it has to be done," became his creed. "The clue is, if he still likes you after you've done it to him. If he doesn't, it proves you've been a son of a bitch." At least one of McNeely's potential contenders lost out precisely because he seemed to lack such empathy, but E. L. McNeely—the "E" stands for Emil, a name he doesn't like—did manage to jump that last hurdle, a "sentimental" Irishman's compassion test.

This and all the other hurdles were still ahead when Rulison told Fitz-Gerald in 1964 that McNeely was exactly the type of guy Wickes was looking for. McNeely, then forty-six years old, was at the time national merchandising manager of the hardware and electrical departments of Montgomery Ward, and living in Winnetka, Illinois, with his family. He had entered that company's training program immediately after his graduation from Northeast Missouri State University in 1940, and his first job had been to unload boxcars of bedsprings, a pedagogic device to show the college kids that were coming in that they couldn't just sit around the Ward offices and meditate. Mc-Neely's early employment rigors as well as occasional meditations were interrupted by World War II. He joined the Navy, served as a gunnery officer in the Pacific for three years, had a destroyer kamikazed out from under him, swam around for three hours before he was picked up, and doesn't mind admitting that when the destroyer that had rescued him came under attack right afterwards, he and another grown man "were holding hands and shaking to beat hell."[3] At Ward's, after the war, things were less tense but hardly calm. After fighting his way up to a buyer's position in the furniture department, McNeely managed to be noticed at executive levels and became prominently involved in developing a new merchandising system for the whole chain. This was followed by a stint as West Coast merchandising manager, during which time he supervised the flow of goods in fifteen stores. Eventually he was promoted to a post that carried nationwide responsibility for two major departments.

When a head-hunting firm, hired by Rulison, first pinpointed McNeely as a promising candidate, he couldn't have been less interested either in Wickes, which was still a relatively small company when compared to billion-dollar Montgomery Ward, or in moving from Chicago to Saginaw. He turned off the first approach on the spot, and when the headhunters called again a few weeks later, telling McNeely that here was a company in which he was sure to move up very quickly, he still refused to go out of his way to be interviewed. "If they want to come and see me," he said, "that's OK."[4]

If Wickes hadn't been desperate to pull in all the talent it could, the matter might have rested right there, and the future of Wickes could conceivably have taken a totally different course. But Rulison went to Chicago and somehow persuaded McNeely that it would be worth his while to meet with Dan Fitz-Gerald and Smith Bolton. Even so, McNeely took his time. It wasn't until about a month later that he flew to Saginaw, where Dan Fitz-Gerald's talent for blarney triumphed once again. He told McNeely that Wickes was sure to do a quarter-billion dollars worth of business in the coming year and that there was nowhere to go but up. He offered McNeely a $10,000 jump in pay, implied that McNeely could expect to be an officer of the company within two years or so, and even asked him what title he would like in the meanwhile. Neither Fitz-Gerald nor McNeely really knew what "director of marketing" meant, but that's the job description they finally settled on, largely because McNeely felt that it would give him some flexibility. He was hooked.

"If I had known about the lack of middle management and the lack of depth in management," McNeely says now, "I probably would have turned down the job. It would have looked just like a company in trouble. There was hardly anybody around who mattered except Dan and Smith, and Smith was about to retire. Well, it turned out to be a blessing that the organization had to be built from scratch. It gave us the chance to bring the right people into the company."

One of these was John Drum, recently named president of The Wickes Corporation, whom McNeely first met when the former was running Montgomery Ward's farm equipment department in the late 1950s, during the period McNeely managed that chain's West Coast stores. Drum must have made a big impression on McNeely at that time, for it wasn't long after McNeely had come to Wickes and had taken over the Lumber Division—after a year as its director of marketing—that he hired Drum away from Ward's in the summer of 1966 and brought him in as his merchandising manager.

On the face of it, no two personalities could be less alike than McNeely and Drum. Where McNeely is verbal, Drum is reticent. McNeely, born on a Missouri farm, fled the rural life. John Drum, an urban child, albeit from the appendages of a small city, Toledo, Ohio, craved it; he had studied agriculture at Michigan State and animal husbandry at Kansas State, and for several years as a young man he had operated the second largest farm in Ingham County, Michigan, about 800 acres including leased lands. He might still be doing this today had it not been for a benign tumor in his neck and the ensuing surgery that made it impossible for him to carry on the heavy physical labor involved in tending 200 head of cattle and 400 hogs. At heart, though, he is really still a farmer, and this has stood him in good stead: city slickers have a hard time keeping up with country boys who come equipped with the smarts.[5]

McNeely, suave and cosmopolitan, is not adverse to the comforts and accoutrements of high position. His office is stylish; Drum's is Spartan, equipped with nothing but a simple sideboard and a small oval table around which everybody huddles without hierarchical overtones. More often than not in shirt sleeves, Drum lives out of a well-worn, million-miler briefcase. Until the day he became president of the corporation, he refused to have a secretary of his own, and still doesn't like the idea. McNeely sips iced tea as he swivels between his immense desk and the phone on his marble-topped credenza. Drum, totally abstemious, is a Fresca fiend. Where McNeely treasures books, Drum is at home with mechanics: his father had been one of the automotive pioneers who drove their home-built cars in Indianapolis before World War I. John Drum himself, after he had sold his farm, worked as a project engineer for Graham Paige in Detroit, designing implements for a new tractor, and later patented a number of farm equipment products when he went on his own for a while as a sales consultant in that field. McNeely, who seems cheerful even when he's serious, is a public person. Lincolnesque John Drum, somehow somber even when he laughs, is a private one. McNeely is a born orator. John Drum, almost as dry a speaker as John Wayne, used to hold his audience for no other reason than that he invariably made sense; only in recent years has he gotten around to polishing his rostrum rhetoric. Where McNeely always had his eyes on the top slot, Drum just wanted to be in a high enough position to get things done his way. Until a few weeks before the announcement that he would be the next president of Wickes, he didn't expect to succeed

TOP OF THE TEAM

John Drum, in his early days at Wickes, endures an interview with the editor of a building materials trade journal (left). Youthful E. L. McNeely (above, right) presents new organizational chart to Dan Fitz-Gerald. (Photos by Bradford-LaRiviere, Inc.)

OLD GUARD
Tom Cline (left), now a board member and secretary of the corporation, and Tom Rulison, most recently vice president of operations at Wickes Lumber.
(Photos by Victor Avila and Bosch)

McNeely, and didn't even covet the job. Quite the contrary. Then approaching the age of fifty-five, he was trying his best to tutor a younger man for the post.

Yet, where it counts, McNeely and Drum are very much alike. Both are analytical rather than impetuous. Neither is given to being swept away by temporary enthusiasms. Both know well that dreams are but seeds of the future, and that while good fortune sometimes grows a healthy plant, it takes expert knowledge and control of the environment to ensure survival. They know that, to a large degree, running a great company like Wickes must be a science.

This, above all, is what differentiates the corporation's new management from yesteryear's. Most of the old-timers felt that if you couldn't fly to the moon by the seat of your pants you shouldn't fly there at all. Or, worse yet, they sometimes tried

188

NEW GUARD
Dick Cotton (right), joined Wickes in 1964, today supervises corporate sales. Dick Fruechtenicht is a later arrival in the top-executive suite. He is corporate profits manager.
(Photos by Avila)

to fly there anyway. Dan Fitz-Gerald's drive for growth had pushed Wickes over into a new world where neither such can't-doism nor such haphazard adventuring was possible any longer. Of course, being the product of a more free-wheeling era, Fitz-Gerald was by temperament inclined to let dreams take off by themselves. But his actions were tempered by good sense: he had the disconcerting habit of calling back his spacecraft. If it happened once, it happened a hundred times that he expounded a great new idea and had everybody walking on the ceiling, but when they all returned the next day, ready for more blue-sky, he had his feet back on the ground while they were still floating.

Not that today all experimentation is out. "That's one of the greatest things about Wickes," says Richard G. Cotton, a senior vice president. "Unlike so many other corporations, the people here are able to do their own thing. They have the opportunity to try something that looks good, and if they fail, it's not held against them, provided they stay within defined parameters." What Cotton means is that experimentation is OK if you don't go off half-cocked. For example, a trader in Wickes Agriculture, or for that matter an executive in any division dealing with basic commodities, is not permitted to plunge on either the short or long side. Should he succumb to the temptation to gamble, then he's had it, even if it turns out in the end that he hunched the situation correctly.[6] On the other hand, every project that shows bottom-line promise is thoroughly explored. If it then fails to fly, the executive in charge isn't blamed unless he has blundered at the controls.

Dick Cotton, who feels strongly that such educated, research-backed experimentation is the only way to go if you want to grow, is another of the new players who were recruited by Wickes after the Wolohan crisis. Not inappropriately, in view of his penchant for the scientific approach, one of Cotton's most recent assignments has been to help launch "Project Twenty-first Century," a McNeely-inspired systematic analysis of all aspects of the company's operations and potentials for future growth.[7] Working with Cotton to get this complex two-year study organized was a later arrival on the Wickes scene, Richard W. Fruechtenicht, a financial man who, like McNeely and Drum, had spent several years at Ward's. Fruechtenicht joined Wickes in 1974 as a corporate vice president and controller, and after putting his imprint on Project Twenty-first Century was reassigned in August 1975 to a post of more immediate moment—corporate profits manager.[8] At the same time, Dick Cotton was handed the hand-in-glove responsibility for managing corporate sales.

Cotton seems tailor-made for this newly created position. When Dan Fitz-Gerald recruited him in July 1964, just one month before McNeely came with Wickes, Cotton was thirty-nine and a divisional manager for Michigan Bell. Fitz-Gerald had met him while they campaigned together on behalf of the United Fund of Saginaw County, and for the establishment of a local Junior Achievement program. It's not surprising that

Fitz-Gerald cottoned to Cotton, who served as general chairman of both drives: Fitz-Gerald recognized that Cotton could become a millionaire selling heating pads in equatorial Africa if he believed in the product. There is today no better salesman or public speaker in the whole Wickes organization, and Billy Graham can consider himself lucky that Cotton didn't take up evangelism instead of business. However, what convinced Fitz-Gerald that he had to bring this young man into the Wickes organization was that, quite apart from the persuasive quality of his voice and his disciplined oratorical genius, Cotton has a steel-trap mind that can instantly put all facts into their logical slots and make them serve him as arguments. Once Cotton is convinced that a certain course is right, nothing but solid information to the contrary can put a dent in his infectious enthusiasm.[9]

Evidently, Cotton has made it with Wickes, as did McNeely and Drum. Not all the players did. When you look at the management team today, you see only four top executives who were with the corporation prior to 1964. There's Bob Dodge, who had come up through Michigan Bean under Al Riedel, and is now a senior vice president. Then there's Roland Pretzer, who figured so prominently in the early Cash Ways and made such a spectacular success of the first lumberyard that actually bore the Wickes name; he is now back where he started, in the country elevator business, except that he's at the top—he runs Wickes Agriculture. There is Ralph Zemanek who succeeded Smith Bolton as general manager of Graphite and who is now senior vice president in charge of all Wickes industrial manufacturing operations. And finally there's Tom Cline, now corporate secretary, senior vice president, and a director of the corporation. In a way, Tom's rise with the new Wickes that came into being in 1964 is a testimonial to the good judgment he exercised as a young man, for it so happens that he's a nephew of Dick Wolohan.[10] Despite this family connection he decided to stay with the corporation, whose legal department he had launched in the 1950s. He never doubted that Fitz-Gerald had the future figured out.

13

The New Game

McNeely's arrival on the scene was to change the whole complexion of the lumber operation. The fact that the Wickes yards no longer stocked 24-foot ladders in parts of the country where one-story homes were prevalent was the least of it, although such inventory control was typical of the new approach. Guesswork was out. Planning was in. There had to be a rationale for every action, not just hope. But one thing even McNeely couldn't change was the cyclical nature of the lumber and building supply business. Within a year after he had taken over the division, the housing industry plunged into one of its periodic slumps. The pattern was a familiar one, if not to McNeely who until then had enjoyed nothing but success in getting the division on track: the nation's cash went into paper that offered higher yields, mortgage money dried up, housing starts plummeted, builders went broke, the building supply centers lost customers and sold less to those who were still around. Inevitably, to make matters worse, the price of lumber dropped drastically at the same time, forcing Mc-Neely's division to take a write-down of around $4 million to get inventories to a competitive level.

For McNeely, who is an optimist by nature, this was an important formative experience, and one that was to serve him well in later years when, as the president of Wickes, he had to tighten the screws on all operations in the face of the unprece-dented inflation-recession syndrome of the 1970s. Retrench-ment is just the opposite of how McNeely likes to operate, and when, in 1966 and 1967, he had to reduce the sales force of the Lumber Division and postpone some planned expansions, he found it hard going, and in fact no fun at all. McNeely almost quit then. "I am not sure you've got the right guy," he told Dan Fitz-Gerald, and once again the latter's talent for the kind of warm, friendly flattery that's half blarney and half bluster saved the day. "I don't know what you're bothering me for," Dan told McNeely. "You just go right back in there and keep the ship from pitching and rolling too much until this thing turns around, and when we get through it, we'll make more money than we ever made." And that's what happened.

But it's not surprising that McNeely suffered the miseries of self-doubt. Ever since he'd come to Wickes, everything had turned up roses for him despite the disorganization he had encountered in the Lumber Division. He couldn't help but feel a hero as its sales volume jumped from $131 million in fiscal 1964 to $201 million in fiscal 1966, and the division's net income nearly doubled from $7.8 million to $14 million even before he'd had time to put most of his innovations into effect. He had been riding high in the upswing phase of the cycle, but while he looked the hero then, he didn't really become the hero until the pinch was on. It takes headwinds to test a sailor's skill.

As it happened, McNeely had been recruited into an almost self-propelled growth situation. Even before he came aboard, negotiations had begun for mergers that would add thirty-eight lumberyards to Wickes's existing forty-eight before the year was out,[1] and would position the company in the part of the country that national retailers have traditionally found the hardest to crack—the South. Two acquisitions were involved, both of companies whose founders had approached the lumber business in much the same way as Joe McMullin did. In fact, both operations predated the first Wickes Cash Way by several years, and one of them had already achieved a degree of sophistication in computer softwear use and personnel training that, for Wickes, still lay in the future. This company was the Varina Wholesale Builders Supply Co. of Fuquay-Varina, North Carolina, the creation of one R. Douglas Powell, who, after two and a half years as a Navy storekeeper in the Pacific, invested his $1,400 savings in a hardware store in 1947. One year later he branched out into building materials, and by 1964, at the age of thirty-nine, he was boss of a nineteen-store chain in seven southeastern states—the Carolinas, Virginia, Kentucky, Alabama, Mississippi, and Tennessee.[2] He racked up $25 million a year in sales, enjoyed after-tax profits of approximately 5 percent a year, and averaged a return of between 33 and 40 percent on capital investment. This very astute businessman was gearing up for doubling his number of stores and going public when Dan Fitz-Gerald and Smith Bolton convinced him that his best bet for the future lay with Wickes. The deal went through on October 14, 1964, involving a consideration of 326,640 shares of Wickes common, then worth $8,091,000, making the Powell family the first in a long line of instant millionaires created by the Wickes mergers of the 1960s.[3]

The other acquisition, also in the Southeast, was that of Ross Builders Supplies, Inc., of Greenville, South Carolina, which had eighteen outlets, plus one under construction, in Georgia and the Carolinas.[4] This merger, completed on November 24, 1964, was The Wickes Corporation's first acquisition of a publicly held company. Ross had about 600 stockholders, who received 375,000 shares of Wickes common, then worth $9,045,000, in exchange for their 500,000 shares of Ross.

The company had been formed in 1945 by a small group of prominent Greenville businessmen led by George Ross, the owner of a local lumber company that formed the base of the new operation. Unlike Wickes and Varina, Ross had started by offering customer credit and delivery—ancillary services that were to become standard everywhere in future years. In the meanwhile, Ross had also come around to the cash-and-carry method of merchandising building materials at just about the time that McMullin launched his Bay City Cash Way. What had given the Ross people this idea was the springing up of competition by "back-haulers"—truckers who had caught on to the fact that they could make money both coming and going whenever they made deliveries to a place where building materials were manufactured or distributed; they simply loaded up for the return trip and peddled the lumber or whatever off the backs of their trucks.

Since 1959, Wade H. Stephens, Jr., a former construction engineer, had been president and chief executive officer of Ross Builders Supplies. He was doing very well with the cash-and-carry operation plus the optional availability of credit and delivery at extra cost. When Wickes acquired the company, Ross Builders had just completed a fiscal year that saw $22 million in sales and $726,000 in earnings. In addition to its building supply centers, it operated two "experimental" home supply stores in markets too small to justify full-scale yards. There is a clue to the nature of the Ross operation in this designation, for Ross not only sold building supplies, but was heavy on all sorts of household goods from appliances and television to bikes and pots and pans. To a degree, this was true also of Varina, and these two companies that now formed a part of the Southeastern region of Wickes Lumber were thus quite different in their market approach from the basic building supply concept as pursued by the Wickes yards. Not surprisingly, Ross-Varina, as it was called after the merger because Wickes wanted to retain the two chains' well-established regional identities, had its own purchasing department, and unlike the other Wickes yards, was not directly controlled by Saginaw for some years. Wade H. Stephens, who eventually succeeded Powell, ran the combined operation in much the same way he had run Ross.[5]

As time went on, it became obvious that this difference in approach must be resolved. Wickes had to decide what business it was really in. Was it to be a general merchandiser, or was it to concentrate on its original franchise? Either avenue promised profits. The question was, which would offer more leverage, i.e., the higher yield in relation to investment and overhead. This problem was not easily solved. In fact, for several years Wickes experimented with home supply stores in different parts of the country, and in 1965 even went briefly into the catalog business in cooperation with a Milwaukee mail-order house, testing the possibility of going into competition with organizations like Sears and Spiegel. Neither tack proved profitable enough to keep Wickes in the business.

Not that the wide range of merchandise offered by the Ross outlets was available at the Wickes home supply stores. Rather, these stores were envisioned as branches of lumber and building supply centers. Located in small shopping centers, they sold the same lines of building materials as the big yards but didn't carry bulky inventory. The deceptively attractive theory was that neighborhood customers would come in on their shopping-center trips and order what they wanted; then the big lumber and building supply center in the area would act as a feeder, and deliver the required supplies to the store two or three times a week. But that's not how things worked out. If the urge hits you to panel your basement, you want the paneling today, not tomorrow. When customers were told they had to wait a couple of days until the material came in from the yard, they asked where that yard was and went there themselves. Wickes usually still got the business, but the store overhead went for naught. Moreover, without lumber and sheathing, the two best-selling building materials, stored on the site, these little outlets lacked identity. They didn't have enough inventory to be really hardware stores, or really plumbing and heat-

THE LATEST IN "LUMBERYARDS"
Design of Wickes Lumber center in Freeland, Michigan, is representative of the corporation's approach to an old architectural challenge: how to make a building attractive as well as functional. (Photo by Bradford-LaRiviere)

ing stores, or really complete paint stores. Only a few were successful, but these, surprisingly, were blockbusters. Just what distinguished the winners from the others, Wickes managers are still trying to figure out. Until they do, expansion of this program is held in abeyance.[6]

Another Wickes Lumber venture, this one into the home improvement business, didn't pan out at all. The idea behind it, of course, was to sell more building materials out of the centers. Salesmen would call on homeowners who had responded to the advertising, and give an estimate. In most cases, this led to a hassle. What the salesmen would sketch out for them might appear the right thing at the moment, but when work was in progress, what the customers saw often wasn't what they had envisioned, and they demanded changes. As a result, jobs almost consistently ran over estimates. Moreover, the game wasn't worth the candle anyway. A $4,500 job might involve only $800 worth of building materials. The rest was labor. This, too, was no way to go.

THE INSIDE STORY
Consumer domain of Wickes Lumber centers offers almost everything a family needs for home improvements and remodeling. (Photos by Bill Wegner and Jim Campbell)

AND THE OTHER SIDE OF THE STORY
Wickes Lumber centers are also fully stocked to fill the needs of building contractors, who account for more than half the volume of the average outlet. (Photo by Bradford-LaRiviere)

What it all came down to was that Wickes Lumber had to define its market stance: a policy that could only be established at the top executive level, and that had to be controlled out of headquarters lest individual store managers or even regional managers yield to the temptation to buy anything they figured they could sell and end up with a hodgepodge of merchandise in stock. The need for a definite policy became increasingly evident as yet another lumber and building supply retail chain was acquired in September 1965. This firm, Timberline Products, Inc., had five outlets in New York State and one in Connecticut,[7] and, just like Ross-Varina, continued to operate more or less independently of Saginaw. Between the Timberline acquisition, for which Wickes tendered 150,400 shares of stock valued at $4,004,000, and the new building supply centers that Wickes established on its own during 1965, the organization encompassed 108 yards by the end of that year.[8] Clearly, it was high time to run the Lumber Division as the big business it had rapidly become. That's when McNeely phoned John Drum at Ward's and asked him to lunch at the Continental Plaza in Chicago. McNeely knew which way he wanted to lead the division, of which he was now senior vice president and general manager, having succeeded Smith Bolton in 1965. But McNeely also knew himself well enough to understand that he was at his best when he dealt in concepts; even in his dawn-to-midnight day, there wasn't enough time to implement all his ideas in detail. What he needed was someone to fine-tune his plans of action. He needed John Drum.

Luckily, John Drum was tired of traveling—and didn't suspect how much more traveling he'd eventually have to do for Wickes. At that time, in the summer of 1966, he was merchandise manager of Ward's third largest department, which sold lawn, garden, and farming equipment, and as part of his job, he had built up a tremendously profitable sideline for Ward's. He'd go to Thyssen in Germany and Fuji in Japan, buy their steel, and sell it at a profit to the manufacturers who supplied his department. Somehow he'd been successful in getting the steel for less than these manufacturers could buy it themselves. Since Ward's never used more than half the output from any source of supply, Drum was able to negotiate contracts under which the cost of the steel he bought would carry no markup. With these known-cost contracts, he was able to achieve very healthy margins in his department in addition to the profits that accrued from selling the steel. But, making all this money for Ward's, he not only found himself jetting around overseas most of the time but also deadlocked in his job. At forty-six, he knew that there wasn't time for him to gain the experience in other departments necessary to become Ward's general merchandise manager and thus an officer of the company, and in any case Ward's didn't want to give him another assignment— he was far too useful where he sat. So Drum was ready for a change and almost immediately accepted the job McNeely offered him over a ham sandwich and a glass of milk. That very weekend, Drum took his wife to Saginaw, where neither had ever been, and on Monday he was the new merchandise manager of Wickes Lumber, the second in command of the division.

Drum's first action was to devise a number of guidelines which are still Wickes Lumber's commandments today. Most important of these was that all merchandise control would lie with headquarters. Beyond the fact that Wickes would furnish all the goods for the average builder of the average house, plus assorted shelter and home-related products, the product lines were not specified. It was determined, however, that no matter what the line, it had to appeal to the mass market. This meant that the exotic 10 percent at the top and the junky 10 percent at the bottom would never be in the merchandise plan. If customers wanted fancy light fixtures or sculptured doors, they'd have to go somewhere else; nothing was to be special-ordered. By the same token, Wickes would never offer factory closeouts, seconds, or shoddy goods.

Dispensing with the cream and the dregs left Wickes aiming at 80 percent of the market, an ambitious goal that could be met only with attractive pricing, intelligent advertising, proper display, and consistently adequate inventories. To offer its customers the lowest prices, Wickes had to buy at the lowest prices, and this meant concentrating all purchasing on the fewest possible sources and using only the most efficient suppliers in their respective lines, like Owens-Corning and Celotex (insulation products), Certain-Teed (roofing), and U.S. Gypsum and Flintkote (primarily gypsum products).[9] No less important than price was presenting outstanding values at times when customers were most likely to buy the merchandise; there'd be no off-season sales. Wickes would never advertise cheap air conditioners in January, but would undersell competitors in July. Moreover, Wickes must never be caught short of inventory. All goods were to be displayed in bulk, especially when advertised: there's nothing that turns off a customer like going into a store to buy one thing and having a salesperson push something else.[10] Last but not least, even though basic prices were to be predicated on cash and carry, credit and delivery had to be made available to customers who wanted those services. Indeed, by 1974, Wickes's cash-and-carry trade had shrunk to 38 percent. People increasingly wanted credit and convenience, and they got it.

What finally determined the merchandise mix was the composition of the audience that shopped at Wickes yards. In an average year, Wickes Lumber does a little more than half its business with contractors and a little less than half with individual customers. Thus, in effect, each center is two businesses under one roof. It serves builders out of the back, and do-it-yourselfers out of the front. But to maintain its own low costs, it must sell essentially the same goods to both sets of buyers. This requirement means that Wickes cannot go into depth in the merchandise lines it handles. It has to be a low-margin, high-volume operation. A center may carry three most frequently wanted kinds of hammers, but not forty. It can't carry hundreds of different kinds of nuts and bolts and screws, but only a basic selection. It won't stock all kinds of appliances and bathroom fixtures, but only a few lines—again those that are most likely to sell and low-priced enough to give a push to the sales.

Similarly, once the basic customer mix of the Wickes market—the small and medium-sized contractor and the advanced do-it-yourselfer—was fully understood, another major problem, that of site selection, also resolved itself, and in retrospect it's amazing that the Lumber Division had pulled so many boners like Grapevine, Texas, in its early years. The Wickes approach obviously works best in burgeoning suburbs and in semi-rural areas in the process of being suburbanized. In such markets there is less difference between the needs of the professional contractor and those of the walk-in customer than there is in areas that are already built up: the suburban contractor is not so likely to ask for customized products, and the customer is more likely to be a bulk buyer.

All that really had to be done was to study certain demographic characteristics of successful locations and pick future sites accordingly. To arrive at these criteria, McNeely and Drum engaged the research services of Transamerica Corp., which identified more than 100 factors that influence buying patterns and applied them to the eighty building supply centers that showed the highest sales. The results of the study were computerized into volumes of statistics, and once these were boiled down, they offered an almost foolproof blueprint for expansion. Like all such studies, this one came up with some surprises, like the fact that a high percentage of clerical workers in a center's market area constituted a definite advantage. And like all studies, there were some things it could not fully explain in terms of other data, as, for instance why Gaylord, Michigan, with a population of 2,500 and a winter-squeezed building season that lasts only about four months of the year, should be the town with Wickes's largest and most consistently profitable lumberyard—the Gaylord center, which was opened in 1960, does millions of dollars' worth of business a year and is so big it's actually a tourist attraction. But the greatest surprise of all was that Florida turned out to be a fine place for lumberyards, something that John Drum, although an experienced merchant, admittedly would never have suspected. "If I'd been asked to pass judgment on that," he says, "my answer would have been no, because in Florida it's all concrete block construction." But in 1970 Wickes did go into Florida on the basis of the Transamerica study, and it's been a bonanza. "It still doesn't make any sense to me," says Drum. "I don't know what they do with all that lumber." And even the Gaylord anomaly taught Wickes a valuable lesson, for the success of this center was clearly due to the fact that the facility provided a service that people in the northwoods had never enjoyed before and couldn't get anywhere else. As a result, Wickes also went to woodsy, sparsely populated Maine and into northern Minnesota and is doing very well indeed.

With Wickes Lumber divided into nine regions, it's up to the staffs on the spot to identify potential growth areas in their respective domains, using the Transamerica blueprint. This research is supplemented by a "shelf study"—an on-the-spot analysis of the movement of merchandise off the shelves of stores in areas with characteristics similar to those of the proposed location. The final consideration is a good look at the potential competition. This is done to see what Wickes might be up against and what market approaches are indicated, and does not really affect the go-or-no-go decision. "We haven't let competition keep us out of any place yet," says McNeely. Adds Drum, "If everything else checks out, I'm thoroughly convinced that we can take almost any community and run a successful Wickes yard."

Market research like this, however, is not the only reason Wickes Lumber has been consistently successful under McNeely and Drum. One of their most important innovations has been to institute the "retail system" of accounting for inventories, a system traditionally used by big retail chains like Ward's, Sears, and J. C. Penney, but brand-new to the lumber business.[11] Getting this system to work at Wickes Lumber was far from easy. In fact, it was one of the most traumatic experiences the division ever went through. Now, if you're not a businessperson, you may well say: So what—who cares how inventories are treated on the books? The answer: Everyone who is concerned with pricing goods—i.e., the store managers—because it can affect how much money they'll take home. To understand why this is so, and why the introduction of the retail system provoked a morale crisis that lasted nearly three years, you've got to bear in mind that, in the lumber business, inventory has always been carried at cost: each store manager keeps his goods on a unit-cost basis and then, in determining selling prices, adds the margin he figures he needs to make a profit. The more profit he makes, the greater his bonus. On the face of it, that sounds fine. But since personal income is almost everyone's prime interest, it stands to reason that this system makes store managers waste a lot of time worrying about cost versus price. Under unit costing, they are constantly fretting whether they can afford to be competitive in view of the margins they must maintain, instead of being out there selling the hell out of their merchandise. That attitude isn't very good for business, since everything hinges on the ability to compete.

The retail system relieves the store manager of this concern. Inventory is carried on a store's books at retail price, and the manager has no idea of what the goods cost. There's no mental block, then, against competitive pricing. By the same token, managers don't have to wrestle with their conscience when they sell a 25-cent item for $1 if they don't know that it only costs a quarter.[12] All responsibility for pricing lies instead with the merchandise manager, whose job it is to buy the goods cheaply enough to guarantee an overall margin. Every store manager gets what is called a markdown budget—so many dollars that can be applied to price reductions—and it's up to the merchandise manager to support the competitive pricing with competitive costs.

When this system was introduced at Wickes, store managers not only resented operating in the dark, but also did not believe that John Drum, who was then merchandise manager, could protect their margins as well as they could themselves. Their natural inclination was to think that their margins would go down, adversely affecting their bonuses. It wasn't until they received fatter bonus checks than ever before that they were finally convinced of the value of this system, which made them concentrate on being competitive without regard to cost. [13]

By late 1968, most of the McNeely-Drum innovations were "in place," as business jargon has it. Wickes Lumber itself was in more places than ever before. In the three years since its acquisition of Timberline Products, Inc., the division had opened 27 new building supply outlets and purchased 4 from the Home Materials Company of Mansfield, Ohio, bringing the total number now to 139. All the new stores, except for one in Kansas, were in states where Wickes was already entrenched, and although the locations map looked impressive indeed with all its colored stickers, there were still a lot of holes. One of the most inviting voids was that of the booming Gulf states, where an old family-owned firm that had restyled itself in line with the Wickes idea was doing a whale of a business. Back in 1966, Smith Bolton had already approached this company, Turpin Wholesale Supply, Inc., hoping to achieve a merger, but the Turpins felt that they weren't yet big enough to get the price they wanted for their operation. That time came in 1968, when the Turpins had expanded their business to eight building supply centers in Louisiana and Mississippi, plus three in Arkansas and one in Oklahoma. [14]

Turpin Wholesale was headquartered in Bastrop, Louisiana, where it had been founded way back in 1919 as the Bastrop

Supply Company, Inc., by Alan T. Turpin, Sr., and a couple of associates, to deal in all building materials used in the light construction industry except lumber. In 1928, when the local sawmill closed down, Bastrop Supply took on that merchandise as well. Turpin survived receivership during the Depression, turned into a construction outlet, and in 1946 added a branch in Monroe, Louisiana. Then, in the 1950s, pressed hard by all the new firms that were coming out of the woodwork to engage in speculative building of FHA (Federal Housing Administration) and VA (Veterans Administration) houses, the Turpins began noticing articles in trade journals about cash-and-carry building supply outfits like Wickes, Ross, and Varina. Being intrepid entrepreneurs, the three Turpin sons, Alan, Jr., Corbin, and Carl, remodeled their warehouses and showrooms, instituted an inventory-control system, and recruited their sister, Dorothy, to handle the advertising. In 1958, the changeover was complete, and ten years later, in October of 1968, the Turpins were ready for the deal, which involved 130,000 shares of Wickes valued at $5,525,000.[15] With the stroke of a pen, Wickes was now up to 151 yards in twenty-eight states,[16] had filled an important gap on the map, and gained the expertise of the four Turpins in the process. Dorothy, Carl, and Alan, Jr., remained with Wickes until the Turpin chain was fully integrated into the Wickes operation in 1970. Corbin Turpin stayed on, handling all the lumber purchasing below the Mason-Dixon line, until 1974, when a heart attack forced this paragon of Southern gentility into early retirement.

With the Turpin acquisition, Wickes Lumber shifted into really high gear. We recall from the opening chapter that, in 1965, Dan Fitz-Gerald and E. L. McNeely had agreed to do their utmost to push the corporation over the billion-dollar mark by 1975, and just as the Lumber Division's new procedures were taking hold in 1968, so now the corporation was launched on its program of comprehensive and synergistic future planning. The push for acquisitions, for the most part, now took place outside the building supply retail area. The closing 1960s and the early 1970s saw Wickes engage in mergers designed to establish vertical and horizontal positions in the shelter field. That's when the corporation acquired Sequoia Forest Industries, Behlen, Lee L. Woodard Sons, Valiant Mobile Homes, Ritz-Craft, Moriarity, Idapine Mills, Colonial Products, Farmaster, Oregon-Pacific, Steel City Lumber, Coast Millwork, and others, which will figure later in this story. The Lumber Division, in the meantime, expanded mostly by building its own new centers. Between January 1969 and December 1972, Nebraska, Delaware, and Maine were added to the division's roster by new construction. There were several minor acquisitions, such as the Rock Island Lumber Company, which had one store in Rock Island, Illinois (in March 1971); Grady Building Supply & Hardware, Inc., with two yards in Kingston and Morehead City, North Carolina (May 1972); the Harrington Millwork Company, in Arkadelphia, Arkansas (October 1972); and a store in Cadillac, Michigan.[17]

But the two truly important acquisitions of those years rooted Wickes firmly in Florida, that highly profitable market which Wickes would never have touched had it not been for the Transamerica study. One of these was the merger, in October 1969, with Lewis Lumber, which had stores in Bradenton, Venice, Sarasota, and Englewood.[18] The other was the outright purchase for $1,374,000, in November 1970, of the Bond-Howell Lumber Company, which added outlets in eight more Florida locations, including four in the Jacksonville area and one each in New Smyrna, Daytona, St. Augustine, and Lake City.[19] With these acquisitions, Wickes was now in thirty-two states with 213 outlets, and the empty space on the locations map was shrinking fast.[20]

This phenomenal growth over a period of just a few years put tremendous strains on the Lumber Division. Expansion isn't just a matter of acquiring new outlets or building new ones, or of buying real estate or leasing it, or of finding suppliers and pinpointing markets. All this has to be done by people, and for the organization to function smoothly, every one of them, right down to peak-hour part-timers at the lumberyards, must be trained properly in the Wickes way.

The obvious route was to pull potential talent out of the older centers and put them in charge of the new ones, as had been done with Roland Pretzer back in the Cash Way days. But this very logical procedure was impossible to implement on a large scale—there were just too many new stores going in all the time. Smith Bolton had already recognized this problem in the early 1960s when he tried to pull together the Lumber Division after the Wolohan split. To provide personnel at the store level, he had leveraged the resources of The Wickes Foundation so that they might benefit the company as well as the community. The Foundation had been a considerable benefactor to the Saginaw area's sole institution of higher learning, the two-year Delta College, located at University Center, about 15 miles from downtown.[21] Taking advantage of this connection, Bolton arranged with the college for six-week seminars in management techniques, salesmanship, marketing, communications, industrial psychology, and accounting for managers and assistant managers of the lumber and building supply outlets. At the same time, working with Dr. Samuel Marble, who was then president of the college,[22] Bolton set up an "earn-while-you-learn" program for high school graduates which was divided into two fifteen-week periods, the first in the classroom, the second on the job at a Wickes operation. This was the beginning of a far-reaching staff development campaign that eventually developed into a two-year training program for potential Wickes Lumber center managers. Trainees are enrolled for two years, with full scholastic terms in classes and summers at Wickes lumberyards. One of the annual projects of the students, in addition to filling a variety of slots at various centers, is to build a house which is then sold, with the proceeds going back to the program. All trainees are paid and Wickes keeps its fingers crossed that, when the two years are up, these young people will decide to stay with the company. So far, most of them have.

Finding leaders presented no less of a problem. There wasn't time, as there is now, to groom junior executives for top positions. At least for the moment, managerial talent had to be

imported. Luckily this process tends to be self-perpetuating. The head-hunting program Tom Rulison had started at Fitz-Gerald's behest began paying compound interest before long, as new executives brought in by the old crowd in turn recruited talented people they knew—the same way McNeely had lassoed John Drum. One of Drum's own major personnel acquisitions, however, was discovered by a headhunter, who somehow put his finger on exactly the right type for a company on the move like Wickes: someone bright to the point of brashness, unusually verbal, eloquent in his arguments, forceful, pragmatic, quick to grasp opportunities, a salesman and retailer par excellence.

Clark A. Johnson was all of those and more. He had been born into the lumber business and understood it in all its ramifications. No wonder his rise at Wickes was meteoric even

WICKES HALL
*Classroom building at
Saginaw Valley State College,
financed by The Wickes
Foundation and named in
honor of H. Randall Wickes.*

MELVIN J. ZAHNOW
*This former Wickes executive
and board member now heads
The Wickes Foundation.*

by that company's speed-of-light standards. Hired in February 1971 as the division's vice president of operations, Johnson took Drum's place as Lumber's boss just three months later, when Drum moved up to the new corporate executive VP slot.

Tall, husky, and heavy-jawed, Johnson was only forty then, and had come to Wickes from Pope & Talbot, one of the grand old Oregon firms in the lumber, hardboard, and plywood business. Johnson's father, a wholesale lumber salesman, had bought a retail lumberyard in Fort Dodge, Iowa, just as Clark entered the University of Iowa in 1949 to study marketing and business administration. After graduation he joined the Chicago-based Edward Hines Lumber Company's training program and was sent to the West Coast as a "lumber student," a job that involved every phase of operations from the office to working in the woods. Clark's penchant for taking the initiative manifested itself immediately on completion of his apprentice-ship. When he found himself assigned to Minneapolis as a senior salesman, the Hines regional manager took one look at him and said, "I've asked for help up here and they send me a damn green kid." Whereupon Clark packed his bag, looked at a map and decided that Sioux Falls, South Dakota, was a fine place to show his true color. On arrival, he phoned the Minne-apolis gentleman and announced that he was hereby picking his own sales territory, one not yet tapped by Hines, and would send in a report every week. Nine months later, Clark had put his territory in the thirteenth rank among Hines's twenty-seven. "That's where I learned that you've got to hunt where the birds are flying," he says—one of his favorite phrases, and a guideline he has followed ever since. Soon he was promoted to the assistant managership of Hines's distribution center in Chicago; later, he joined Kaiser Aluminum, where he ended up as general sales manager of the building products division; then he switched to Evans Products as general manager of its thirty-two distribution warehouses and fifteen plywood mills. From there he went to Pope & Talbot as vice president for marketing and public affairs.

One of Johnson's first actions at Wickes was to reorganize the Lumber Division's field organization. Until this time, district managers in charge of eight-store groupings sat between the centers and the regional bosses. That had been OK when the operation was still relatively small, but hampered communications in a division which was now grossing more than $300 million a year. Johnson knocked out the district management, put approximately thirty stores under each of nine regional managers, and gave each regional manager a staff of experts in sales, administration, operations, and credit, thus increasing efficiency in the field.[23] He streamlined the division's computerized credit program for builders, and insti-tuted consumer credit cards as well.[24] At the same time, he improved the delivery system.[25] To attract more walk-in trade, he revamped advertising to appeal more to the consumer, and

CLARK A. JOHNSON
*Wickes Lumber's former chief now heads all the corporation's lumber produc-
tion and wholesale distribution operations.* (Photo by Lake Oswego
Photographers)

Wickes Lumber Centers

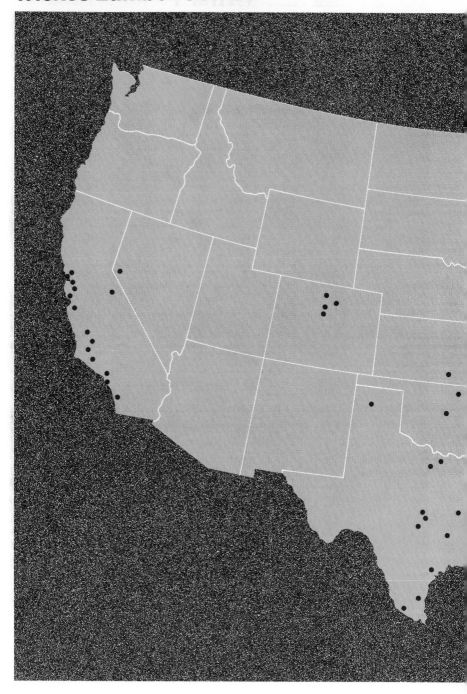

LES HAGEN
*Wickes Lumber's newest coach once played
end for the University of Oregon football team
in the Cotton Bowl.* (Photo by Rummel
Studio)

glossied up the front end of the stores so that women would
feel at home in this heretofore almost exclusively male
domain. Moreover, he promoted the Lumber Division's highly
lucrative sideline of financing the construction of residential
complexes. Johnson also steered Wickes back into the installed
sales business, but this time along a straighter and less hectic
route—by working not with the homeowners but with the
contractors.

Under Clark Johnson's leadership, the Lumber Division
grew even faster than it had before. In the less than four years

216

of his management, during which he did away with 35 of the marginal home supply stores, the number of major building supply centers jumped from 181 to 256, and the division's sales volume increased at an average of $70 million a year, topping the half-million mark in 1973. Despite the adverse economic conditions that then descended on the country, the division still did nearly that much business in 1974 (Wickes's fiscal 1975), which it closed out with $483.4 million. Toward the end of that year Johnson was reassigned to head a new superdivision (called a "group" in the organizational structure) of all Wickes units involved in forest products operations, lumber and plywood wholesaling, building-material warehouse distribution, and all international programs, including the Wickes stores in Europe.[26] Meanwhile, the number of Lumber Division outlets rose to 261 in December 1974, with two new states—Colorado and Nevada—joining the list of Wickes territories. The Colorado foothold was achieved with Johnson's $3,180,256 purchase in February 1973 of the Hogsett Lumber Company, which had stores in Boulder, Greeley, and Longmont. Other purchases of existing facilities added stores in Tustin, Fremont, and Mammoth Lakes, California; Reno, Nevada; Burlington, North Carolina; and Lafayette, Indiana.[27] Then, in January 1975, the division bought out Home Mart Building Centers, Inc., of Atlanta, Georgia, a $3,228,237 coup which firmly established Wickes in that important, constantly growing metropolitan market.[28]

Clark Johnson's successor as Wickes Lumber's leader is senior vice president Leslie L. Hagen, a husky 220-pounder with a cement-mixer voice who looks the prototype of the ex-college jock he is. On New Year's Day of 1949, he played in the Cotton Bowl as end for the University of Oregon team. The next year, when he was a senior, he broke his leg and they put a steel plate in it and that was the end of his athletic career except for the four years he coached football at a senior high school in Hermiston, Oregon, where he taught social studies. But business life held more appeal for him, and like his predecessor at Wickes Lumber, Clark Johnson, he joined the

Edward Hines Co. training program. For several years he sold lumber and plywood in Illinois, Minnesota, and Wisconsin, and in May of 1960 went with Oregon-Pacific Forest Products, a brokerage type of lumber and plywood wholesale operation, of which he later became one of the two major shareholders. Clark Johnson had met Les Hagen in their Edward Hines days, but that's not how Les happened to come to Wickes. In 1972, Oregon-Pacific Industries, thus renamed by Hagen and his partner Darrell Robinson, was acquired by The Wickes Corporation, and a few months later Hagen was transferred to Lumber as vice president of merchandising.[29]

In early 1976, as the country pulled itself out of two years of stagflation and the housing industry slowly picked up once again, Les Hagen had 268 lumber and building supply outlets in his charge.[30] The goal is 500 by 1980, the year the Lumber Division aims to cross its own billion-dollar line, which it must do to maintain its relative position in the Wickes scheme of things, for by that time the corporation expects to hit $2 billion.

Lumber's share includes sales from its component plants that manufacture trusses, floor joists, paneling, and prehung doors.[31] This operation is expected to mushroom in the coming years as the production of housing becomes increasingly "rationalized"—a European term that means doing things in the most rational way. Which is exactly what Wickes is after.

14

Vickess

That's how Wickes is pronounced in the Low Countries and in Germany, where the corporation's building supply centers display signs that read, respectively, **VOOR BOUWEN EN WONEN** and **FÜR BAUEN UND WOHNEN**—"for building and living"—an immediate clue that the marketing approach here is different from that at home.[1] In fact, the European outlets are vastly expanded variants of the home supply stores that were tried, and for the most part failed, back in the United States. But Europe, despite all its "Americanization," isn't America by a long shot. Its Americanization, or more appropriately its shift to a mass-market economy, is still largely external. Once *de huisvrouw* or *die Hausfrau* has brought her groceries home from the *Supermarkt*, and her husband has returned in their sporty little car from a business meeting at the Holiday Inn or the Hilton, and they've closed their door behind them, they are back in the Old World where every gadget is treasured as the adventurous major purchase that it was. Except in the most affluent households, and even in the new beehive blocks of planned suburbs, appliances are minimal. Most people live in antiquated apartments, which they own or rent in semiperpetuity. Either way, the responsibility for improvements is theirs.

Meanwhile the Common Market countries have prospered immensely, with discretionary income increasing at all levels of society, even in bungling, devil-take-the-hindmost Britain. Today's Europeans, their professed disdain for "American materialism" notwithstanding, are obsessed by an almost ludicrous infatuation with modernity. Anything new sells, and since everybody now has a car and a with-it wardrobe, the turn for home improvements has come. It's a fabulous market, with a pent-up demand far greater than in the United States: for water heaters, bathtubs, sinks, wallboard, counter tops, flooring, carpeting, tile, tools, paint, structural lumber, doors, moldings, flashlights, copper pipe, fittings, kitchen tables, refrigerators, dishwashers, veneer, toilet bowls, mowers, screws, nuts, and bolts. As McNeely likes to say, "If it fits our bag, we'll try it." The new Europe certainly does.

Wickes hit the Netherlands first. After all, Holland was the home of Cornelis van Bergeijk, who had forged the company's initial link with Europe back in the days of government-surplus beans, and although the aging Corky had long ago retired from business and was taking it easy at his country villa in Doorn, he and Dan Fitz-Gerald still were great friends. In search of foreign opportunities, McNeely had dragged Dan to Australia, which also looked promising—so promising, in fact, that one of Dan's oldest and most knowledgeable Wickes associates, Art Pufford, like Fitz-Gerald a former Lybrand's man, was sent to Australia for a whole year to check out chances for a Wickes invasion.[2] But just about that time Australia's economy sagged, and in any case the mood was not exactly pro-American business: a new prime minister held office who had run on an Australia-for-Australians platform. So that was no way for Wickes to go at this time. Not that Dan Fitz-Gerald minded very much. He would not have admitted it to his best buddies, or even to himself, but the long flight "down under" had proved fairly exhausting. On the other hand, Amsterdam's Schipol Airport lay a mere dozen martinis from Saginaw's North Washington Avenue. Dan could entertain his cronies in the cocktail lounge of Tri-City Airport in the afternoon, and breakfast with old Corky the next morning.

And so it happened that Tony Swies, then Wickes Lumber's merchandise manager for all hardware and electrical products, was summoned to see John Drum one day in January 1969, and after some pleasantries, found himself escorted to McNeely's office. McNeely asked Drum, "John, did you tell him?", and Drum, ever an expert in monosyllables, replied, "No." Whereupon McNeely turned to Swies. "We want you to go to Europe," he said. Swies thought it was a joke.

Just why Tony Swies was chosen to head Wickes N.V.,[3] which at this moment did not yet exist, nobody can say for sure today, except that he was a top-notch merchandiser. True, he had some reputation around the shop of being a linguist. Son of a Polish-born Pennsylvania coal miner, he spoke second-generation Polish. Also, he had studied Latin in parochial school and minored in French in college.[4] None of these languages, however, was widely used in Holland at that point in history. Tony'd had some experience with hardware in Europe, but it had been confined to highly specialized equipment: he'd been in Army Ordnance in World War II. By temperament, he was anything but the professional international type. Always speaking straight to the point, never backing and filling or wasting time on gratuitous diplomatic trivia, he epitomized the efficient, old-fashioned American bulldog approach to business. Well, the same no-nonsense attitude had worked in Europe for Drum when he was dealing in steel for Ward's. Why shouldn't it work for Swies of Wickes?

Georgetown graduates take note: It worked astoundingly well. The Dutch can cope with deviousness. World traders for more than five centuries, they are used to artifice, taking it as well as dishing it out. But directness in commerce tends to take them by surprise, and that can give you an important edge once they learn you mean exactly what you say. Then they know that if they want your business, they have to meet your terms.

The same directness helped Tony over innumerable governmental hurdles. Anyone less persistent would have been lost, as well as interminably hung up in that continental specialty, red tape. As it was, he almost went to jail.

The first Wickes N.V. building supply center was to be launched in June 1970. A few weeks earlier, Fitz-Gerald and McNeely had simply notified Swies that they'd be there on the eleventh of that month for the grand opening—but Swies still didn't have the remodeling permit he needed to convert the warehouse he'd bought Utrecht into a store. So he proceeded without the blessings of bureaucracy, and soon found himself under arrest. Only some fast talking, half in English and half in newly acquired Berlitz Dutch, backed by the intervention of some Corky contacts, saved Tony from jail. The permit was issued, and the store opened on schedule.

Corky also had helped in establishing Wickes N.V. as a legal entity. Under the Netherlands law, a new company must have at least one native resident among its founders, and Corky had come up with a likely candidate: Dick De Rooij, partner in a firm that made household appliances. Fifty Wickes N.V. shares were issued at 1,000 guilders each, then the equivalent of about $285, of which DeRooij took one and Wickes the rest. Indola, DeRooij's household appliance company, had done some studies on the potentials of home supply stores, but Tony found the resultant statistics to be virtually useless, since they were concerned only with Indola's own products, like power tools and hair dryers, and there was a lot more that Tony wanted to sell.

As Wickes N.V.'s managing director, the transatlantic equivalent of general manager, Tony needed a staff of at least seven to help him get started—a legal officer, a controller, a merchandise manager, a construction superintendent, a personnel manager, an administrator, and an operations boss. Saginaw

"OUR MAN IN THE HAGUE"

Tony Swies, shown here visiting the famed Dutch miniature city of Madurodam, established Wickes in Europe. The corporation's approach to retailing has revolutionized the traditional way of doing business on the continent. (Foto-Kino Dekker, Delft)

eventually sent him a financial man, Ray Roeser, an old Wickes hand,[5] but for the moment Tony had to do all the spadework himself. He was Wickes Europe, period. Probably no one before him, and certainly not in a foreign country, ever had to change hats so often in the course of a single day.

Among his first major problems was finding merchandise sources. There was no point in his building a store before he could be sure that there'd be stuff on the shelves. Sounds easy enough, but wasn't.

Had Tony Swies been with Wickes Lumber in its early years, he would have known that lining up suppliers for an unorthodox business is one of the hardest things in the world to do. Back in the old Cash Way days, when Wickes lumberyards began to catch on, Wickes was anathema. Everybody in the building materials business—from suppliers to distributors to retailers—had umbrellas over everybody else, and everybody made a good profit. It was about as close to a cartel situation as you could get without Uncle Sam dispatching assorted investigators. Then Wickes burst in, brashly cut prices, and sent the whole industry into a tailspin.

Wickes was working on fifteen to seventeen points of margin, while the traditional lumber dealer took thirty-three points for granted. Even for a do-it-yourselfer who bought in relatively small quantities, this difference represented considerable savings. To bulk-buying builders, it was big money in the bank and they deserted their regular dealers in droves. Naturally the dealers had to defend themselves, and they did this by trying to stop manufacturers from selling their products to Wickes directly, i.e., at the manufacturer's wholesale price. They couldn't do much about structural lumber, which any dealer had been able to buy straight from the mills ever since Weyerhaeuser established this policy way back in 1900. The same applied to plywood. For these materials, Wickes could afford to charge less simply because it sold more. Any dealer willing to take lower profits should have been able to compete. Such was not the case, however, when it came to other basic building materials like gypsum, insulation, sheathing, flooring, ceiling tile, plumbing, etc. These products were sold by the manufacturers to distributors, who added 15 to 18 percent to the manufacturer's wholesale price on orders of less than a carload, which was about all the average lumberyard needed at one time. This arrangement left a fair profit for the retailer, provided he stuck to his 33 percent margin on sales. But he couldn't make out if he cut his price to compete with the Cash Ways.

Now here was Wickes, which never thought in terms of smaller-than-one-carload "fill-in" orders, and usually bought not just one carload at a time but, more likely, twenty. On carload-and-up transactions, distributors pocketed 7 percent in carrying charges although they never saw the merchandise: large quantities were shipped from the factory straight to the retailer. Why not simply buy directly from manufacturers, and pass on the resultant savings to the customers? Certain-Teed and U.S. Gypsum were among the first manufacturers to go along with this new approach. They saw that the Wickes way—the shortest possible route between producer and consumer—was the wave of the future. But it took years to get through to the diehards and break down the old system.

If you can envision this situation in the United States, where cartels are illegal, you can well imagine what Tony Swies faced in Europe, where cartels are part and parcel of the system. They may not be sanctioned as such, but they do exist; they control distribution right down to the retail level, and get away with charging outrageous prices. Take paint, for instance, a high-profit item in any case and one of those products where you pay mostly for the can and the promotion of the brand name. Holland, small as it is, has about 160 paint manufacturers, which ought to leave plenty of room for competition. But the retail prices are fixed so high that when Tony managed to persuade one of the best of the paintmakers to supply him, he found he could sell the product for 40 percent less than the going rate and still show a highly satisfactory profit margin.

That didn't happen until later in the game, however. For all intents and purposes, Wickes Europe found itself blacklisted by suppliers from Day One. GIZA, one of the biggest of the trade associations, had the plumbing and heating business in Holland all tied up. Tony knocked on door after door trying to find merchandise to retail below the decreed market prices and met nothing but frustration for months. Finally he convinced Stokvis, the country's largest wholesaler of these product lines, to deal with Wickes. Tony kept hammering away at the fact that sooner or later Wickes would find a supplier, that Wickes would crack the cartel, that price fixing could not be sustained in the new consumer economy, and that Stokvis might as well get in on the ground floor. Once Stokvis was aboard, other suppliers followed, among them the paint people, and after Wickes opened for business and cut prices, its competition cut prices, too, and swallowed lower profit margins. And that was the end of GIZA, felled as it were by a short, chunky Pennsylvanian with an habitually worried look on his craggy face. Tony must have worn one of his rare, utterly entrancing smiles on the day of GIZA's demise, but it couldn't have lasted long. There were more windmills to tilt at.

HIBIN, for instance. This trade association of producers and wholesalers of heavier building material lines, such as cement blocks and bricks, as well as of windows and insulation, has survived Wickes's campaign for lower retail prices to this day, but even here, despite HIBIN's resistance, Tony Swies and his interim successor, Paul Hylbert, have brought some manufacturers and distributors around. The Netherlands government, which does not favor cartelism, has been of considerable help in this regard, since it is aware that the Wickes approach leads to lower pricing, not only in the building supplies industry, but also in other areas where retailers are following the Wickes example. In the last couple of years, authorities have repeatedly intervened when suppliers were reluctant to deal with Wickes.

When Wickes went into Belgium, it again had to tackle suppliers one by one. Here Paul Hylbert brought around van Marcke, that country's leading manufacturer of plumbing and heating equipment and appliances, just as Tony had cornered Stokvis.

Not only cartelism but also the continental way of bargaining took the Wickes ambassadors somewhat by surprise. For instance, when Tony was first looking for a line of appliances, he went to three manufacturers in Germany and told each of them the same thing. "Look," he said. "I don't have the time or the staff to go through a long procedure. Tell me right off the bat what you want—terms, products, prices, backup allowances, and so on." When the proposals came in, Tony snapped up the best one. Soon he had a phone call from one of the bidders who wanted to know what Wickes thought of his terms.

"I gave the business to so and so," Tony said. "They offered me a better deal." There was a pause, then the manufacturer's representative blustered, "What do you mean you gave it to that firm? If you had asked me a second time, I would have beaten their terms."

And that's the way it went. Europeans may josh condescendingly about the way business is done in the bazaars of the Middle East, but they actually follow the same pattern themselves, even at the highest levels.

Partly for this reason, and partly because of the cartels, Wickes Europe draws on a surprisingly small number of suppliers. Where, in the United States, Wickes Lumber at various times might have anywhere from 150 to 200 major merchandise sources, Wickes Europe has only about 20, and this despite the fact that its outlets carry a far greater range of products. The big-turnover items that make up about two-thirds of the volume are concentrated in the hands of less than a half-dozen wholesalers and manufacturers. One German firm, for example, provides all kitchen cabinets marketed by Wickes Europe.[6]

Obtaining sites and building permits proved no less of a problem. Indeed, it's amazing that first Tony Swies, and later Paul Hylbert, managed to expand the chain as rapidly as they did in the five short years after Tony opened the first Wickes outlet in Utrecht at the jeopardy of his personal freedom. The store in Breda, also in the Netherlands, was the second, and its opening date in December 1970 had been no less firmly decreed than that of its predecessor—but again local authorities dragged their heels. In fact, it took nearly eighteen months to wrap up the arrangement. It wasn't that Wickes was unwelcome. Here, as elsewhere, the obstacles were internal political deals and squabbles. Tony never could figure out what had held up the Breda permit, but later, in Apeldoorn, he learned that there was a man on the city council who was afraid that Wickes was going to put his brother, who owned a hardware store, out of business.

Personnel turned out to be another challenge. Under the semicapitalist, semisocialist systems of government now prevalent in Western Europe, you have to be darn sure of people before you hire them. Once you have them in the organization, it's almost impossible to fire them, regardless of how incompetent—or even dishonest—they may be. On one occasion, a store manager in Holland was caught pocketing money he claimed he was paying to part-time help. Wickes eventually did succeed in getting rid of him, but it cost the company a pile of severance pay because the labor bureau felt that the man's actions hadn't been sufficient cause for dismissal. While there are bound to be some rotten apples in any barrel, Tony Swies and Paul Hylbert managed to keep them at a marginal minimum. The European work force, which now numbers more than 300 full-timers, is at least as conscientious and productive as its American counterpart, and the envoys from the home office have been impressed by its performance. Similarly, the two Wickes men were extremely fortunate in their recruitment of local executives. For example, Willem Bouten, a wholesaler who had handled the first plumbing order for Wickes Europe, had performed so well that Tony latched on to him immediately. Bouten is now general manager of Wickes's Dutch operations.

Tony Swies made another excellent choice in Paul de Rooij, Dick de Rooij's son. In Paul's case, Swies had to overcome a bias unknown in the United States—the prejudice against starting at the bottom if you are a member of the educated middle class. Paul was studying for the equivalent of a master's degree when Tony hired him in early 1970 as a part-time accountant and general factotum to translate Wickes's American procedures into their nearest Dutch equivalents. Recognizing immediately that the young man showed definite promise, Swies sent him for three weeks to Wickes Lumber in Saginaw to learn the ropes. Later, after Paul had discharged his military obligations, Swies offered him the managership of one of the early stores. You'd think that Paul would have grabbed this chance, but the de Rooij family debated for a whole week whether their son, with an advanced academic degree no less, should waste his time on something so mundane as running a lumberyard. Good sense prevailed, however, and young de Rooij accepted at last. Not surprisingly, it did not take him long to work his way up. He is now director of administration in Holland, although he is only in his late twenties.

Indeed, if there is a major corporation anywhere that gives

young talent a chance to come to the fore, it is Wickes. The company's leaders recognize that with the fast-moving organization they've got on their hands, they can't afford to be tied to yesterday's routines and day-before-yesterday's dreams. New blood, bubbling with new ideas and eager to try new approaches, is vital. Without it, the corporation couldn't hope to grow, or even to survive. While most of the top jobs, inevitably, are still held by people in their prime, the young generation is coming up fast. Paul W. Hylbert, Jr., who succeeded Tony Swies after the latter's first tour of duty with Wickes Europe, is a case in point. Paul was only twenty-seven years old when he joined Tony as marketing manager at the corporation's first European headquarters in Utrecht (since moved to The Hague). A few months later, he inherited Tony's job as managing director. In 1975, back stateside himself after taking his three-year turn abroad, Paul Hylbert, at thirty-one, became Wickes's youngest corporate vice president, with an array of responsibilities that would give anyone pause: acquisitions, sales and marketing, coordination of international sales and of intracompany sales, corporate market research, corporate research and corporate purchasing, plus the ever more important field of "energy" (i.e., conserving energy without sacrificing efficiency).[7]

Within a short time of Hylbert's return to the States, however, it became apparent that Wickes's foreign business was growing at such a rapid rate that it required Hylbert's undivided attention. By early 1976, his other functions were distributed among several staff executives, and he was named vice president of international development—a prestigious post, indeed, for so young a man: as we shall see, the world market of shelter products is now one of the corporation's major areas of expansion.

Hylbert couldn't help but make good. His very appearance and bearing are bound to kindle a recognition, and also a considerable amount of nostalgia, in anyone of the older generation who grew up when the puritan work ethic still held sway. Hylbert dresses businessman-conservatively. He wastes little time on chitchat. He is pleasant and polite, but never presumptuous. His every gesture conveys purpose, like those of athletes who have learned to economize their movements for maximum effect. He is trim and straight, unwavering of blue-eyed gaze, still knows how to use the old-fashioned address of "sir" without sounding servile; in San Diego, he could easily be mistaken for a promising young Navy career officer in civvies. All that's missing is an Annapolis class ring. He even wears his hair reasonably short, which, however, is no criterion at with-it Wickes today.

McNeely, who coached Little League in his Chicago days with Ward's, had known Paul Hylbert as one of the players on the team. But this acquaintance no more explains the young man's rapid rise than does his anachronistic demeanor. Anyone who'd assume such a thing doesn't know either McNeely or Hylbert—aggressive types like that disdain the crutch of nepotism. While still a senior at Denison University in Granville, Ohio, where he majored in history and minored in economics and political science, Hylbert was courted by many companies for management training. Wickes, which had no such structured program, was not among them, however. So Hylbert, hoping for something more exciting than what he'd been offered, wrote to McNeely, who referred the letter to the personnel department, and Paul didn't even meet McNeely again until several months after he had joined the company following his graduation in 1966. His first job, as befits an incipient Horatio Alger hero, was to unload boxcars and trucks and perform other manual labor at the Wickes yard in Elwood, Indiana. Then, still in Elwood, he went into clerical work, inventory control, and sales. Seven months later, with the McNeely-Drum team clicking along and the billion-dollar goal set, Wickes finally got around to establishing a twelve-month management development group for which five young men were chosen, and Hylbert was one of them. He moved to Saginaw, where he was exposed to all the various departments from finance to merchandising to operations, and at the same time continued his night school studies at Ann Arbor for his master's degree in business administration. Subsequently, Hyl-

Wickes Europe

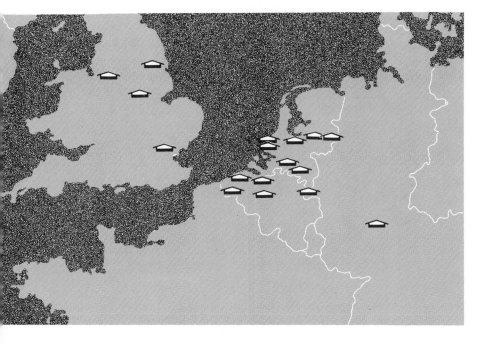

bert became assistant manager of the lumber and building supply center at Grand Blanc, south of Flint, and after that returned to Saginaw as a buyer of trusses and other building components. His next break came when McNeely set up a "corporate exploration and planning group" under Ronald J. Woods, whom we shall meet in a later chapter, and who then held a position known as "Office of the President," a type of aide for special presidential assignments. Here, Hylbert became involved in checking out the potentials of various new lines of business for Wickes.

With all this experience crammed into five years, and given the fact that he'd had at least a brush with life in the Low Countries (his father had represented Culligan, Inc., in Brussels), Hylbert ranked high to start with among likely candidates for the Wickes Europe post. True, he was still very young and looked it, but it had long been apparent to his bosses that he was not only possessed of unflagging ambition but blessed with a sharp mind and a phenomenal memory for facts. Moreover,

"VICKESS" IN EINDHOVEN

This store, one of twelve in the Low Countries, was opened in May 1973. (Photo by V. Beek)

PAUL HYLBERT

*He headed Wickes Europe for three years,
returned in 1975 to become the corporation's
youngest vice president.*

he was capable of making difficult decisions, and of seeing
them through. What better proving ground for such upcoming
executive talent than that wide-open new enterprise on the
other side of the Atlantic? John Drum's decision, as executive
vice president in charge of foreign operation, to send the
promising youngster abroad probably surprised no one except
Hylbert himself.[8] These, then, were the Wickes Europe
pioneers: Tony Swies, who had laid the groundwork and was
about to return home for a spell; Paul Hylbert, raring to go at

new goals; and the down-to-earth, never-to-be-fooled old-timer, Ray Roeser, the financial man, who remembered more relaxed, but no less future-directed, days when he'd walk in on Dan Fitz-Gerald and ask for an afternoon off to take care of some important family affairs, and Dan would tell him, "Hell, if all your work's done and you want to go play golf, just say so." Tony had established the original 20,000-square-foot Utrecht store; had followed up with the Breda store; and in cooperation with a Dutch firm, Edah, had gone into business in Helmond near Eindhoven (a small outlet that's since closed) and had opened the first store in The Hague itself.[9] He had also paved the way for Apeldoorn, launched in June 1972, and worked out the first phases of Wickes's fifty-fifty joint venture in the United Kingdom with J. H. Sankey & Son, a British builders' merchant firm, to establish a Wickes Europe subsidiary that does business under the name of Wickes Building Supplies. John Hazel, the managing director of Sankey's, a

NOT SO LIMITED

First store of Wickes Building Supplies, Ltd., the United Kingdom branch of Wickes Europe, was launched in Whitefield, a suburb of Manchester, in 1972. Among guests at grand opening were (above, left to right): Dan Fitz-Gerald; Lord Alfred Robens, of Vickers, Ltd.; and John Hazel, managing director of J. H. Sankey & Son, Ltd., Wickes's partner in the British subsidiary. R. E. T. Clark (left) is in charge of the U.K. outlets. There are four of them now, including one at Harrow, near London (right). Plans call for eighteen stores in the U.K. by 1980.

dynamic gentleman now pushing sixty, who doesn't let his somewhat rotund figure interfere with his perpetual motion, is one of those "new" Britons who may drop their aitches occasionally but never the ball. Relishing the labor as much as the fruit it produces, he is likely to insist on holing up in a resort hotel on Spain's Costa Brava for a budget review, splitting the time between golf, siestas, and hard talk, but come the weekend, he's back at his 700-year-old house in England's movie-scene countryside. Hazel had first touched base with Wickes in 1968 in North Carolina, intent on learning that burgeoning American firm's way of doing business. Through Barrett Green, then regional manager for Wickes Lumber (and since with Grossman's, a Wickes competitor), Hazel had been introduced to John Drum, and when the decision was made to have a shot at Holland, a partnership with Hazel in the British Isles soon followed.

The first store in the United Kingdom, in Whitefield, a suburb of Manchester, opened in September 1972, and a second, in Nottingham, in July 1974. Two more outlets, one in

Hull and the other on the outskirts of London, in Harrow, were added in 1975. The "bloke" in charge of the British show, as he'd refer to himself, is a tall, darkly handsome Wiltshireman, R. E. T. ("Dick") Clark, thirty-three years old, a graduate in law of London University who had been a sales director of one of the regional operations of Sankey's and a financial director of that company. Despite the snarls that British bureaucracy is prone to and which slowed the initial expansion in the United Kingdom, Clark has managed to achieve an excellent profit record.[10] In the meantime, as the British branch struggled to expand, Paul Hylbert went ahead full speed on the Continent—or at least with as much dispatch as the local authorities would allow. In 1973, he opened stores in Brussels, Antwerp, and Ghent in Belgium, and in Eindhoven and Heerlen in the Netherlands, the last so close to the German border city of Aachen it almost looked as if Hylbert were following Eisenhower's footsteps and getting ready to fight his own battle of Huertgen Forest. But, like his martial predecessor, Paul found out that it was one thing to get close to the German border and another to punch through, although in his case he didn't mind the infiltration of great numbers of Germans who flocked to the Heerlen store from across the line.[11] Although Paul Hylbert had done the pioneering, Germany, in fact, did not fall to Wickes until Tony Swies, returning for his second tour of overseas duty in 1975, zeroed in with unerring instinct on the heartland, the vibrant Frankfurt-Darmstad-Mainz triangle at the confluence of the Rhine and Main rivers.

The first Wickes store in Germany, at Egelsbach, about 18 miles south of Frankfurt, was a huge success from the moment it opened its doors on December 5, 1975. A volume of 30,000 DMs (around $12,000) had been projected for its first day in business, although everybody naturally kept his fingers crossed for a bit more than that. What actually happened no one could have foreseen; by evening, the store had grossed 110,000 DMs, or about $44,000. It could have racked up a yet greater total if it hadn't run out of delivery vehicles in the face of this unexpected deluge of customers. Even John Drum, who had always considered Germany Wickes Europe's most promising target, was surprised. The average ticket sale ran over $25, nearly double that of the Utrecht store's $13, which until then had been the highest in the chain. Rainer Kerber, the 36-year-old general manager of the German operation, was delighted: some 60 percent of the buyers were clearly large-project oriented, and this boded well for his second store, which was scheduled to open in March 1976 in a similarly favorable location also near the Frankfurter Kreuz, Europe's busiest superhighway intersection. Already at the end of December 1975, even without that second store, the German branch was breaking even, despite its disproportionate initial overhead— about a year earlier than had been anticipated. That's what happens when you're doing three times budget.

Not that a heavy population concentration, such as in this German metropolitan corridor, is essential for a Wickes store to succeed in Europe. Of course, it doesn't hurt to sit smack in the center of a busy, affluent community. But the Wickes men learned some time ago that their original location requirements had set unnecessarily high standards. To begin with, both Tony and Paul had followed guidelines that demanded a minimum population of 150,000 to 200,000 people within about a 6-mile radius of a store. Then it turned out that 100,000 was quite enough—as Dick Clark's store in Nottingham proved conclusively. By the same token, there had been some reservations about moving into Heerlen, which had been initially classified as a secondary or even tertiary target because of the decline of coal mining in that region. Contrary to expectations, however, Heerlen's sales were far more than adequate. Its first year's volume considerably exceeded projections, and the operating income immediately hit an impressive 7.9 percent. The discovery that neither great affluence nor a large population base is required for success now makes it easier for Wickes to develop new markets. As Paul Hylbert saw the Heerlen business blossoming, he pressed ahead with plans for stores in Enschede[12] in the east-central Netherlands, and in Kortrijk in northwestern Belgium, neither of them territories the corporation would have dared tackle in the early days. By the end of 1975, Wickes Europe had seventeen outlets in operation— thirteen on the continent and four in the United Kingdom— and at least seven more were scheduled to be opened in 1976.[13]

Paradoxically, the depressed economy of 1974–1975 aided in this growth. With major industrial expansion in Western Europe at a near standstill, there was less squabbling about real estate prices when Wickes dickered for new sites. In Holland alone, nearly fifty new location possibilities have been identified and will be pursued. Not all of them are expected to mature, of course. Present plans, which call for a total of seventy-five stores in Europe by 1980, project twenty-two for the Netherlands, seventeen for Belgium, and eighteen each for Germany and the United Kingdom. With this expansion, sales are expected to rise to $115 million from fiscal 1975's $20.7 million. Over the same period, the annual operating income is projected to grow from fiscal 1975's $375,000 to nearly $7 million.

Such grandiose growth figures may sound like blue-sky prattle, but they aren't. They are predicated on locations that have been thoroughly researched, and where Wickes's entry is a virtual certainty. Moreover, Wickes Europe's prior experience backs up these expectations. Even in the shaky economy that prevailed in fiscal 1975, the division's sales were up 65 percent, putting them 8 percent above projections. As for the operating income, that was an astounding 40 percent higher than Paul Hylbert had ventured to predict in his budget that year.

Fiscal 1976 looked better yet, for the German Egelsbach store was far from Wickes Europe's only success. The new, third outlet of Wickes Building Supplies Ltd., in Hull, was also doing very well, and the London/Harrow store, Britain's economic difficulties notwithstanding, enjoyed an initiation that was nearly as triumphant as that of the first German store. Harrow grossed about $40,000 on its opening day, almost four times as much as had been expected. Since then it has routinely run two-and-a-half times budget, and it easily slipped into the black in its second month of operation, ten months ahead of schedule. In the Netherlands, the second store in Utrecht, which opened in late November 1975, did not dilute the first Utrecht store's sales, as some had feared. In fact, the original Utrecht store chalked up one of its best weeks right after the second's successful, money-making inauguration at the other end of town. All this is rather convincing evidence that the Wickes ambassadors don't make empty promises.

European manufacturers and wholesalers of building materials are beginning to appreciate this in even greater numbers: Wickes Europe has become a prime outlet for their goods. Certainly, the local people working for Wickes have learned under Tony's and Paul's tutelage that there is something to be said for that new unorthodox way of doing business they introduced in Europe. There was the time, for instance, when Jan van der Woord, the second center manager Tony Swies had hired, refused to put bathtubs on the showroom floor. At first van der Woord pretended he didn't understand Tony. Then he made it clear that he thought that bath "tubes" didn't belong in a public place. Tony insisted, and Somebody Up There must have liked him, for, within a few minutes after van der Woord had reluctantly complied and put a really gaudily colored one on display, it was snapped up by a young couple. Van der Woord has now caught on that big items can be mass-merchandised too, and he has become one of the most valuable men in the organization.

The competition, too, is also learning fast that there is something to the Wickes method. Not a day passes when you don't see middle-aged men in conservative business suits peering interestedly through the windows of the Wickes stores and occasionally taking notes. The Wickes personnel is used to that by now. They don't even nudge each other anymore when they spot the latest spies. After all, draped over the front of the stores are big sheets that proclaim "**VRIJE TOEGANG VOOR IEDEREEN**" and "**FREIER EINGANG FÜR JEDEN**," meaning "free entrance for everybody."

Which is just as it should be. For years, most people in Western Europe felt they shouldn't go into a building supply store, that they didn't belong there, and that even if they went in, the store would refuse to sell its merchandise to them. If they wanted do-it-yourself supplies, they had to shop around in any number of little shops and then pay high prices to boot. All this is changed now. The Wickes concept has become established, much to the delight of a continent where manual labor is even harder to find than in the United States, and where everybody has to be a handyman if he wants to get anything done.

Like the executives of any company, the Wickes leadership must be concerned primarily with its responsibility to make profits for the corporation's stockholders, but the growth thus fostered to achieve this goal now provides a long-needed consumer service in Europe, as it long has in the United States. Stuffy spokesmen for big business, pontificating from their rostrums, may call this "enlightened management." Maybe so. But the real point is that Wickes has learned that the easiest way to make a profit is to sell what people truly need at prices they can afford to pay.

15

Instant Millionaires

Every time Tony Swies drives to Antwerp from his Wickes Europe office in The Hague, he is reminded that Wickes is not only in the lumber and building supplies business. Right after he crosses the Rhine and barrels down the superhighway through Doordrecht, he catches a quick glimpse of a warehouse perched on a bluff to the right. What distinguishes this steel structure—the specialty of another Wickes division—is the fact that despite the building's 220,000 square feet, nothing holds up its roof but the walls.

That such a sizable area can be enclosed without internal supports may seem of no great consequence to people not involved with industrial and other large-space architecture. But think about it for a minute, and you can see how important it can be and how practical it is to do away with built-in obstructions in airplane hangars, factories, auditoriums, and the like. As a matter of fact, the warehouse at Doordrecht isn't even one of the giants of its genre. The Wickes-Behlen plant in Columbus, Nebraska, under whose license this Dutch building was erected, itself shelters 19 acres under one continuous roof. That's enough to accommodate fourteen football fields, including end zones, plus six regulation tennis courts for doubles, and with still enough square footage left over for all the rooms in an average house. True, the roof of this huge plant does have internal supports between its 50-foot-wide bays—but each of these bays runs on for 800 feet without a single structural member blocking the way.

Now it obviously wasn't Fitz-Gerald or McNeely or Drum who decided one day that Wickes engineers must get to work on the practical applications of the principle that makes clear-span steel structures of this type possible. The major strength of Wickes as an organization lies in its ability to integrate viable projects into its marketing scheme; in short, to acquire existing organizations that fit the corporation's aims. This is not conglomerating in the traditional sense. Wickes isn't about to buy a movie studio, no matter how profitable it promises to be, nor a chain of resort hotels. Not that the corporation would mind the extra volume and earnings that might result from such diversification, but the process of running an acquisition outside one's realm of expertise is a chancy proposition at best.

Let's take a look at the sort of properties that are most often available for mergers. They are companies that are without the financial resources to realize their full potential, and/or are closely held entrepreneurial organizations whose prime movers want to cash in and get out. The former kind makes a fine acquisition if you're able to provide the wherewithal for expansion, and if, as the purchaser, you can count on the ability and loyalty of the existing management, or else know enough about the business to run it yourself. Merging with one of the latter entails the risk of landing in limbo. The one or two innovators whose concepts propelled the property to prominence and made it a desirable candidate for acquisition now want to savor the rewards of their labor on the golf course or the bikini-bedecked foc's'le of a yacht, and you had better be ready to replace them with good people who can carry on the task. And even if the old management is eager to stay, you're likely to find yourself racked by more merger migraines than you anticipated in the first flush of corporate courting. Remember Al Riedel of Michigan Bean. Individualists like that don't take kindly to becoming cogs.

The agonies of acquisition are familiar to the leadership of any expansionist organization. Yet, as indicated earlier, a gargantuan growth such as Wickes has enjoyed is almost impossible to sustain from within. That's why the search for appropriate (and manageable) acquisitions has been, and will continue to be, one of the corporation's greatest challenges, and why it is always in the hands of its most trusted top-level officers. Wickes's earliest mergers had been presided over by Dan Fitz-Gerald personally, assisted by Art Pufford, the financial expert whom we met when he served as the corporation's envoy to Australia, and by Tom Cline who, as the Wickes legal beagle, had to beard the merger prospects' lawyers in their lairs. In the late 1960s, George W. Kelch, who had come to Wickes from Borg-Warner, was charged with the responsibility for investigating mergers, and the interesting and highly profitable company in Columbus, Nebraska, that put Wickes into the clearspan building business was one of Kelch's coups.[1] Word that Behlen was available had come to Wickes through the Continental Illinois National Bank and Trust Company, whereupon George Kelch flew to Omaha and then drove west across the prairies to have a look at this unusual homegrown operation, the brainchild of a basement tinkerer who made good.

Behlen Manufacturing had started as "The One-Minute Soldering Iron Company, Walter D. Behlen, Proprietor," which never got off the ground because of lack of funds. Born in 1905, Walt was in his early thirties then and made his living as a Railway Express delivery man. He was a farm boy without formal education beyond high school, but his imagination was not limited by his lack of degrees, or for that matter by the scarcity of cash that was the order of the day for family farmers in Nebraska's Platte County. Walt was no more successful with his second product, a corn-husking hook, which became obsolete just about the time he started manufacturing it. He then

decided that steel toe caps for wooden-soled shoes might sell—
and they did, to industries like Detroit's automobile plants,
where some workers are exposed to extremely hot floors and
spills of acids. The toe caps didn't exactly net a fortune for Walt
and his brothers Mike and Gilbert, who were also moonlight-
ing, but they did learn some business basics, like studying the
Thomas Register of American Manufacturers to find out where
necessary materials and equipment could be purchased. A
fastener for egg-case lids was next, inspired by Walt's experience in handling poorly closed egg cases on his delivery job.
This item, too, was a success, as was a subsequent venture, the
production of dental clasps used by dentists and dental labora-
tories in making partial plates. By 1944 the Behlens found
themselves so busy they had to expand from their garage and
basement to an old repair-shop building, and the leading local
bank considered the enterprise sound enough to risk a $6,000
loan.[2]

From then on, Walt Behlen's enterprise grew in a hurry. It
so happened that a Minnesota farmer with a talent for
mechanics, A. H. Siemen, had patented an important
improvement for corn pickers—the very machine that had
contributed to the demise of Behlen's corn-husking hook.
Siemen's patent was a new type of rubber roller that greatly
enhanced the husking capability of mechanical corn pickers.
After one of the local Columbus, Nebraska, men had become
a distributor of the new product, Siemen came down to check
out the Behlen Manufacturing Company as a possible production source. Soon an agreement was reached that Behlen
would make up Siemen rollers on a royalty basis. This, however, was easier said than done. World War II was approaching
its climax: all the nation's resources were directed toward
building up the fighting force that would soon invade Hitler's
Europe, and raw materials were scarce. To get into mass
production by April 1944, as agreed, Walt had to improvise. He
designed a high-speed jig and press that could be built from
salvaged junkyard materials, and to obtain the rubber for the
rollers he concocted a machine for removing the steel beads

from scrapped auto and truck tires. All the makeshift equipment and procedures worked so well that within a few months Behlen had outgrown its new plant. Once again Walt's practical ingenuity paid off. Building materials were no easier to come by than anything else, so he bought an antiquated and long-unused brickworks in Columbus, dismantled it, used the bricks to build his addition, and at the same time acquired a site for a possible new factory.

This was the turning point. In 1943, Behlen Manufacturing had shown pretax earnings of only $3,095. In 1944, the company closed its books with a $45,000 profit.

A few months later, Walt's consistently straight-line thinking—from need to idea to practical application—led him into yet another profitable venture. In 1945, a spell of rainy weather held up the spring planting, and it was a foregone conclusion that there would be an all-but-worthless harvest of soft and soggy corn. Walt decided that the situation called for a device that would reduce the corn's moisture content, and he came up with an inexpensive ventilator of die-expanded sheet-metal tubes that could be put into corn cribs to aid air circulation. As a companion piece, he designed a heater-dryer with a burner that used kerosene or fuel oil and a fan that could be powered by a tractor to send the heated air through the ventilator. Soon ventilator sections were selling by the thousands. By the end of the year, Behlen had a $100,000 backlog of orders for corn dryers, and pretax earnings jumped to $151,629.

The variety of products Walt Behlen managed to dream up in the two decades that followed was staggering. It included zinc-coated wire-mesh corn-crib panels; oil-hydraulic power-steering gearboxes for farm tractors and road graders; grain bins and grain dryers; augers and farm elevator legs; sophisticated heat blowers and perforated bin floors; stitching presses; and self-framed corrugated steel-mesh farm gates. One idea led to another, and so it happened that in 1949 Behlen invented a structure of such sturdiness that its prototype withstood the explosion of a nuclear device at Yucca Flat, Nevada. The 30-megaton A-blast blew out the Behlen building's doors and

THE GENIUS
FROM NEBRASKA

*Countless inventions
flowed from the fertile
mind of Walt Behlen (left),
who made Behlen Manu-
facturing one of Wickes's
most important
acquisitions. Among
Behlen products are giant
grain tanks (below).*
(Portrait by Fabian
Bachrach)

Behlen stressed-skin steel building withstood A-bomb test in 1955. Competitors did not fare nearly so well. (Walt Behlen photo)

Behlen horizontal roof system, which requires no internal supports, allows obstruction-free viewing for 10,000 people at Church of God of Prophecy, Cleveland, Tennessee. One of Behlen's biggest sellers is the "Curvet" (below), which gives farmers more space per dollar than any comparable building. (BMC photos)

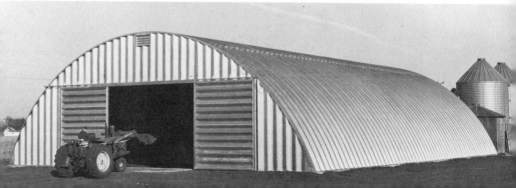

NINETEEN ACRES
UNDER ONE ROOF

Behlen plant in Columbus, Nebraska, has enough floor space to house fourteen football fields and then some. (BMC photo). *Harold E. Joiner (left) is general manager of this vast complex– and other units of the Behlen division.* (Portrait by Landgren Studio)

windows, but that was all. Other test buildings, also at a distance of 6,800 feet, were crunched.

"We had been using corrugated mesh panels as a structural material, first in farm gates and then in corn cribs," says 6 foot 2 Walt Behlen, a 225 pounder who looks as if he himself might have been able to make a pretty good showing in an A-bomb test in his younger years. "These mesh panels, when flat, had no strength to speak of and could not even support their own weight. But when deeply corrugated they became very rigid. So we reasoned that sheet-metal panels might be made so stiff by deep corrugating methods that they could serve as both the enclosing frame and the roof of a building." The first experiment involved a 16-gauge panel, 8 feet long and bent into a peaked-hat section. The two ends were supported by sawhorses. Walt himself, piece by piece, stacked 3,000 pounds of steel rods across the top. And then something very interesting happened. The corrugated panel held the load. Pressure applied from above strengthened rather than weakened it. In effect, Walt had come up with a roof whose ability to carry a load increased as more load was put on it.[3] Bolted to walls of similarly corrugated panels, you had a shell that was virtually indestructible.

Needing more working space in the plant, Walt designed a 50 x 200 foot building based on this principle, and with his old-fashioned flair for a carnival type of showmanship, arranged a public demonstration in which sixteen International Harvester tractors, weighing a total of 64,000 pounds, were hung from the new addition's roof ridge. Thus, the frameless stressed-skin (or monocoque) building was born.[4] It could be constructed with a horizontal or pitched roof linked to corrugated walls as in the early models. Or the whole structure could be a single vast corrugated-panel arch, theoretically of infinite dimension. Indeed, if someone were willing to finance the world's biggest building, Walt Behlen is ready to supply the plans: they're for a multisports stadium roofed by a Behlen Dubl-Panl Arched-Span System that could shelter a horserace track, football field, baseball field, and seating for 78,000 spectators; it would enclose 44 acres without a single obstruction, and its 1,600-foot-long arch would rise to 250 feet. Countless smaller, less costly versions have been built by Behlen in the United States and by its licensees in Australia, Argentina, and Italy. More common still are Behlen buildings of the original horizontal-roof design, including the 15,000-seat basketball arena of the University of New Mexico at Albuquerque; the 10,000-seat Church of God of Prophecy in Cleveland, Tennessee; a 322-foot-long cut-flower terminal in Haifa, Israel; and a 527-foot-long candy factory in Verona, Italy. Needless to say, since Behlen became part of Wickes, the corporation itself has used Behlen Clear-Span structures in abundance as building supply centers, furniture warehouse-showrooms, and various manufacturing facilities, including that of Behlen-Wickes, Ltd., the Behlen Division's wholly owned Canadian subsidiary in Brandon, Manitoba.

On the face of it, the acquisition of Behlen Manufacturing in 1969 did not fit into the Wickes scheme. At that time Wickes was only in the business of retailing building materials, wholesaling navy beans and other crops, and handling the manufacturing and mining franchises it had inherited from the original Wickes companies. But actually, Wickes and Behlen were akin in their basic thinking. Both recognized the great opportunities in the fields of shelter and food. Wickes sold 2 × 4s and shingles, Behlen sold enclosed space. Wickes handled agricultural products; Behlen produced equipment to aid in their harvesting, processing, and storage. There was a definite logic in getting together. Dan Fitz-Gerald was convinced of that, as was Walt Behlen, and it took them only a few months to agree on the terms after the initial visit by George Kelch. As usual, Dan pulled a Fitz-Gerald when it came down to the nitty-gritty. Walt wanted to entice Wickes, but there were enough admirers around so that he could afford to bargain. Dan's offer of share for share didn't strike him as quite good enough, so he called Saginaw one day and asked for two shares of Wickes for one of Behlen. Dan protested that he'd have to take it up with his board, and Walt said he didn't mind, he had lots of time.

Less than an hour later his phone rang. It was Deloris Menthen, who had been Dan's secretary for nearly twenty years. "Mr. Behlen," she said, "the directors have agreed to your terms." Walt was amazed at the speed with which Dan could muster his far-flung board at such short notice, and it wasn't until three years later that Fitz-Gerald admitted that he'd just been stalling. He'd had the power all along to agree to any reasonable arrangement, and two for one—that is, 535,000 shares of Wickes, then worth a little more than $27 million—was certainly reasonable enough for a company like Behlen, which had grown to king size in its own right and had reached annual sales of nearly $23 million.

The whole $27 million chunk of Wickes didn't go to Walt, of course, or to his aged father, who had taken care of the company's office matters in its early days, or to Walt's two brothers, who were still helping him run the show. Behlen had gone public in 1959, and counted nearly 3,000 stockholders, although the Behlen family continued to control the company. Walt's own holdings entitled him to only about 29 percent of the proceeds, or 153,000 shares of Wickes, but even so, this made him the largest single stockholder of the corporation, with more equity than held even by Ran Wickes.

As mergers go, the transition was fairly smooth. Although Walt Behlen formally retired from major management responsibilities on March 14, 1969, the date of the acquisition, he retained the title of chairman of the subsidiary until the following year when he reached sixty-five, the mandatory retirement age at Wickes, and he served on the corporation's board of directors until 1975. His brother Gilbert stayed on as executive vice president, treasurer, and head of the purchasing department until the beginning of 1971, and later served as a consultant to the subsidiary, as did brother Mike, who retained the post of president for another nine months. Since then, Behlen has been in the hands of Harold E. Joiner, who came into the organization as vice president shortly after its merger with Wickes. He has been general manager of the division since 1971, and in fiscal 1975 pushed Behlen's sales volume close to

$65 million, thanks largely to his development of a highly effective coast-to-coast network of 600 dealers, most of whom represent Behlen exclusively.[5]

Since August 1971, Farmaster Products, Inc., acquired for 66,904 shares of Wickes stock then worth slightly over $3 million, has been part of the Behlen operation. Headquartered in Shenandoah, Iowa, and with additional plants in Georgia, Texas, Ohio, and Nebraska, Farmaster is by far the nation's largest manufacturer of farm gates and farrowing stalls, and in the agricultural prosperity of 1974 it contributed a hefty $8 million to Behlen's sales.[6]

While stressed-skin steel structures of immense clear span may hold more appeal for the imagination, the Behlen Division's other products are its bread and butter.[7] About 60 percent of its volume derives from the manufacture and sale of grain-handling, grain-conditioning, and grain-storage equipment and agricultural buildings, and another 22 percent from farm fencing and gates, hydraulic presses, and tractor power-steering. Industrial and commercial steel buildings account for only 18 percent of the division's sales, which is not surprising since the Behlen stressed-skin structure is the Cadillac of that business. Wickes doesn't mind in the least. The corporation also sells its Vegas.

Wickes's lower-priced lines of utility structures are manufactured by the Wickes Buildings Division, formerly the Moriarty Corporation, of Argos, Indiana, which was acquired in August 1969, five months after the Behlen merger. Moriarty was a much smaller organization, and its acquisition involved only 62,500 shares of Wickes stock, or about $3 million. This was a drop in the bucket in a year that marked Wickes's biggest buying spree to date—some $81 million worth of properties. In the Moriarty case, however, practically the whole bundle dropped into the lap of one individual, Mrs. Georgia Moriarty, whose husband had started the firm in the early 1950s. At that time Doanne's Agricultural Service, headquartered in St. Louis, Missouri, had developed a design for pole buildings for use on farms as barns, tool sheds, and the like, and was marketing the plans and the know-how. The pole-building concept was revolutionary and an instant success, since such shelters were easier and faster, and therefore cheaper, to erect than traditional frame structures.

The pole-building principle is really the same as that of modern skyscrapers whose walls are not load-bearing and where steel pillars hold up the works. In pole buildings, the supportive skeleton is wood. The vertical members, chemically impregnated under extreme pressure against rot and decay, are set on concrete pads at a depth of 4 feet. The poles support the roof trusses, and the siding is, in effect, hung from the roof. Owen Moriarty, who ran a small retail lumberyard in Argos, deep in the lush farm country of north central Indiana, decided that putting up such buildings would be a good business to get into, and he was absolutely right—except that he didn't foresee that there would be a divorce and that his wife would end up owning the company.

For several years, Georgia Moriarty, who had served in the Marine Corps and felt at home in the world of men, then ran the outfit by herself, which couldn't have been an easy task. The competition was terrific. Everywhere in the farm belt, lumberyard owners and small contractors were trying to establish themselves in the lucrative pole-building field. Nevertheless, the Moriarty operation grew into a sort of junior conglomerate of nine little pole-building companies, of which five were owned outright by Mrs. Moriarty, and another four had managers who held 49 percent of the stock in their respective companies.[8] By 1969, Mrs. Moriarty was doing $4.8 million in sales and was ready to take her capital gains. Although tired of the hassle that's an inevitable concomitant of growth, she agreed to stay on as president of the subsidiary for several months to ease the transition after Wickes took over.

Her successor at the Moriarty helm was Wickes's Roland Pretzer, that young manager of the Cash Way days who had spearheaded the Lumber Division's first venture outside Michigan, the phenomenally successful building supply center at Rootstown, Ohio. Pretzer's acumen had not diminished in the intervening years, while his experience had considerably widened. For more than a decade, ever since the Wolohan split, he'd been intimately involved in the division's growth as a high-level troubleshooter reporting directly to Lumber's successive bosses, first Smith Bolton, then McNeely, and finally John Drum. Pretzer was by far the most logical person to become the Wickes man in the new Moriarty subsidiary, since the close future relationship between the Lumber Division and this wood-construction operation could easily be envisioned. Pretzer went in as vice president under Mrs. Moriarty, assumed the presidency on her resignation, and when the

VERSATILITY IN BUILDING

Wickes Buildings Division engages in commercial construction, such as the Sears store at Boyne City, Michigan (above), also specializes in a variety of agricultural buildings, ranging from utility structures to cattle barns.

OTTO C. KROHN

He succeeded Roland Pretzer as head of Wickes Buildings.

subsidiary became a division in 1973, continued as its general manager until his reassignment as vice president and general manager of Wickes Agriculture a couple of years later.

Under Pretzer's leadership, the volume jumped to more than $23 million in fiscal 1975, a nearly fivefold increase in five years. At the time of the acquisition, the Moriarty firm had sales offices in Indiana, Michigan, and Ohio, from which construction crews were dispatched to erect the pole structures. These five profit centers were backed up by two Moriarty-owned lumberyards, which supplied the materials. [9]

But with the merger, all of Wickes's lumber centers also became potential suppliers. Wickes Buildings could go practically anywhere it wanted to and be assured of its raw materials without having to spend a lot of money on inventories and their storage. To open a new territory, all Pretzer had to do was put up one of his own buildings (an advertisement in itself), assign salesmen, hire and train construction crews, buy a few trucks, and order specific materials from the nearest Wickes lumberyard, and he was in business. This low investment requirement resulted in a phenomenal return on net assets, consistently in the 30 to 40 percent range. Moreover, by following in Wickes Lumber's footsteps, the big problem of the initial sell was at least partially solved. Wickes Buildings, invading virgin territory, might have had a hard time getting its trade name across. Not so, however, in an area where Wickes Lumber was already an established institution, and where the slogan, "Wickes is a good name to build on," was familiar from advertisements. When Otto C. Krohn took over the division in February 1975,[10] Pretzer had established additional pole-building profit centers in the three original Moriarty states and expanded into Georgia, Illinois, Iowa, Kansas, Kentucky, Maryland, New York, North Carolina, Pennsylvania, and Wisconsin. Additional offices were opened in 1975 in Missouri, South Carolina, and Tennessee, bringing the total to thirty-nine.[11]

Today, the division's pole buildings—their wooden post-pillar-beam frames sheathed in weather-tight aluminum or painted steel—serve far more than the agricultural market, although this is still the prime source of business, accounting for about half the volume. Nonfarm utility and garage-type structures represent 30 percent of sales. And with improved truss design, making clear spans up to 80 feet possible, commercial and industrial buildings produce another 15 percent of the volume. Horse barns, apparently a growing market, add another 5 percent.[12] In addition, Wickes Buildings markets Behlen steel buildings out of several of its locations—another example of how a specialized diversification like Wickes's can lead to mutually profitable hand-in-glove relationships.

To stimulate such intracorporate cooperation is high on the agenda of Clark Johnson who, in his post of senior vice president, has several division managers reporting to him, including Harold R. Pearson,[13] of Yorktowne, an acquisition made in March 1970. Yorktowne, which started as the Dallastown Furniture Co., based in the town of that name in central Pennsylvania near York, had been a maker of kitchen cabinets since 1937. It also manufactured slats for venetian blinds, survived World War II by turning out Navy footlockers,

YORKTOWNE KITCHEN

Yorktowne produces top-of-the-line kitchen cabinets, also makes counter tops and vanities, as well as specialized cabinetry and other furniture for schools and libraries.

climbed into postwar prosperity with TV cabinets, bathroom vanities, and top-quality kitchen built-ins. By 1970, known as the Colonial Products Company, it could demand an acquisition price of 488,925 Wickes shares, worth nearly $20 million at the time.[14] Practically all this money went to Charles Pechenik, who had started the business with the modest proceeds of a window-glazing and door business he had operated in his native Brooklyn, New York.

Yorktowne now employs about 800 and makes and sells all sorts of cabinetry, case goods, and related items, including highly specialized furniture for school and college kitchens, science rooms, libraries, music rooms, and general storage. Its Yorktowne-brand kitchen cabinets, counter tops, and vanities are sold to developers on a bid basis, and to individual customers through independent distributors. At the same time—putting Wickes's internal strength to work—it markets private-label kitchen cabinets, counter tops, and vanities through the outlets of Wickes Lumber. Conversely, Yorktowne buys a large share of its raw materials from still other Wickes divisions. For instance, it has been working closely with Wickes Forest Industries in the development of an industrial grade of particle board. As a result, Yorktowne, which is one of the country's largest users of that kind of board, has become an important Wickes Forest Industries customer. And although Yorktowne's purchases of West Coast lumber are relatively small, every little bit helps, and it's of course the Oregon-Pacific Division of Wickes that gets those orders.

Evidently, the advantages of internal sales are many. As we have seen with Wickes Buildings, there is the leverage of minimum investment to achieve a maximum return on assets that's made possible when appropriate facilities exist elsewhere in a company's framework. There is, moreover, a greater certainty of obtaining required materials when their vendor is a member of the corporate family. By the same token, if a company has effective retail outlets, its manufacturing arms get a leg up when it comes to distribution. And while one division of a company, when buying from another, doesn't get a special price break, the profits arising out of in-house transactions accrue to the corporate kitty—they don't leave the premises. Thus, the wise approach to acquisitions must be predicated not only on their appraisal as potential contributors of earnings and cash flow, or as a diversification of safeguards, but also as building blocks that fit a corporation's scheme. In the merger frenzy of the late 1960s, the world seemed full of entrepreneurs who wanted to take their millions and run. Nearly a thousand acquisition leads crossed George Kelch's desk every year. Most of them, of course, he zinged into the circular file. The handful that looked promising he bucked up the line to Fitz-Gerald and McNeely. Some died right there; others fizzled in the negotiating process. Only a relative few made it to the final handshake—and all these fell into certain categories as Wickes's perception of its purposes sharpened.

The penetration of the shelter market being one of these purposes, that's where most acquisition dollars went. Behlen and Moriarty put Wickes into the farm and commercial end. The merger with two mobile home manufacturers, also in 1969, marked the corporation's entry into factory-built housing. The first building blocks for vertical structuring went into place the same year: Sequoia Forest Industries, a California manufacturer of particleboard and other wood building products, and Idapine Mills in Idaho. Subsequently this tree-to-truss positioning was strengthened with the acquisition of Oregon-Pacific Industries and Steel City Lumber Company, which added the wholesale link, and the purchase of additional building supply warehouses from Evans Products.

Going into human shelter in a big way led quite naturally to furniture. Dan Fitz-Gerald had long been intrigued by the fact that this was a "blind item," one whose manufacturing costs were a mystery to buyers, and thus could be sold—and traditionally have been—at markups far greater than those on most other consumer goods. Eventually, Wickes was to become a major furniture retailer: there was enough room for profits even if chairs, couches, and beds were marketed substantially below customary price levels. But, to start with, Wickes went

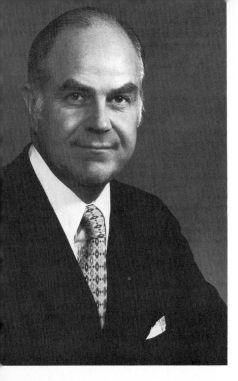

JOHN H. HEKMAN

His Lee L. Woodard operation, headquartered in Owosso, Michigan, concentrates on exquisite wrought iron furniture, as exemplified by the grouping below.

into furniture manufacturing—Colonial Products, whose built-ins and case goods dovetailed with other Wickes operations, and even before then, Lee L. Woodard Sons, Inc., a firm that made top-quality wrought iron and other casual furniture.

Woodard, a prosperous old firm headquartered in Owosso, Michigan, and with two other plants in Maxton and Salisbury, North Carolina, was acquired as a subsidiary in May 1969 for 162,000 shares of Wickes, with a market value then of $7,634,-250. The Wickes-made millionaires in this case were three aging descendants of Lyman E. Woodard I, an architect and builder who had migrated to Michigan in its pioneer days to seek his fortune. Unlike the original Wickes brothers, however, he didn't have to start from scratch. He had about $1,000 in his pocket, enough for a Shiawassee River sawmill, which happened to be for sale when he stopped overnight in Owosso on his way to Grand Rapids in 1866. He immediately began making windows, doors, caskets, dressers, and beds. Fires and tornadoes kept Woodard busy rebuilding. During one of these renovations he decided to switch from waterpower to steam, and a Wickes boiler was ordered from Saginaw.

It would be nice to report that it was still in use when Wickes acquired Woodard, but that would be fiction. By then, Lyman E. Woodard I was long dead and his company out of business. It had been liquidated during the Depression; in any event, with the depletion of Michigan's hardwood and pine, the wood-furniture boom was over in the state. Then, shortly before World War II, three grandsons of Lyman I—Joe, Russell, and Lyman—were able to repurchase part of the land and buildings, and the production of metal furniture was launched. Soon Lee L. Woodard Sons became one of the most prominent firms in its field.[15] Interestingly enough, it was Lybrand's, Dan Fitz-Gerald's old base, that passed on the word that Woodard might be ready for a merger. The three brothers had no heirs interested in running the company, and they wanted to be sure of a continuity of effective management. Lybrand's told George Valentine, a longtime Wickes financial man,[16] and Valentine told Kelch. Recalls the latter: "Well, we had been talking some about the furniture business. McNeely had some experience in it and he was kind of interested. Frankly, we were concentrating then on the home and home building industry, but as a practical matter we looked pretty hard when we came across a real moneymaker."

But almost immediately after the acquisition, Wickes ran into one of those difficult situations that are typical of mergers. It wasn't a case here of the old owners wanting to get out of the business after its sale, or, conversely, of their trying to hang on too hard. Rather, it was because the inherited Woodard middle-managers deserted in droves. Apparently, they'd been under the impression that eventually they'd get a piece of the action, and now this wasn't in the cards. To make matters worse, Russell Woodard died in September, four months after the merger, and Joe, ailing, withdrew more and more from the business until he, too, died in 1971. Only Lyman Woodard was left, and his real love wasn't management but furniture design—the best pieces in the Woodard lines are his work. For all practical purposes, the company was leaderless, making do with a series of trial bosses, until John H. Hekman, the scion of another Michigan furniture firm, was recruited as president and general manager of the subsidiary in June 1971.[17] Hekman has since been elected a vice president of The Wickes Corporation.

Like Pearson at Yorktowne, Hekman is pursuing the sale of his products through Wickes outlets. Only one of the Woodard lines, however, fits the formula here—Salisbury Craft, which is designed for the middle-income mass market. The prestige, big-ticket Woodard line of patio, outdoor, dining, and informal furniture is sold through department stores and elegant specialty shops. Despite this emphasis on luxury, Woodard did not suffer unduly during the economic downturn of 1974-1975. Earnings for fiscal 1975 were actually up 15 percent.

The same month Woodard got Wickes into furniture in a small but solid way, the acquisition of Valiant Mobile Homes put the corporation in the manufactured housing field, a most logical development—at least that's how it seemed at the time. The Valiant merger, which involved 122,000 shares with a market value of $5,810,250, was but the first step in that new direction. Three months later, in August 1969, Wickes also acquired a far bigger mobile home manufacturer, Ritz-Craft, Inc., and now was really in the business. The price was 420,320 shares, worth $19,597,420 on the day of the merger, and Walt Behlen would have become Wickes's second largest individual stockholder had it not been for the fact that Ritz-Craft's John A. Ritzenthaler, keenly aware of inheritance taxes, had shared the ownership of his controlling interest with his wife and children. The Ritzenthaler family thus received some 210,000 shares of Wickes, and his three partners in the closely held corporation—Carl Henricks, Charles Cole, and Vernon Saltsgiver—collected the other half.

John Ritzenthaler's was another American success story not unlike Walt Behlen's. He was born in Columbus, Indiana, in 1915, son of an iron molder. He graduated from high school, then worked in a chain store for eight years, starting as a stock boy and rising to assistant manager. He tried the used-car

JOHN A. RITZENTHALER

*Wickes board member
started his career hauling
travel trailers, became
prominent as a manufacturer
of mobile homes.*

business for a while, and when that didn't pan out, became a life insurance salesman. In 1942, when many small northern Indiana companies were building house trailers to satisfy the demand for temporary homes around Army and Navy bases, he took a job with an Elkhart firm that specialized in the delivery of these primitive boxes, which were so jerry-built they were usually damaged in transit. Ritzenthaler didn't mind that at all. He was paid for the towing by the mile, and made extra money sticking around afterward to repair the clobbered cargo. Having learned all about the construction of these bungalows on wheels, he knew he could do better by building them himself. He therefore gladly accepted the offer to run a new mobile home manufacturing company, the Mid-States Corp., which started its operations in the back of an old department store in Bourbon, Indiana, and finally grew into the largest manufacturer of its kind, with nine factories. Then, in 1954, Ritzenthaler quit, and went into business on his own.

His mobile homes, considerably more sophisticated, were a big success. When Ritz-Craft was merged into Wickes fifteen years later, Ritzenthaler and his partners owned two big plants in Argos, Indiana; and one each in Shamokin, Pennsylvania; Maxton, North Carolina; Sarasota, Florida; and Vivian, Louisiana. The company he had started from scratch was doing about $30 million of business a year. It was a veritable gold mine.

No wonder the acquisition looked good to Wickes, and for the best of reasons. Not only were mobiles selling like crazy in those days, but the market seemed to be changing. In ever-increasing numbers, these units were towed to their destinations not on their own wheels but on flat-bed trailers, and then put on foundations just like any other house. Often two were spliced together to make a "double-wide." Even triple-wides were not unknown. This was honest-to-goodness shelter in a new form, far more reasonable in cost per square foot than any other existing construction method could provide. With on-site building costs climbing out of reach, shelter produced on the assembly line was clearly the wave of the future. All it took was some capital infusion, intelligent design, efficient marketing, and you'd have your investment back in spades by filling a real social need.

Wickes was definitely on the right track with this assessment, but it hopped the wrong trains, and at the wrong time at that.

16

Houses on the Hoof

If Wickes often accomplished the seemingly impossible, and in a hurry at that, it was in large part due to Dan Fitz-Gerald's unwillingness to take no for an answer. Once he considered a project "doable"—a favorite word in the Wickes executive suite—it had better get done. Until he mellowed somewhat in his later years, his modus operandi was to let his staffers know that they were not indispensable. When some hapless aide told him a given objective couldn't be met, Fitz-Gerald would flash the kind of sweet Irish smile that heralds a Sunday punch. "If that's the case," he'd say most pleasantly, "maybe you'd like to recommend someone who can do it—to replace you." He wasn't kidding. No wonder he got results.

But there were times when Dan brandished his psychological shillelagh in vain, and when the perseverance so characteristic of E. L. McNeely and John Drum went for naught as well. Such was the case when, after the Ritz-Craft acquisition, Wickes rushed headlong into modular housing.

George Romney, the resuscitator of American Motors and ex-Governor of Michigan, a devout Mormon, was then Secretary of Housing and Urban Development (HUD)—and a salesman of missionary zeal, the kind who is utterly believable because he believes in what he sells. Romney was out to solve America's shelter shortage once and for all. He envisioned a brave new world in which everyone had at least adequate housing. Slums would be replaced by healthy modern cities. World War II's baby crop, rapidly maturing and founding families, wouldn't have to double up with in-laws. Quite rightly he foresaw that traditional construction methods could not fill the need at prices the nation could afford and with the speed that was required. On-site labor was getting too expensive, bad weather delayed target dates more often than not, and the flow of materials to building sites was haphazard at best. The answer, Romney knew, lay in factory assembly-line production, and he promoted that goal with all his remarkable vigor. To back up his personal persuasiveness, HUD's Operation Breakthrough, announced in early 1969, held out the carrot of the federal government's financial support to firms willing to take a swim in that murky sea. Overnight, the terms "industrial housing," "prefab construction," "sectionals," and "modular" assumed magic in corporate board rooms and on the security exchanges. Here was one of the greatest opportunities in years to participate in the country's growth. Or so it seemed.

Wickes wasn't the only company that found itself HUD-winked into trying to ride Romney's wave of the future. So did Boise Cascade, ITT, Stirling Homex, National Homes, Scholz in Toledo, Ohio, and a host of others.[1] Many drowned. Only the strongest managed to struggle back to shore. At the very least, as the old Wall Street saying has it, everybody took a bath. It wasn't that Romney's vision was invalid, but that his ideas could not be implemented on a large scale under the limitations imposed by the existing marketplace. With building codes differing all over the map, there was no way to dovetail distribution with productive capacity. You couldn't take full advantage of centralized assembly-line economies when a prefab destined, say, for a lot in Indianapolis had to meet entirely different requirements from one going to Milwaukee. Besides, to withstand the rigors of long-distance shipment, where such was possible, a modular shelter unit had to be of sturdier construction than a house built on site. This added yet another cost factor. Not until 1972 did the industry arrive at the conclusion that a modular housing plant could survive only if it fulfilled at least one of four requirements.

One was a low overhead, so that the firm's cash flow would not suffer unduly when production stopped for any reason. Another was that the plant had its own development arm to erect and market the buildings it produced. The third called for an established dealer organization in a position to sell factory-built houses. Lastly, a company might be successful if its basic output was in other lines of shelter component manufacture so that the modulars could be worked in on demand, taking up slack time on the principal production line. No firm in the business was blessed with the complete constellation of desirable characteristics. Lucky were those with just one. The Wickes operation qualified in none. But by the time the *Manufactured Housing Newsletter* summarized these criteria for success, most of its readers were already painfully aware of them. Operation Breakthrough had turned into a bust.

Yet, in the first flush of expectation, Wickes had appeared eminently qualified to participate in the modular housing effort. All the basic facilities, i.e., the mobile home plants acquired through Ritz-Craft, were in place, and essentially there was, and is, little difference between the methodologies of mobile homes and modular construction. Both products are three-dimensionals, and both call for practically the same mode of delivery. You manufacture a complete shelter unit and truck it to the site. In the case of mobiles, the unit is called a "floor," and it is usually transported on its own framing. If the customer wants a bigger home, you hook two floors together. In modulars, you build a home in sections, called "boxes," load them on flat-bed trailers, and unite them on the construction site. Of course, the mobile home comes furnished, and the

SECRETARY ROMNEY

*His utopian Operation
Breakthrough broke down
at the reality barrier.*
(Photo courtesy of the
Union-Tribune
Publishing Co.)

modular home—at least that of the past—does not. But that's
a marginal difference.

John Ritzenthaler already had leveraged this similarity for a
number of years, producing on an average of 500 modular
homes annually and selling them at a profit of about $1,000
each through contractor-dealers in Pennsylvania and New
York, all within a radius of approximately 300 miles of Ritz-
Craft's Shamokin plant. These were "scatter-lot" homes, not
intended for subdivisions. The ultimate buyer owned a plot of
land a few miles outside some urban area where codes were not
restrictive, and the Ritz-Craft modular was put on it. Ritzenthaler thus met one of the basic requirements: he was able to
integrate his modulars into his mobile home production line,
thereby incurring no additional overhead. So when Operation
Breakthrough dawned, Wickes was right in there with a fine
production facility and the know-how, and Shamokin went full
time into modular housing. Wickes then invested in an entirely
new, fully automated plant in Mason, Michigan. Recognizing
the likeness between all factory-built living units—whether

they be mobiles, modulars, or campers—the corporation set up a Manufactured Shelter and Recreational Vehicles Group under Douglas P. Crane, formerly president and general manager of Coleman Instruments, a subsidiary of Perkin-Elmer. Wickes had hired Crane in August 1969 as vice president on special assignment, and he was now promoted to senior vice-presidential rank.

At first, prospects looked promising indeed. In February 1970, Wickes was one of twenty-two firms selected by HUD to build variously priced modular models, houses as well as apartments; the latter were to be constructed by stacking modular sections as self-contained structural components. For this HUD project, Wickes joined a twelve-company consortium headed by The Keene Corporation of New York, among whose plans was an ambitious "Townland" housing system for high-rise apartments utilizing precast concrete structural frames and lightweight factory-made housing units like Wickes Modulars. It was an admirable and wholly logical concept. Townlands

ASSEMBLY-LINE HOUSE

Wickes modular homes, like this two-story model, were practical and well designed. (Bradford-LaRiviere)

would be built in the air space over shallow-water bays, shopping centers, parking lots, deteriorated factory sites, and slum dwellings. Tenants would be relocated in the completed upper stories to allow the lower levels to be demolished and redeveloped. This sort of thinking was right up Romney's alley. Of course, it never came to realization. Utopian concepts, no matter how intrinsically sound, don't fare too well in a world beset by the insolence of office and the law's delay. But unfortunately, those who build on dreams rarely recognize reality until it is too late. Caught up in the momentum of their work, they believe they're flying high when they're actually headed for a fall.

Mobile homes were selling at a good clip, as were the Monitor, Swinger, and Ace recreational vehicles manufactured by the Monitor Coach Company subsidiary, which had been acquired by Wickes in July 1969 for 84,000 shares of stock then valued at slightly more than $4 million.[2] Wickes then produced a full line of travel trailers, truck campers, motor homes, and fifth-wheel units in Wakarusa, Argos, and Elkhart, Indiana; in Alfred, Maine; and in Lethbridge, Alberta, Canada. The oil countries had not yet turned the world upside down, and the rec vehicles business was doing great.

But the Wickes Modulars built in Shamokin and Mason were up against hard times almost immediately. The most pretax profit the new Manufactured Housing Division made was $142,000 in fiscal 1970. After that everything went straight downhill. In fiscal 1971, when the Shamokin plant was converted to automated operation, and the 100,000-square-foot Mason installation went on stream, there was a loss of $224,-744. Then the bottom really dropped out. In fiscal 1972 (i.e., calendar 1971), the division plunged into the red to the tune of $3,260,000. With orders for modulars few and far between, it was necessary almost every month to run a cost analysis to see whether less money would go down the drain if the division closed the plants and ate the overhead, or if it kept the plants open and made the few boxes that were on order. Often the lines were shut down, even though suspending production meant damaging the product's image by keeping customers waiting. Clearly, something had to be done.

In retrospect, it's easy to identify the basic blunder. Instead of letting the marketplace dictate the extent of capital investment in modular production, the Manufactured Housing and Recreational Vehicles Group concentrated on building factories and buying machinery, apparently lulled by hope that the market would respond to capacity. This Pollyanna policy was set in 1970 with the decision to hire a production man rather than a marketer to head Manufactured Housing. The man who got the job was Stuart Heagy, formerly of Scholz Homes, a prefab firm famous for its technological expertise. Having committed itself to go the production route, Wickes, at least on the face of it, probably couldn't have done better than to pick someone who had been exposed to the acknowledged genius of Don Scholz. But, ironically, it was the marketing expert who had been interviewed for that very job and didn't get it to whom Wickes finally turned two years later, in 1972, to bail out the sinking operation.

Robert H. Welsh was then thirty-nine years old, slightly bulky and beginning to get bald, a whirlwind of a man so full of ideas that they come tumbling from him in torrents, like fruit from a tipped cornucopia. Welsh had been a brilliant marketer all his life. At the age of ten he sold magazines door-to-door. By the time he was fourteen he peddled cookware to housewives. He did so well that he soon formed a little company, branched out into the seasonal decoration business, and hired part-time salesmen while he devoted himself to merchandising. His organization kept expanding during the years he attended Loomis, a prep school in his native Connecticut, on a full scholarship, and later Trinity College in Hartford. In his senior year, his extracurricular enterprises netted him $19,000. Dozens of companies vied for him when he graduated. He narrowed the field to IBM, Procter & Gamble, Jones & Laughlin Steel, Bethlehem Steel, and Owens-Corning, finally choosing the last, although it was the lowest paying, because he judged its sales training program to be most up to date. His first selling job, out of New York City, was in the industrial fiber field. Home building products came next. At twenty-eight, he was a division manager. Then Welsh left Owens-Corning and in 1965 went to Atlanta as director of marketing of Kingsberry Homes, a division of Boise Cascade. This phase of Welsh's career turned out to be the most important so far as Wickes was concerned, for it was to influence the corporation's approach to manufactured housing after the modular debacle.

Kingsberry Homes, which is still going strong today, proved to be an exception in the generally dismal manufactured housing picture of the late 1960s and early 1970s. That's because it didn't try to sell boxes but made "two-dimensionals," as they are known in the trade—exterior walls with siding, interior walls as put-together studs, roof trusses, precut floor systems. The knocked-down components of Kingsberry could be jigsaw-puzzled together on site in a great variety of combinations. There were some forty basic floor plans, and several different elevations for each.

Kingsberry was selling about 1,200 homes a year when Welsh took over its sales and marketing. A few years later, it was selling 10,000, and he was soon asked to take on additional assignments at Boise Cascade. These included administering intensive care to those of Boise's European manufactured housing properties that were on the critical list, as well as starting up a whole new division for the marketing of vacation housing. Eventually Welsh got a phone call from Dick Cotton, who was then Wickes's senior vice president of personnel. Cotton admitted somewhat sheepishly how sorry he was that he hadn't had the chance to meet Welsh personally on the first go-round two years earlier, but that he very much wanted to see him now, and the sooner the better. A two-hour talk at United's Red Carpet Room in Denver followed, whereupon Welsh was invited to Saginaw to meet McNeely, Drum, and George O'Dair, and by the end of that day Wickes Manufactured Housing had a new vice president and general manager.

Heagy had resigned about a month earlier, and shortly after Welsh came aboard, Douglas Crane, the shelter group's vice president, resigned as well.[3]

To a student of The Wickes Corporation, the mess Welsh found is somewhat reminiscent of that encountered by Smith Bolton when Fitz-Gerald called on him to make sense out of the early Lumber Division. Even if a market for modulars had existed, Wickes Manufactured Housing was in no shape to deal with it anyway. Most of the staff didn't show up for work on time. The modulars produced deviated from their blueprints. Nobody kept track of inventories. The sales force had to make do with out-of-date literature. Expenditures were committed without authorization. Products were priced anywhere from 10 to 20 percent under cost.

Welsh burst into this appalling scene with his customary energy. He machine-gunned the organization with directives and made sure that they got action. After one month on the job, he had unraveled most of the administrative tangle. At the end of his first quarter, Manufactured Housing was organizationally in good shape. But that did not change the general picture. Welsh could not help but come to the conclusion that there was only one way for Wickes to go—and that was out of the modular housing business. With some misgivings, he prepared a recommendation to that effect. For all he knew he was about to talk himself into the ranks of the unemployed.

Welsh reasoned that Wickes's continued production of modulars could be justified in only one of two ways. Either the operation had to bring in substantial profits, or it had to assist the other divisions of the corporation in expanding theirs. Neither held true. Modular housing was indirectly in competition with Wickes Lumber, the corporation's most important profit center, and, to make matters worse, lost money in gobs. Wickes had invested approximately $3,320,000 in property, plant, and equipment for its manufactured housing operations. Add the operating losses, and the investment to date totaled over $7 million. How much more should Wickes pour into this bottomless pit, and in the hope of what? Might there not be a better way to approach manufactured housing?

Welsh had the answer for that, something that had occurred to him while working at Kingsberry. Builders, faced by high on-site labor costs, were always in a hurry to finish a project before their front money ran out. This created a ready market for two-dimensional components like roof trusses, floor systems, prehung doors, windows, wall panels, and gable ends. Nothing was more natural than to sell such components through the Wickes lumber and building supply centers, where some 40,000 contractors across the country already bought their 2 × 4s, plywood, shingles, and other materials. Knocked-down, panelized-structure packages for single-family and vacation houses and for garages might be sold through the same channels, and not only to builders but to advanced do-it-yourselfers as well.

Still, it was certain that giving up its modular franchise would be a bitter pill for Wickes to swallow. Its leaders were not accustomed to surrender. They knew that somewhere, somehow, there had to be a future for modular housing in some form; common sense dictated it. Besides, the corporation was rapidly approaching the billion-dollar mark in volume. Seen in this context, a start-up operating loss of a few million dollars wasn't really out of line. The news on Wall Street that Wickes was retreating might cost stockholders a good deal more. On the other hand, the investment community had become sophisticated enough to accept, and moreover to value, firms smart enough to cut their losses, especially in a business that nobody seemed able to make really go. The once-touted high-flyer Stirling Homex had filed for bankruptcy. Boise Cascade was having second thoughts. National Homes hovered near the brink. Swift Modular and Gulf Oil's Cubex had closed their doors. Fruehauf had written off $20 million in eighteen months in its effort to go into modular production. Levitt Building Systems had distinguished itself by its indecision, first announcing that it was going out of the business, then that it

was going to stay in after all, and finally going out anyway. No, by now, investors could take the Wickes news. They understood that modular housing had been the victim of an overkill in investment—a case of too much too soon, before anyone knew where the industry was headed.

Welsh first took his recommendation to close shop to his new boss, Clark Johnson, then senior vice president of Wickes Lumber, who had inherited Manufactured Housing after Crane's departure. Johnson immediately agreed. The next step was more difficult: John Drum, that most practical of all Wickes's pragmatists, turned out to be at heart no less idealistic than McNeely, in fact perhaps even more so. Letting go was hardest for him. He called a meeting for August 30, 1972, at which Welsh and Johnson would present their arguments to the corporation's executive committee—Fitz-Gerald, Mc-Neely, Drum, and O'Dair—plus George Valentine and Paul Tatz, who, as McNeely's special-assignments aide, then headed the Office of the President.

It was one of the most sobering get-togethers of Wickes executives in many years. "Sure," Welsh told his bosses, "the modular industry is a good idea. But I think it has to be localized, with the investment kept well under control. It has

HE PUT HIS TRUST
IN TRUSSES

Robert H. Welsh (right)
bailed Wickes out of the modulars
business, switched to the
manufacture of trusses and
other components that could be
trucked to site (left) and there
assembled (below) with a
minimum of expensive
on-site labor. (Portrait by Bosch,
Saginaw; industrial photos,
Wickes)

to be labor-intensive, so that in bad times you can cut your costs by letting people go. At Wickes Manufactured Housing we're technology-intense. We've always got to fight that overhead. We just can't make it that way."

Welsh and Johnson waited outside while the powers deliberated. Then John Drum came out. "Close it down," he growled, evidently disappointed. "When?" Welsh asked him. "Tomorrow," Drum said.[4]

And so Wickes's venture into modular housing ended, and a new era of manufactured housing began. Wickes Lumber already had seven small truss plants, four of them in Florida and one each in Michigan, Ohio, and Pennsylvania. These manufacturing units, until then under the control of the local center managers, now became part of Welsh's operation. So far, most of them had been losing money, and in fact were budgeted that fiscal year to drop around $100,000. Welsh was charged with turning them around and making $100,000 instead. Recovered from the blow to its pride, Wickes was its old self again. After McNeely told Welsh to net $100,000, Drum suggested that $200,000 would be better. After some further discussion with Clark Johnson, the target was set at $300,000. By the end of fiscal 1973, Welsh had attained this goal: his operating income that year came close to $400,000.[5]

The Shamokin plant was closed and eventually sold.[6] Mason is still in operation, heading a network of ten component plants that make twenty-eight different types of trusses, including 60-footers for industrial buildings. One of the plants specializes in doors.[7] Wickes Shelter Systems, as the operation is now called, is still part of Welsh's responsibility in his current position as Wickes Lumber's vice president of marketing. He projects that by 1978 or 1979, when the division is expected to gross $1 billion, around $100 million of it will be in the component field, with additional products being added every year. Shelter Systems contributes to Wickes Lumber's volume in yet another important way. It piggybacks a lot of other sales at the building supply centers. Along with every dollar's worth of trusses and components, builders buy at least $4 worth of lumber, shingles, and wallboard.

Only in Canada did Wickes continue modular production on a small scale. But here it was not a case of throwing good money after bad, but rather, a special philanthropic project of a Canadian subsidiary acquired in 1969, HaiCo Manufacturing, Ltd., of Lethbridge, Alberta.[8] HaiCo, like Wickes itself, was something of a mixed bag. Along with manufacturing and selling mobile homes and recreational vehicles, retailing farm supplies, building irrigation systems, and running a Toyota dealership, it had entered into a unique partnership, in July 1970, with the Blood Indians of southern Alberta. This committed the company to an annual contribution of $1 million for up to five years for the operation of a modular housing plant, which was built by the tribe with the help of Canadian government loans. Unlike in the United States, a good market for the output—so good that the Bloods started out with a three-year waiting list. This demand for sectional housing within a feasible delivery radius protected the operation from major losses, but wasn't enough to turn a profit, and the main accomplishment—as intended—was providing employment on the reservation.[9]

HaiCo, meanwhile, was split into two separate organizations, Behlen-Wickes Building Systems and Wickes Canada Ltd. The former, in a new plant at Brandon, Manitoba, makes Behlen grain storage tanks and steel farm buildings, and administratively is part of the Behlen Division in Columbus, Nebraska. The other organization, Wickes Canada Ltd., inherited all the original functions of HaiCo, including the manufacture and sale of recreational vehicles and mobile homes, and became part of the Wickes Homes Division, which was headquartered in Argos, Indiana, home of the John Ritzenthaler enterprises.[10]

Here, Wickes Senior Vice President Ronald J. Woods was placed in charge of what was then envisioned as one of the corporation's most promising projects: to make Wickes a leader in the mobile homes industry. This was an ambitious plan, to say the least. With its existing facilities, Wickes could turn out only 17,500 floors a year, or about 3 percent of the U.S. total. But this was only the beginning, the foot in the door. The

Wickes scenario was designed to revolutionize the whole industry from drawing board to point of sale. For the first time, a big company had recognized mobile homes for what they really were—factory-built three-dimensional shelter modules, the only form of manufactured housing that had managed to find a market, and with it a springboard for future development. Treated as such modules, mobiles could be wedded into houses that were at least as attractive as most development homes, and, like the latter, put up on their own residential lots instead of being jammed together in parks. Even so, square foot for square foot, they would be the cheapest form of shelter available.[11]

Of course, this wasn't meant to happen overnight. The mobile homes industry was sitting pretty at the time, and it's hard to budge anyone out of an easy chair. As the country's population leaped from 130 million in 1940 to 210 million in 1970, mobile home makers had been inundated by a constantly rising demand. Not surprisingly, they concentrated on production rather than marketing. With their annual growth rate of 10 to 15 percent they couldn't miss. All they had to do was to pipeline "floors" from factory to dealer. Such merchandising as manufacturers engaged in took place at the trade shows in Louisville, Dallas, Atlanta, Tulsa, Harrisburg, Tampa, and South Bend. It was all hoopla: fancy flags, straw hats and canes, magicians, and girls. Booze, broads, and ballyhoo— that's how orders were written. Hardly anyone gave a thought to the eventual buyer. There was no need to. He was stuck with the product. He couldn't afford anything else.

As a result, there was little, if any, product differentiation. Aesthetics were based on the primitive notion that rocks or bricks painted on mobiles would make them look prettier and more respectable. Dimensions were standardized, largely governed by state highway regulations. The interiors were no less cookie-mold, with the materials coming from the same sources, being processed the same way, living up to the same codes and specifications regardless of who made the mobile. The sales points were strictly exterior treatment, like curlicued eaves and look-like-something-else paint jobs, and the terms offered by the dealer. Keep in mind now that this dealer was selling into a fairly impecunious market whose main interests were low price, minimal down payment, and as many months as possible to pay. Naturally, the dealers shaved the retail price as near to cost as they could, asked for next to no cash on the barrel head, stretched the installments—and made their living on finance charges, insurance kickbacks, and manufacturers' rebates. It was the used-car business all over again.

Wickes intended to change all that, and since these changes affected everything right up to the signatures on the sales contract, the corporation decided to tackle the mobile homes pipeline vertically. Not long after the Ritz-Craft merger, it thus acquired a core of mobile home retail outlets, financing arms, and insurance companies. But more of that later.

Ron Woods had been running the Office of the President, McNeely's think-tank of bright young men, when he was reassigned to Argos, Indiana, to become the group senior vice president of what were then three separate divisions: Wickes Mobile Homes, Wickes Recreational Vehicles, and Wickes Canada. The day was April 1, 1973, and a true April Fool's Day it turned out to be.

No sooner had Woods taken over than everything went on the skids. To start with, the housing industry experienced its worst downturn in twenty-five years. It suddenly became agonizingly evident that Wickes Mobile Homes could stay afloat only so long as the mobile homes industry enjoyed its heretofore customary growth. As if this weren't enough to cope with, the recreational vehicles business collapsed as well. The oil embargo, following that fall's Arab-Israeli skirmish, made vacation trailers and motor homes anathema to the gas-pinched public. Woods found himself with 477 motor homes and more than 200 trailers on his hands, a stubborn inventory worth in excess of $5 million.

With every economic circumstance against him, including the skyrocketing cost of renting money, Woods was suddenly the most unenviable of Wickes executives. Until then, he had

enjoyed a brilliant career. Another former Lybrand's man, he had risen rapidly through a series of highly responsible positions—director of planning and administration, executive vice president of Colonial Products when it was still a Wickes subsidiary, vice president of corporate planning and development, head of the Office of the President. At the age of 37, he had attained the exalted rank of senior vice president.[12] Conceivably all this was now in jeopardy. Fitz-Gerald, McNeely, and Drum couldn't help but recognize the inexorable power play of external forces, but even a good man like Ron Woods has a tough time looking his best while being shafted by the arrows of outrageous fortune.

Luckily Woods was born for the line. He knew that, just to survive the 1973 crunch, he had to dump his inventory of recreational vehicles and make sure that he didn't get stuck with more. A quick analysis indicated that selling what he had on hand at about half-price would be, as he put it, "digestible." So he ate that 2.5-million-dollar write-off, but the danger

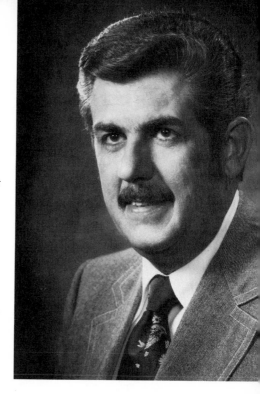

ON THE LINE

Ronald Woods, right, headed off rec vehicles rout, but prime-rate push dislodged his Wickes Homes bridgehead.

ON THE GO

Wickes RVs survived oil embargo and recession. Camper, left, is a real Swinger.

wasn't over yet. In the RV business (as with mobile homes), it is the practice to saddle manufacturers with a contractual one-year obligation to repurchase the inventory of dealers who run into financial difficulties. Thus Woods was liable to lose another big chunk in buy-backs. This prospect would have set a less self-confident man to chewing his fingernails. Given the sluggish summer sales of 1973, followed by the gas scare, Woods didn't know how much of his fire-sale inventory he might have to haul in again. Well, there wasn't much he could do about that. What he could do was to trim production to minimize potential future losses. But where do you cut—at the top of the line or at the bottom? Experienced merchandisers like Woods know the answer to that one. He cut from the bottom, limiting his lines to more expensive motor homes and truck campers, and upgraded their construction and decor. Not only do high-end goods carry a better cost-value relationship (i.e., the value you add in producing them is worth more to the customer than the value added at the low end of the

283

line), but there's another, often forgotten, fact of life. When the going gets tough, people with little money run out of it faster than people with a lot of it. In an economic downturn, Cadillacs keep selling long after Chevrolets go begging. That's how it works with discretionary purchases.

Woods closed down the Ace Travel Trailer plant in Alfred, Maine, and put it up for sale. Swinger, in Elkhart, Indiana, which had come to Wickes with the acquisition of Action Industries in 1970, he kept operating on a limited schedule. Wickes's first acquisition in the mobile homes business, Valiant, of Elkhart, Indiana, had been converted to an RV plant during the Ritzenthaler regime. Woods now reconverted it to mobile home building. Monitor, in Wakarusa, Indiana, remained the only RV production facility in full operation. By the summer of 1975, Woods was pretty well over the hump. He wasn't making a fortune on motor homes, but he wasn't going broke either. More than a year had passed since his inventory purge. From here on, the economic risk was practically nil. The prospects of profits from the operation were modest but sound enough. Should the RV industry ever see bonanza days again, Wickes would be sure to share the bounty. Meanwhile the RVs were worth keeping in the stable, but nothing to lose a night's sleep about.

But with mobile homes it was another matter. Soon after he had moved in on Argos, Woods unified Mobile Homes, Recreational Vehicles, and Wickes Canada into a single division, allowing a more effective integration of effort and more direct control. Mobile Homes was of course the biggest component, accounting for about 80 percent of the combined volume. It was equipped to generate well over $100 million a year. The relatively small RV facilities could be closed or liquidated and the write-offs taken, if somewhat shakily, in stride. But when the bottom drops out from under a 100-million-dollar business, there seems to be no end to the abyss. Smaller units of the same profit center, no matter how healthy, can't compensate for the losses. Wickes Canada's Toyotas could sell like hotcakes and so might the Canadian RVs, but you can't douse a holocaust with a soda siphon.

In 1972, the peak year of housing starts to date, mobile home manufacturers had shipped 618,000 units. By 1974, shipments were down to about 300,000. Then, in 1975, the bottom really dropped out, and production plummeted to an annualized rate of less than 200,000. Wickes Homes fared little better than the rest in this industry-wide tailspin. With his customary decisiveness, Woods closed five of his plants, slowed production at ten others, and indefinitely delayed opening a sixteenth factory that was all set to go on stream.[13] At the same time, he swung full force into his scenario. The mobile homes depression might yet turn out to be a blessing in disguise: he could revamp his production lines, make model changes, and reorganize his marketing without much risk of sacrificing sales. Then, when the business turned around again, he'd have a head start.

The key to success, Woods was convinced, lay not in a mobile's exterior, as manufacturers and dealers had always wanted to believe, but in the interior.[14] He standardized production to three basic lines, each with four price levels—the difference being in floor plans, appointments, and trim. His low-end 12 × 64-footer, fully furnished, was engineered to fall within the Federal Housing Administration's $10,000 mortgage maximum for single-wides. Similarly, his double-wide met the FHA's mortgage limitation of $15,000 for such housing. Even at that absurdly low price, considering the ballooned costs that came with inflation, Woods managed to squeeze in a host of desirable consumer appointments—a neat Yorktowne kitchen, a 14-foot frost-free refrigerator (instead of the usual 12-footer), walk-in closets, wood siding instead of aluminum skin, a house-type roof. He developed what he termed "life-style" features, modifying the same basic home to appeal to different market segments, to young marrieds, middle-marrieds, and older couples. The young marrieds got a sewing center (surveys showed that nearly 75 percent of young brides did a lot of sewing), a queen-size bed, a wet-bar option. Middle-marrieds, who are likely to have school-age kids, could buy the same mobile with a "study center" alcove. Retirees found a heat lamp in the bathroom and grab bars on the tub, and glass-enclosed bric-a-brac shelves for their knickknack collection.

Instead of a second bedroom, a hobby room was available. One 16 × 52-footer had sliding glass doors across the end and a cathedral ceiling. Once inside one of the new Wickes-made mobiles, it was hard to tell that it wasn't of conventional construction, except that the rooms were of course somewhat smaller. In the double-wides and triple-wides, there was no discernible difference. Production lines in Argos, Indiana, in Jordan, Minnesota, and in Riverside, California, turned out such to-be-spliced-together floors as parts of sectionalized homes to be erected on permanent foundations, and eligible for the same mortgages as any contractor-built house.

The Louisville Mobile Home Show is the big shindig that ushers in the industry's new model year. At the 1974 show, which came around before Woods had time to launch his new approach, Wickes had sold only 50 floors. In 1975, an even worse year for the mobile homes industry, dealer attendance was down about one-third. But Woods returned from Louisville glowing with pride. He had 228 orders for Wickes Homes in his pocket, more than any other manufacturer had been able to pull in. In May of that year, Woods invaded Detroit's Northland Mall with a display of his multifloor, sectionalized "mobile" homes. This single promotion resulted in more than sixty sales, thirty-three of them on the spot and the rest through leads.

It looked like Woods was on his way. True, Wickes Homes was still losing money in gobs, but at the manufacturing end, at least, his scenario seemed to be working out. He could now begin to tackle his next project: to develop an effective distribution system. That's where the modulars had missed out, and as a result these sectionals had ended up as custom-builts, losing their price advantage because they were produced only on order. Woods wasn't going to let this happen to his mobiles. He needed a dealer organization that could absorb inventory. To build it, he would back dealers with service and warranty commitments, with financial assistance and counseling, with support promotional programs, and with instructions on how to handle FHA. Indeed, he was going to teach dealers how to sell—how to recognize what customers really want and to sell them on the basis of these wants. None of this had ever been attempted in the mobile homes industry before.

But it wasn't going to happen at Wickes Homes either. All of Woods's perception of the market place, all of his managerial flexibility, went for naught. The industry as a whole, and Wickes Homes with it, was running against impossible odds, hobbled by high interest rates, and saddled with the unbearable weight of its own past excesses. The pipeline sales practices that Woods so deplored—the acceptance of poor credit risks, the low down payments, the disproportionately high monthly installments that had to cover insurance and financing kickbacks—all these had now come back to haunt the industry.

Hard as it was for dealers to sell mobiles into the housing slump, they couldn't make money even on what they did sell. In the earlier, prosperous years, repossessions had run about 5 percent of sales. In 1975, they jumped to around 50 percent; in other words, half of the sales made that year were offset by merchandise returned to the sellers. Worse than that, 1975's repossessions told the grim story of a depression-depressed populace. When mobile home buyers couldn't meet their monthly payments they didn't just walk out, as they used to, leaving the place in fairly decent condition. Now a substantial portion of the mobiles were left vandalized and rifled, refrigerators gone, furniture ripped out. The expense of putting these shambles back in shape averaged about a quarter of the original cost, more than the profit margin on the sale had amounted to. Service companies were forced out of business in droves as banks increasingly shied away from such credit risks. Dealer after dealer, unable to finance his inventory, his sales volume down to nearly nothing, repossessions eating up his margins, toppled over the brink of bankruptcy. It would be years before anyone could put this Humpty Dumpty together again.

Had Wickes been content with starting out gradually in the business, it might have survived those years. The corporation conceivably could have gone into manufacturing mobiles in a small way, allowing Woods to slowly play out his scenario; it could have gradually established its own financing and insurance arms, letting their volume adjust to the market; it could have based its distribution network on the Lumber Division's building supply centers. Maybe—and just maybe—such a modest approach might have worked. But in the flush of rushing toward that first billion-dollar year, and with the country's boom looking like it would go on forever, and with the absolutely correct assessment that fewer and fewer people could afford conventional housing, Wickes had gone it whole hog.

In quick succession, between November 1973 and January 1974, it had consummated the acquisitions of three mobile home service companies by means of pooling. All became wholly owned, unconsolidated subsidiaries. The first was Universal Mobile Services Corporation, a Houston-based mobile home financing and insurance organization that operated in twenty-four states.[15] Next came Western Diversified Financial, Inc., a closely held company that sold and reinsured credit life, credit accident, and health insurance through its own general agency in Chicago, and its Ram Life Insurance Company chartered in Arizona.[16] The third was American Homes Industries, of South Bend, Indiana, which engaged in financing dealer inventories of mobile homes and servicing mobile home installment contracts. This firm also provided, as agent, casualty insurance and credit life insurance to buyers of mobile homes, reinsured credit life insurance risks through a subsidiary of its own, and, on top of all this, owned thirty-five mobile home dealerships in four states.[17]

With these acquisitions, Wickes was in mobile home servicing up to its neck—a business that no one at Wickes really knew much about. Wickes had hoped to import specialized leadership along with the properties, but this didn't pan out in every case.[18] William R. Peterson, who had built Universal Mobile Services, decided he had worked long and hard enough; he stayed on as president of the subsidiary only briefly, then retired to Arizona. This was bad enough, but not the worst of it.

The money flow in paper-shuffling organizations like Universal Mobile has always been complicated at best, if not outright nebulous, and there was a far greater chance that some negative aspects of the operation—outstanding tax obligations that were unknown even to the owners, for example— would not be reflected in the balance sheet. Prior to the acquisition, Hyman J. Lee, Jr., one of the Wickes general attorneys in Art Kirchheimer's legal department,[19] had computed for how long Wickes might get hurt by such potential obligations, and how much they could conceivably cost the company.[20] Having studied statistics at San Diego State before he took his law degree at Harvard, Lee was right in his element with such calculations. In a legal hassle that lasted six months, he worked out an agreement under which the original owners of Universal would be liable, on a decreasing scale, for six years for any claims of that sort. It was a brilliant legal construction—but of course it protected Wickes only against unwittingly inherited obligations, not those that it had knowingly bought as part of the acquisitions package.

As the housing slump deepened, and mobile home repossessions mounted, and Universal-held paper turned worthless by the ream, Wickes could do nothing but pay and pay. For a long time, indeed, the corporation didn't even know how much cash was flushing down the Universal drain. Even at the subsidiary's headquarters in Houston, they had a hard time figuring it out. The situation was so confused that the precise amount of the operation's substantial losses was still in doubt even on the deadline day for the Wickes fiscal 1975 report.

McNeely, whose almost invariably cheerful demeanor masks a multitude of pressing concerns, had sensed that a serious storm was brewing already two months earlier, in January of calendar 1975. He was beginning to have doubts about the whole mobile homes operation, and its financial aspects in particular, and he had assigned Art Nasso, one of Wickes's ablest young troubleshooters, to steer the service companies through the troubled seas that swelled ahead. In March, when the true extent of Universal's difficulties was at last revealed, Nasso moved to Houston to deal directly with that mess. He found Universal a company of numerous bits and pieces, each intent on running its own show. Nasso closed two of the regional offices, then centralized the operation, unifying all its scattered accounting, banking, and credit activities in one system. This not only established a central management control heretofore lacking, but saved on manpower—always an important consideration but never more so than when a business wallows in red ink. Within a few weeks, he had subdued the free-for-all and shaped it into an efficiently functioning organization. But that, in effect, was all he could do.

He could not turn the country's economy around, force unemployed mobile home owners to meet their monthly payments, or lower the prime rate. When Wickes had first ventured into the mobile homes business, the prime rate had hovered around 7 percent. This left room for a small profit on mobile home loans even in states like Missouri whose usury law limits the interest rate on such transactions to 8 percent. But now the prime rate had soared to 11 percent, 11½ percent, and even 12 percent in some places, putting the effective cost of money close to 15 percent, about two to three points higher than the interest you could charge on mobile home loans in most states. The situation actually was such that the more mobile homes Wickes sold and financed through Universal, the more money it lost. American Homes Industries was of course similarly affected. Only Western Diversified Services and the Coronado Life Insurance Company, offspring of its original Ram Life Insurance Company, whose fortunes were not wholly dependent on the mobile homes industry, were more or less immune to the malaise. Deep inside him, McNeely couldn't help but shudder when he thought of the enthusiasm with which the financial service companies had been welcomed into the Wickes fold just a year and a half earlier. As a result of these acquisitions, he now faced the toughest decision of his career.

The recession had cut into the net of nearly every division. Earnings were down and likely to remain low for the rest of the year. But overall, the corporation itself was making money— and here the mobiles were gobbling it all up, almost as fast as it came in.

Unlike some other companies, Wickes had always made it a point to pay dividends. The majority of its shareholders, many of them dating back to the corporation's Saginaw origins, counted on this income. They were investors rather than speculators: they hadn't gotten into Wickes just for quick capital gains. Despite the corporation's phenomenal growth, its common equity had never found its way into many glamour-stock portfolios.

When George Valentine, the assistant controller, got done with his quarterly chore of computing the corporation's earnings that July of 1975, he came up with an after-tax profit of 2 cents per share for the first half of Wickes's 1976 fiscal year. Without the drag of the mobile homes operations, the earnings would have been ample to cover the dividends, and then some.

GEORGE VALENTINE

True to his Scottish origin, Dumbarton-born Valentine has been keeping track of the Wickes finances since 1947.

But as matters stood, the corporation would have to dip into its reserves to maintain the quarterly dividends of 25 cents a share. In effect it would have to borrow money from itself, or put another way, indirectly borrow the money from its shareholders in order to pay them. Governments engage in this sort of practice regularly, and we've all found out to our dismay what happens as a result. But governments can get away with it for a while by printing money. This, a corporation can't do, and wouldn't want to: it must protect the equity of its owners. Wickes had declared its usual dividend in July 1975, but there couldn't be a next time. If any dividend was declared at all, it would have to be in kind, i.e., in a proportionate amount of stock, and this indeed was done. The corporation had to get back on a sound financial footing before any cash was paid again. If there was a real possibility of the mobile homes business turning around fast enough, not necessarily in this very next quarter but within a reasonable period, certain allowances could be made. If real progress could be shown, stock dividends instead of cash would be acceptable for a while. If not, getting out of mobiles was the only solution.

The crucial question was what happened to the prime rate. Would it stay up? Would it come down? And if it came down, would it come down far enough to make a difference? Not a week passed that summer and early autumn when McNeely didn't consult with the corporation's bankers and other financial advisers, and every week their concensus was the same: if the prime rate came down it wouldn't come down very far. With massive government spending and the concomitant monumental government borrowings, interest rates were bound to remain high. Only a total collapse of the economy could bring back the rates of yesterday, and if such an unthinkable disaster occurred, everybody, including Wickes, would be broke anyway; so this was nothing to base one's planning on.

McNeely postponed the showdown as long as he could. Quite understandably, he didn't want to get burned making the wrong decision. His top financial officer, David J. Primuth, told him Wickes had better get out of the business, and fast.[21]

John Drum, of iron will as always, felt that he and Woods could certainly make the manufacturing end go. These were agonizing meetings. All three men were convinced that Wickes had been absolutely right in principle, if not necessarily in timing and choice of acquisitions, to get into the mobiles business. The Ron Woods scenario made eminent sense. To retreat from such an important objective was totally against their personal philosophy and that of the corporation.

For one last time, McNeely summoned Woods and Nasso to San Diego in October. What were their estimates as seen from the front line? It wasn't a long meeting. There wasn't much to say. Woods smiled a little sadly, knowing what was in the wind. His outfit was jelling; there was real faith in the future now at Wickes Homes. "I guess we'll lose about 5 million dollars this year on an operating income basis," he said, "but next year, if we're as good as we all think we are, we'll break even. After that?" and he shrugged his massive shoulders. Nasso, who didn't have Woods's attachment to the mobile homes business was harsher. To 37-year-old Nasso, a financial man by inclination, training, and experience, it was all a matter of dollars and cents, a cold-turkey decision.[22] "We're never going to make any money in this business," he said, a trace of his native Brooklyn still in his speech. "We'll probably drop about 15 million this year, 10 million the next, and 5 million the year after that, and somewhere, way out there, we might break even. But I don't think I'll live that long."

McNeely needed to hear no more. With such negative reports from two of his most trusted lieutenants, there was no point in going on. True, Woods hadn't been pessimistic about the long-range prospects of his operation, but if 1976 turned out to be an up-beat year, as everybody seemed to expect, then breaking even wasn't good enough. Even John Drum, albeit reluctantly, agreed that it was time to shut the shop and bite the bullet.

With some trepidation, McNeely called a special directors meeting for October 28. It wasn't that he expected an uprising. But there, in one of the chairs, sat John Ritzenthaler who had

ERECTOR-SET HOUSE

So far only marketed as "vacation homes," small houses completely built of Wickes components may turn out to be one answer to high on-site construction costs. An advanced do-it-yourselfer can put this one together without undue difficulty. (Photo by Milo V. Stewart)

made such a big success out of mobile homes, and whose original property was about to be put on the block. McNeely wouldn't have been surprised if that outspoken Hoosier had said something like, "You damn fools, you don't know how to run it." But nothing of the sort happened. Quite the contrary. Ritzenthaler was the first to support McNeely's recommendation that Wickes rid itself of all its mobile home operations. The motion, unanimously approved, called for an "orderly divestment," meaning that Wickes would continue to run the properties until buyers could be found.

This didn't take very long. Offers came in rapidly, particularly for the manufacturing plants. Despite its recent losses,

Wickes Homes had, as one industry observer put it, "kicked a lot of butts," and several competitors eagerly submitted bids for the factories whose products had caused such a stir. In short order, Wickes also divested itself of the Universal Mobile and American Homes Industries subsidiaries. By year's end, for all practical purposes, Wickes was out of the mobiles business.

The corporation had taken its balance sheet licking on the discontinued operations to the tune of $7,608,000. A reserve of $17.4 million had been set aside for after-tax losses following the disposal of the properties. The per-share loss for the first thirty-nine weeks of fiscal 1976 came to $1.86, including this reserve.[23] The financial hurdle had been vaulted. The books were clean. Nobody exulted, but everybody sighed with relief. Wickes had weathered its only really big failure.

With the dismantling of the Wickes Homes Division, Woods returned to San Diego headquarters, where he is now in charge of all corporate planning and research. Wickes Recreational Vehicles is a separate division once again: Woods' strategy had paid off, not only in averting imminent disaster but in turning that business around so that it's making good money again. The manager of the reborn division is L. J. Dawson, and along with Hal Pearson, who runs Yorktowne, he reports to Senior Vice President Clark Johnson.

Meanwhile, Wickes is by no means to be counted out as a contender in the manufactured housing arena. Since 1972, when Bob Welsh put the company into the building component business, that operation has grown by leaps and bounds. Its lines now include low-priced prefabricated knock-down garages and one- and two-story vacation homes that are sold through the Lumber Division's building supply centers. Make some modifications in the designs of the knock-downs, build them a little bigger, take advantage of the same efficient marketing system—who says this won't be done when the time is right? Wickes's houses on the hoof may have galloped off, but that doesn't mean that they won't be roped in again.

17

Everything but
the Squeal

" **A** sawmill is a poorly arranged collection of inadequate and obsolete machinery used to convert logs into sawdust and slabs. It is constantly submerged in a series of cataclysmic disasters of fluctuating intensity. Owned by one or more optimistic idiots, it is operated under a thin guise of respectability known as 'Lumber Company.'"

So wrote an anonymous humorist some years ago, and he wasn't far from wrong. You got yourself a little piece of timber, and before you knew it you had a sawmill, and you were doing just dandy until you ran out of either timber or buyers. That last part is still true today. The lumber business is one of great ups and downs, more drastic even than housing's, since it's subject not only to the vagaries of building cycles, but to those of other markets as well. Paper, for instance. When the economy is bad and housing plummets, lumber goes begging. At the same time, newspapers slim down for lack of ads, shippers with less to ship use fewer cartons, office managers clamp down on paper waste, and as a result, there's little demand for the wood chips needed to make pulp. When that happens, a lot of sawmills that haven't already shut down because they can't get rid of their construction lumber now call it quits because, without selling wood chips, they can't make it at all. So suddenly there's a paradoxical shortage of 2 x 4s, and their price shoots up. On the futures market, anyway. But still nobody wants the construction lumber, and you're in for another dive. All you can be sure of is uncertainty. That, and of getting kicked in the pants every so often, especially when you think you're sitting pretty. Rich today, poor tomorrow. Rare is the operator who hasn't had his share of disasters.

One of those who didn't was the late Gus Luellwitz, a big, husky guy nearly as strong as Paul Bunyan and no Babe the Blue Ox in the brains department either. With his unusual name, a lot of people thought he was Jewish, an idea he didn't discourage. Maybe he even promoted it to get Sam Goldwyn's business. In Hollywood's prime, Metro-Goldwyn-Mayer built lavish sets and almost always burned them down after the shooting. Luellwitz sold MGM its lumber.

He'd gone into the forests at the age of sixteen and had made one fortune after another. Every log he touched seemed to turn to gold, or—as lumbermen would put it—to "a deep clear." In 1936, he partnered up with a fellow by the name of E. P. Ivory, and they purchased a mill in Oregon that cut about 15 to 17 million board feet a year until the timber supply in that area dwindled. Then in 1948 they bought into a stand of more than a billion feet of sugar pine, white fir, and ponderosa pine in the Sequoia National Forest, and sank $400,000 into a highly sophisticated sawmill in Dinuba, a small, sun-drenched town in central California's Tulare County. This was the beginning of Sequoia Forest Industries—now Wickes Forest Industries—which the corporation acquired in 1969.

Gus Luellwitz was close to ninety when Thomas Jefferson Hedrick, known as "T.J." in the tree trade, went to work for him in 1960. Hedrick's job didn't seem to have much future to it. He'd been hired specifically to liquidate a millwork factory, the Continental Moulding Company, which fell into Luell-witz's lap when it couldn't pay what it owed him. Hedrick, who at forty-eight had years of experience behind him in most phases of the lumber business, including millwork, soon real-ized that if Continental were managed properly it could make lots of money.[1] There was only one place to get front money to make more money, and that was old Gus, whom Hedrick had heard much about but had never seen.

The lumber business always has been extremely informal. Even today, million-dollar deals are made on a nod, a hand-shake, and a smile. Hedrick phoned Luellwitz. The latter cut short Hedrick's explanation. "Meet me on the San Bernardino Freeway in an hour," he said, and hung up. Hedrick was in a quandary. It was his first time in Los Angeles, but he did know that the San Bernardino ran on for miles and miles. He quickly called Grant Potter, who was managing Sequoia for Luellwitz out of the company's sawmill in Dinuba. Potter laughed, and

BEGINNINGS IN THE WESTERN BOONDOCKS

Scenes like this were familiar to young Gus Luellwitz when he first headed into the woods. His operations formed the core of today's Wickes Forest Industries.

explained to Hedrick how to get to a particular point where the freeway widened, and told him to park there. Sooner or later, Luellwitz would come by in his limousine and pick him up.

Sure enough, the chauffeured limousine arrived, and Hedrick got in. He still had no idea what it was all about. Gus wasn't grumpy, just silent. Hedrick didn't know then that the old man was deaf and didn't like to talk. At last the car drew up at the Union Bank of Los Angeles. Luellwitz gave his briefcase and hat to the doorman, and said, "Take this gentleman to Mr. Dansby," and stalked off. Frank Dansby, it turned out, was the bank's vice president, and he didn't know what this visit was all about either. So he and Hedrick passed the time of day until at last Luellwitz joined them (after a brief old-buddy visit with the bank's president), and without any preamble demanded of Hedrick, "How much do you need to run that business?" Hedrick, stunned, thought for a minute. He guessed about $125,000 for starters. "OK, Frank," Luellwitz said to Dansby, "put it in his account." Then something yet more amazing happened. Dansby, the lender, asked Luellwitz, the borrower, how much interest he wanted to pay. "I think we ought to be fair," the old lumberman said. "Let's make it 5½ percent." With that he got up, informed Hedrick that he was going to get a rubdown at the Jonathan Club across the street, and to have the chauffeur take him back to his car. Hedrick, more puzzled than ever, asked Dansby since when borrowers had started setting their own interest rates on loans. "Oh," said Dansby, "Mr. Luellwitz practically owns the bank."

It wasn't long before T.J. had turned Continental around, making Luellwitz richer still. In fact, after only a few months, Continental was doing so well that the old millwork plant ran out of capacity. Hedrick found a likely 22 acres way out in what were then the boondocks of Orange County (since booming due to the proximity of Disneyland), bought it from the Southern Pacific, and, being a jack-of-all-trades, planned the layout of the buildings and designed them himself. When he presented the blueprints to Gus Luellwitz and Grant Potter for approval, the former rolled them up without looking at them and pushed them aside. "Sonny," he said to middle-aged T.J., "you build what you want to build. But there's one thing I want you to do. I want you to paint it all kinds of colors. Because these old lumbermen will say, 'I'll be damned, look what that old son of a bitch did.'"

And so Gus Luellwitz, who died in 1963 soon after the new plant was completed, left his personal imprint on the lumber business: a mill complex glowing with delicate pinks, blues, greens, and yellows, the first such installation that was painted anything but barn red, if painted at all.

Pastel exteriors are still the hallmark of Wickes Forest Industries facilities, of which Hedrick, now a corporate vice president, is general manager. Like Luellwitz, Hedrick seems to have an innate talent for taking the temper tantrums of the lumber business in his stride without ever missing a step. While economists all over the world were hollering timber and timbermen were getting clobbered by the economy, Hedrick stood up at the annual Wickes Management Conference in January 1975, and, in a deep, matter-of-fact drone still slightly tinged with the twang of his native Missouri, reported that while calendar 1974 hadn't been Wickes Forest Industries' best year, at least it was its second-best. He appeared almost to regret that the big year of 1973, in which Forest Industries chalked up a pretax profit of $15 million on a $65-million volume, had set such an impressive precedent for his division. All he could show this time around was a pretax profit of $7.5 million on a volume of $49 million. The fact that other lumbermen were only dreaming of 15 percent profits didn't console him much.

One of the reasons for the division's amazing successes is Hedrick's ability to look coldly at any situation without getting sidetracked by marginal factors that would confuse a more if-and-but mind. Wickes Forest Industries produces about 200 million board feet of dry lumber a year. During the housing doldrums, there were always a few freight cars of 2 × 4s left over that were not committed. Hedrick would gauge the tempestuous futures market and sell into it every time it ran up enough for him to make a profit. If the market chanced to stay

T. J. OF THE TREE TRADE

Thomas J. Hedrick, boss of Wickes Forest Industries, is a woodsman from way back, pursues program of full log utilization with great success.

up, he was ready to deliver on his short. If it dropped again, as usually happened, he bought the contracts back, leaving him that much more lumber to sell into the next high. With that kind of hedging he couldn't lose. But, as in Wickes Agriculture, the futures method of protecting the division's posture in the marketplace is merely ancillary to the basic mission. At Wickes Forest Industries, that basic mission is the manufacture of a multitude of timber products—and that's where Hedrick's organization benefited immensely from Luellwitz's legacy of a company that knew how to squeeze every last drop of sap out of a tree.

Shortly after the original 41-acre facility—since then grown to cover 100 acres—had been built on the northern outskirts of Dinuba, a *Fresno Bee* reporter commented that the Ivory Pine Company, as it was then known, "will do better than meat packers who use everything in the pig except the squeal. Someday even the bark will be used by this timber company."

The reporter's prediction came true much sooner than "someday." In 1951, a subsidiary company, Dinuba Planing Mill, Inc., was organized by Luellwitz and Ivory, and its $180,-000 plant leased to Ivory Pine. When both the lumber and planing mills had gained enough operating momentum, a research program, supervised by Peter Fields and J. D. Bolle, undertook to achieve commercial utilization of all bark and scrap-lumber residues. Two successful products of bark compost were developed almost immediately: Forest Humus, a general soil conditioner that sold in great volume—and of course also did very well in the mid-1970s as farm production followed rising food prices; and Orchid Bark, a coarser product of less commercial significance that found considerable following, however, among the cymbidium orchid growers throughout California.

This was but the beginning of full log utilization as envisioned by Grant Potter, who had become president and chairman of the company on Luellwitz's death, and as practiced today by Wickes Forest Industries, whose technology makes it possible to convert all but a fraction of 1 percent of any given log to some constructive and profitable purpose. Remember those beehive-shaped furnaces that used to puff away at every sawmill? They still exist, and when blue smoke curls from their chimneys, you know that more than one-third of any log brought in from the woods is being wasted, for only about 50 percent by volume is of the quality to end up as finished lumber. True, as previously mentioned, there is a market for wood chips. But that still leaves a lot of residue, and lucky is the sawmill that's close enough to a Wickes installation so the leftovers can be sold for further processing. Indeed, between the residues of his own operations and those bought from outside sources, Hedrick's sales of bark, sawdust, slab, edging, and trim have developed astounding proportions. The bark business alone has reached an annual volume of around 400,-000 cubic yards, including by now not only Forest Humus, Orchid Bark, and other growing mediums and planting mixes,[2] but also a specialty product known as Decorative Pebble Bark—bark chunks of various graded sizes that provide an attractive ground cover for anything from flower beds to playgrounds.[3]

Then there is wood flour, the softest, most powdery of the residues, which serves as an absorbent and filler in roofing felts; grape-packing sawdust, which is dried, screened, and grated for cushioning grapes bagged for export shipment; industrial sawdust, which is used as an oil-filtering medium in diesel engines; lath (also called carstrips) that can be used in a variety of ways, including snow fencing; processed shavings, which are sold as poultry litter and as bedding for cattle and horses; and a specially screened sawdust that has proven itself an effective absorbent on butcher shop and slaughterhouse floors. All that plus wood chips for pulp manufacture, of which Wickes markets the impressive amount of some 7 million cubic feet a year.[4] In total the residue business now accounts for revenues in excess of $3 million a year.

Important as it was to develop a production system that lets leftovers help pay the freight, Grant Potter's greatest contribution was to integrate a particleboard plant in the operation.

SERVING IT UP ON THE CHOWCHILLA LINE

Mill scrap goes in, particleboard comes out of the Sequoiaboard plant of Wickes Forest Industries near Chowchilla, California. In one year, this plant makes enough of that sturdy construction material to roof a few Manhattans and then some.

Particleboard is, in effect, an engineered wood product whose basic component is any and all mill scrap except for that tiny amount that's inevitably contaminated by metal and other foreign matter. Mixed with liquid glue as a binder, it is heat-cured in a 500-pound-per-square-inch press into panels that possess more dimensional stability than regular wood, and offer considerably more warp resistance. There is an immense market for this product: as walling, sheathing, roof and floor underlayment in conventional construction as well as in manufactured housing, for particleboard is truly a ready-made, two-dimensional component. Moreover, it is an excellent core-material substitute for solid or edge-glued lumber in furniture panels and flush doors, making it possible to produce quality surfaces that can be finished to a high gloss, since there is no danger of sunken joints, particleboard being all of one piece. Thus, although it is essentially a by-product in the sense that it is made of residues, particleboard is a major building material in its own right, and its manufacture is an industry of no mean proportions.

The Sequoiaboard plant (or *Wixwand*, i.e., Wickes Wall, as particleboard is identified at the corporation's building supply outlets in continental Europe) is an automated 5-million-dollar wonder that was built on a 59-acre site west of Chowchilla, California, shortly after Sequoia's acquisition by Wickes, and has now been in operation for more than five years, often on a seven-day, around-the-clock schedule. Its annual capacity totals some 30 million board feet—the equivalent of nearly 110 square miles of paneling. The plant's press, especially constructed by Bahre Bison, of Springe, Germany, is the largest of its kind. It produces 8½- by 45-foot sheets, which may range in thickness from ⅜ to 1½ inches. The operation is so efficient that it even utilizes its own residues. Not only is the trim from every stage of the processing fed back into the mix, but sawdust helps fuel the natural gas-fired oven that heats the particleboard compound as it goes into the press.[5] The resultant utility-bill saving comes to 15 percent.

There is some indication that if it hadn't been for Grant Potter's plan to build such an ambitious installation, Wickes might never have gotten a crack at acquiring Sequoia. Ever since Luellwitz and Ivory joined forces, the enterprise had been closely held, and, like many such tight organizations, it faced the future with some trepidation, for it was beginning to run out of steam. Soon after Potter had taken over, he embarked on a coordinated program of expansion. To start with, in a capital-consolidating move, Ivory Pine had purchased the assets of Dinuba Planing Mill, Inc., and the Klamath Equipment Company; the latter was also an Ivory-Luellwitz partnership, which operated the logging, trucking, and special products manufacture of Ivory Pine. Potter then went on to acquire Southern California Lumber Sales, a wholesale distribution yard in Monrovia.

In 1961, Luellwitz bought out the Ivory interests, and the name of the company was subsequently changed to Sequoia

Forest Industries, Inc., which also embraced the Continental Moulding firm, then going full blast under T. J. Hedrick's stewardship. Diversification into other wood-related enterprises soon followed. Sequoia's first major acquisition was that of Emmert Forest Products, of Clovis, California, in late 1963. United Plywood Distributors, of Fremont, was brought into the organization the following year, and in 1967 Sequoia bought the California Reel Company, located in Lindsay, a manufacturer of those big wooden spools on which cables are coiled. To accommodate Sequoia's increasing need for raw material, Kings River Pine, Inc., a lumber mill in Auberry, California, was absorbed at about the same time.

Thus matters stood as the 1960s drew to a close. In his decade at the helm, Potter had steered Sequoia through a period of remarkable growth. Annual sales were up to around $14 million, and while raising capital for additional expansion was not a problem as such, what with the Union Bank of Los Angeles closely tied to the enterprise ever since Luellwitz's day, Sequoia lacked the wherewithal for the quantum jump it must now take to become a truly big business. Millions would be needed to get a particleboard plant on stream, and more millions for the timber resources required to feed Sequoia's wood-gobbling manufacturing facilities, for it is neither cheap nor easy to obtain rights to forest lands. For all practical purposes, buying privately owned timber is out of the question; there isn't as much of it as most people would think, and what there is goes at sky-high prices. If you want to do any logging without going broke in the process, you are committed to lease lands from the U.S. Forest Service, which allocates allowable cuts on a bid basis. To make sure that no more timber is cut than grows, the quantity that becomes available each year is fairly limited, and if you need more wood than you can get hold of in this manner, you must acquire existing rights; that is, you have to buy out sawmill operations with prior claims to timber lands.

In short, Sequoia found itself on that familiar merry-go-round of expanding within a framework of total vertical integration. To utilize residues, it had to have a plenitude of timber; thus, to fully realize its manufacturing potential, it had to grow proportionately at the level of raw material production. No longer could either end be tackled in bits and pieces. Both had to be attacked at the same time. But this wasn't the only problem.

Like so many mushrooming entrepreneurial companies, Sequoia was dangerously thin in management: the bigger you get, the more good people you need, lest your bonanza turn into an insufferable burden. Potter, Hedrick, and a couple of other prime movers couldn't be everywhere at the same time.[6] There was also a more personal problem that's characteristic of closely held corporations. Sequoia had nearly 100 shareholders, but most of the stock was in the hands of Luellwitz's aging widow, and of Potter, Hedrick, and Bert Dennis, the company's long-time sales director. Without Sequoia's securities being routinely traded on the open market, there was no way to determine a value base for negotiability. If anything were to happen to any of the principals, none of whom was exactly a youngster anymore, the company as well as the deceased's estate would be beset by overwhelming legal and tax difficulties. Going public was one way to get out of this particular pickle, but an intelligent merger would solve everything.

Now it so happened that just about then, back in Saginaw, Fitz-Gerald, McNeely, and Drum had come to the conclusion that Wickes should be in lumber all the way from tree to finished product. The corporation was then about to go into the mobile home business, manufactured housing loomed on the horizon, and above all else, the Lumber Division had become firmly established as the biggest retailer of its kind. But Wickes had no intention of merely picking up a few sawmills here and there. To cross the river into the trees, Wickes needed a woodsman who knew them from the stump up— someone like Grant Potter.

The introductions were performed by William Shannon, one of the Sequoia directors, and in January 1969, after some fairly stubborn negotiations, for Potter was not a man to settle for 50 cents when he could get a dollar, the acquisition was accomplished. The pooling involved 207,060 shares of Wickes, then worth $10,353,000. Preceding the Behlen acquisition by two months, it was the corporation's biggest merger up until that time, exceeding by more than $1 million in market value the 1964 deal with Ross Builders Supplies. Before the year was out, nearly another $10 million had been committed to Sequoia's expansion—the Chowchilla particleboard plant whose construction was started that December, and the purchase of Idapine Mills for $3,645,000 worth of Wickes shares the same month: this was the required two-legged leap, for Idapine Mills was a sawmill operation with cutting rights to large stands of timber in Idaho. Wickes couldn't have chosen a better moment to make this sizable investment in its return to the forest, the erstwhile domain of the original Wickes brothers, Henry Dunn and Edward Noyes Wickes. Not that Fitz-Gerald's or McNeely's mind meandered along such sentimental channels, at least during business hours. What mattered was that, once again, here was a chance to harvest green gold: with lumber prices on the rise, Wickes earned back its total Forest Industries investment within three years.

Grant Potter, the woodsman Wickes had counted on, paved the way for this success, but he lived barely long enough to see it. He died in October 1972 of cancer at the age of fifty-two, but at least he'd realized his dream of a full-utilization operation, for by that time Chowchilla was in high gear, Sequoia's sales had more than tripled to $50 million, and the company he had built had grown into one of the bigger lumber producers in the country: some 200 million board feet that year. Potter's death was a grievous loss to the corporation, but luckily T. J. Hedrick was available to step up from Continental Moulding, and at the millwork plant Roger Marsh was ready to take Hedrick's place in turn. There was now good backup for management at all levels.

Meanwhile, expansion had continued. Additional sawmills in Idaho were purchased in August 1970 from Idaho Western, primarily to take over its timber leases, and Wickes logging in that state increased dramatically from 79 million board feet to 130 million in 1974. At Grangeville, the home of Idapine, where all Idaho operations are now headquartered, an additional $3.5 million was invested in improvements that included several double-track dry kilns, a debarker system, a new sawmill, and a unique small-log stud mill.[7] One of the three installations at Grangeville is a "chip and sawmill," a new concept for sawing the log and at the same time chipping the side pieces off into separate bins for transfer to pulp operations—another forward step in the division's full log utilization program. To increase production of reels and pallets—boards of less than structural-lumber quality used primarily for loading materials by lift truck—a second reel assembly plant, the Foster Manufacturing Co. of Lodi, California, was purchased in 1972.[8]

With Wickes Forest Industries' combined capacity for cutting and processing somewhere between 270 and 300 million board feet per year, the division is in a position to supply almost two-thirds of the wood-product needs of other Wickes operations. This does not actually happen, of course, since geography dictates local pricing. Forest Industries is more likely to be competitive in the West, while Wickes Lumber and other Wickes divisions in the Midwest can get better deals from sawmills in the closer South. But it's a distinct comfort to have Forest Industries in the family in the event that shortages limit outside purchasing. At present, intracompany sales by this division total only about 7 percent of its volume. This figure, however, is bound to increase in the future as more and more of the output is channeled through those recent Wickes acquisitions that forged the corporation's final link on the route from tree to truss, namely Oregon-Pacific and its chain of Sequoia Supply, Inc., warehouses.

Clark Johnson, then the Lumber Division's general manager, had hailed Oregon-Pacific aboard Wickes in 1972. It will be recalled that Johnson had spent practically his whole life in the lumber business, working in various marketing capacities with a host of prominent firms that included Edward Hines

Lumber and Evans Products. While at Hines, he had become acquainted with Les Hagen and Darrell Robinson, formerly college fraternity buddies and fellow football players who looked enough alike to be mistaken for brothers. At that time in the mid-1950s, they were going through the Hines sales training program preparatory to being sent into the field. Both Hagen, who in late 1974 succeeded Johnson as Lumber's boss, and his friend eventually had quit Hines to join a Portland company, then known as Oregon-Pacific Forest Products. They started as lumber traders—specialists in buying lumber from the mills and selling it to retail dealers.[9] When the two young men went with Oregon-Pacific, it was a brokerage-type operation that coordinated the shipments of carloads of lumber and plywood from the sources in the Pacific Northwest to wherever retailers were in need of such goods. By 1964, Darrell Robinson had become Oregon-Pacific's general manager and Les Hagen its sales manager. They pushed Oregon-Pacific's volume to 37 million a year, but as time passed they felt that the company, if constituted differently, could perform far better than that—especially if they could run it in their own way, without the constraints inevitably felt by even the most trusted employees. What they wanted to do was to wholesale the complete range of bulk building materials, not only lumber and plywood, but also everything from ceiling tiles and roofing to nails, doors, and windows. This involved considerable risk but had immense potential. The answer was to buy the outfit.

Oregon-Pacific's principal, Jack Saltzman, tired by then of the hustle of telephone wholesaling and well-fixed for life in any case, was not averse to their idea, and in fact made it easy for them to take over the company. The transaction involved no exchange of cash. Saltzman took $275,000 worth of preferred stock which Robinson and Hagen agreed to redeem over a period of seven years. This $275,000, however, although it actually constituted a debt, was considered part of equity, and therefore enabled Robinson and Hagen to borrow against it. That was the crux of the deal, for, in the wholesale business, the receivables are insured and the assets are so liquid that equity exercises tremendous leverage. The result was another one of those Horatio Alger stories. The bank loaned the two men about $2.5 million and, although they each had only about $10,000 in the business, they now controlled a multi-million-dollar company.

As soon as the opportunity presented itself, they changed the setup by adding warehouse distribution to their brokerage service. Less than a year passed before, in October 1968, they used the money they'd borrowed to buy out M. Trumbo, an Oregon wholesale building materials company which had three warehouses, one at its Portland base, another in Eugene, and one in Salem, and which was doing $3.5 million in sales. Robinson and Hagen shut down the two branch warehouses, and by 1971 were doing $11 million out of Portland alone. Together with its brokerage operation, Oregon-Pacific had now reached a volume of $50 million. How did they accomplish that dramatic rise in warehouse sales? The answer is really very simple. Like most such businesses, Trumbo had run a traditional warehouse operation which required dealers to come to the warehouses to pick up their goods. This was an inconvenience, since retailers prefer to spend their time selling. But more than that, it was just as easy for them to go shopping at some other warehouse. Only by buying a fleet of trucks and guaranteeing immediate delivery could Robinson and Hagen be sure of building a real following, and that's what they did.

Moreover, unlike other warehouse operations, Oregon-Pacific stuck to its commitment only to sell to dealers. The company did not compete for the contractor business of its customers. Not surprisingly, the firm soon became the leading bulk building material wholesaler in the Portland market. This had a secondary, no less salutary, effect, for with Oregon-Pacific's big volume it could preempt the output of a number of sawmills and thus in effect serve as their sales organization. The firm, by providing a needed service, had achieved the ideal position of being practically indispensable not only to its customers but also to several of its major suppliers. For instance, it handled the total production, something like 100 million board feet a year, of Olympic Forest Products, in northern Oregon, and of Gram Lumber, a stud operation in Kalama, Washington. That accounted for about $6 million a year right there. Oregon-Pacific also became the biggest outlet of venerable Pope & Talbot, and a major customer of Louisiana-Pacific, Georgia-Pacific, Willamette Industries, Boise Cascade, and later Sequoia (now Wickes) Forest Industries.

You'll have noticed by now that there is a distinct similarity between the lumber business and the country elevator business through which Wickes Agriculture got its start. In each arena the same names crop up over and over again and participants meet each other coming and going. Everybody knows what everybody else is up to. So it was quite natural that, one day in January 1972, Darrell Robinson picked up the phone to hear Clark Johnson say in his straight-to-business manner, without any preliminary small talk, "You've got the best wholesale company in the country and you'd fit great in the Wickes picture. Do you want to talk about it?"

Once again, as with Sequoia Forest Industries, it was the right moment for both parties. Robinson and Hagen hoped to expand Oregon-Pacific's franchise into other parts of the country but lacked the capital for such an ambitious step. If Wickes were willing to provide the necessary funding, it was "Go" as far as they were concerned. The terms finally settled on after several months of negotiation, mostly between Robinson and Johnson, was a pooling that involved 46,900 Wickes common shares, worth $1,664,950 when the acquisition was consummated in June of that year.

Oregon-Pacific branched out almost immediately. Everybody at Wickes agreed with Robinson and Hagen that the first logical step was to establish a wholesale position in the southern pine market. Again, as with Wickes Lumber, it wasn't practical to start from scratch as outsiders: the South is the one part of the country that has so far managed to retain its regional integrity. Thus it became a matter of acquiring an existing wholesale firm. Barrett Green, then general merchandise manager of the Lumber Division, who had also established the contact with Wickes's British partner, took Robinson around to scout for likely candidates.

The choice soon came down to Steel City Lumber, of Birmingham, Alabama, probably the best-known lumber wholesaler in the South. The company dated back to 1907, and had built its strength on intimate contact with its markets. All its sales reps lived right in the areas they worked, and their average length of service was fifteen years; they were local institutions. Luckily, despite its sixty-odd years of success, Steel City was still owned by only a handful of stockholders, all of whom worked there. Its president was David P. Whiteside, who held about 25 percent of the equity and was the corporation's largest shareholder. The firm, acquired by Wickes in December 1972 for 55,995 Wickes shares then valued at $1,553,114, retains its own identity.

A new Oregon-Pacific warehouse in Wilsonville, Oregon, 15 miles south of Portland, came next, soon followed by a similar facility in Fairfield, California, about halfway between San Francisco and Sacramento on Interstate 80. The next major move was the purchase of the A. J. Johnson Company, a small, undercapitalized building materials distribution center in Tacoma, Washington. The $509,136 purchase of this family-owned operation, which did about $2.5 million in sales a year, was of no great moment except that it brought good people to Wickes and opened a wholesale gateway in the Puget Sound area, which serves not only western Washington but also Alaska, one of our fastest growing states. It's expected that the Tacoma warehouse will soon reach an annual sales volume of $15 million.

Another small acquisition, in February 1973, of Coast Millwork in Santa Ana, California, for $110,512, had given Oregon-Pacific the sole distributorship for Andersen Windows in California, Arizona, and Nevada, a franchise the division had previously obtained for the state of Oregon. Everything was beginning to fall into place. By late 1974 the distribution division was firmly established in the Pacific Northwest, in northern California, and in the South. Now it was a matter of covering the rest of the nation, and the opportunity arose far sooner than expected.

The housing slump of that year had hurt almost everyone in the shelter business. Few firms were as fortunate as T. J. Hedrick's Wickes Forest Industries, or for that matter The Wickes Corporation itself, whose profits suffered somewhat but which, thanks largely to its diversification, remained financially in good shape and could even think in terms of expansion. Many other companies, however, found themselves so sorely pressed by the recession that divestitures rather than acquisitions were on the agenda. Such was the case with Evans Products, which had been one of the most successful building materials companies in the 1960s. Being oriented basically to manufacturing rather than to retail, Evans had, up to then, generated higher after-tax profits than Wickes on roughly similar volumes. This was only to be expected, since manufacturing requires a greater capital investment than retailing, and this capital must show an appropriate return to compete in the money marketplace. But when a squeeze is on, manufacturing profits easily turn into losses; capital-intensive companies, unable to reduce fixed overhead, are then among the first to suffer. The low margins of wholesaling cannot compensate for this drag, and thus Evans Products, pinched for cash, had to retrench and sell off a number of its properties, including a chain of thirty-three building supply warehouses strategically located in twenty states.

That Evans Products was in temporary difficulty was well known throughout the housing industry and was of particular interest to Clark Johnson, who had been general manager of that company's building materials division from 1964 to 1966, and during that period had nursed its volume from $85 million to $125 million a year. In addition to a number of mills, the warehouses were part of this division, and when Johnson heard the rumor in mid-November that Evans intended to sell these distribution centers, he realized that the situation presented a rare chance for Wickes to establish a nationwide wholesaling base overnight.

Johnson was still in Saginaw then, running the Lumber Division, but since Oregon-Pacific reported to him, wholesaling was one of his responsibilities, and he knew that it would become even more important in the future. He phoned J. Kenneth Brody, the Portland-based executive vice president and chief administrative officer of Evans Products, to get the lowdown. Yes, Brody said, what Johnson had heard was true enough. Would Wickes be interested in buying?

As soon as Brody had sent all the required financial data, Johnson flew out to San Diego to present the proposition to Drum and McNeely. Drum, in particular, had always been enthusiastic about the warehouse distribution business, and Johnson got the go-ahead to proceed with negotiations. Within a few days, he found himself in a most ironic situation, one that made him reflect how small the world of lumber really is. Ten years earlier, as an Evans executive, he had regularly extolled the virtues of these warehouses to Monford A. Orloff, the brilliant entrepreneur who had put Evans Products together.[10] Now Johnson was once again sitting across the desk from Orloff, and Orloff was telling him how wonderful those warehouses were. Johnson didn't have to be sold. He knew.

The parameters of the deal were defined in less than half an hour, and although the purchase was not officially closed until February 19, 1975, Wickes took physical possession of the warehouses in late January. By that time Clark Johnson had been named group senior vice president of Oregon-Pacific, Wickes Forest Industries, Wickes Europe, and the new Sequoia Supply warehouses, and Hagen had succeeded Johnson at Wickes Lumber. Wickes paid approximately $20 million for the distribution centers, including some $3 million worth of receivables for inventory in the warehouses on the date of the Wickes takeover.[11]

Since then, interestingly enough, Oregon-Pacific has become once again what it used to be—a brokerage type of wholesale

operation which takes title but not physical possession of goods, in this case primarily wood products of all kinds, and arranges for their shipment in carload lots from source to retailer. The division, now called Wickes Wholesale, includes the Oregon-Pacific sales office in Wilsonville, Oregon; the Steel City Lumber Company in Birmingham, Alabama; and brokerage branches in Fairfield and Fullerton, California.[12] The three warehouses Robinson and Hagen had built after Oregon-Pacific first merged with Wickes have become part of Sequoia Supply's twenty-two-state chain of thirty-four distribution centers that deal in building supplies in less-than-carload quantities.[13]

Sequoia is presumably the country's fourth largest network of such warehouses. Only Georgia-Pacific, U.S. Plywood's Champion International, and Weyerhaeuser may have bigger warehouse-distribution systems. But Sequoia enjoys one telling advantage over these competitors, one that helped it

BUSINESS IN BULK

*Headquarters of Wickes Wholesale
and Sequoia Supply are
appropriately sited in rustic
Oregon setting (above).
Warehouses (left and right)
distribute building supplies
in twenty-two states.
Andersen Windows, being
assembled below, are a
distribution specialty.*
(Photo at top by
Photography Northwest)

**Wickes
Wood Products**

Manufacturing and
Distribution Facilities

▲ WICKES FOREST INDUSTRIES
DIVISION
■ OREGON PACIFIC INDUSTRIES
● SEQUOIA SUPPLY, INC.

make healthy profits even as the building bust extended into 1975. This advantage is that Sequoia, unlike the others, is not apron-stringed to mill facilities. Champion International, for example, must concentrate on selling the plywood made by its parent company, and if there is no market for plywood, things get tough. By the same token, the warehouses of Georgia-Pacific and Weyerhaeuser have to be sales arms for their respective mills. Sequoia, on the other hand, can buy and supply whatever the market calls for at the moment, and with housing starts down and therefore building materials in only sporadic and small-volume demand, Sequoia's warehouses were doing very well indeed even at the depth of the shelter depression.[14] The fact that Wickes Forest Industries manufactures wood products does not interfere with Sequoia's total independence, if for no other reason than that the primary market area where Hedrick sells his output—Southern California—is one where Sequoia is not yet represented. There are

318

a couple of other holes on the Wickes Wholesale map as well: Michigan and New England. But Johnson plans to plug these in the near future. By the end of 1977, he intends to run a country-wide chain of more than forty warehouses.

Indeed, Clark Johnson, under whose four-year leadership the Lumber Division showed its greatest growth, expects a no less impressive performance from his new operation—and that's saying a lot, for although Johnson may act the optimist, he is not one by nature. One reason he always seems to make out is that he expects everything to come unglued at any moment, and he always tries to have some stickum ready before that happens.

He plans to continue to broaden the product mix distributed by Sequoia far beyond the items traditionally handled by warehouses—plywood, particleboard, paneling, sidings, laminates, and the like. He is adding roofing insulation and other basic building materials. The products of the other Wickes divisions, insofar as they apply, will be distributed by Sequoia too, and of course the warehouses will in turn also service the other Wickes operations. But as Johnson puts it, "We're going to keep everybody at arm's length, especially Wickes Lumber. We're not going to be an in-house pipeline. We're going to supply everybody in the shelter business on equal terms." Johnson intends to give the warehouse arm the same flexibility as that enjoyed by retailers; hence, the enlarged product spectrum. "The way we're going to make our money," he says, "is through what I call velocity. That figure is margin multiplied by turnover. Say you've got an item on which you make 15 percent profit, and you turn it over eight times a year. That gives you a velocity of 120. For my money, that's a heck of a better figure than a 40 percent item you turn only twice."

18

From Boards to Beds

As vice president of corporate communications, Peter W. Willox is stuck with one of Wickes's wooliest jobs. Concerned with everything that involves the Wickes image, he must be in constant touch with all divisions, and this calls for catching their executives on the fly. His frantic working day at San Diego headquarters frequently starts at 6:30, and sometimes even earlier, so that he can call people in the East and Midwest on the phone before everybody is all tied up for the rest of the day. Clearing materials with the San Diego moguls is no less harassing. Reaching E. L. McNeely and John Drum when they are in the office between trips often demands breathless sprints down the hall to beat other executives on equally urgent missions. That Willox's impressive mop of hair hasn't turned white is only because, as a longtime advertising man, he has learned to take his lumps and hope for a better tomorrow. Witness his experiences in helping to launch Wickes Furniture, a chain of warehouse-showrooms that aims to eventually become the country's biggest furniture discounter.

In his current position, fifty-eight-year-old Pete Willox normally wouldn't be directly concerned with such divisional promotion campaigns. They are the responsibility of the respective marketing managers. But in 1970, when Wickes Furniture was being put together, Willox was still a partner in the Saginaw advertising agency of Parker, Willox, Fairchild & Campbell, whose principals had been handling most of the Wickes business for many years, long before they merged into one firm. It had been a highly unusual situation: a corporation hitting the big time without a communications department of its own. Jack Parker, of what had originally been Parker Advertising, represented Wickes Bros. and Wickes Boiler. Pete Willox, of Tanner, Willox & Fairchild, had managed the U.S. Graphite account since shortly after World War II, and had been involved in Wickes corporate public relations since the formation of the new Wickes in 1947. Even after Dan Fitz-Gerald finally took Jack Parker's advice and established a public relations department of sorts in the mid-1960s, Parker and Willox still did most of the work. Not until September 1972, when Wickes moved to San Diego, did Willox join the corporation as an officer.[1] At least by that time one of his most frustrating assignments—midwifing the birth of the furniture operation—was largely behind him.

Getting this project off under the best possible auspices was particularly important. Not only was Wickes entering an entirely new business and one that involved considerable investment, but, for the first time since well before the turn of the century, the Wickes name was on the line right from the start. Wickes Lumber, as will be recalled, saw the light of day as "Cash Way." Almost all acquisitions kept their original names long after their mergers into Wickes. But the establishment of the furniture division marked a psychological turning point. After its many successes, the corporation had finally gained enough confidence to proclaim its own identity. To be sure, outside consultants had been retained to suggest a splendid label for the new enterprise. A medley of Madison Avenue etymologists dreamed up such supposedly motivational mon-

GETTING
WICKES FURNITURE
OFF THE GROUND

To draw big crowds, exciting
grand openings with a circus
flair are a must when
Wickes Furniture moves
into a new location (left).
Peter W. Willox (right),
corporate vice president of
communications, has
to program the shows.
(Photo, left, by
Bradford LaRiviere,
Inc. Willox portrait
by Custom Photography)

ickers as "Go-Way." The Unimark outfit of Chicago (which also designed the red-and-blue Wickes "W") suggested a logo that almost made it: Compass Furniture. Unimark reasoned that unless furniture had a different name, some customers might be confused and try to buy their sofas at Wickes Lumber. But then Dan Fitz-Gerald put his foot down. At the executive committee meeting where all the possibilities were paraded before the Wickes power elite, he suddenly thrust his chin up and sideways in a motion that always signaled his impatience. "Why don't we quit horsing around," he growled. "We've got a great name in Wickes. Let's use it."

So Wickes Furniture it was, and Pete Willox went to work, plunging headlong into a series of near-debacles. It almost seemed as if the gremlins had it in for Wickes. The opening of the first furniture store in July 1971 at Fridley, Minnesota, a suburb of Minneapolis, was to be a gala affair, with band music, gymnasts, beauty queens, and other ballyhoo, including the giveaway of an $8,000 Swinger R.V. as door prize. Then, on July 14, one of those Midwestern thunderstorm spectaculars lowered on the Twin Cities. Torrential rains washed away the newly pinned-down sod around the 142,610-square-foot Behlen building—the most logical of structures for a warehouse-showroom complex—and the mess clogged up the sewers on the 352-car parking lot. The sewers backed up, and within minutes Wickes Furniture was moated by thigh-deep water all around.

The following year, at the opening of the store in Warren, Michigan, a malevolent breeze blew up, making it impossible to launch the much-heralded propane-burner "Balloon Platoon," lest the balloonists' baskets bean bystanders attracted by the $75,000 that had been spent on grand-opening advertising. "No more balloons," Fitz-Gerald told Willox, and Willox switched to heavier-than-air.

For the opening at Norfolk, Virginia, on July 26, 1972, he hired a member of the famed Flying Wallendas to do a special stunt. Upside-down Carla Wallenda, one foot in a sling, was to zip along a cable strung from the 150-foot light tower on the store's parking lot to deliver a symbolic, oversized store key to Dan Fitz-Gerald at the showroom's portals.

A hush settled over the crowd. Drums rolled. Necks craned, Carla started her daredevil slide—and suddenly, out of nowhere, an errant garbage truck roared onto the lot, right under the wire. Carla missed the truck by a couple of feet, and then she all but slammed into the Wickes sign when her slide was stopped a fraction of a second too late and the momentum swung her up within inches of the wall. Willox was wiping his brow in retroactive shock when it turned out that she'd forgotten the key. Luckily Willox is a specialist in emergencies. He carried a spare. No more high-wire acts. What next?

At Livonia, Michigan, on November 29, 1973, fate's fickle finger wiggled at Wickes Furniture again, but this time Wickes ran with the ball. The *Detroit Free Press* headlined its story on the store opening "Wickes Bets Against Slowdown," and in big display type, next to a picture of McNeely, quoted him as saying, "We're either brave or dumb." It was true enough that he had said this, but in all that surrounding white space, the quote found itself dangling out of context.

What had happened was that at a breakfast for Livonia's civic dignitaries prior to the ribbon cutting, *Free Press* reporter Ellen Hume had burst into the Cordoba Restaurant and had parked herself behind E. L. McNeely as he sat at the U-shaped banquet table toying with his scrambled eggs. It was pretty obvious what kind of story she was after. The Arabs had just turned off the oil and nobody knew when they'd let it gush again. General Motors and other car makers, trimming their production schedules, were laying off thousands of workers. Economists were predicting worldwide depression. Nixon was up to his neck in the effluent of Watergate and sinking deeper. The Dow-Jones had plunged below 800 and was headed south. What could Wickes be thinking of, starting a high-volume furniture operation in the face of dismal times like these?

Her questions put McNeely in a difficult position. Evidently this was not the time or place to explain what Wickes was all about to someone who admittedly was still fairly new to the business of business reporting: how Wickes had decided to position itself in every phase of the shelter industry; how thoroughly the retail furniture business had been studied and how carefully conclusions had been drawn; how booming suburban areas like Livonia are where it's at, slump or no slump; how a corporation must invest in the future, much as society must foot the growing-up bills for its young. Even under the most favorable interview conditions, it's difficult to get such points across to newspaper people whose main concern is a quick getaway so they can hurry to their next assignment. McNeely, trying to keep it light, smiled charmingly at persistent Ms. Hume, shrugged his shoulders, and at last gave her the kind of quotable quote reporters pray for. It's not often that a top-level executive will describe his company's actions as "either brave or dumb."

At first glance it seemed that this was a real public relations fiasco. But not so. Just as the Minneapolis storm hadn't stopped hundreds of customers from wading through a flood to get into the Wickes furniture store in Fridley, so the *Detroit Free Press* story created nothing but positive comment. The McNeely interview was the only optimistic note in a newspaper full of gloom. Every other story saw doomsday just around the corner, but here was a company that still had faith in the future. At a meeting of the Michigan Advertising Industry Alliance soon afterward, dozens of image specialists kept slapping Jack Parker on the back, shaking their heads in admiration, and commenting how clever Wickes had been to get that article into the paper.

The warehouse-showroom in Livonia was the twentieth Wickes had opened in less than three years. Its location epitomized the market Wickes Furniture knows it must reach, for Livonia is archetypical of the nation's surburbia. In 1950, when this then sparsely settled township on the northwestern outskirts of Detroit incorporated, it had counted fewer than 17,000 inhabitants. By the time the 1970 census taker came around,

116,000 people called it home. Most lived in single-family developments scattered over the 36 square miles that make Livonia the state's third largest city in area. It is basically a white-collar community, whose 1970 median household income of $15,700 topped that of any other American town of more than 100,000 population. The local Sears store—across the street from where Wickes moved in—consistently beat all others in the chain in retail volume and customer traffic.

Other sites where Wickes established its early furniture stores were not necessarily endowed with quite the same statistical superlatives, but they all manifested the same essential characteristics. They were, without exception, in rapidly growing suburban communities of home-proud middle-class families, whose taste and purchasing power fell in that solid 80 percent of "best-value" merchandising (neither the top 10 percent cream nor the bottom 10 percent schlock) John Drum had zeroed in on ever since he'd first joined Wickes Lumber. There were Wickes furniture stores in Wheeling, outside Chicago; in mushrooming El Cajon, 20 miles east of San Diego; at Anaheim, Woodland Hills, and West Covina in the burgeoning Los Angeles basin, as well as in a careful selection of other spreading urban concentrations that included Cincinnati, Milwaukee, Pittsburgh, St. Louis, and Charlotte, North Carolina. By late 1974, three more outlets had been added, among them an experimental showroom-catalog store in the Woodfield Shopping Center of Schaumburg, Illinois, a famous cluster-housing community in vast Chicagoland.[2]

Most of the Wickes warehouse-showrooms run between 100,000 and 150,000 square feet of floor space. Anaheim, with its 171,272 square feet, of which about 100,000 are devoted to warehousing, is the biggest and has been the most consistently profitable. In the showrooms, which generally take up a little more than one-third of the complexes, the furniture is exhibited in as many as 300 room settings, complete to wall hangings, pictures, and decorative accessories. That's very helpful to average people who don't buy furniture very often and are not certain of their judgment in selecting appropriate colors and designs. Seeing the goods in decorator environments gives them the assurance they need to make the purchase. Every item on display is for sale, and can be picked up right then and there from the warehouse in the back, or delivered at a small extra charge. Even with delivery, there is no protracted waiting period, as is the usual procedure in furniture buying unless you take the floor sample. "Who wants to wait six weeks for a new

THE NO-WAIT WAY TO BUY FURNITURE

Wickes's warehouse/showrooms display about 50,000 different items of furniture and accessories in room-like settings (above). All items are available on the spot from 30-foot-high racks in the warehouse part of the building (right). The average inventory runs around 500,000 pieces.

chair?" says Drum, as ever eminently practical. "By that time your mother-in-law has come and gone, and the new chair wasn't there for her to admire."

No less important than the extensive stock (up to about 50,000 different items) and the warehouse inventory backup (around 500,000 pieces) is that the prices are significantly below those charged by conventional furniture dealers and department stores for the same quality of merchandise.[3] Mass orders from the manufacturers and a fast turnover of inventories make these substantial discounts possible. Here again, as in its retail sales of lumber and building supplies, Wickes avoids the high cost of special-order servicing. The savings end up in the buyer's pocket.

The idea, as such, of retailing furniture through warehouses was not original with Wickes. Credit for putting this concept into practice rightfully belongs to the Levitz brothers, one of whom started selling discount furniture out of the warehouse of his store in Tucson, Arizona, back in 1958.[4] Even that wasn't really the first time it had been done. Warehouse sales of furniture had been conducted long before that on a sporadic basis, but until Levitz came along, nobody had ever considered making a steady business out of them. Nor is Wickes today Levitz's only competition. Crossroads, a division of Unicapital Corp. of Atlanta, has a number of warehouse-showrooms, as do J. Homestock, in New England, and Gold Key, a division of Federated Department Stores, in California. Wickes still trails behind Levitz, but all others trail behind Wickes. "The competition doesn't worry me," says Drum. "What would worry me is to be in a business where nobody wants to compete."

It wasn't just Levitz's success that prompted Wickes to enter the furniture arena. Dan Fitz-Gerald had flirted with it for years, even as he persuaded Al Riedel to have Michigan Bean join forces with Wickes way back in the mid-1950s. Fitz-Gerald didn't think specifically of warehouse-showrooms then. What intrigued him was how much money all those mom-and-pop furniture stores made. "I had two good friends," he liked to explain, "both in the furniture retail business. One was in

Pontiac, the other in Saginaw. The one in Pontiac told me he made all his money on the interest on the time payments of his customers, and the one in Saginaw said he made all his money on the markup. He said he invariably priced his merchandise higher than anybody else's. Then if he couldn't get rid of it at 300 percent margin, he'd put up a great big sale sign, and let it go at 150 percent margin. And I asked myself, 'What the hell am I doing here with beans?' In the furniture business you could undersell everybody, and you'd never run out of money."

Fitz-Gerald's occasional furniture daydreams got lost in the shuffle of the ensuing hectic years. Somewhat surprisingly, when they resurfaced, consideration was first given to going into furniture manufacturing rather than retailing. That was in 1969, Wickes's big acquisition year, when it bought Lee. L. Woodard Sons and was preparing to merge with Colonial Products. Eugene Gordon was then general merchandise manager of the Lumber Division after several years in charge of its marketing. Since his background prior to coming with Wickes had run the gamut of the furniture field from retailing to manufacturing, he was assigned to take on the two new subsidiaries, and at the same time to study further expansion along similar lines.

There was no doubt in Gene Gordon's mind that making furniture presented great opportunities, but so far as Wickes was concerned, he felt that three factors militated against getting in any deeper at that point. To begin with, it was almost impossible to pick up successful manufacturers of meaningful size. Most of the big firms already had been absorbed, and the rest were highly independent people like the Broyhills and Bassetts, and there wasn't a chance to buy out any of those. As for the vast majority of the country's more than 5,000 furniture factories, they were considered big if they were doing $25 million a year. The best growth rate one could possibly expect would be in the 10 to 15 percent range, an extremely modest increment by Wickes standards. This led directly to the second argument against the corporation's becoming any more

GENE GORDON

He launched Wickes Furniture. (Portrait by Mel Fox)

involved with production, namely that enlarging factories is a costly proposition, quite apart from buying them in the first place. The mathematics of expansion were far more favorable to retailing all around. And there was yet a third argument of equal weight. Wickes had much built-in expertise in merchandising and marketing, but none really at the production level. Even Gordon had spent only a minor portion of his career with a manufacturer.[5]

Retailing presented a totally different picture, however. It was an annual 6-billion-dollar business, fragmented between some 35,000 dealers of whom only a few hundred did $1 million or more a year in volume. There was as yet no national chain. Levitz had gone like gangbusters in California and the South, but even that operation was only just beginning to cover the rest of the country. Meanwhile, the public was clearly frustrated with things as they were, with the high prices, the confusing displays, the limited selections, the long waits. Furniture makers were well aware that a retail revolution was overdue. There would be no serious supply problems such as

Wickes Lumber had faced in its early days; the furniture industry had no stake in keeping an umbrella over its antiquated distribution system. By the same token it wouldn't be difficult to find good people to staff the Wickes operation. The good ones could tell which way the wind was blowing. If Wickes were ever to tackle this business, now was the time.

Of course, no one expected that Wickes Furniture would prove to be a gold mine overnight. Just getting started would require a sizable investment, for warehouse-showrooms are a totally different breed from lumber and building supply centers. Wickes Lumber, we recall, concentrates its efforts in areas where city and country meet. Here, if an outlet gets 5 to 10 percent of the building materials business, it can turn a healthy $2 to $3 million a year. The real estate required is relatively cheap; generally $50,000 to $60,000 will suffice. But semiurban, semirural areas cannot support a furniture warehouse-showroom. A 10 percent share of local furniture sales might give you an annual volume of $700,000 in that sort of market, and that's far from enough to operate such a machine. To show profits, a warehouse-showroom complex has to do around $3 million a year, and that's only possible in metropolitan centers where an appropriate building site can cost close to $1 million. By the time you've erected the complex, and the asphalt has set on the parking lot, you've got anywhere from $2.5 to $3.5 million in the business. To cut the start-up cost by reducing the size of the operation isn't the answer: that way you'd lose customer impact. So now you have to fill this huge place with expensive inventory, and there goes another chunk, say about $1 million.

And the higher costs don't stop here. Now you've got to move these goods. In the Lumber Division, an advertising allocation of 2.5 percent of consumer sales, i.e., less than 1.7 percent of total volume, is sufficient to attract new customers in big enough numbers to compensate for natural attrition; if a Wickes building supply center were suddenly to stop advertising today, the consequences probably wouldn't be felt for many months. But furniture is big-ticket stuff that involves difficult buying decisions. To attract customers, you not only have to be known as a reliable institution—which necessitates developing an image and maintaining it—but you must keep the market constantly aware of all the merchandise you have available, and then lure customers with special sales promotions. Thus, in addition to the image advertising, for which Wickes uses television, there have to be broadside mailers that show off your assortment, plus the spot ads on now-or-never buying opportunities. Before you know it, you're stuck with an advertising budget that runs around 9 percent of sales.[6]

There was no question that going into furniture retailing called for a major commitment, especially since Wickes had to build up the division as rapidly as possible. To go at it piecemeal would only serve to dissipate image-promotion efforts. Moreover, the prorated advertising costs could be pared whenever several outlets were put into the same market area; hence Chicago's quintet, the trios of Detroit and Los Angeles, and the twins in Pittsburgh and Minneapolis were on the drawing boards almost from the moment the decision was made to get into that business.

One of the reasons the Minneapolis store at Fridley became the first of the chain was that this territory was very familiar to Robert Weinstein, whom Gene Gordon brought in from Boutells, then an eight-store furniture retail operation in the Twin Cities, to run the aborning division in October 1970.[7] The Minneapolis market area comprised a population of about 1.4 million, whose annual furniture expenditures totaled about $80 million. An 8 or 9 percent market share would provide Wickes Furniture's required volume. Levitz had succeeded under similar demographic conditions, so this was a good opportunity to test the Wickes approach against established precedent. At the last minute, however, Fridley almost fell through. The complex had been designed, and the opening day set a few months hence, when Burlington Northern Railroad, which owned the siding-served industrial park where Wickes wanted to locate, suddenly backed out of the deal.

Gene Gordon heard the bad news at Pinehurst, North Caro-

lina, during a gin rummy game. It was already November, and
the store was supposed to open in April. Gordon slammed the
phone receiver down so hard it made the place rattle. "Don't
get all worked up," Fitz-Gerald told him. "If you really want
that piece of property, we'll manage it. The boys at the Burlington Northern real estate department probably don't realize that
we're one of the largest shippers of freight in the United States.
That's all we'll have to tell them." A few weeks later, the
agreement was signed.

Fitz-Gerald had been absolutely right. The railroad's real
estate people hadn't done all their homework—in fact, they'd
never even heard of Wickes. What had decided them against
selling to the corporation was that they simply couldn't believe
that a furniture store would require 200 carloads or more a
year, which was the projection Gordon had given them. But it

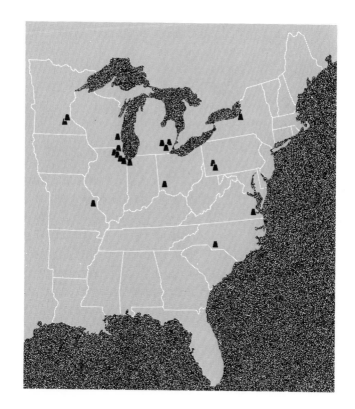

Wickes Furniture

turned out to be true enough. From the day of the thunder-storm, when Minneapolis police finally asked the store to close because backed-up traffic had become a hazard, Fridley has been a noble performer, much to Burlington's delight, if not to Boutells: that chain couldn't stand the Wickes heat, and has since gone out of business.

Not all the furniture warehouse-showrooms were so imme-diately successful. But in four short years, Wickes Furniture grew from nothing to nearly $100 million in annual sales—the fastest growth enjoyed by any retail organization in recent years—and despite the 1974–1975 recession, it was coming ever closer to being profitable.[8] For several months in the worst of the economic crunch, a husky ex-lawyer from Des Moines, Iowa, found himself in charge of the furniture operation. This was Paul H. Tatz, a Wickes senior vice president, one of the organization's most promising comers on the staff side, who earlier had headed McNeely's Office of the President.[9] Although Tatz lacked retail experience, he was pulled out of headquarters in late 1974 and shipped to Chicago to run the new division because he was known to be a forceful administra-tor, just the kind of guy to cut overhead and solidify the system of this still almost entrepreneurial organization so that it might withstand the pummeling of bad times. Tatz sharply reduced expenses all around. One of his first steps was to concentrate the whole organization's merchandising at its Wheeling, Illi-nois, headquarters. This made it unnecessary to staff these posi-tions at the individual complexes as had been the practice earlier when Wickes Furniture was still trying to find its way. As a concomitant measure, he centralized all inventory replacement so that, thanks to the Wickes computer center, the division knows the status of every single item in stock at any given time. Furniture showrooms are now open from noon to nine, and on certain days of the week to ten, eliminating the morning hours of least traffic, which saves considerable over-head. This much accomplished, Paul Tatz suddenly resigned quite unexpectedly about a year later, apparently for personal reasons, and Dick Cotton, Wickes senior vice president and corporate sales manager, the in-house sales evangelist, was thrown into the breach. It was an inspired emergency decision: with the organization tightened up by Tatz, it was now time for Cotton's talents; the economy was picking up again, and with it the opportunity to concentrate on building sales. Gordon, as divisional vice president, is in charge of merchandising, his specialty and the key area for establishing profitability since a retailer must have the right goods at the right price to make it in the marketplace.[10]

But it's amazing how little things, and not just big decisions, contribute to the success of retail operations—and that's where ingenuity on the scene comes in. For instance, a former manager of the store at Maryland Heights, in St. Louis, Missouri, once scheduled a wine and cheese party in his showroom. Again, as in Fridley, Minnesota, the weather man had it in for Wickes. It was January, and the rain of the day before had congealed into a sheet of ice. On the morning of the party, first sleet and then snow fell until, by late afternoon, traffic was practically at a standstill. Things looked pretty grim, and indeed only 259 customers showed. But the store ended the night with nearly $35,000 in the till. Two-thirds of the customers bought, and the ticket average came to $421.

What did it was the way the manager handled the situation. He tended the bar himself, and seeing that, with so few customers, he'd have a lot of wine left over, he spontaneously handed a bottle to a lady who had just bought a $450 bedroom set. This simple gesture made her feel so good that she and her husband spent another $650 on a dining room table and chairs they'd been looking at. Quick on the uptake, the manager immediately instructed his salesmen to bring any customers they had near closing to the bar. All these prospective buyers were presented with a bottle of wine they liked best, and sure enough, most of them went through with their purchases. One salesman alone racked up $10,480 that evening in return for eight bottles that had cost only about $2 apiece. When it comes to leverage, you can't beat ingenuity.

Wine is with it today—and so is personalized decorating. In a world that increasingly enforces uniformity, life-style accoutrements become a label which says "that's me," or perhaps more honestly, "that's the type I'd like you all to think I am." How important this individualized segment will become in the home furnishings mass market is open to speculation, but there is no question that it is gaining strength. To test it, Wickes Furniture recently set aside 10,000-square-foot areas in its three Detroit warehouse-showroom complexes, and remodeled them as "Decorator Centers" that carry everything from drapery and carpeting to knickknacks and cabinetry, including of course Yorktowne Kitchens. These experimental centers, supervised by Robert Thele, whose regular job is vice president of administration of the Furniture Division, opened in June 1976, and are staffed by decorating specialists competent to give individualized service. What this innovation may accomplish in terms of the division's bottom line—whether it will bomb or blossom—won't be known until after this book is published. And it's really not all that important in itself. What makes it significant is that it exemplifies the flexibility of Wickes, big as the company is, to ride new waves; particularly in a young operation like Furniture, that's what it takes to get out of growing-pains pink into beautiful black.

19

The Here-and-Now Business

A sk almost any lady on the ninth floor of the Bank of California Building in San Diego, and she'll tell you that Dave Primuth is one of the most attractive men to walk the spacious halls of Wickes's top-executive domain. Primuth is well over 6 feet tall, with an angular face that seems sculpted of granite. He has a disconcerting look about his green eyes, which is caused by the fact that his right one is made of glass. It's a sophisticated model, though, with a magnetic plate behind it and a magnetic ball sewn onto the muscles, so the eye moves. In his younger years, he had a lot of fun with it. Deep in a serious business conversation, he would suddenly tap it with his fountain pen when he got bored, causing considerable consternation all around. Despite his handicap he took up flying, just to prove that he could do it, and eventually joined that elite trio of one-eyed pilots who hold commercial multi-engine ratings. Which goes to show that having an eye poked out at the age of seven by a pencil-wielding school chum teaches a fellow to take life as it comes, with tenacity and with a sense of humor. Both these qualities come in handy in the money business. Executive Vice President David J. Primuth is the chief financial officer of Wickes, and it's at his office, literally, where the buck stops.

And starts. On August 7, 1971, ten days short of his thirty-third birthday, Primuth, already the corporation's senior vice president of finance, sat in his living room in Saginaw, where Wickes was still headquartered at that time, and watched President Nixon announce Phase I of his wage and price control program. The speech was a real shocker, like so many other episodes in that enigmatic politician's checkered career. Until the very day before, Nixon had insisted that no such measures ever would be taken by his administration, and the business world had believed him and acted accordingly.

Wickes common was then trading at 24 times earnings and the corporation's capitalization was becoming highly leveraged. It was certain that the corporation must obtain equity capital in the not-too-distant future. Sitting there in front of his TV set, Dave Primuth was convinced that Phase I marked the beginning of a long and bumpy slide. There was no way that he could see for the earnings and multiples of United States corporations to go anywhere but down until the country's economic problems were resolved. As a result, the value of equities was bound to drop, and very likely in the near future, as Wall Street anticipated developments. Here and now was perhaps Wickes's last chance, for quite a number of years, to go for a common stock offering at a favorable price. There was no telling when values might tumble. Every day counted.

From his past experience, Dave Primuth knew that Dan Fitz-Gerald was a man with an habitually open door. A few months earlier, when Dick Cotton had invited Primuth to Saginaw in the hope of recruiting him away from Symons Corp., of Des Plaines, Illinois, he had received a phone call from Fitz-Gerald within five minutes of checking into the Holiday Inn West late on a snowy January night. In his characteristically informal way, Fitz-Gerald asked Primuth if he would mind their spending some time together that very evening. Primuth could hardly believe it. Here was the chairman

DAVID J. PRIMUTH
Not quite thirty-three years old when he became the corporation's chief financial officer, he was elected executive vice president four years later, in 1975.
(Photo by Victor Avila)

of a very large company eager to get together with a candidate for the controller spot in the middle of the night. Of course, Primuth didn't mind, and Fitz-Gerald drove all the way across town to the motel, never mind the blizzard, and they talked until nearly three o'clock.

So the morning after Nixon pulled that big surprise out of his bag of tricks, Primuth rushed into Fitz-Gerald's office first thing, and laid out his appraisal of the situation. One of the great strengths of the Wickes organization is the speed with which it can act. There is no black book of rules, no hang-up about formality, tradition, and protocol. It's a rolled-up-shirt sleeves, briefcase-decision operation. Fitz-Gerald immediately called in McNeely, Drum, and George O'Dair. Before noon, the preparation of the registration statement required by the Securities and Exchange Commission had begun. Within six weeks, probably a record time, an issue of 1.2 million shares was on the market, co-managed by Goldman, Sachs and Merrill Lynch, and heavily supported by William D. Witter & Co. Just in time, too. Wickes common traded at $42 a share when the offering was announced. On the day it was priced, the stock was up to $49¼, a most unexpected bonus since stocks normally go down when potential per-share earnings are being diluted, in this case by increasing the number of outstanding shares from 7 million to 8.2 million.

In fact, the wave of enthusiasm did not crest until a couple of weeks after the offering was sold out. In October, Wickes shares reached their all-time high, up in the 50s, with a multiple of 30 times earnings. After that the price plummeted, along with everything else. Thanks to Primuth's foresight, the issue had hit the market at about its peak—a coup for which everyone in the company now likes to take credit. Net proceeds came to well over $56 million, which went into strengthening the equity base.[1]

Since then, raising money has been considerably more difficult. As Primuth had predicted, the years that followed were no time to offer stock. The financing game always has been a fast-paced affair, but never more so than in this turbulent period with its currency upheavals, trade-balance distortions, runaway inflation, and roller-coastering of interest rates. In 1974, which, one would hope, saw the end of the country's dalliance with despair, Primuth had eight financings on the burner at the same time, and found himself in almost daily huddles with two other prominent members of Wickes's behind-the-scenes brain trust, William W. Boyle, the corporate treasurer,[2] and Arthur E. Kirchheimer, the corporation's general counsel.[3] Between them, they devised purse-string projects ranging from a $10 million lease-back of Wickes-developed properties to a $50 million revolving credit agreement with a number of leading United States banks.

Most interesting of these financing strategies was the brilliant Boyle idea for Wickes to "rent" equity until such a time as the market again favored common stock offerings. The plan—which is still in abeyance—was to privately place $20 million of ten-year preferred stock, callable after three years, with casualty insurance companies and credit corporations. In that way, Wickes would have been able to obtain capital without going into debt and without diluting the corporation's common equity when it was quoted far below book value. The lease-back financing, a more usual practice, involved four Wickes furniture warehouse-showroom installations in Merrillville, Indiana; Charlotte, North Carolina; Pittsburgh, Pennsylvania; and Chicago. As is customary in such transactions, the developed properties were sold, each for about $2.5 million, to a "conduit company" financed by institutional lenders, and then leased back by Wickes. All this strategy is accomplished off the balance sheet, and the major advantage to a company using it is its pass-through tax effect. Only the lease payment is deducted from the income statement, but for tax purposes the depreciation and all operating costs are written off.

The third financing venture was the establishment of a five-year revolving credit line in Eurodollars with European banks to back up $15 million worth of commercial paper sales in the United States. The reasons Primuth chose this route were several, the most important of them being that it was a cheaper

way to obtain funds because of currency differentials, and that
Wickes wanted to establish a relationship with those banks in
order to ease future financing for Wickes Europe.[4]

The fourth was a domestic $50 million revolving credit
agreement, with Security Pacific as the principal bank, and
with the Union Bank of Los Angeles, the First National of
Chicago, the Mellon Bank of Pittsburgh, Chase Manhattan of
New York, and the Michigan National Bank as participating
institutions. This innovative package, designed for general corporate financing, allowed Wickes to take $20 million of the
credit in Eurodollars, which happened to be favorable at the
moment, and to use these Eurodollars, like those obtained
abroad, as backup for commercial paper. This gave Wickes the
flexibility to treat as long-term loans what would otherwise
have had to be handled as short-term commitments.

The fifth was a senior debenture debt of some $40 million;
and the sixth, another lease-back financing arrangement on a
large manufacturing facility in the Midwest, which was then
being planned. As with the furniture stores, this was to be an
off-balance-sheet transaction.

The seventh plan called for the repositioning of about $80

million worth of bank credit lines on a current basis. This primarily involved the First National City Bank of New York, the corporation's principal bank, which had done business with Wickes and its predecessor companies for nearly sixty years, and the Continental Bank of Chicago, also of longstanding association.

The eighth was a program to exchange outstanding 5⅛ subordinated convertible debentures for a new straight subordinated debenture carrying a higher coupon. What this did for the company was to reduce the debt on the balance sheet. At that time, the old debentures were trading at about 57. Being replaced with a security with a value of between 65 and 70, the difference became a reduction of debt, and at the same time created a gain of the same amount, which could be used by Wickes to offset divestiture losses, to write off deferred charges, or simply to increase earnings. The principal benefit to holders of the old debenture was that they received a higher yield on their paper. The convertibility was hypothetical in any case, since it was pegged at 53, about 5 times the market value of Wickes common at the time.

Not all these strategems worked out, but even so, Primuth

managed to obtain more than $100 million, a tidy sum to support the corporation's orderly expansion in the face of that year's adversity.[5] Getting it all together took a bit of doing, and one would assume that such intricate financial acrobatics are more than enough to occupy anyone full time. But as Wickes' chief financial wizard, Primuth has many other responsibilities. Not that the heavy load fazes him.

Born on his grandfather's farm in Racine County, Wisconsin, he started helping out at an early age, and soon almost lost more than just an eye. He was out with his grandfather one day, rolling the soil with a horse-drawn crusher, when a falling branch spooked the horses. They reared, and young Dave was catapulted between the team and the machine. Almost immediately, the horses yanked the crusher forward again, running it over Dave. He was pressed so deeply into the earth that he had to be dug out with shovels. Luckily this happened in the spring, after long rains, and the soil was soft enough to yield; otherwise, the boy would have been pulped. In the ninth grade, he embarked on a less dangerous career, working three hours a day after school and all day Saturday as an all-around helper at a fish market and delicatessen, a job that saw him through high school and paid for his first two years at Wheaton College, in Illinois. His original intention had been to study chemical engineering, but he took some business courses and became so interested that he switched to finance and accounting. Even before his graduation with a B.A. in business administration in 1960, he started working full time for an accounting firm in Aurora, Illinois, and he continued on that job for another year afterward. In the process he learned that, for someone of his temperament, keeping books wasn't challenging enough. He was a young man in a hurry.

His first job in industry was with Foundry Allied Industries in Racine, Wisconsin. He joined that firm in 1961 as a divisional vice president and controller, and left six years later as corporate vice president of finance and a director of the company. He then joined Symons Corp., of Des Plaines, Illinois, a manufacturer and marketer of concrete construction equipment, as vice president and controller. And that's where Tony Eastman, of Eastman and Beaudine, Inc., Wickes's favorite Chicago headhunter, found him.[6]

To pave the way for an eventual offering of common equity was high on Primuth's agenda from the moment he joined Wickes in February 1971. He had no idea, of course, that it would be as soon as the coming September, but an effort of this sort takes a lot of preparatory leg work. He got to know Wickes's Wall Street contacts in short order, and soon was on very friendly terms with Bill Stutt, one of the New York partners of Goldman, Sachs.

People in the financial world inevitably talk money, even when they're out together for an after-dinner drink, and so it happened that, in a Manhattan pub one night that spring, the conversation came around to Sears and J. C. Penney, and how much these retailers made from financing credit purchases at their stores. With the strength of their big organizations behind them, these firms were able to obtain the required funds at prime rate or close to it, and then relend the money to install-ment buyers at anywhere from 12 to 18 percent a year, depend-ing on the type of contract.[7] On millions of dollars, the differ-ence was enough to account for a large and ever-growing percentage of earnings. No wonder Sears and Penney's were higher than Wickes on the list of *Fortune* magazine's top fifty retailers, but take away the financial services, which at Sears also included Allstate Insurance, and the gap wasn't all that great.[8] Why shouldn't Wickes be in that business too, espe-cially with the new furniture stores coming into the picture? Furniture was big-ticket stuff, and 80 percent of it, so statistics indicated, was bought on credit.

After Primuth and Stutt had kicked the idea around for a while, it didn't seem far-fetched at all. True, Wickes knew next to nothing about handling credit, and didn't yet have the financial capacity to fund a large consumer debt. But perhaps an experienced company could be brought into the picture to supply the cash and the know-how. Impatiently, Primuth started scribbling on his napkin. There were many things that had to be done. The tax treatment and accounting aspects must be studied, the matter had to be cleared with the Securities and Exchange Commission, and a firm found to take on the venture on a temporary basis until Wickes was ready to stand on its own feet. Primuth took that napkin back to Saginaw with him, and from it sketched out the framework of what grew up to be Wickes Financial Services.

Primuth's plan to use an outside firm to help Wickes break into the installment credit business was unprecedented, although the benefits to both parties fairly hit you in the face. The finance company had a new outlet to employ its funds profitably. At the same time, this arrangement would not in the least impair the deferred tax benefits Wickes could derive from installment sales. If the outside company, in effect, lent Wickes the money with which to fund the installment purchases, then these transactions would not have to be treated as if a receivable had been sold to a third party. Wickes would have the full price in pocket at the moment of purchase, but could spread the taxable portion of it over the life of the installment contract. Say a sale brought in $1,000, of which Wickes's profit was

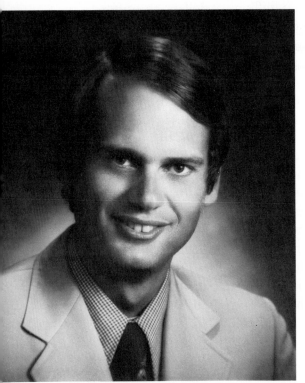

RICHARD H. CHAMBERS

He is general manager of Wickes Credit. (Photo by Victor Avila)

$200. Wickes could immediately draw the whole $1,000, but had to declare as income only one-fifth of the profit portion of each installment payment—and in furniture, the payments usually spread over three years. It was truly a nifty concept.

Still, it being so unconventional, the first two credit corporations Primuth approached turned Wickes down. Finally, General Electric Credit Corporation (GECC) agreed to the temporary arrangement, with the understanding that Wickes would take over the financing before too long. Thus, even as Primuth, Boyle, and Kirchheimer worked on the big common equity offering of 1971, the Wickes Acceptance Corporation was organized as an unconsolidated subsidiary, and before the end of the year the project was underway.

Equity gives leverage. The more you've got, the more you can borrow. With the $56 million from the new stock issue in its treasury, Wickes was in a position to handle its own consumer financing. By late 1972, Primuth was secure in the knowledge that he and his staff could supervise the credit operation. Robert N. Beck, of Federal Department Stores, was brought in from Detroit to head the subsidiary, whose headquarters were set up in Wheeling, Illinois, at the Furniture Division's hub. As the early installment debts were paid off, GECC drifted out of the picture. In that period, about 27 percent of Furniture's sales were on time payments. Today, such purchases account for nearly half the division's volume, and they're all carried by the Wickes Credit Corporation, as the subsidiary has been renamed. The major factor in this growth was the heavy promotion of the Wickes credit card, introduced in November 1972 and tucked into 200,000 wallets across the country since then. It's good for $500 of revolving credit at all Wickes retail outlets, including Wickes Lumber centers, the furniture warehouse-showrooms, and the Big Acre Stores of Wickes Agriculture. In early 1975, furniture sales on credit cards ran at the annualized rate of about $45 million, and building supply sales at about $12 million.[9] The subsidiary, now under general manager Richard H. Chambers,[10] was solidly in the black.

COMPUTER CHIEF

Ralph E. Pfaff programmed his career with a bachelor's degree in physics and a master's in business administration.

But the fact that Wickes Credit made money wasn't its only virtue. While its profits accrue to The Wickes Corporation's bottom line, the borrowings of the unconsolidated subsidiary bypass the corporate balance sheet and therefore do not put a drag on the corporate treasury's borrowing power. This is vital, since Wickes can't let consumer debt financing impede its ability to obtain funds for expansion. But there is yet another, equally important, plus. Credit cards foster repeat business. Already more than half of Wickes Furniture's customers are second-timers or better.

None of this would have been possible if Wickes had not gone whole hog for computerization. When Gene Gordon took McNeely upstairs in the 150,000-square-foot building in Wheeling, Illinois, that was to serve as a furniture warehouse-showroom at street level and as division headquarters above, McNeely for once came close to losing his temper. His face got beet-red as he looked at that vast space. From the inside, the Behlen steel building appeared even more overwhelming, since there were no internal supports. "This is going to break us," McNeely said, only half in jest. "You get that much office

350

space, and before you know it, it'll be full of people." McNeely shouldn't have been concerned. It turned out that the space was needed more for machines than for people. For, in addition to the movable-partition offices of the Furniture Division and Wickes Credit, it's the home of the corporation's Management Information Systems (MIS), whose mechanical brains take care of just about everything. They are hooked up to Wickes Furniture outlets all over the country twenty-four hours a day, and every single transaction is instantly fed into the circuits. At any given moment, Wickes knows exactly what's in inventory and where, what must be reordered and shipped to what point, what credit customer is trying to shoot over the $500 limit—indeed, in a broad sense, how much the corporation is worth at that instant. This intricate system was set up by Ralph E. Pfaff, a gangling, easygoing Wheaton College physics major who later took an M.B.A. at the University of Chicago—an unusual combination and just what's required to cope with a computer operation. Pfaff had come to Wickes from United Air Lines, where he had been controller of the computer services division during those hectic years of air-travel growth from 1966 to 1972. Now thirty-seven, he is a vice president and the director of MIS.[11] In this position, Pfaff reports to Primuth, as do William W. Boyle as treasurer; Richard L. Barker, the controller; Richard J. Ainslie, the corporate tax director;[12] and Arthur J. Nasso, the vice president in charge of the Wickes Financial Services Group.

Wickes has a great penchant for moving its people around. Executives are apt to be reassigned at a moment's notice, and dispatched to some sore spot that requires concentrated care. If they can't grab hold instantly, they are not Wickes material. Art Nasso evidently is. Since he joined the company in 1970, he has been director of the corporate tax department, vice president for administration and finance of the Lumber Division, and once even found himself briefly in charge of the American end of the Wickes Europe leash, a position that's now in Clark Johnson's province.[13] In 1974 Nasso was handed the responsibility for the financial service operations, and he

TROUBLESHOOTER ART NASSO

He got stuck with the unenviable assignment of trying to shape up the Universal Mobile Services subsidiary.

had barely moved from Saginaw to San Diego when he had to pack up again, this time for Houston, in a last-ditch attempt to bail out sinking Universal Mobile Services. The sad story of what happened here has been told in detail in Chapter 16— how, in the face of the high prime rate and the housing slump, it was impossible to turn the mobile homes business around. After Wickes had divested itself in late 1975 of all its mobile homes operations, and had written off the substantial losses these businesses had imposed on the corporation's bottom line, Nasso returned once more to San Diego.

As this is written (in early 1976), Nasso's Financial Services Group includes the Wickes Credit Corporation as well as two of the financial service subsidiaries Wickes had originally acquired in its push for vertical positioning in the mobile homes industry. One of these is Western Diversified Financial Inc., a company that sells credit life, credit accident, and health insurance; the other is the Illinois-chartered Coronado Life Insurance Company, which underwrites this type of insurance. Western's principals at the time of its acquisition are still aboard: Edward G. Edelstein, who is president of the subsidiary; his older brother, Milton, who is vice-president; and Fred E. Wollock, who stayed on in a sales capacity.[14] Coronado Life is closely linked with Western Diversified: it is an outgrowth of Western's own Ram Life Insurance Company which, after their joint acquisition by Wickes, was merged with similar credit life companies that had been brought to Wickes by the two mobile home–financial service companies, Universal Mobile and American Homes Industries, of which Wickes divested itself in late 1975 and early 1976.

The fact that the corporation's remaining financial service properties are all in Chicago, while Nasso, their boss, sits in San Diego, may appear somewhat ill-considered. But there's a good reason for keeping Nasso at corporate headquarters and close by Primuth's side. For some time now, Wickes has been shopping around for a regular life insurance company (as opposed to a credit life operation), and San Diego is of course where it's at when it comes to mergers. That Wickes acquire such a firm was first recommended by Transamerica Corp., a frequent Wickes consultant,[15] and has since become an announced goal of the company. The rational, of course, is that no other business, with the exception of banking, produces so much cash flow. To be meaningful, it would have to be a sizeable acquisition, probably the biggest yet undertaken by Wickes. However, the capacity for a king-size merger has been provided for ever since 1972 when the corporation's stockholders approved an increase in the number of shares from 15 million to 25 million. With only about 8.5 million shares outstanding at this point, Wickes has plenty of room to maneuver in. Negotiations already have been conducted with several life companies. So far all have come to naught. It's an interesting thought that sooner or later such conversations might lead to a merger. If and when that happens Wickes will have extended its franchise from man's castle to the castle's king. Dave Primuth, for one, is all in favor of that.

20

Cavalcade

It was fourteen months after the billion-dollar dinner in Chicago when Daniel M. Fitz-Gerald flew home for the last time. If he knew it, he didn't let on. Weak though he was from repeated surgery, chemotherapy, and radiation treatments, he refused to lean on Art Nasso, who picked him up at St. Joseph's Hospital in Houston to escort him to Saginaw. On the plane, Fitz-Gerald played the boisterous Irishman as ever,[1] cracked his usual jokes, made light of his pains, and insisted that he had his cancer licked. Sure, at the upcoming board of directors meeting later that week, on May 22, 1975, he'd hand over the chairman's reins to E. L. McNeely, but not because of illness. After all, Fitz-Gerald was sixty-five, and he himself had instituted the retirement-at-sixty-five dictum at Wickes. So now it was his turn.[2] That didn't mean, however, that he'd let go altogether. He could remain a member of the board and chairman of its executive committee for another five years, until his seventieth birthday, and such was his avowed intention—a fiction he maintained until the very last. Within a few weeks he was taken to Saginaw's St. Luke's Hospital, where he died on July 24, 1975.³

Fitz-Gerald's death marked the end of an era that in actuality had passed some time ago. When surgery first put him out of action in early 1974, the new Wickes already was in place. By then, but for Fitz-Gerald's advice and consent, McNeely was running the show. Wickes was hardly even the same company anymore. Another name might have served it just as well. The new look had taken shape even as Fitz-Gerald groomed McNeely as his successor, naming him senior vice president in 1965 and making him the driving force in the push to the billion-dollar goal. In 1969, Fitz-Gerald had entrusted E. L. McNeely with yet more of Wickes—the presidency. Two years later, when McNeely also assumed the role of chief executive, the transition was complete. Only the final veto power still rested with Fitz-Gerald. It almost seems as if he'd sensed all along that he must hurry. When his body suddenly refused to do his bidding, he had everything tidied up. Even the billion-dollar target was about to topple one year ahead of schedule.

Most emblematic of the new era's arrival had been the move of corporate headquarters from Saginaw to San Diego in the summer of 1972—and the fact that Fitz-Gerald chose to stay in the old Wickes town. It goes without saying that a no less suitable office suite was set aside for his periodic visits to the Coast. But he still hung his sporty houndstooth hat on the seventh floor of 515 North Washington Avenue, and through his southern window-wall looked across Saginaw's roof tops to the familiar Michigan Bean Elevator.⁴ To answer his imperious buzzer he still had Deloris Menthen, who had been his secretary for almost three decades. In the early days he had shared her with Ran Wickes: she was the discreet repository of the company's innermost secrets.⁵ And down the hall were more faces from old times: Tom Rulison, now field operations vice president of the huge Lumber Division; Group Senior Vice President Bob Dodge, who as a young man had served as Fitz-Gerald's foil in the Al Riedel confrontation; Bill Hensler, with Wickes since 1960, who had risen through the ranks to

FAMILIAR FACES

*During his last months
at the Saginaw office,
Dan Fitz-Gerald relied as
always on Deloris Menthen
(left), often chatted
with Wickes old-timer
Bill Hensler, administrative
vice president of Wickes
Lumber (right).* (Portrait
by Bosch, Saginaw)

become Lumber's administrative V.P.;[6] and Tom Cline, the member of the Wolohan clan who had decided to stick with Fitz-Gerald when his uncles split from the firm.[7] Retired Smith Bolton, Wickes' elder statesman, dropped by on occasion.

Fitz-Gerald's decision to keep his personal headquarters in Saginaw somewhat softened the blow to the town's pride, but there was still much resentment of the corporate relocation, and many a sharp barb was fired across the communal lunch tables at the Saginaw Club.

In fact, only forty Wickes families had been involved in the move. Although the departed executives collected most of the top salaries, the city's payroll loss was negligible, for the corporation's Lumber Division, which employed more than 1,000

THEY TURNED OUT FOR THE CHIEF

Wickes staffers all over the country sent their best wishes to ailing Dan Fitz-Gerald. The Saginaw crew is shown above (Photo by Bradford-La Riviere, Inc.), the San Diego headquarters contingent at left, and the Chicago bunch below.

people at headquarters, did not leave. Nor did Wickes Agriculture, Engineered Materials, Wickes Tool, and Saginaw Machine and Tool.[8] But removal of the corporate nerve center had become inevitable for a number of highly practical reasons. GM's Saginaw Steering Gear, as the area's biggest employer, almost preempted the skilled clerical labor pool. Recruiting executive talent had become increasingly difficult. The Saginaw telephone exchange of Michigan Bell already was taxed to its limits by the demands of General Motors and of Wickes Lumber with its nationwide network of building supply centers. To add computer hookups to this phone load, as had been intended, was impossible. Moreover, transportation was turning into a real problem. A single month might find McNeely, Drum, or any other Wickes wallah chasing to Los Angeles, Chicago, Amsterdam, Washington, South Bend, Oregon's Cascades, California's San Joaquin Valley, and Red Lion, Pennsylvania. Typically, they spent four out of five days on the road. Saginaw's air connections were not up to this demand. San Diego averages nearly 200 arrivals and departures a day (as against Tri-City's 26); eight scheduled airlines offer direct, often nonstop service to most major cities (while Saginaw only has two carriers, and you almost always have to change in Chicago or Detroit to reach your destination). What's more, in San Diego, it's fifteen minutes from the Wickes office to the boarding gate.[9]

Psychological orientation as well as financing considerations also entered the picture. As Wickes followed the acquisition route from lumberyard to lumber source, the Far West increasingly figured in the corporation's scheme. Besides, between the building supply centers and the furniture stores, California was rapidly developing into a major market for Wickes. It accounted for a quarter of the volume, more than any other state or geographic region, and its share was likely to go up as annual sales approached the second billion.

Originally, when Wickes hurdled the billion-dollar barrier in calendar 1974, the target date for doubling this volume had been set as calendar 1979, i.e., fiscal 1980. Five years is about as far ahead as Wickes details planning. Now and again the top executives get together for what McNeely calls "in-house fun and games" where everybody leans back and dreams of what's going to happen ten or fifteen years hence. These sessions do not take place in a blue-sky vacuum, however. What gets kicked around on those occasions are studies by the Stanford Research Institute, Transamerica Corp., Massachusetts Institute of Technology, and the like. But these scholarly speculations are looked to merely as contingencies. A review of what studies of this type, conducted ten years ago, foretold about the present indicates that even the best thinking on the part of some of the world's best brains turns out to be more often wrong than right. To run Wickes in conformance with such hypotheses would put it on a troubled zigzag course. To survive day-to-day challenges, an organization must be pragmatic about the present while trusting that it is flexible enough to change step when the Pied Piper switches tunes: all preparations for the distant future are of no avail if you go bust before it comes. True, the future has a way nowadays of arriving ahead of schedule, but Wickes tries to be set for that. McNeely makes it a point that his staff must learn to live with future shock. The corporation's five-year plans are reasonably precise but always open to instant amendment. At the very least, they are revised every year. That makes for a fast-moving company.

Take that two-billion-dollar target set in 1974. Within a year, and despite the rapidly deteriorating economic situation at that time, the 1980 goal was upped to $2.8 billion, not because McNeely and Drum had sidetripped to Tijuana for some peyote, but because that's what the adding machine said: it was the total of what the general managers of the various divisions thought they could reasonably accomplish. If things don't quite work out that way, nobody will hold it against them. It's recognized at Wickes that the only way never to strike out is never to swing. Although it may appear that the Wickes executive suite is equipped with an automated revolving door, most of the people who did get checked out were pushing their organizations around so hard that they became useless as leaders, or they weren't standing up and taking their own heat, or they really didn't care, or they didn't try to work with the others on their team, or they were so defensive about situations that they lost their objectivity. Nobody's been bounced yet because he put money on the wrong horse when the horse looked good. Intelligent mistakes are taken for granted, provided they don't happen too often—but then they wouldn't be intelligent.

Needless to say, McNeely is not blind to the fact that the world is changing and that Wickes has to change with it. "Starting in the 1950s," he says, "Wickes was very entrepreneurial for a company that had been around so long. We moved forward on quick, intuitive decisions, and things were done less than professionally sometimes, but it worked. Times were such that you could make little mistakes and get away with it. We all got big kicks out of our rapid growth, folding in companies that added to the sales and profits. It was more or less a joyous kind of free-wheeling activity. That's over. At the size we are now, and the way the economy looks for the future, we can no longer rely on pure intuition. If we make a mistake now, it's a giant mistake.

Again, because of our size, because of Federal Trade Commission regulations, and because of our position in some markets, we have to look to other ways to grow. Whether we like it or not, we must be more exact in our planning, must have greater control, must do more following up, and must have brighter, better-trained managers."

In saying this, McNeely is not ringing the death knell for the entrepreneurial spirit. He believes with Alvin Toffler, author of *Future Shock*, that things are moving along at such a pace that by the time you've learned to do something properly it's almost gone out of style. This means there has to be some leapfrogging to find the best way to run a business. And leapfrogging does mean taking chances, for you don't know exactly where you'll land. "We're not trying to exercise caution to the extent that we'll stand still," McNeely says. "I think the bright young people we've brought into the corporation in the past few years possess the entrepreneurial spirit. But they'll have to be a lot more thorough than we used to be. They'll have to be able to survey the situation in a much broader way than we who were great risk takers without always having the knowledge of what we were doing." In other words, McNeely's symbolic ski racer still won't be snowplowing down the hill, but will have to learn to cut turns with more precision.

It was this kind of thinking that prompted McNeely to make his Office of the President a training ground for Wickes's young lions. The talent that came up through this postgraduate, on-the-job project was radically different in background, education, and intellectual discipline from the leaders of old, or even those of today. John McCullough had to ride Dan Fitz-Gerald to make him crack his schoolbooks, and even then young Dan barely scraped by. Only his innate shrewdness saved him. Tom Rulison had had only one year of college. Al Riedel didn't even finish high school. Nor did Joe McMullin. McNeely is a voracious reader, but not per se a scholar; not having the time to research Toffler's sources, for example, he must make do with the author's conclusions. Drum, who has an extraordinary talent for practical engineering and a solid technical as well as marketing background, can deal effectively with foreign businessmen on the basis of his profound practicality, but the national nuances, the little differences in the ways that, say, Hollanders and Germans tick, and which do influence their buying attitudes—such matters are not Drum's cup of tea.

Contrast that type of person with Paul Hylbert, who is no less pragmatic than his predecessors but who majored in history, lived abroad in his youth, and is fairly fluent in a couple of foreign languages. Or with thirty-year-old Tom Hannah, who took his masters in political science at Michigan State and is altogether the type of fellow you'd expect to meet at a university faculty club rather than in a business office; he was the corporation's director of acquisitions for two years and is now breaking into international bean marketing at Wickes Agriculture. Or take Ron Woods, who saved the company's recrea-

THE NEW LOOK AT WICKES

Here are some of the faces you see around Wickes these days. McNeely calls them his "thundering young herd." Above is the legal department's Hyman J. Lee (Photo by Victor Avila). *On the opposite page, clockwise from top left are Roy Ashbrook, of Forest Industries; Richard Passaglia, of the Lumber Division; Doug Hofeldt, of Behlen; and Jonathan Fish, who got stuck with the difficult and disheartening assignment of writing the financial epitaph for Wickes Homes* (Photo by Victor Avila).

tional vehicles business, and who might well have shoved the whole mobile homes industry into a new, enlightened era if financial circumstances had not militated against him. Nor is the youthful Wickes braintrust confined to Office of the President alumni. For instance, there are Bill Boyle, the treasurer; Ralph Pfaff, the computer wizard: physicist and financial man in one; and Hyman Lee, who straight A'd himself through college, fellowshipped at Yale, and then went on to Harvard Law. Or take Dave Primuth and Art Nasso. M.B.A.'s rather than B.A.'s have become the standard in many management areas around the shop.

Throughout the corporation, youth is on the move. More than one-third of the center managers are under thirty-five. Up at the divisional level too, more and more responsible

ROBERT B. THELE

*At thirty-six, the vice-president
of administration of the
Furniture Division often finds
himself on special assignments.*

positions are being filled by the new generation. Look at the lineup in late 1975: At Behlen, thirty-year-old Doug Hofeldt is controller.[10] Dick Passaglia had barely turned thirty-five when he was named the Lumber Division's vice president of merchandising, a job held by John Drum not too long ago.[11] Bob Thele, thirty-four, is vice president and controller of Wickes Furniture.[12] Roy Ashbrook, also thirty-four, manages the Dinuba operations of Forest Industries.[13] Art Simmons, thirty-two, has been general manager of Saginaw Machine and Tool for nearly a year.[14] Jonathan Fish, thirty-one, the corporation's former director of financial planning and analysis, served most recently as controller at Wickes Homes, working on the disposals of the discontinued properties. Indeed, there are so many promising young people with Wickes today that they cannot all be named—a book is not a personnel roster. If brains and schooling can accomplish what pure intuition would muff, then Wickes is all set for the future.

What does this future look like?

First let's consider the areas that seem unrelated to Wickes's central thrust in the shelter area, namely the manufacturing divisions. On the face of it, the most marginal of these would be the machine tool companies. After all, the automotive industry, which is their major customer, is suffering serious convulsions. But that's viewing the machine tool properties with blinders on. The business of these divisions may be down at the moment, but in the percentage of profit incrementation, their chances are extraordinarily good. How so? Well, that's where the leapfrogging comes in.

Some 100 million cars on the road today will have to be replaced for the simple reason that they're gulping too much gas. When Detroit's ponderous giants finally let out the clutch on more sensible vehicles, they'll come up with models that will reduce use of petroleum products by at least 20 to 30 percent. Among other things, these new cars will require smaller crankshafts and transmissions—and tools for these are among Wickes specialties. If anything, Wickes Machine Tool and Saginaw Machine and Tool would do worse if automobiles remained the same. Similar benefits will accrue to Kux Machine and Wickes Engineered Materials. The former's die-casting machines will be in demand for the retooling, and its powder metallurgy presses for components of new dimensions; in turn, Engineered Materials will be engaged in the production of hundreds of thousands of powdered-metal rings, bearings, etc., all to new specifications.

Agriculture seems more in the Wickes bailiwick, if for no other reason than that it's concerned with needs rather than wants, a distinction that has always figured prominently in Wickes thinking. So far as corporate profits are concerned, we already know that this has worked out very well indeed. Like the housing industry, agriculture tends to yo-yo, but the way the world's economy is shaping up, their respective ups and downs are inclined to be countercyclical these days. It doesn't always work out exactly like that, but in fiscal 1974 and 1975, for instance, Wickes's involvement in commodities saw the corporation through a frighteningly deep dip in housing starts.

Wickes
Manufacturing
Facilities

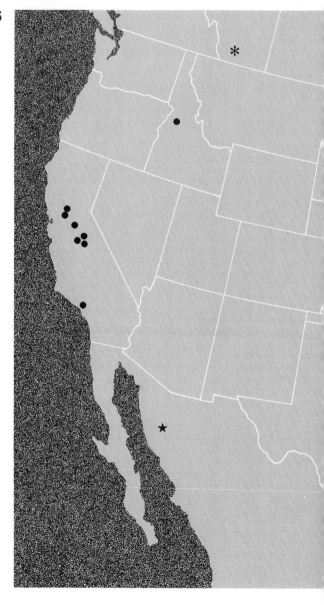

BEHLEN MANUFACTURING COMPANY ▲   WICKES ENGINEERED MATERIALS ★

KUX MACHINE ■   WICKES FOREST INDUSTRIES ●

MARON PRODUCTS, INC. ✪   WICKES HOMES ✳

GINAW MACHINE AND TOOL COMPANY □   WICKES MACHINE TOOL △

WICKES BUILDINGS ☆   LEE L. WOODARD & SONS, INC. ✷

WICKES BUILDING COMPONENTS ⬠   YORKTOWNE ○

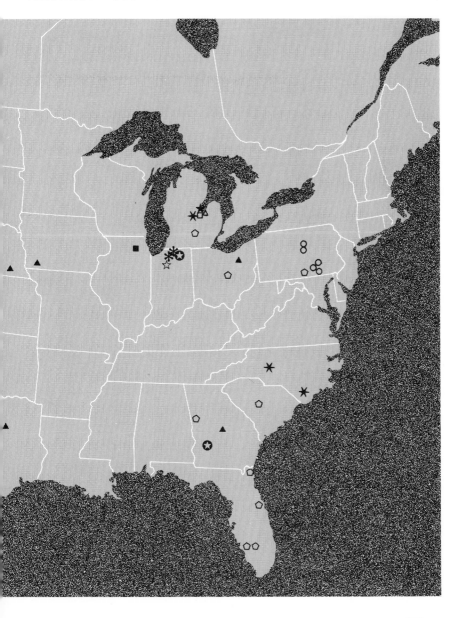

369

Housing and agriculture conceivably could both be going down at the same time, too. Barring a worldwide fiscal fiasco, however, that isn't too likely in view of the general food shortage. By the same token, they could both hit the upbeat at the same time, and if that should happen, says McNeely, "We won't know how to spend all that money."

The great advantage Wickes enjoys in the agricultural area is that the company deals in dry, machine-harvested, easily bulk-stored crops that are, moreover, of high nutritional value—especially protein-rich beans.

Teach a farmer to sow and ye both shall reap. The 1975 merger into Wickes of two bean companies in Idaho was another step in this direction: M. J. Bean and Hunter Bean are producers of seed beans, the kind of beans you need to efficiently turn large acreages into bean country. Wickes is even proselytizing Brazil, an ideal region for bean culture of all varieties, where pintos, too, should do well. Eventually, Wickes Agriculture may tackle some Asian countries, and perhaps Yugoslavia and Hungary, and make them pinto exporters—through Wickes Agriculture, of course.

Right here at home, prospects appear no less promising. As demand for foodstuffs continues to rise, marginal acreage increasingly will come into play, but, with new technology, this land won't be marginal anymore. Productivity is bound to improve substantially. One thing is sure: Farmers won't be allowed to starve. Ever diminishing in number, they may not have much clout at the polls, but the country needs a healthy agricultural sector, not only to feed itself but to export the produce—America's big-bore weapon in its war against trade deficits, and its potentially most important bargaining tool in the coming struggle to obtain essential raw materials from other parts of the world.

This situation inevitably will enhance not only the position of Wickes Agriculture, but also of Behlen Manufacturing and Wickes Buildings. In Columbus, Nebraska, and Brandon, Manitoba, Behlen has reached the limits of its present production capacity. When Behlen was acquired, McNeely projected its five-year goal at a volume of $50 million. In fiscal 1975, Behlen did $60 million. But that was as far as it could go. What held up plant expansion here was the steel shortage of the early 1970s: there was no point in building another manufacturing facility or two if the raw material required for increased production was unavailable. Now the steel pinch, which is an on-and-off proposition, has passed. As soon as funds are available to green-light Behlen's expansion, an increase in volume and profits—maybe as much as fivefold, depending on the size and number of facilities built—wouldn't surprise McNeely at all. Among probable moves is construction of a Behlen plant in Europe.

As for Wickes Buildings—that perpetual money machine whose sales have increased nearly eightfold from the time the Moriarty pole-building operation was acquired—this division may well show the greatest percentage growth of all. Only twenty of the Wickes lumber centers are now used as Wickes Buildings outlets. That leaves another 250 markets to be tapped. Wickes Buildings' 1980 volume—conservatively figured—is expected to be about $100 million, up more than three times fiscal 1975 sales.

The future of Wickes Furniture is almost a foregone conclusion. Except for Levitz, it is the biggest furniture discounter in the business. There's still a big gap, to be sure. Wickes only has twenty-three outlets, and Levitz more than sixty. But with the big-daddy Wickes Corporation backing up its new baby, the Furniture Division will be fed everything it needs to grow up big and strong. A modest projection foresees 1980 sales of about $160 million, with profits of about $13 million. This would put the division's anticipated growth rate at 16.5 percent for volume and 25 percent for earnings. Somewhat similar expansion patterns are envisioned for Yorktowne and Lee L. Woodard Sons, the Wickes arms engaged in furniture manufacture.

Now for the homes where all that furniture will go. While Behlen and Wickes Buildings are part and parcel of the corporation's major franchise—the production and distribution of shelter in its many forms—the provision of housing for people remains Wickes's central purpose. True, Wickes stumbled onto this scene. If it hadn't been for Joe McMullin, Wickes might still only know from beans. The Cash Ways were a lucky strike. Wickes couldn't have done better by design: Never before had there been so much need for housing, and for faster, more efficient, more economical methods of meeting this demand.

As a first step, the Wickes lumber and building supply centers supplanted the clumsy lumberyards of yesterday. Then Wickes had slipped into the other end of the shelter pipeline with the acquisition of Sequoia Forest Industries. The manufacture of steel buildings and pole buildings followed, as did the aborted efforts to make "modulars" and to become established in the mobile homes industry. But despite these failures, more and more pieces kept falling into place: wrought iron furniture, kitchen cabinets, truss and door plants, millwork, factory-built garages and vacation cottages, furniture outlets, consumer credit. Along the way, Wickes invaded the wholesale echelons of the shelter business by embracing Oregon-Pacific, Steel City Lumber, and finally the extensive web of Evans Products warehouses. No master plan could have achieved a more perfect positioning for what's about to come.

The winter of 1975 marked the 355th anniversary of the Pilgrims' landing at Plymouth Rock. Between 1620 and today, roughly 150 million houses have been built in this country. In the next thirty years, about 50 million more will have to go up. This means that in every single year between now and 2005 nearly five times as much building will have to be done as in an average year in the nation's past. World War II's Manhattan Project seems child's play by comparison.

Much as the current economic turmoil has raised the question of whether the United States can maintain its traditional standard of living, this is an academic rather than a practical issue. Society—and business—must answer in the affirmative. There is no other way. Otherwise, everybody might as well heed the advice of those no-growth proponents of a return to cottage industry who would have us sitting around in patched blue jeans, making baubles, bangles, and beads. Those idyllic cottages would be unpleasantly overcrowded—but never mind that. More important, they had better be equipped with moats and barricades, for the have-lesses of our society will insist on having all that has been promised to them in TV commercials and the time-fillers between. So it becomes an extremely critical problem, well out of range of bull-session seminars. An adequate standard of living—adequate in terms of expectation rather than bare necessity—must be provided lest there be blood and not just discarded candy wrappers in the gutters. One of the essentials to maintain our standard of living is obviously the availability of shelter at the lowest possible cost. And that's precisely Wickes's line of business.

Apart from the eventually inevitable resurgence of housing starts, which alone should increase the sales of Wickes Lumber manifold, there is the potential for increased penetration of the markets where Wickes already is established. By all odds, Wickes Lumber, even as it is situated today, is the country's largest distributor of building supplies. This also makes it the world's biggest, but for the moment that's beside the point. Surprising as it may seem, however, to people brought up to think of the "biggest" in terms of a General Motors type of market dominance, Wickes Lumber actually serves only a small percentage of the total building business. In any given area where Wickes has stores, its share may range from a low of 1.5 percent, and sometimes even less, to about 20 percent at best. Evidently there's plenty of room for additional sales. That these additional sales can be made is evidenced by special promotions staged by Bob Welsh, Wickes Lumber's indefatigable marketing manager.

After the Wickes acquisition of the six Home Mart stores in Georgia, Welsh arranged for a grand opening on April 17, 1975, a full-of-pizzazz affair in which the four existing Wickes centers in the area joined for a two-week "celebration." Each store featured its own come-on events, ranging from jazz concerts and antique-automobile rides to a sawdust box where youngsters searched for hidden money. More than 10,000 hot dogs and Cokes were consumed at a nickel each. The promotion cost a pile. But in that two-week period, the average sales volume per store increased nearly fivefold—and this was accomplished despite the 1975 recession. Just to cite one item of this sales gala: More than 100,000 building studs went out in three days.[16] A similar sales push in the Saginaw area stores followed in May, and with equal success. Evidently you don't need a "grand opening" to drum up customers. So much for locations where Wickes already is in business. And there is still a lot of country left where location studies haven't even been started.

As we know, Wickes's premature but by no means illogical venture into "modular" housing came a cropper, but since then Wickes has profited in a real sense from this sad experience. The manufacture of two-dimensional shelter components and their sale through the building supply centers now play an increasingly important role in the Lumber Division's volume, and there is every indication that this business will grow even faster in the future. It's a matter of cost efficiencies: contractors can build houses more cheaply when they use factory-made components than when they have to hammer the whole structure together on the building site.

Nor has the corporation's more recent retreat from the mobile homes business turned off thinking about some sort of more complete manufactured housing unit. Wickes had to get out of mobiles. Under the conditions prevailing in that industry, there was no other way to go. But the fact remains that conventional stick-built housing, principally because of high on-site labor costs, is too expensive for an ever larger, already very substantial segment of the population. Some way must be found to provide shelter at a lower price, and Wickes intends to hang right in there.

Not that McNeely plans to play Don Quixote; if he were a windmill tilter, Wickes would still be making mobile homes. "All right," he says, "we've taken our bruises. We know enough now not to move against inexorable forces. But we also know that the need for cheaper housing is still unfulfilled, and that with our positioning, and with what we have learned, we have a definite place in that picture."

Just what approach Wickes will take is not yet clear. Only one thing is certain: the project will not involve substantial investments before it's proven out in the market place. No doubt, it will be based on the corporation's existing component-manufacture capability, and its already successful production of factory-built vacation homes and garage units. A new Wickes manufactured home may well be smaller (say in the 800 to 1500 square foot range) than conventional homes currently being built. There's also a good chance that—whatever form it takes—it will be distributed through the building supply centers, as the trusses and other two-dimensional components, the garages, and the vacation cottages are today. In fact, many of the centers sit on property with real estate to spare, so that local production facilities can be added easily and at no great expense. But this wouldn't be a problem anyway. Everybody loves a winner, and if Wickes does succeed, as well it might, in developing a marketable, partly or wholly manufactured low-cost house, it'll be the rare investor who won't want to climb on the bandwagon.

Still, the matter of the corporation's overall profitability, as discussed up to this point, can come under question. Volume is one thing. Net earnings are something else again. There is little doubt that about the time Wickes crosses the $2 billion line, profits after taxes will total around $60 million. Assuming that by then about 12 million common shares will be outstanding, earnings per share should amount to approximately $5, certainly more than double the $2.20 of fiscal 1974, Wickes's most profitable year to date. At a conservative 10-times-multiplier (conservative by the standards of normal times), a share should then be worth about $50—a pleasant prospect. But looking at it cold turkey, $60 million is only 3 percent of $2 billion, and that's not how McNeely and Drum view their world. They recognize that, in pursuing mainly high-volume businesses so as to supply consumers at the lowest possible prices, they are committed to low margins. This applies even more to the wholesaling of lumber and the distribution of building materials, which are the functions of Wickes Wholesale and Sequoia Supply.

To compensate for its low-margin operations, as well as to support retail sales—particularly those of Wickes Furniture—the corporation definitely plans to expand its financial services, a field with traditionally high margins. The double thrust of this approach is evident: You make money on the loans, and on credit insurance where that's applicable, while giving customers that much more incentive to buy from you. To add a captive life insurance company to the already extant financial service units is an announced goal of the company. The cash flow inherent in such an operation is but one aspect of the impetus for an acquisition of that kind. Its insurance policies, of the same types offered by any other "straight" life insurance company, from term to cash-value contracts, will be made available to a whole array of customers: to Wickes's contractor-builders and their clients in turn, to individual buyers at Wickes building supply centers and Wickes furniture stores, and even to Wickes employees. Mail-order will no doubt also be used—Wickes Credit, with its 200,000 screened cardholders, and very likely many more by that time, should send that project off to a flying start.

And now we come to the most romantic part of the tale that wags the future Wickes. A home built of materials and components from a Wickes Lumber center, or a factory-built Wickes house if it comes to that, may be cozy to live in, pleasant to look at, and probably more reasonably priced than other houses. A piece of Wickes furniture may be decorative and easy on the rump. But where it's really at is the basic source of most of these products. That's where you smell the sap of sun-warmed trees, walk on soft carpets of needles and hear the shriek of the saws, where you wipe the dust of logging trucks out of your eyes, and finally listen to the whine of winches loading lumber. It's here at the forest frontier that you find perhaps the greatest potential for the corporation's future. Wickes Forest Products is only the beginning.

That division now cuts timber largely on government land

leased in Idaho and California. But this activity presents many problems. Logging government forests is a take-it-when-you-can affair limited by many restrictions, some of them needed but some a sop to conservation zealots, many of whom don't want to know that most timber stands can't flourish without periodic fires or cutting. At the same time, the price of private forest land has become prohibitive, and there is no prospect that valuations will go down to the point where a return on the required investment becomes reasonable. Thus, Wickes's own lumber production is not likely to accelerate greatly. But timber and other woods can be purchased in other parts of the world. Wickes Forest Industries gets a steady stream of feelers from countries without softwoods—Japan, the Philippines, the African nations—as well as from geographic regions without hardwoods or exotic specialty woods like Scandinavia and Australia. "I am convinced," says McNeely, "that with the knowledge we have gained from our operations here, and marketing experience we have through Wickes Europe, we can carve a substantial place for ourselves in the distribution of timber and timber products abroad."

McNeely's and Drum's thinking along these lines has not yet been translated into any five-year plans. But the first step in this direction was taken in early 1975, when Wickes's most experienced lumberman on every level from sawmill to sales office, Clark Johnson, became senior vice president of a group that most significantly includes not only Oregon-Pacific and Forest Products, but also Wickes Europe, and with all this, the as-yet-undefined category, "international operations." In the thinking stage along these lines is the establishment of a partially owned subsidiary, perhaps to be called Wickes International, like Corky van Bergeijk's bean business of old, whose stock would be offered to foreign investors to raise capital for global expansion.

There's more to this scheme than merely buying wood in one place and selling it somewhere else. Remember how Tony Swies and Paul Hylbert wore down the building supply cartels in the Low Countries. Similar archaic four- and five-step distribution systems are the rule throughout the world. Interposed between the forest and the consumer, there are export agents, import agents, superdistributors, distributors, dealers, and contractors. Everybody takes his cut along the way, with the result that expensive as housing is in the United States, it's still a lot cheaper than anywhere else. In many countries, the insult of inefficiency is added to economic injury. For instance, in Australia, every single piece of gypsum board is custom-made for the particular job it's ordered for. To simplify such cumbersome, costly practices—and to profit from the simplification— is John Drum's crusade.

"Everybody is concentrating on staying in his own little niche and filling his pocket," he says. "That's true right here, too. Lumber dealers over the years have said, 'Oh, we're not going to sell to the mobile home manufacturer. He competes with our builders.' So a whole new chain of distribution was created to supply the mobile home manufacturer with exactly the same kind of service that the lumber dealer could have offered in the first place. But he chose to close his eyes and he put an umbrella over what he thought was his customer, and this helped neither himself nor his customer nor the ultimate consumer. In foreign countries, you've got this situation in spades. The reason we've been successful is that we have kept the customer in mind constantly and how we get him better value. We've never been mesmerized by margins, and so long as I'm around, we won't be. Our most important export will be our philosophy about that."

Drum's first foreign project is to develop a facility in Rotterdam for the receipt of goods for distribution through Wickes's own outlets in Europe. The inflow will not be limited by the market of the in-house distribution chain. Drum's intention is to sell to Wickes's competitors as well. This, he feels, will eliminate several intermediary levels and result in lower consumer prices. As for the competition at the retail level, Drum figures that Wickes will do O.K. The way he sees it is that, if Wickes can't compete by being more efficient, it shouldn't be in there pitching in the first place.

"We don't care how people want to buy building materials," he says. "We're going to sell them. The cost of vacation homes

JOHN DRUM

*The new president of Wickes is a visionary at heart, a pragmatist in
action. "There's no other way," he says, "to achieve one's dreams."*
(Photo by Victor Avila)

like we're producing at Wickes Lumber is about 60 percent materials. Labor amounts to 12 percent. So we're merely talking about a method of marketing building materials. If there are a couple of million people in this country who want to buy their building materials in that form, that's fine with us. And if it takes the form of a garage, that's fine, too. If they want to buy the material prefabricated, or for building on site, or whatever else it is, we're going to keep ourselves in a position to ride with the market. And that goes for every part of the world where we'll be in business."

By happenstance, Wickes already is in business in the Middle East. In June 1975, an influential Saudi Arabian businessman, Fallah Ben-Jabr, whose family has extensive interests in Jeddah, Riyahd, and Yanbu, contacted the Wickes Furniture warehouse-showroom in Anaheim, California. At that time, this was all he thought there was to Wickes: he wanted to buy furniture for a hotel he was building back home. When Ben-Jabr learned of Wickes's other dimensions, a meeting with John Braun, of Oregon-Pacific, was arranged, and before long, in addition to the hotel furniture, Wickes had orders for lumber, plywood, and other building materials for six speculative houses in Jeddah. The shipment, sourced by Oregon-Pacific, Sequoia, and Wickes Lumber, arrived in Jeddah in October, coordinated by Paul Hylbert and accompanied by Braun, who immediately received additional orders for more rough lumber, as well as finished materials, such as electrical, plumbing, and appliances.

Ben-Jabr then introduced Braun to some other potential customers in the Middle East, and Braun found himself selling 140 air conditioners in one case, and bidding on a 100-house development in another. On his way back to the States, Braun wrote up more orders—about one million dollars worth—in Italy, France, Germany, Belgium, Spain, and the United Kingdom. By the end of 1975, Oregon-Pacific had chalked up yet an additional million in export business.

The success story doesn't end here. Thanks to Ben-Jabr's good offices, Behlen Manufacturing also got into the act.

Behlen's national accounts manager, John Duffy, was put into contact with the airport expansion program in Riyahd, which holds out the possibility of more Wickes business in Behlen stressed-skin hangars. And while he was over there, Duffy went on to Teheran, Iran, for the Agwa (agricultural) Trade Fair. Here, he encountered immense interest not only in Behlen products, but in building materials and Wickes Agriculture as well. These leads were left to be followed up later. For the moment, Duffy was busy enough on behalf of Behlen, bidding on twenty separate projects around the world. All in all, as 1976 rolled around, it seemed that Wickes International was well into its launching, and that John Drum's daydreams are far closer to reality than he himself would have supposed just a few months earlier.

On those rare days when he is in his San Diego office, the new Wickes president likes to look out of its big window now and then, across San Diego Bay. Parked out there, often in impressive ranks, are carriers, missile cruisers, and other lesser Navy craft. But what Drum sees in his mind's eye is a freighter, one of many with big red and blue Ws painted on their sides, that's just pulling into port. That imaginary vessel's voyage started in Eugene, Oregon, where it picked up Douglas fir destined for Europe. Since then the ship has loaded soft woods on the north coast of Africa and delivered them to India, hauled mahogany from the Philippines to Taiwan for processing, and there filled its holds with finished case goods, which it is about to deposit at its San Diego pier. Next it will sail to Vladivostok with Behlen buildings bound for Russian farms, and there it will take on Siberian timber.

This is but a fleeting vision. Soon Drum's nose is back in his peripatetic briefcase, which bulges with more immediate matters. But almost all these, in one way or another, concern the same mission as that of the Wickes ship—the movement of building materials from their origins into the possession of the ultimate user. Their form matters not: raw or finished or at any appropriate stage between, wood or steel or composition. If some day plastic houses should pop out of molds, then so be it.

Notes and Comments

Chapter 1

1. The guest book of the Wickes Billion-Dollar Dinner shows the following names:
James Bere, chairman, Borg-Warner Corp., Chicago; Harold Berry, chairman
of the investment banking committee, Merrill Lynch, Pierce, Fenner & Smith,
New York; James H. Binns, chairman, Armstrong Cork, Lancaster, Pennsylvania; William Boeschenstein, chairman, Owens-Corning Fiberglas, Toledo, Ohio;
Edward Bronstein, president, Englander/U.S. Bedding, St. Paul, Minnesota;
Colon Brown, chairman, National Gypsum, Buffalo, New York; Paul Broyhill,
president, Broyhill Furniture Industries, Lenoir, North Carolina; H. W. Campbell, vice president, Frigidaire Division of General Motors, Dayton, Ohio;

Monte Carpenter, executive vice president, Flintkote, White Plains, New
York; Arthur Carroll, vice president, North American Division, Sanders Associ-
ates, Nashua, New Hampshire; Hammond Chaffetz, of Kirkland and Ellis,
Chicago; William Cohn, marketing vice president, U.S. Bedding, St. Paul,
Minnesota;

Philip L. Defliese, managing partner, Coopers & Lybrand, New York; George
DeFranceaux, chairman, National Corporation for Housing Partnerships,
Washington, D.C.; William J. Dixon, president, Chicago, Rock Island and
Pacific Railroad, Chicago;

Joseph Hall, group vice president, GAF Corp., New York; Carl E. Hartnack,
president, Security Pacific National Bank, Los Angeles; Jack Hayes, group vice
president, National Gypsum, Buffalo, New York; James C. Hemphill, partner,
Goldman, Sachs & Co., Chicago; Melvin A. Holmes, president (now vice
chairman), Frank B. Hall & Co., New York; Paul R. Judy, president, A. G.

Becker and Co., Chicago; Charles Keller, president, Pioneer Plastics, Auburn, Maine; Richard Knipe, vice president and general manager, Kaiser Aluminum & Chemical, Oakland, California;

Warren W. Lebeck, president, Chicago Board of Trade; William G. Lees, executive vice president, Jim Walter Corp., Tampa, Florida; Gustave L. Levy, senior partner, Goldman, Sachs & Co., New York;

Guy O. Mabry, division general manager, Owens-Corning Fiberglas, Toledo, Ohio; George Clarke Martin, president, National Association of Homebuilders, Louisville, Kentucky; John J. McCullough, retired partner and former member of the executive committee, Coopers & Lybrand, Detroit; Malcolm Meyer, chairman, Certain-Teed Products, Valley Forge, Pennsylvania; Walter Mischer, chairman, The Mischer Corp., Houston, Texas; J. D. Moran, president, Flintkote, White Plains, New York; Graham J. Morgan, chairman, U.S. Gypsum, Chicago; Lewis Murdock, senior vice president, First National City Bank, New York;

Robert J. Newhouse, Jr., president, Marsh & McLennan, New York; Howard Niederman, president, Howard Parlor Furniture, Chicago; Karl Nygren, of Kirkland and Ellis, Chicago;

Joseph Quarles, president, Simmons, New York; B. C. Radaker, president, Certain-Teed Products, Valley Forge, Pennsylvania; T. A. Russell, president, Federal-Mogul, Southfield, Michigan;

Paul C. Souder, president, Michigan National Bank, Lansing, Michigan; Robert Spilman, president, Bassett Furniture Industries, Bassett, Virginia; Robert D. Stephan, vice president, U.S. Gypsum, Chicago; William C. Stutt, partner, Goldman, Sachs & Co., New York; Robert Suhr, executive vice president, Continental National Bank, Chicago; Earl C. Swanson, chairman, Andersen Corp., Bayport, Minnesota; George Swindells, Jr., marketing vice president, Willamette Industries, Portland, Oregon; T. Taniquichi, executive vice president, Mitsubishi International, New York; Albert P. Teetzel, partner, Coopers & Lybrand, San Diego; Richard L. Thomas, vice chairman, First National Bank of Chicago; Clifford C. Van Dyke, vice president, National Bank of Detroit; Harry J. Volk, chairman, Union Bank of Los Angeles; Bland W. Worley, president, Wachovia Corp., Winston-Salem, North Carolina.

Present from The Wickes Corporation were E. L. McNeely, then president; John Drum and George O'Dair, at that time executive vice presidents; and the following other officers of the corporation: Thomas W. Cline, Richard G. Cotton, Robert G. Dodge, Eugene Gordon, Clark A. Johnson, David J. Primuth, Paul H. Tatz, Peter W. Willox, and Ronald J. Woods, as well as Karl Dahlem and Tom Kaminski of the corporate communications staff. The outside Wickes directors who attended, in addition to Souder and Hartnack (mentioned above), were Walter D. Behlen, Thomas C. Harvey, and John A. Ritzenthaler.

General Lauris Norstad hosted the gathering. Actor Peter Lind Hayes, widely known as the husband of Mary Healy, was the master of ceremonies.

2. These were the numbers of lumber and building supply centers in operation at the beginning of 1976. The number of United States outlets changes constantly, with some being decommissioned and more added every year (see Chapters 10–13). In early 1976, Wickes Europe had eight stores operating in Holland; four each in Belgium and the United Kingdom; and one in Germany (see Chapter 14).

3. The pretax profit percentages cited for the agricultural commodity and agricultural equipment operations relate to corporate earnings exclusive of the firm's unconsolidated subsidiaries.

Chapter 2

1. The Wickes Corporation of today, which dates back to October 3, 1947 (see Chapter 6), was first listed on the New York Curb Exchange, which later became the American Stock Exchange. Since October 16, 1961, the corporation's stocks and bonds have been traded on the Big Board. Dividends have been paid by Wickes and its predecessor companies for more than eighty years.

2. The name Wickes derives from le Wrey (of Norman origin), which changed successively to Wykes (at about the time of Richard II), Weekes (in the early part of the seventeenth century), and Weeks (retained until 1671). An American branch of the family still carries the name Weeks.

   The earliest known ancestor was Robert le Wrey, who was recorded as alive in 1135, and whose father had probably come to England with William the Conqueror. Thomas Weeks, the fourth great-grandfather of Henry Dunn Wickes, was born in Devonshire about 1612; with his brothers George and Francis, he sailed for Massachusetts in 1635. Later he moved from Watertown, Massachusetts, to Wethersfield, Connecticut, and from there to Stamford, of which he was one of the original proprietors in 1640, and finally settled in Huntington, Long Island. Upon his death in 1671, his sons changed the name to Wickes, very likely to distinguish themselves from their cousins, the sons of Francis, who lived in the adjoining town of Oyster Bay. From Thomas Weeks's eldest son, Thomas Wickes, we can follow a direct line through Joseph, Silas, and James Wickes to James Harvey Wickes, father of Henry Dunn, Edward Noyes, and Charles Tuthill Wickes.

   James Harvey Wickes, born at Schaghticoke, New York, on February 24, 1802, engaged in the occupations of farming and cabinetmaking. On May 29, 1823, he married Maria Tuthill, born October 13, 1803, of Starkey, Yates County, New York. The couple moved to Reading Center, New York, in the late 1830s (some records give the date as 1837; others, as 1839), and in 1856 they returned to Yates County, locating at Rock Stream, where James Harvey Wickes died on August 13, 1866. His widow then lived at Watkins Glen, New York, until her death on June 10, 1884.

3. This figure is based on an average wholesale price of $13 per 1,000 board feet over the 1847–1897 period. See Rolland H. Maybee, *Michigan's White Pine Era* (Lansing: Michigan Historical Commission, 1960), p. 11. This publication also supplied other statistics cited in Chapter 2, as did the following books, all of which are recommended reading if you want to learn more about that colorful time.

   Most amusing of the list is Stewart H. Holbrook's *Holy Old Mackinaw: A Natural History of the American Lumberjack* (New York: Macmillan, 1938). Most statistical is George W. Hotchkiss, *History of the Lumber and Forest Industry of the Northwest* (Chicago: George W. Hotchkiss Co., 1898), whose chapter 10 deals specifically with the development of the lumber industry in the Saginaw Valley. For excellent pictures as well as informative text, see Irene M. Hargreaves and Harold M. Foehl, *The Story of Logging the White Pine in the Saginaw Valley* (Bay City, Mich.: Red Keg Press, 1964).

   Other informative material may be found in *Saginaw, Michigan, U.S.A. 1857–1907, A Semi-Centennial Souvenir*, published under the auspices of the Saginaw Board of Trade in 1907; and *1819–1969*, the historical program of the Saginaw Sesquicentennial, copies of which were still available at the Saginaw Chamber of Commerce in 1975. For biographies of leading citizens of that era, including the Wickes family, see James Cooke Mills, *History of Saginaw County, Michigan*, vol. 2 (Saginaw: Seemann & Peters, 1918).

    Perhaps the best all-around book on Michigan history, which was also used for backgrounding this chapter, is F. Clever Bald's *Michigan in Four Centuries* (New York: Harper & Row, 1961), and for just plain good reading, see Edmond G. Love, *The Situation in Flushing* (New York: Harper & Row, 1965), whose pages 5 through 9 provide some fascinating detail on the Chippewa Reservation.

4. *Industries of the Saginaws* (East Saginaw, Mich.: J. M. Elstner & Company, 1887), p. 106.

5. Edward Noyes Wickes, second oldest of the three Wickes brothers, was born at Starkey, New York, on November 11, 1835. Like Henry Dunn Wickes, he first lived on the maternal family farm and went to the district school at Reading Center. If anything, he was even more gifted mechanically than Henry, and according to James Cooke Mills, op. cit. (see Note 3, above), p. 60, he possessed "a genius for invention, and much of the success of the improved gangs and engines built by the firm was due to his ability. . . ." Never married, he lived with Henry and his family at 324 N. Jefferson in Saginaw for many years. He was a member of the Board of Water Commissioners of East Saginaw, and was instrumental in the installation of the city's original waterworks system in 1873.

6. Saginaw, at that time, was actually divided into two municipalities, the City of Saginaw and East Saginaw. For simplicity's sake, however, it is generally treated in this text as one.

7. The Bancroft Hotel had its own plant for making illuminating gas, another indication of its status, since gas was not yet publicly available. Both East Saginaw and the City of Saginaw, however, were among Michigan's first communities to install gas lamps, well ahead of Bay City and probably also of Flint. The East Saginaw Gas Light Co. was founded in 1863, and the Saginaw Gas Light Co. in 1868. Both were predecessor companies of Consumers Power, of which Daniel M. Fitz-Gerald, the late chairman of the board of the Wickes Corporation, served as board member for several years. For background data on the growth of Michigan's utilities, see George Bush, *Future Builders: The Story of Michigan's Consumers Power Company* (New York: McGraw-Hill, 1973).

8. There seems to have been yet another partner involved for a time—a gentleman by the name of Mr. Smith, on whom no further data are available. More confusion arises on examination of other early records. According to some old local histories, the Genesee Iron Works had existed prior to Henry D. Wickes's arrival and was then called H. W. Wood Iron Works. Yet another source has Mr. Wood arriving in Flint in 1852 and purchasing the Genesee Iron Works at that time. Similarly, some early papers gave the year of the move to Saginaw as 1858, and yet others as 1862. The dates used in the text appear to be the most reliable, since they are most often encountered.

9. The first of the new type of gang saw was built for Hackley's of Muskegon, Michigan.

10. For about ten years, starting around 1865, the youngest of the Wickes brothers, Charles Tuthill Wickes, also worked for the company, but it is doubtful that he contributed much engineering expertise. According to Mills, op. cit. (see Note 3, above), "he was of a studious temperament and possessed marked literary tastes."

    By the time the firm was incorporated in 1883, he had moved to Stanton, Michigan. Like his brother Edward, he never married. He died in Stanton on Feburary 19, 1909.

11. It seems that Henry and Edward were out of the logging and sawmill business by that time. According to *Industries of the Saginaws*, op. cit. (see Note 4, above), p. 147, they built a mill in 1866, and sold it to Jesse Hoyt in 1870. This mill was later enlarged, and it cut its lumber with a Wickes gang saw of fifteen blades that gave it a capacity of 100,000 board feet a day.

    Now we come upon a mystery, however. The East Saginaw *City Directory* of 1868, p. 150, cites J. L. Wickes as the owner of "sawmills." The puzzle is that there was no J. L. Wickes so far as this author can determine, and the Wickes family of this story was and is the only one connected with Saginaw. Moreover, it is highly doubtful that pseudonyms were used at that time in a community of that size. Which leaves us exactly where we started.

12. During the height of the lumber era, the Genesee Avenue drawbridge was lifted on the average of 1,500 times a month.

13. The combined population of Saginaw and East Saginaw grew from 4,704 in 1860 to 46,322 in 1890, with the biggest jump (about 16,000) in the first decade of this period. Flint counted only 9,803 inhabitants in 1890. Bay City had 40,730 at that time, and its population drop was not nearly so precipitous as that of Saginaw. In fact, while Bay City's growth for that period peaked out in 1894 with 42,382, it had a few more people in 1900 than in 1890. See Maurice Edron McGaugh, *The Settlement of the Saginaw Basin* (Chicago: University of Chicago, 1950), pp. 124-125.

14. These lines later became part of the Pere Marquette System.

15. A model of Henry Wickes's steam engine is in the collection of the Henry Ford Museum at Greenfield Village, Dearborn, as is a Wickes gang saw that had been in continuous use for more than fifty years.

16. The assumption that this advertisement was published in the 1890s is based on the fact that, soon thereafter, the Edison incandescent system replaced the earlier method of arc lighting.

17. On September 21, 1858, Henry Dunn Wickes was married in Flint to Ann S. Bailey, who had been born in Genesee County on October 4, 1839, the daughter of Jarvis and Eliza Sharp Bailey. Henry and Ann had two sons, Harry Tuthill Wickes, born in Flint on November 2, 1860, and William Jarvis Wickes, born in Saginaw on August 2, 1862, and a daughter, Mary (1859-1920?), who was married to one Robert M. Randall.

    Both sons went into the business. Harry Tuthill Wickes was to head Wickes Bros., and William Jarvis Wickes took over the boiler business.

18. Henry and Edward had been so close to each other that a physician had actually predicted at one time that neither would long outlive the other. After the death of Henry's wife in 1889, they were practically inseparable. Edward died on January 13, 1901, in Saginaw. Henry died in Guadalajara, Mexico, where he'd returned after the funeral, on February 14.

Chapter 3

1. Along with talc, a magnesium silicate, graphite is number one on the Moh scale of mineral hardness. Diamonds are at the top of the scale, at Moh 10. They'll smear on nothing and will scratch everything.

    Graphite can come about in three different ways. It can be formed scientifically through the conversion of coke by extreme pressure and heat. In nature, it may have been created by the deposition of organic life, which was compressed into peatlike bogs, then went through the coal metamorphosis and down through all the various geological stages to the most recent geosynclines of the earth, about seventy million years ago, whose foldover pressures and resultant temperatures transformed this deposit into graphitic structure. The people at Wickes Engineered Materials are more inclined, however, to believe that at least their Mexican graphite came from the magma of the earth's core, a theory propounded by Eldred Wilson, a geologist at the University of Arizona. Wilson suggests that the magma gave up elemental carbon gases, such as methane, which rose through tremendous crevasses to be deposited in fissures near the surface. Then, under the terrific heat and pressures of the earthquake period, these gases solidified into graphite carbons.

Unlike coal, graphite has a definite crystal structure regardless of its outward form. In Mexico, it appears as almost solid, rocklike ore. On the islands of Sri Lanka (Ceylon) and Madagascar, graphite occurs in crystalline flakes. There are also deposits of various kinds in Korea, Norway, Austria, South Africa, and Brazil. In Japan, the native graphite resembles anthracite coal, and it is used as a fuel.

Interestingly enough, United States Graphite managed to register the highly unusual trademark "Mexican Graphite" for its product. It was unusual because USG's mine was not the only one in Mexico.

2. The company's first officers were A. M. Marshall, president; Thomas A. Harvey, secretary; and Harry Tuthill Wickes, treasurer. In 1905, Eugene McSweeney succeeded Marshall as president, holding this office until his death in 1914. He was followed by William Jarvis Wickes (until his death in 1901), Harry C. Woodruff (until he retired in 1930), Albert S. Harvey (until his death in 1941), and Harvey Randall Wickes (until the merger of U.S. Graphite with Wickes Bros. and Wickes Boiler into The Wickes Corporation in 1947; see Chapter 6).

3. Woodruff's comment is quoted from the brochure *Achievement*, published in 1938 by The United States Graphite Company.

4. And your lungs. But, dangerous as that sounds, this graphite coating actually protects miners against silicosis. Not one case of that notorious ailment has occurred in the Mexican mines in all the eighty-odd years since the operation began. At the same time, graphite, being greasily soft as well as inert, does not seem to be harmful in itself. The biggest problem is cleaning up after you've been down the mine.

5. Woodruff, op. cit. (see Note 3, above).

6. The gold mine at La Colorada never reopened. Its tunnels filled with ground water, and an assay in the early 1930s showed the ore to be of insufficiently high grade to make rehabilitation of the mine commercially feasible. With the recent increase in the price of gold, there has been talk that a new effort might be launched to exploit the deposit.

7. Salvador Aguirre denounced (as mine terminology has it) the Moradillas claim of 60 *pertenencias* (144 acres) on April 15, 1918, which meant that he turned it over to U.S. Graphite. That spring, then still in Aguirre's possession, the mine had shipped 1,650 tons. On a trip in May and June of 1920, Woodruff ordered that the original Moradillas tunnel be extended to a length of 400 feet. The following winter, on another trip which lasted until February 1921, Woodruff made the decision to clean out the Santa María's remaining ore, to stockpile it on the surface, and to establish a production level of 100 tons a week from Moradillas.

8. A mechanic had discovered boiler graphite accidentally. He was using graphite as a lubricant and some of it entered the feed water—one of those rare cases where sloppiness pays off. Boiler graphite went out of use about fifty years ago,

but there is the possibility that it may be reintroduced, since water softeners are not so effective as they used to be: pollution makes water tremendously hard.

9. Woodruff, op. cit. (see Note 3 above), slightly rephrased for greater clarity.

10. Mining is one of those callings that seems to have an irresistible attraction for some people. Victor H. Verity, born in 1903 in Seattle, Washington, is an example. Among his earliest recollections is playing around a small coal mine owned by his maternal grandfather in Nelsonville, Ohio, where he lived from the time he was three months old until he was halfway through the seventh grade. The next experience that made a big impression on him came in 1922 when, after graduation from high school in Toledo, Ohio, and having saved a little money doing odd jobs for a year, he persuaded his parents to take a trip back west. En route, the family visited the Homestake gold mine in Lead, South Dakota, which was then, and still is today, the biggest working gold mine in the United States. The tour included a descent in a cage, watching the stamp mills, and a souvenir of ore containing tiny specks of gold. That did it for Verity. He took two years of engineering at University of Toledo, then specialized in mining engineering at the University of Arizona. After graduation he went to work first for a lead and zinc mine in southern Arizona and later for a Phelps Dodge copper mine in Sonora, Mexico, as a metallurgist and assistant mine superintendent. The latter operation closed down in the Great Depression, and Verity spent the next four years knocking around between jobs, prospecting unsuccessfully for gold, and getting his law degree at the University of Arizona because he felt that administrative positions in mining offered greater chances for advancement than the line.

Unable, because of lack of funds, to start his own law office, and with no one offering him an administrative job, Verity obtained the right to work out of the office of a Tucson attorney, Ben Shantz. At about that time, Billy King of Douglas, Arizona, who had been handling U.S. Graphite's legal affairs in Mexico, was killed in an airplane crash, and Albert Harvey engaged Ben Shantz. The two men, however, did not get along, and Shantz turned the business over to Verity.

11. Such heat is not a characteristic generally associated with graphite mines. Beyond a certain point, the temperature in any mine, regardless of the ore, depends on the mine's location in relation to "recent intrusives"—"recent" meaning several millions of years ago, and "intrusives" referring to magmas that then welled up from the earth's core. Where such intrusions were recent enough, the heat still remains. In Superior, Arizona, temperatures of the wall rock in deep shafts range up to 150 degrees, and the same is true of some of the deeper gold mines at Winterstrand, South Africa.

12. Smith Bolton, who became general manager of U.S. Graphite in 1948 (see Chapter 4), tells this story:

"We maintained a school through the fifth grade, and had three teachers, two women, and the principal was a man. We noticed that this principal was spending more and more time talking to the miners when they would come up for their lunch periods. He asked them on several occasions why didn't they just take the mine over—it belonged to them anyway. We tried to get rid of him and finally did after a year or so, but by that time he had accomplished his mission pretty well, and the union leader of the miners was becoming more and more militant.

"One day Victor Verity and John Splane, the superintendent, and I were sitting in the office discussing the problems of the day and we heard all these people outside the little adobe building, which sat in sort of an amphitheater, and there were all these men sitting around in a circle on the slope. It didn't present a beautiful scene because there were all these men and they just squatted there like vultures waiting for a corpse. Their leader came in, the fellow who had been trained very well by this schoolteacher, and I saw that he had a revolver stuck in the belt of his pants. He got louder and louder and more threatening, and there was only one thing to do and that was to appease him, and we promised to take all his demands into consideration, etc., and he finally calmed down.

"Well, a day or so later, one of the men who ran the store came over in the evening and said, 'Understand you had trouble with so-and-so.' And I said, 'Yes, we do,' and he said that he knew of a way to solve the problem. 'I've got a man,' he said, 'and if you'll give him a horse and $50, you won't have to worry about this fellow at all.'

"Now obviously we couldn't do that, but eventually we did get rid of him through political connections, got the government to give him another job in the labor department of the State of Sonora. Then, what do you know, a few months later he came out to the mine in a brand-new Buick and all dressed up, and he was very friendly and shook hands with all of us. It was very simple. He had got his, and there went his communist principles."

13. Fausto Miranda, who studied as a postgraduate at Harvard, must be one of the most brilliant lawyers ever to have come down the *camino*. He actually won a tax case against the Mexican government for U.S. Graphite before the Mexican Supreme Court in the late 1950s. In brief, what happened was this:

Both the export and the production taxes on ores were pegged to a specific percentage of the valuation of the ore. One day, authorities simply raised this valuation so high that the taxes exceeded the market price. When these taxes were added to the operational overhead, the mine lost money every day it was open. Furthermore, this valuation, imposed in late 1955, was made retroactive for one month so that the mine was in a hole right from the moment it got the bad news. When Smith Bolton, up in Saginaw, heard about the 2200 percent tax increase from Victor Verity by phone, his first thought was to have the mine shut down immediately. This, however, would have deprived the Saginaw manufacturing operation of a continuous flow of its raw material. So the Moradillas was kept open and some of the taxes were paid until Miranda finally prevailed in court. At that time the price of Mexican amorphous graphite was in the neighborhood of $18 per ton and the taxes the authorities wanted to collect came to about $33. Thanks to Miranda, the spurious valuation was lowered from $100 to $38, still more than double the mineral's actual worth, but the company could live with the resultant taxes.

Verity had been introduced to the dapper young Miranda by Herman Horton, then manager of the Phelps Dodge properties in Mexico. Miranda at that time was employed by American Smelting and Refining but also maintained a private practice. He could thus take on a couple of U.S. Graphite's early tax matters, and in this connection he obtained refunds from the Mexican government—something that had never been done before. It was then arranged for Miranda and another Harvard-trained Mexican attorney by the name of Prieto to set up their own law office in Mexico City in a partnership with the big Houston firm of Baker and Botts. The Mexican offspring, called Baker, Botts, Miranda and Prieto, henceforth handled all the government relations for USG and attracted many other important accounts. Prieto dropped out because he was devoting practically all his time to Anaconda Copper Co., and he eventually rose to the top of Anaconda Copper in Mexico. Miranda, now in his middle sixties, retired recently but is still a director of Union Carbide of Mexico, John Deere, and Kimberly-Clark.

14. Since 1922, in compliance with a law then passed, the Cía. Minera de San José had not actually owned the Moradillas itself but merely the right to mine it and to maintain appurtenant structures on the surface. What was in question, however, was not the ownership of the mine, but the removal by a foreign company of an "irreplaceable resource."

15. John Lindsay Splane went into mining along the most direct route: he was born into it. His paternal grandparents had been miners and ranchers in Mexico, Arizona, Nevada, and California. He was born in 1916 in Los Angeles, attended the University of California at Los Angeles for a year, then quit school, took his small independent income, and "just goofed around Mexico for a year and got it out of my system." However, he still had no interest in schooling, and on his return to California went to work as a "mucker," the lowest-ranking job in a mine. He advanced quickly and soon became an assistant foreman, at which time an engineer talked him into going back to school. His education at the Arizona College of Mines in Tucson was interrupted by four years in a combat engineer battalion, including service with the Ninth Army in Europe. He graduated in 1948, and was immediately hired as superintendent for the Moradillas: Victor Verity had asked the dean of the college to recommend the best man he knew— and Splane was that man.

Splane left Wickes in 1954 to become the superintendent of the largest underground mine in Mexico at San Francisco del Oro in southern Chihuahua, where the Union Corp. of London mines lead, zinc, and copper. The fact that adequate schooling was not available for his children prompted him to move back to Tucson, America's unofficial mining capital, and he quite naturally stumbled into consulting, although he originally intended to become a real estate operator.

Besides Wickes, his clients include Phelps Dodge Corp., American Smelting and Refining Co., Southern Peru Copper Corp., Newmont Mining Corp., Quintana Petroleum Corp. of Houston, Texas, Occidental Petroleum, and Humble Oil.

Chapter 4

1. William Jarvis Wickes was president not only of Wickes Boiler, but also of the Saginaw Plate Glass Company, the Consolidated Coal Company, and, for a period, of the United States Graphite Company (see Chapter 3). Moreover, he was a director of the Bank of Saginaw. Tall and husky, of serious mien and wearing a pince-nez, he hardly gave the impression of a person likely to spend beyond his means. He was born in Saginaw on August 2, 1862, and attended public schools in that city. Upon graduation from high school in 1880, he went to work in his father's office and soon manifested a remarkable aptitude for handling business details. On July 14, 1886, he was married to Cornelia Mershon, daughter of Augustus and Helen Mershon of Saginaw.

Of William Jarvis Wickes's seven children, only William Jarvis, Jr., of Saginaw, born in 1895, is still alive. He is childless.

The other children of William Jarvis Wickes were James C., who died at the age of ten in 1894; Helen (1887–1962); Ann (1891–1963), who was married to

Hugh Reed of New York, and left no issue; John (1896-1972), who was also childless; Elsie (1911-1974), who married an Englishman, Ian Rough, and died in Florida, leaving no issue; and Edward Bailey Wickes (1889-1940), who left numerous descendants.

Helen Wickes, married first to Melville Brooks, had a daughter, Cornelia, who died. Helen Louise, the issue of Helen's later marriage to William Davis, survives.

Edward Bailey Wickes, who married Helen Hill, had four children: Edward B., Jr. (wife, Mary Gorden) of Toledo; Susanne (married to Dr. Robert Nelson) of Bethesda, Maryland; William Jarvis III (married to Emily Mathewson) of Saginaw; and Prudence Wickes Thompson of Essex, Connecticut.

Edward B. Wickes, Jr., has four children: Edward B. III, William J., Molly, and Elizabeth.

Susanne Wickes Nelson has three children: Page, Susan, and Robert Jr.

William J. Wickes III has three children: Ashley, Lisa, and William J. IV.

Prudence Wickes Thompson has one daughter, Jordeen.

[The above information was provided by the late Mrs. Albert S. Harvey, Sr. (daughter of Harry Tuthill Wickes) and by William J. Wickes III.]

2. In previous models, the heat source was encased within the boiler and surrounded by water. What made this new model so revolutionary was that it reversed the procedure. The water was now in a tube surrounded by the heat source. It was easy to empty the tube and scrub down its insides.

3. Herman Bickel was born on a farm at Frankenmuth, Michigan, in 1899. He attended Ferris Institute (now Ferris State College) in Big Rapids, Michigan, and then studied engineering at Michigan Agricultural College (now Michigan State). He came to work as a draftsman in Wickes Boiler upon his graduation in 1921, reporting to Henry Aldrich, who was then head of engineering. Bickel worked his way up through the ranks and became the company's chief engineer in the 1930s. He now lives in Saginaw.

4. Municipal utilities that purchased Wickes boilers included Manitowoc, Wisconsin; Virginia and Hibbing, Minnesota; and Lansing, Michigan. They bought the biggest models, which sometimes cost as much as $1 million. There were many other utilities that bought smaller steam boilers for the generation of electricity.

One of Wickes Boiler's most effective salesmen was the gentleman who ran the Milwaukee office, Don H. Barnes, later divisional president and general manager (1956 to May 1961). Barnes was born in Youngstown, Ohio, in 1911, graduated as a civil engineer from Michigan State in 1934, and immediately went to work as a welder at Wickes Boiler. During World War II, it was his job to supervise installation of the boilers at shipyards on both coasts and on the Great Lakes. Retired, he now lives near Sturgeon Bay in Door County, Wisconsin.

5. Wickes Boiler's best year was 1957, when its sales totaled $9 million and its 9.2 percent profit came to $828,000, nearly double the bottom line of the next best year, which was 1958.

6. As the result of a civil antitrust suit brought by the Justice Department in 1970, Combustion Engineering was ordered to divest itself of the Wickes Boiler facilities. The suit had alleged that the acquisition eliminated competition in the industrial boiler field. The divestment order, however, was rescinded, since Combustion Engineering was unable to find a buyer.

7. Harry T. Wickes, a robust man of medium height whose portraits show him to be square-faced with a determined chin, his hair parted down the middle, and a hedonistic twinkle in his eye, had been born in Flint on November 2, 1860.

When his family moved to Saginaw, he attended the old Crary School, and later Central School, where he completed his education in 1878. After two years as a shop apprentice in his father's factory, he entered the office as bookkeeper and correspondent. At the death of his father, Henry Dunn Wickes, he took over as president of Wickes Bros. and in effect remained the head of the Wickes family enterprises until his own death in 1931, when his son, Harvey Randall Wickes, moved into that role.

Harry T. Wickes and his wife Fanny (née Hamilton), who died in 1901 at the age of thirty-six, had five children. The firstborn was Arthur Hamilton Wickes (1887–1953), who never married. The second child, Harvey Randall Wickes (1889–1974), was married to Ruth Brady of Saginaw (1891–1957). Their daughter Nancy was born in 1920.

Harry T.'s eldest daughter, Elizabeth, born in 1892, was married to Albert Sargent Harvey, Sr. (1890–1941), onetime president of United States Graphite. They had three children: Elizabeth Hamilton Harvey (1918–1972), who was married to Robert Preston Davis; Albert S. Harvey, Jr. (born 1929), who married Geraldine Kirchman; and Thomas C. Harvey (born 1921), who is married to Constance Brady (born 1926).

Mrs. R. P. Davis left four children: Stephen Sargent Davis (born 1941), who has one daughter, Frances Ann; D. Harvey Davis (born 1943), who has two children, Elizabeth Brooke Davis and Scott Davis; Laurie Davis (born 1946); and R. Preston Davis, Jr. (born 1948).

Albert S., Jr. ("Sarge") and Geraldine have four children: Albert S. Harvey III (born 1954); Geraldine W. Harvey (born 1955); William L. Harvey (born 1959); and John H. Harvey (born 1960). Sarge Harvey is a Ford dealer in Saginaw.

Thomas C. and Constance Harvey have three children: Catherine (born 1950), who is married to Randall Almirall; Sara (born 1955); and Thomas C. Harvey, Jr. (born 1956). Thomas C. Harvey, Sr., is a director of The Wickes Corporation.

Elizabeth Wickes Harvey (Mrs. Albert S. Harvey, Sr.) died January 3, 1976, at the family's cottage enclave at Higgins Lake, Michigan.

Harry T. Wickes's second daughter, Frances, was married to George Bliss (1894–1959). She moved to Los Angeles in 1926 and now lives in Carmel, California. She has no children.

Harry T.'s youngest daughter, Helen Louise, was married to William Stone (1895–1959), president of the First National Bank of Peoria, who served as a director of The Wickes Corporation for a number of years. This marriage also was childless. Helen Louise Stone still makes her home in Peoria, Illinois.

[Information from Mrs. Albert S. Harvey, Sr. (see Note 7, above) and Miss Deloris Menthen.]

8. Kendall retired in 1971 and now lives in northern Michigan.
9. The Kux Machine Company was started in 1919 by Albert Kux as an engineering firm specializing in the design of custom machinery. Later Albert Kux, a self-taught engineer who never took his hat off his head or his pipe out of his mouth, was joined by Carl Loner, and with this associate expanded the operation into the construction of machinery as well as its design. Kux Machine's first products were compacting presses for the candy industry and die-casting machines for the toy industry. Initial customers were the Mars Candy Company and Tootsie Toy. Later, Kux expanded into making presses for office equipment, the automotive industry, hardware, ceramics, and powder metallurgy. Albert Kux died in 1959 at the age of eighty-two.

Contact for the sale of Kux Machine to Wickes was made through United

States Graphite, which by that time was in the powder metallurgy business and a user of the Kux powder metal press. For the first eighteen months after the acquisition, James Kux handled the sales of the division on a commission basis.

Roland Jacobson is now the division's general manager, reporting to R. J. Jacobs, and Don Kaufman is Kux's sales manager.

10. The Saginaw Machine and Tool Company dates back to 1921 when it was started as a supplier to the then-new radio industry by two brothers-in-law, Frank G. Woidka, a foreman at Saginaw Steering Gear, and Phillip Kessel, plant superintendent at the Baker Perkins Corporation. These men built a couple of engraving machines, which they set up in Phillip Kessel's basement, and proceeded to engrave radio panels. Soon the basement became too small and the equipment was moved to Frank Woidka's barn. The operation then officially became a partnership and was first named Saginaw Engraving and Machine Company.

Like so many other small seat-of-the-pants plants, it managed to survive and even grow by drifting through various product phases, ranging from castings and brackets for ironing boards to jig and fixture work. With business booming prior to the Great Depression, property was purchased on Niagara Street in Saginaw, which remains the location of the plant. After the deaths of Kessel and Woidka, Sr., in the 1930s, Frank Woidka, Jr., took over operation of the company. In 1953 the company was incorporated, with Woidka, Jr., and his mother, Mary, as stockholders. It wasn't until the late 1950s that Saginaw Machine and Tool began specializing in vertical turning and boring machines, a step precipitated by the arrival of Robert W. Cashman as chief engineer and plant superintendent.

Under Cashman's technical leadership, the company was able to design and build its own machinery, and to completely cover it with patents. This happened at a most propitious time, for the automatic transmission market was then still in its infancy, with installations in only about 35 percent of cars manufactured. By the late 1960s, however, there were automatic transmissions in about 90 percent of all automobiles. Saginaw Machine and Tool simply grew along with this extremely lucrative market.

11. R. J. Jacobs was born in New York City in 1918, graduated from Stuyvesant High School (a public school for students of technical aptitude) and later from the College of the City of New York, then joined Goodyear Aircraft in Akron, Ohio, as an engineer. After the war, Jacobs and three of his friends started a small tool design company in Madison, Wisconsin. The partnership was disbanded after a couple of years and Jacobs joined Mercury Engineering, a manufacturer of paper carton and paper cup machinery, in Milwaukee. Next he worked at Black Clawson Company in New York, which had specialized in the building of pulp mill machinery, but needed a new product line. During the next ten years, Jacobs developed a new line—paper-converting machinery—for them, built the business volume up tenfold, and rose to the position of vice president in charge. A headhunter then recruited him for the Midland-Ross Corporation, another firm specializing in paper converting and drying machinery. Here, Jacobs became vice president and general manager of three plants in the New Brunswick, New Jersey, area, one that made plastic extruders, another paper converting and coating machinery, and the third couplings for transmitting power. In 1963 he was invited to join the Beloit Corporation, the world's largest paper machinery company, as vice president of that organization's plant in Downingtown, Pennsylvania. During the next six years, until his recruitment by Wickes, he developed a program to get the company into the plastics machinery business.

12. It's somewhat puzzling that The Wickes Corporation didn't stop Oeming from going into competition with it in the first place. Industry usually guards itself against such contingencies by paying discharged or voluntarily separated key personnel considerable stipends in return for noncompetition agreements that cover a number of years. What makes the lack of such an agreement so surprising in Oeming's case is that this was not the first Wickes experience along such lines. As we shall see in Chapter 11, the original manager of the Wickes Lumber Division also went into competition with Wickes after his separation from the company. This doesn't mean Wickes is slow on the uptake, however. T. W. Cline, the senior vice president of personnel and corporate secretary, who used to be the corporation's general counsel, thinks that most such contracts aren't worth the paper they're written on. "If somebody wants to," he says, "he can always find a way to get around it."

    In any case, though Jacobs did have some sleepless nights, Oeming was never able to make it really big in the crankshaft business. C. M. Systems Company, with which Oeming, incidentally, is no longer connected, is now mainly engaged in marketing cam machines, i.e., machines that make the cams that lift the valves. But there was the time when Jacobs felt indeed threatened, particularly in Europe, where much of Wickes Machine Tool's business originated.

    "I felt there was every chance that they would open a manufacturing facility in Europe, and if they had done that we would have been very vulnerable," explains Jacobs. "We had this big plant here dependent on the manufacture of machines for export, while they had a very small plant that had absolutely nothing to lose, so we were wide open."

    Jacobs solved this problem by setting up a licensing arrangement with Snyder Limited in England, so that now Wickes crankshaft lathes are also manufactured in the United Kingdom. Of course, with the devaluation of the dollar, Wickes Machine Tool is in a much more favorable export position, but in the early 1970s it certainly seemed that if Wickes didn't build in Europe immediately, it might find itself on the outside looking in.

13. These are not Wickes Machine Tool's first exports to the Soviet Union. During World War II, Wickes Bros. sold a great number of lathes to Russia.

14. Fiscal 1975 was a record year with $18.5 million in sales. The backlog for that year was $16 million. Orders backlogged for fiscal 1976 totaled about $12 million, and the expectations in 1976 are for sales of $17.4 million, which would make that year still the second best in the history of the Wickes Machine Tool Group.

15. As early as 1914, United States Graphite had started to publish its own internal house organ, *Road and Office*, an expensively printed semimonthly magazine on heavy coated stock, whose content was far less pretentious than its execution. It contained Edgar Guestish homilies, a few technical articles, personal items, appeals for greater sales efforts, and new marketing ideas like selling graphite paint to barnacle-proof the bottoms of ships. The idea in this case was that the mollusks would have a tough time latching on to anything as slippery as graphite. After a pause for World War I, *Road and Office* gave way to *The Greaser*, which was of smaller format but still a rather ambitious undertaking, considering the fact that United States Graphite had fewer than fifty employes in the white-collar category for whom the magazine was intended. *The Greaser* ceased publication in 1928.

16. In the late 1930s (see *Achievement*, op. cit. Chapter 3, Note 3), R. H. Khuen was in charge of engineering and research. His assistant was Harold F. Mitchel, the chief engineer, who later succeeded Khuen. Others in the development end

included George Cay, the chief chemist, and his assistant, Irwin Moessner; Don Urquart and Harold Bradley in Gramix engineering and research; Chalmer Thomas, Emil Hildebrandt, George Grant, and Otto Penskofer in new-product testing; as well as Fremont Ruhl, formerly a salesman, who took care of special engineering assignments.

17. The first successful Graphitar product was a clutch throw-out bearing, which United States Graphite manufactured in great quantities for Chevrolet and Pontiac in the late 1920s and early 1930s.

    To compact Graphitar components requires some 10 tons of pressure per square inch. Gramix, with its copper ingredients, needed 20 tons per square inch for compaction. Most current iron powders become seeming solids at 30 tons per square inch.

18. Smith Bolton derived his unusual first name (unusual as a first name, that is) from his mother's family. He attended Hoyt School (named after Jesse Hoyt, the prominent lumberman) in Saginaw, then was sent to board at the Irving School at Tarrytown, New York. He was graduated from the University of Michigan in 1924.

    Smith Bolton's career with Wickes included positions as sales manager of United States Graphite (1940–1948); vice president and general manager, and later divisional president, of United States Graphite (1948–1961); vice president of operations of The Wickes Corporation (1961–1965). He served two long periods on the corporation's board of directors from 1947 to 1972, and between his terms was a member of the corporation's executive committee. He was a longtime member of the Society of Automotive Engineers, and he served on the War Production Board during World War II and on the board of governors of the National Electrical Manufacturers Association from 1956 to 1960.

    He retired in 1967. He and his wife, Eleanor, now divide their time between Saginaw and Tucson, Arizona.

19. This is not to imply that these men were incompetent. In fact, most of them were highly experienced and talented salesmen. They had just gotten too smug. Later, when Smith Bolton took over and abandoned the sales offices and instituted technical backgrounding, most performed admirably.

    Oldest member of the sales staff was Frank B. Godard, who had joined Graphite in 1903 and in the 1930s was manager of the Pittsburgh office. Godard later served as a member of the board of The Wickes Corporation.

    Other old-timers at USG included James G. Drought (since 1905), who was assigned to Chicago; Roy A. Corrigan (since 1909); Eric H. Warmber (since 1911); George D. Robinson (since 1912); Ray A. Nauer (since 1912); Arthur J. Heindel (since 1913); Leon B. Lavigne (since 1916); Ralph J. Edmiston (since 1918); Joseph J. Edmiston, his son (since 1919); and Joseph J. Vallette (since 1920).

    When Bolton joined USG, O. R. Miller was secretary of the company and its general sales manager, and Albert J. Lent was superintendent of the plant.

20. H. Ward was assistant secretary and assistant treasurer of the company.

21. Today, steelmaking and refractories consume approximately two-thirds of Mexico's total graphite output, of which the Moradillas mine accounts for approximately 35 percent.

22. Ralph J. Zemanek was born in Saginaw in 1913, went through the Saginaw school system, and graduated from college in 1935. Although he had a job offer from Dow Chemical, he chose to join United States Graphite, where he worked in the engineering department for his first year with the company. In 1938, he was appointed chief metallurgist, and in 1940 was placed in charge of graphite

products. He became sales manager in 1948 and divisional manager in 1961, succeeding Smith Bolton in both positions. He was named a senior vice president of The Wickes Corporation in 1974.

23. Raymond Amberger, a gentle 6 foot 3 engineer with a sly sense of humor, was hired by Smith Bolton on the recommendation of the latter's secretary, Betty Amberger, Ray's sister. When she mentioned to Bolton that her brother was available, Bolton told her, "Well, Betty, I don't know your brother, but if he has half the personality and smile you have, I would certainly be anxious to talk to him."

    Ray, who was then in the metallurgical department of the Wilcox-Rich Corp. in Saginaw, first came over to United States Graphite to work in the plant. After a Navy stint in World War II, he went into the sales department, became a product manager, then sales manager, and finally director of marketing. He held the title of Special Projects Coordinator of Wickes Engineered Materials when, at age sixty-two, he retired in June 1975 after thirty-three years with the company.

Chapter 5

1. Of course, it wasn't Churchill's purpose to find a rationale for heavy smoking. A man like that takes it for granted that everything one does in life carries its attendant risks. His point was that human affairs couldn't simply be the result of a "blind interplay of events," but that the various terms used to describe "fate"— chance, fortune, luck, destiny, providence—were merely different ways of expressing the fact that man's "own contribution to his life story is continuously dominated by an external superior power." [Winston Churchill, *My Early Life* (London: Butterworth, 1940). Also published as *A Roving Commission: My Early Life* (New York: Scribner, 1930).]

2. Ibid. See Note 1, above.

3. Lybrand, Ross Bros. & Montgomery, commonly referred to as Lybrand's in the business world, is now Coopers & Lybrand, the result of a partnership with the British firm of Cooper Bros. As this is written, the firm has 79 offices in the United States and 231 abroad.

4. White, Bauer, and Prevo which was ultimately merged into Arthur Young & Co. Like Lybrand's, this firm is another of the "Big Eight" in public accounting.

5. Among these accounts were not only many Michigan companies, but Charles S. Mott's personal business as well as a number or companies controlled by Mott, such as the Long Island Water Co., Northern Illinois Water Co., Illinois Water Co., and St. Louis County Water Co. Robert McCullough, one of John McCullough's younger brothers, was still working for the Mott Foundation and the Mott family in 1975.

6. Dan Fitz-Gerald's mother, whose maiden name was O'Connor, had also been born in Ireland. His Irish lineage on both sides anteceded the grandparents and went back as far as he could trace his family history.

7. Dan's sister, the only girl in the family, died in 1929 at the age of sixteen of peritonitis following a burst appendix.

8. At that time, the Lybrand's office was on the thirteenth floor of the Book Building.

9. It's quite possible that Richard Fitz-Gerald at that point wouldn't have been able to send Dan to college even if he hadn't considered it better for the boy to work

his own way through school. Between 1920 and 1930, Richard Fitz-Gerald had built the Detroit office to a staff of about forty, but the number quickly diminished during the Depression until there were only about a dozen people working at the branch. As a Lybrand's partner, Richard Fitz-Gerald was entitled to a share of the profits, but as Dan Fitz-Gerald once put it, "nobody had any profits in those days." In what may be an apocryphal anecdote, he recalled that "one of my first jobs for Lybrand's was working in some of the brokerage offices. I well remember, in one brokerage office, it was my responsibility to get certain information from one of the partners. I asked his secretary if I could see him. She said to go right in. I opened the door and found the window open. He had just jumped."

Dan was then making about $100 a month. For a newly married man, this wasn't much to get along on. He later remembered coming home one night "and all we've got in the house is a half bottle of milk, a little sugar, and some corn flakes. We had that for dinner. I kind of made up my mind right then that I wasn't going to be hungry anymore."

Dan Fitz-Gerald's first wife, Mary Margaret, whom he married in January 1930, died in 1954 at the age of forty-three. They had one daughter, Eve (Barris), who, now divorced, lives in Saginaw with her three children, two boys and one girl. Fitz-Gerald remarried in 1957. His second wife, Grace, had a daughter, Sandy, by a previous marriage, whom Fitz-Gerald adopted. A boy, Michael, was born in 1959.

10. Fisher & Company, after the merger of the original Fisher Bros. concern into General Motors as Fisher Body, had built the Fisher Building, an art deco edifice, as part of the New Center development across from the General Motors complex on Detroit's West Grand Boulevard. There were to be two other buildings—one, exactly mirroring the Fisher Building, at the next corner (Third Avenue), and between the two, set back from Grand Boulevard, an office tower about double the height of the other buildings. A deal had even been worked out with the Pennsylvania Railroad to bring its trains into this development. These plans had been made on the basis of the assets of the five Fisher brothers as of December 31, 1929, when they were worth about $5 billion. By 1934 these assets had diminished to about 20 percent of their previous value, and the Fisher brothers were now worth less than $1 billion, as McCullough and Fitz-Gerald found out in the course of their audit. This was still a lot of money, but not enough to back so grandiose a project, and it died on the drawing boards.

11. Extreme accuracy is required in audits of this type, since the auditors must assume responsibility for errors that might occur in the financial statements presented in the stock offering. Any stockholder suffering a loss on the sale of stock purchased pursuant to an erroneous registration statement could recoup damages in substantial amounts from the auditors.

12. Among other accounts that hadn't been credited properly was that of Wright Aeronautics (later Curtiss Wright).

13. The lady's name has been omitted, although she is probably deceased by now. There is no point in destroying the reputation she evidently worked so hard to build for herself, albeit illegally. If any people remember her today, they may as well remember her as the person she wanted to be.

14. After leaving the accounting department of Manhattan Life Insurance Company and before joining Lybrand's, McCullough had worked for two smaller firms while attending night classes in New York City. Of the two, which are still in existence, one was David Berdon & Co., a CPA firm; the other, Woodward, Fondiller & Ryan (now Woodward & Fondiller), an actuarial firm that performed

services for life insurance companies. Three years' practice in an accounting firm or in the office of a CPA was required to qualify for the CPA degree.

McCullough became a Lybrand's partner in 1944 and later was in charge of the seventeen or so offices in the firm's central region. According to McCullough, Lybrand's, although highly competent, was an extremely conservative firm with no real growth policy when he first joined the company. "I felt we were becoming a regional firm, not a national or international firm, and that this policy was self-defeating, and I feared that sooner or later we would begin to lose some of our larger clients," he told me in an interview on August 12, 1974. "I tried to prevail on the firm to grow externally as well as internally, and participated in the merger negotiations toward most of the acquisitions that occurred during the period of, say, ten years prior to my retirement."

McCullough was a member of Lybrand's executive committee when he retired in 1969 at the mandatory age of sixty-five. He then joined Wickes as a consultant for five years, which ended on his seventieth birthday on January 21, 1974. This being in turn the mandatory retirement age of Wickes executives, he was given a "throwing-out party" at Wickes's annual Management Conference at John's Island, Florida. But he still remains active, performing consulting services for Forrest C. Lattmer, whom McCullough met through Mott some twenty-five years ago, and who owns a substantial interest in the Central Louisiana Electric Company. To this day, McCullough and his wife Rose (née Kaiser), whom he married in 1930, live in the comfortable three-bedroom home they built in Grosse Pointe in 1937 for $9,000 on a $2,000 lot. His salary then was somewhere between $6,000 and $7,000.

15. H. (Harvey) Randall Wickes, son of Harry T. and Fanny Hamilton Wickes, was born in Saginaw on September 1, 1889, earned his engineering degree at the University of Michigan, and after his graduation in 1911, joined Wickes Bros. as an apprentice machinist. He was president of the three Wickes companies from 1941 to 1947, continued as president of The Wickes Corporation until October 1964 and as board chairman until 1969, relinquishing both positions to Daniel M. Fitz-Gerald. He then served on the corporation's board of directors until June 1972. On July 22, 1974, he suffered a stroke from which he never fully recovered, and he died on October 6 of that year, at the age of eighty-five, at Saginaw General Hospital. He was buried in the family plot in Saginaw's Forest Lawn Cemetery. His wife, Ruth (née Brady), had died in 1957.

Ran Wickes was survived by his daughter, Nancy (Mrs. Robert Blanford, of Montrose, Michigan); three grandchildren; and three sisters, Elizabeth (Mrs. Albert S. Harvey of Saginaw), Helen Louise (Mrs. William Stone, of Peoria, Illinois), and Frances (Mrs. George Bliss, of Carmel, California).

Chapter 6

1. But that wasn't the end of the *Capitola*. What was left of her was sold through Lloyds of London to a banana-shipping company, which put her on a run between New Orleans and the Yucatan Peninsula. Soon thereafter she ran aground on a sandbar, and before anything could be done so much sand had collected around her that it was cheaper to leave her where she sat. Now her hull, once the purveyor of good times on the Great Lakes, is the steel center of a tiny island in the Gulf of Mexico.

2. The borrowings by W. J. Wickes and H. T. Wickes were all in Wickes Bros., from which Wickes Boiler had been split in 1907 for the purpose of satisfying that division's executive personnel. (See Chapter 4.) Since these managers were

permitted to purchase considerable amounts of Boiler's stock, it was agreed that any advances to the Wickes brothers from Wickes Boiler would be reimbursed by Wickes Bros. By the time of the IRS claim, this distinction had become academic, since practically all the Boiler stock was back in Wickes hands.

Since the death of E. C. Fisher, Wickes Boiler had gone straight downhill. Once in a while, as during World War II, it made a pretty good living, but for the most part it just limped along, not necessarily losing a great deal of money but not making a great deal either. At the depth of the Depression, Boiler's stock, which had sold as high as $18 a share, dropped down to $1.50, and its owners started asking Ran Wickes to buy back the stock. In view of the fact that his family had started the company and still owned a chunk of it, he felt obliged to help out, and every time a desperate investor showed up, Wickes bought more and more of the shares, paying whatever was asked, which in some cases was as little as 50 cents. Some of the stock he repurchased in his own name; other shares in the names of his wife, daughter, and sisters. In the end, the family holding was back up to about 95 percent.

3. It was Ran Wickes's good fortune that all his life he was surrounded by people driven by the urge to succeed. This helped him not only with The Wickes Corporation but in other ways as well.

For instance, at the time of his death he owned 137,000 shares, worth in the neighborhood of $5 million, in the Michigan National Corporation. What had happened was that he'd had a deposit in the Bank of Saginaw, which failed in 1938. At that time, Howard Stoddard (who later was to become one of the directors of The Wickes Corporation, a post he held until his death in 1971) had come to Michigan at the request of the Reconstruction Finance Corporation to see what he could do about the disastrous state of banks in Michigan. Stoddard got the idea of launching a new bank chain, starting with the defunct Bank of Saginaw. Because the Wickes family name meant a great deal in Saginaw, he asked Ran Wickes if he would be willing to accept stock in settlement of his account. Ran Wickes consented. As time went on and Stoddard's chain grew, he prevailed on Ran Wickes to buy more and more of the stock. In the end, Ran Wickes, without ever having planned it, owned a substantial interest in the Michigan National Bank and several other banks in the Detroit area, Lansing, and other parts of Michigan, all under the umbrella of the Michigan National Corporation. And every single bit of these holdings had been financed by loans pressed on him by Stoddard!

4. At the time of the consolidation, the stock of The Wickes Corporation (symbol WIX) was the only strictly Saginaw stock traded on either of the two national exchanges.

5. To start with, the stock of the new Wickes Corporation paid dividends of 60 cents a year. At the exchange ratio of three Wickes common for one U.S. Graphite common, this immediately upped the dividend income of the Graphite stockholders by 80 cents a share, since Graphite's regular dividend was only $1 per year. Due to a special dividend of 75 cents, however, Graphite dividends in 1947 totaled $1.50 a share.

6. The original roster of the new corporation's officers was as follows:
   H. Randall Wickes, president and chairman of the board of directors
   Carl Bintz, vice president and general manager, Wickes Bros. division
   Robert J. Stormont, vice president and general manager, Boiler division
   Smith Bolton (formerly secretary and sales manager of United States Graphite), vice president in charge of Graphite division sales

William E. Stone (president of the First National Bank of Peoria, Illinois, and a brother-in-law of Ran Wickes), vice president

Charles G. Morrell, treasurer

Melvin J. Zahnow, secretary

Daniel M. Fitz-Gerald, comptroller

All these men, plus Frank B. Godard, the Pittsburgh sales representative for Graphite, were named to the board of directors. The directorate also included Walter J. Harris, vice president of Symons Bros. & Co.; Elbert G. Rounds, manager of the Saginaw division of Standard Oil of Indiana; and Herbert F. Russell, general manager of the Saginaw (Wilcox-Rich) division of Eaton Manufacturing Co.

Chapter 7

1. The Wolohan holdings have been cited in the text. As for the others:

    Wallace & Morley at that time was in Bay Port, Caseville, Linkville, Pigeon, Gagetown, Elkton, Fairgrove, Gilford, Bradleyville, North Branch, Akron, Bach, Munger, Mitchell, Grassmere, and Sebewaing.

    There were two Frutchey elevators in Saginaw and two in Columbiaville, plus one each in Greenleaf, Kingston, Cass City, Deford, Clifford, Mayville, Millington, Pinconning, St. Charles, Montrose, Vassar, Lennon, Gaines, Kawkawlin, Linwood, Oakley, Shepherd, Fostoria, Auburn, Grand Ledge, and Clare. Three others, in Ashley, Carson City, and Vickeryville, were not owned by Frutchey directly but were controlled by them.

    Michigan Bean was in Saginaw, Alma, Blanchard, Caro, Chesaning, Croswell, Deckerville, Fenton, Hendersonville, Merrill, Midland, Owendale, Sandusky, Silverwood, and Vestaburg.

    Bad Axe Grain had elevators in Bad Axe, Applegate, McGregor, Port Austin, Port Hope, Ubly, Ruth, Kinde, Six Lakes, and Harbor Beach.

2. It takes about 60 pounds of beans to fill a bushel.

3. This consolidation would have resulted in an initial marketing force of seventy-five country elevators. See Note 1, above.

4. Wallace & Morley also refused to participate, despite the fact that Mrs. Albert Harvey, the sister of Ran Wickes, owned about 20 percent of the Wallace & Morley stock.

5. The Michigan Elevator Exchange, a farmers' cooperative, had more storage capacity in its grain terminal at Ottawa Lake at that time, and has since built another mammoth, also on the Carrollton bank of the Saginaw River and only about 2 miles downriver from Saginaw Grain.

    The Saginaw Grain Terminal, whose contractor was John S. Metcalf of Chicago, was originally designed only to hold grain, but has since been converted in part also to handle beans. Annual operating costs in the early years were estimated by Albert L. Riedel to be around $51,300.

6. Michigan Bean did not have the necessary cash, so Wickes Corp. bought $75,000 worth of newly issued Michigan Bean treasury stock to enable the latter company to invest in the venture.

7. For a short period, Riedel did become a director of Saginaw Grain, replacing one of the original members of the board, C. L. ("Lew") Taylor, Michigan Bean's agriculturist. Riedel resigned his directorship when he sold his bean company's share in Saginaw Grain to Wickes.

Chapter 8

1. When Dan Fitz-Gerald was interviewed for this book, he was often bemused by his youthful excesses. "What a fool I was," he chuckled on one occasion. "I didn't want to get Al mad at me, and I shouldn't have. But at the time it looked as if it couldn't be helped. The deal was going through, and Al wasn't around, he was down in Mexico, no way to get hold of him, and the papers had to be filed, and they had to have names on them. So I just went ahead without him."

2. Marginal country elevators used to burn down with amazing regularity. Be that as it may, by the turn of the century Minden City had become a far more preferable location than Forestville. A rail line had just been built to serve the Minden City area, and the days of shipping crops by lake steamer, as had to be done from Forestville, were pretty well over.

3. Wallace & Morley was eventually merged with the Wallace Stone Company, also owned by W. H. Wallace, an enterprise whose basic business was the manufacture of aggregates. Simultaneously, Wallace Stone acquired J. P. Burroughs & Son of Flint, adopting the Burroughs name in the process. The new Burroughs company now merged Bad Axe Grain into its corporate fold, and in addition acquired A. T. Ferrell & Co., a maker of grain and bean drying equipment, as well as several firms producing aggregates. The resultant complex eventually merged with Blount, Inc., of Montgomery, Alabama, whose prime mover, Winton M. Blount, served as a postmaster general early in the Nixon administration.

4. The original stock was held as follows: W. J. Orr, Sr., 3,500 shares; Frank W. Merrick, 3,089; Alfred Chamberlain, 2,361; Gustav Hill, 200; Albert L. Riedel, 200; William J. Dufty, 300; Norman L. Wales, 350.

5. For an idea of what country elevators were worth in those days, here is the value for these properties as carried on the Michigan Bean books of 1916: Croswell, $8,575.95; Harbor Beach, $7,714.67; Vestaburg, $22,183.90; Owendale, $37,-593.84. The Producers Elevator facility in Port Huron was valued at $25,694.21 at the time of formation of Michigan Bean. Additions were made, however, and when Chamberlain bought it back in 1919, he paid $53,175.66.

6. After all this time, Al Riedel, whose reputation as an elder statesman in the Michigan commodities business now far outshines W. J. Orr, Sr.'s fame in the latter's day, is no less impressed with his mentor's perspicacity today than he was as a young man. One telling anecdote should suffice:

   "I came back to the office one day at noon," Riedel remembers, "and W.J. said to me, 'I just bought a car of oats from your friend Burkholder at Marlette Farmers Elevator,' and I said, 'How many bushels did you buy?' W.J. hedged around a little bit and then he said, 'Well, I didn't specify bushels. I just said carload. Was that a mistake?' And I said, 'It's a hell of a mistake. Burkholder is a good friend of ours, but if the market goes up he'll ship a 1,600-bushel car and if it goes down he'll ship us a 2,400-bushel car. That's the way he operates.'

   "The old man didn't say a word. He turned to his stenographer and dictated a letter to Mr. Burkholder. 'Dear Milton,' he says. 'I just reported the purchase of a car of oats to Albert when he returned from lunch, and he told me that I made a horrible mistake. He explained that if the market goes down, you will ship us the biggest car possible to ship, and if it goes up, the smallest. Now, we don't know what the market will be at the time you will ship the car, but when that time comes, we'll expect you to do just exactly as Albert says, and don't you disappoint us.'

   "Of course the market went down and the damn guy shipped 2,400 bushels, and we had to take the rap. But it was one of the greatest letters ever written by the company and it did us an awful lot of good, because this fellow Burkholder used to take this letter, together with a copy of the invoice, and show it to all his friends, showing off how he took the old man, who was regarded as one of the most astute men in the business. And the result was that we became human to everybody. We weren't a company anymore that was just trying to take the last penny from the farmers."

7. Frank W. Merrick was Michigan's commissioner of banking. The new vice president taking his place was Albert E. Sleeper, who had been Michigan's governor during the World War I years. Evidently Michigan Bean lacked neither financial nor political clout. Also among the officers was Andrew W. Orr, W.J.'s older son. A. W. Orr served as secretary, as well as on the board of directors.

8. It was the acquisition of Cass City Grain that had brought the Frutcheys into Michigan Bean in the first place. First of all, there was the old man of the clan, Amuel, and his two sons, Joseph and Herbert Frutchey. Associated with them in Cass City Grain were Archibald D. McIntyre and his brother George McIntyre. As a result of the Cass City acquisition, Riedel, who already had been promoted to vice president and general manager of Michigan Bean, temporarily stepped a rung back down the ladder. So, for two years, Michigan Bean's executive lineup included Merrick as president, Joseph Frutchey as vice president and general manager, Riedel as treasurer and assistant manager, W. J. Orr, Jr. (W. J. Orr, Sr.'s younger son) as secretary, and A. D. McIntyre as assistant secretary. After the separation of the Frutchey interests, Riedel moved back up to vice president and general manager. For the eventual lineup of Frutchey elevators, see Chapter 7, Note 1.

9. C. K. Eddy & Sons had also owned the Saginaw Milling Co., an earlier Michigan Bean acquisition (see main text).

10. Precise statistics on merchandising distribution are not available for the war years, although evidently protein-rich beans were predominant, as they already had been for several years, and they were to become even more so after 1944 when the federal government asked that the Michigan Bean crop be expanded by 40 percent to one million acres. For a general picture on relative percentages prior to this big bean jump, let's grab-bag a typical inventory listing from the Michigan Bean minutes of 1934. At that time, beans constituted 38 percent of inventory; grain, 22 percent; feed, 11 percent; seed, 10 percent; coal, 6 percent; building materials, 5.5 percent; and miscellaneous (still including wool), 7.5 percent.

11. Michigan Bean's bank was and still is the Second National Bank of Saginaw, Michigan, whereas Wickes Corp. in Saginaw primarily dealt with the Michigan National Bank. Al Riedel, now a consultant in the agricultural business, still maintains an office—and regular office hours—in Saginaw's Second National Bank Building. In fact, Michigan Bean's association with the Second National had been an important factor in its growth quite apart from the financial aspects, much as Lybrand's influenced Wickes far beyond auditing its books. For instance, the Saginaw Milling acquisition by Michigan Bean from C. K. Eddy (see Note 9 above) was financed by the Second National, whose president was R. Perry Shorts, who was also president of C. K. Eddy & Sons. To go one step farther, Shorts was also involved in U.S. Graphite. No wonder experienced Wall Streeters become extra cautious when they meet "just a country boy."

12. One of the things that still rankle Riedel is that, in hindsight anyway, Michigan Bean could have been big enough to make it on its own. "What I should have done," he says, "is really build it up during the war [World War II]. Instead of

paying excess profits taxes, we could have used the money for construction and investment. I guess you never think of those things until it's too late."

13. One of which, at Silverwood, had in fact been bought from Michigan Bean in 1953. This elevator was later sold to a small processor for—believe it or not—a carload of beans. It has since been abandoned.

14. Wickes stock had risen from a low of $7\frac{7}{8}$ in the fourth quarter of 1954 to $16\frac{1}{4}$ in early December 1955. Of the 1,185,000 shares ($5 par value) outstanding, H. Randall Wickes was the record and beneficial owner of 76,384 shares, or approximately 6.45 percent of the outstanding voting securities. Other associates (i.e., mostly family) of Ran Wickes beneficially owned 102,814 shares in the aggregate, or approximately 8.68 percent. Other major stockholders, as of November 11, 1955, included Robert E. Wolohan, with 18,151 shares; Richard V. Wolohan, 10,898 shares; Dan Fitz-Gerald, 8,000 shares; Frank B. Godard, 7,599 shares; and Smith Bolton, 5,599 shares. With the Michigan Bean merger, Albert L. Riedel and his family now also became major Wickes stockholders, holding in the aggregate close to 14,000 shares.

15. At the time of the merger, 17.5 percent of the Michigan Bean stock was held by the Orr family, 13.8 percent by the Riedel family, 14.3 percent by the Second National Bank as trustee in estates, and 13.7 percent by Michigan Bean employees. Al Riedel had always pushed for heavy employee interest in the company.

16. At the special directors meeting of the Michigan Bean Company of December 30, 1955, which convened for the purpose of approving the merger, The Wickes Corporation's attorney, Jerome Weadock, read a letter to the employees of Michigan Bean, dated December 19, 1955, and signed by Ran Wickes. The letter said in part: "A. L. Riedel will be *Vice President* and Divisional General Manager, also a *Director* of The Wickes Corporation, with substantially the same or even more authority in directing affairs of Michigan Bean as he had heretofore . . ." (author's italics). This letter, like all other specific Michigan Bean Company data, is quoted from Michigan Bean Co. Minute Books.

17. The lineup was as follows: H. Randall Wickes, president; William E. Stone, corporate vice president; Carl Bintz, president and general manager of the Wickes Brothers Division; Smith Bolton, president and general manager of the United States Graphite Division; Richard V. Wolohan, president and general manager of the Charles Wolohan, Inc., Division; Robert E. Wolohan, president and general manager of the Saginaw Grain Company subsidiary; Dan Fitz-Gerald, treasurer of the corporation; and Melvin J. Zahnow, secretary of the corporation.

The board of directors also included Elbert G. Rounds, the retired general manager of the Standard Oil Company of Indiana's Saginaw division; Herbert F. Russell, general manager of the Saginaw division of Eaton Manufacturing Company; and James M. Shackleton, senior vice president of the Michigan National Bank. (Gone from the board now was F. B. Godard, sales representative of U.S. Graphite.)

18. Wickes's share of the bean market is so substantial that, quite predictably, the government at one time considered antitrust proceedings, and Wickes spent much effort to prove that it was not in a monopoly situation.

The world's biggest producer of edible beans is Brazil, with an annual output of between 30 and 40 million hundredweight. The United States, which annually produces an average of about 20 million hundredweight, ranks next. But beans are also grown in many other countries, including the Balkans, Canada, Russia, and Japan.

Michigan produces at least one-third of the total United States bean crop. The state accounts for 99 percent of navy beans (also called pea beans), about 95 percent of cranberry beans, about 95 percent of yelloweye beans, and about 30 to 40 percent of red kidney beans, as well as a smattering of several other varieties, such as marrow, black turtle soup, and pinto. On a worldwide basis, the Michigan navy bean has consistently led all other varieties in volume of production. Following in second place is the pinto, and in most years—again on a worldwide basis—the great northern ranks third, followed closely by the red kidney. With the recent acquisition of Gormley Bean Company, Wickes is now also firmly established in pintos, though it is by no means the leader in that field.

For a sample year prior to the agricultural upheaval of 1973-1974, let's look at some of the 1971 statistics (the figures refer to hundred weights of cleaned beans). That year Michigan produced 5,959,000 (of which about 5,200,000 were navy beans); California, 2,141,000 (mostly small white, lima, baby lima, pink, blackeye, cranberry, pinto, small red, and red kidney); Idaho, 2,024,000 (mostly small white, great northern, cranberry, and red kidney); Colorado, 1,929,000 (mostly pinto); Nebraska, 1,517,000 (again pinto); New York, 794,000 (mostly white and red kidney, marrow, and some navy); Wyoming, 450,000 (great northern and pinto). The other principal bean producers are Washington, Oregon, Montana, North Dakota, Minnesota, and Kansas.

19. Robert G. Dodge, born in Gratiot County in 1926, moved with his family to Merrill in 1935, attended public schools there, and in 1940 moved back to Gratiot County to the community of Middleton, where he graduated from high school in 1943. At seventeen, he enlisted in the Naval Air Force, attended training programs at Emory and Henry College and Mercer University, then was washed out by serial number and entered the NROTC program at Georgia Tech, where he received his degree in naval engineering (for all practical purposes, industrial engineering). After his discharge as a lieutenant, j.g., he took a job with Dow Chemical in Midland, working in the spectroscopy laboratory, which didn't interest him very much. At that time, a short course in elevator management had been started at Michigan State University, and he decided to apply. But he discovered that to be eligible, he had to be sponsored by a local cooperative, and so went to work for the Michigan Farm Bureau in Saginaw. (The reason for this requirement was that the Michigan Farm Bureau had put up the front money for this program.) Disenchanted after a year with the cooperative's way of doing business, he quit, was interviewed at Frutchey, and then immediately went to work for Michigan Bean. At the same time, he took a correspondence course in traffic management from LaSalle University, training that happened to feed into his career when in later years, among other functions, he took charge of the traffic department of The Wickes Corporation.

After succeeding Albert L. Riedel at Michigan Bean, Dodge remained general manager of Michigan Bean until 1972, and during this period also became a vice president of the corporation. On February 1 of that year he was promoted to senior vice president to take charge of a group of operations that included Michigan Bean, Behlen Manufacturing, Farmaster Products, and Moriarty (now Wickes Buildings). Later the corporate staff functions of construction, real estate, and corporate traffic and distribution were added, as was supervision of Gormley Bean, which was acquired in August 1973 (see Chapter 9).

20. The properties purchased by Wickes from defunct Frutchey Bean included six country elevators at Cass City, Kawkawlin, Lennon, Linwood, Shepherd, and Vassar, and a major storage facility at Bay City. All these installations are still in service.

For scholars of agricultural history and collectors of Americana, here is what happened to all the other country elevators Dan Fitz-Gerald originally wanted to merge into one big organization. The facts are abstracted from the meticulous notes of Al Riedel, who promised John A. Hannah, former president of Michigan State University, eventually to turn over all the old Michigan Bean documents and other assorted historical materials to the archives of that once primarily agricultural campus. For the present, however, this is, so far as I know, the only summary in print:

Michigan Bean: Saginaw (Bean Terminal), Alma, Blanchard, Caro, Chesaning, Croswell, Deckerville, Fenton, Forest Hill, Henderson, Merrill, Midland, Owendale, Sandusky, Silverwood, and Vestaburg. All are still operating under Wickes except Silverwood (sold, then abandoned; see Note 13, above) and Forest Hill, which was discontinued.

Charles Wolohan, Inc.: Still operating as part of Wickes Agriculture are Birch Run, Davison, Hemlock (vastly expanded), Merrill, Freeland, and Emmett. The Gera elevator has been sold to the Star of the West Milling Co. of Frankenmuth, Michigan. Gladwin was sold to the Gladwin Milling Co. The feed store in Saginaw was discontinued.

Bad Axe Grain Co.: Still operating as part of Blount, Inc., are the elevators at Bad Axe, Applegate, Ruth, Kinde, and Six Lakes. The property at McGregor was destroyed by fire and not rebuilt. The properties at Port Austin were discontinued. The properties at Port Hope and Ubly were sold to employees. The elevator at Harbor Beach was sold to "a competitor."

Wallace & Morley: Still operating as part of Blount, Inc., are Gagetown, Elkton, Fairgrove, Gilford, Bradleyville, North Branch, Akron, Munger, and Sebewaing. Seven elevator locations were discontinued: Bay Port, Caseville, Linkville, Pigeon, Bach, Mitchell, and Grassmere. In Riedel's opinion, only the last two should have been closed down when they were.

Frutchey Bean Co.: Here the story is more complicated. We already have listed the properties sold to Wickes. As for the others:

Frutchey owned three elevators in Saginaw, all of which were destroyed by fire. Two of these had originally belonged to the Brand & Hardin Milling Co., which was started in the 1850s by Daniel Hardin to grind flour. The site of these former grist mills is now the location of the Lyon Street Terminal. Frutchey's third Saginaw elevator burned, was rebuilt, and finally discontinued.

Still operating under various ownerships, besides those in the Wickes stable, are Greenleaf, Kingston, Clifford, Mayville, Millington (where there used to be two, but one was destroyed by fire and not rebuilt), Pinconning, Montrose, Oakley, Ashley, Carson City, Vickeryville, Auburn, Grand Ledge, and Clare. Of these, Kingston and Clifford were sold to R. Walker; Mayville, to Allied Mills; Pinconning, to the Michigan Farm Bureau; Ashley, Carson City, and Vickeryville, to Central Elevator Co., and since acquired by new owners; Auburn, to Auburn Bean & Grain, and since transferred to new ownership; Grand Ledge, to Grand Ledge Seed & Supply; and Clare, to J. Johnson.

The elevator at St. Charles burned (making a total of five that fell victim to fire), and Deford, Columbiaville, Gaines, and Fostoria were closed down.

Chapter 9

1. Van Bergeijk's experiences during World War II are no less interesting than his peacetime exploits as a commodities trader. To start with, his Rotterdam office was bombed to smithereens in the notorious German raid of May 10, 1940, which wiped out the heart of the city. With the Nazis occupying the Nether-

lands, there was no longer any export to Britain. Whatever crops were left in Corky's terminal, the Germans confiscated. Now, even though there was no more business to be done, Corky kept on paying all his employees throughout the war, thus depleting his considerable fortune. His major occupation during that time was to stand in the garden of his country place near Apeldoorn with binoculars and watch for crippled American planes returning from attacks on German industrial centers. One evening alone, seven Flying Fortresses crash-landed within a few miles of the van Bergeijk house. Then Corky went out on his bike to look for survivors. When he found any, he hid them for the night and then arranged to have them taken out along a pipeline of "safe houses." The Nazis never caught him in this precarious activity, but they almost shot him anyway one night when—possibly having heard that Corky had lots of valuable French wine stashed somewhere—they started digging in his garden and discovered a car he had hidden under a pile of charcoal dust. His son Theo, then fifteen, saved his father's life by somehow hunting up tires for that by now well-rusted vehicle, and the Germans, appeased, pulled it away with horses.

2. Corky had a special trick to gild his guilders. By importing crops from the Iron Curtain countries and Africa first to the Netherlands for processing before exporting them to their eventual destinations, he achieved an extra profit margin. Here is an example: the import duty in the Netherlands was 7 percent, in France it was 17 percent, but from the Netherlands to France—both Common Market countries—the beans could be shipped duty-free, so Corky exported "Dutch" beans to France and saved himself 10 percent.

3. Not that Corky ever did reconcile himself fully to paying United States taxes. Eventually he liquidated the Agricultural Products Company and established a holding company on Curaçao in the Netherlands Antilles. In turn, Wickes eventually formed the Wickes International Division (since disbanded) for its agricultural exports, and headquartered the division in Puerto Rico, which was then and still is a sort of Liechtenstein under United States auspices. Payments for the exports to foreign countries went to San Juan, whence the Wickes half went to Saginaw (and Wickes Corp. was of course obliged to pay U.S. taxes on its corporate profits), but van Bergeijk's share, nearly tax-exempt, was then transferred to Curaçao, which in turn was a tax haven for the Dutch. This arrangement, however, didn't last too long: by the time it was established, Wickes had set up its own direct channels for international sales and did not need an intermediary. Containerization of fully processed beans also helped expedite direct deliveries.

   Wickes, too, could have escaped paying full taxes under this John Mc-Cullough-inspired scheme if there had been enough employees in Puerto Rico to qualify the corporation for this exemption, which had been established to boost Puerto Rico's economy. But of course the San Juan office was really nothing but a letter drop—a manager by the name of Eugenio Rodriguez and a couple of secretaries—and any potential Wickes tax saving wasn't even considered when the arrangement was set up.

4. His tall and slim son Theo, no less handsome and charming than Corky must have been, is now a successful manufacturer of hospital equipment in Breda, south of Rotterdam. Like his father, he is a bon vivant, a connoisseur of wines, and an habitué of the best restaurants on every continent. The only reason he keeps his trim figure, I suspect, is that he is an ardent sailor, a sport to which he devotes most of his spare time (and often weeks at a stretch).

5. The Wickes Marine Terminal traffic diminished and is now almost down to nothing, since edible beans are no longer shipped in "break" bulk. With the

advent of mechanization in sorting, sizing, screening, and cleaning of the bean crop, it became possible to ship a perfectly graded product, which is packed in 100-pound bags. Four hundred of these bags (i.e., 40,000 pounds of beans) fit into a 20-foot-long moistureproof container. These are often loaded right at the country elevators; the rest at the Wickes Terminal facilities. They are then trucked out to the ports. Grains, on the other hand, are still shipped in bulk, primarily by water but also by rail, and usually directly from the Saginaw Grain Terminal.

6. Of Michigan's beans, about 20 to 25 percent is sold to foreign canners and packers, and this proportion also holds true for the beans shipped by Wickes. Wickes's major customers abroad today are Heinz England; H. P. Sauce; and Nestlé (of which Crosse & Blackwell is a subsidiary). Its major domestic customers are (and generally in the order given) Campbell Soup, Stokely-Van Camp, H. J. Heinz, Libby McNeil & Libby, followed by Bush Brothers, Mammoth Springs, and Morgan Packing.

Wickes's biggest competitor on the bean scene is the Michigan Elevator Exchange of the Michigan Farm Bureau.

Of course, the volume of Michigan's bean crop varies from year to year. Depending on a number of factors, it may range anywhere from 4.5 to 7.5 million hundredweight bags. Navy beans are always in preponderance, and constitute about 90 percent of all of Michigan's bean crops. For instance, in 1973, which was a fairly typical harvest year, Michigan produced a total of 5.32 million bags of beans, of which 4.64 million were navy beans. That year, Wickes processed roughly 1.1 million bags (of which about 900,000 were navy beans) through its country elevators, and from other sources purchased about another 500,000 bags (again primarily navys) which were directly processed through the Michigan Bean Elevator in Saginaw and the company's other terminals. In 1974, the Michigan crop totaled 7.2 million bags (of which 6.48 million were navys), and that year Wickes sold about 1.8 million bags.

7. Current Wickes country elevator locations are Cass City, Kawkawlin, Lennon, Linwood, Shepherd, Vassar, Alicia (on the diked "Prairie Farm" development south of Saginaw), Alma, Birch Run, Blanchard, Brown City (which had been purchased from Carl Wendt), Caro, Chesaning, Croswell, Davison, Deckerville, Emmett, Fenton, Freeland, Hemlock, Henderson, Merrill, Midland, Owendale, Sandusky, and Vestaburg.

In terms of hundredweights, the average annual volume of these elevators totals about 1.25 million bags of navy beans, and 350,000 bags of other varieties, including cranberry, yelloweye, dark red kidney, light red kidney, pinto, and the black turtle soup bean.

8. These facilities include the Bay City Terminal of 1.25 million-bushel capacity (not to be confused with the Marine Terminal), a facility which was purchased from Frutchey in 1967, as well as a 600,000-bushel former flour mill in Owosso, which was purchased in 1973 for the storage of soybeans. Wickes's total storage capacity therefore at any given time is approximately 7 million bushels.

9. In the average year, this breaks down to 2 million bushels of wheat, 5.5 million bushels of corn, 1.9 million bushels of soybeans, and 700,000 bushels of oats.

The elevators of The Wickes Corporation (for their locations, see Note 7, above) are strategically placed to handle a maximum of the crops of Michigan's leading bean counties: Huron, Tuscola, Saginaw, Gratiot, Sanilac, Montcalm, Shiawassee, Genesee, Clinton, Isabella, Midland, and St. Clair. Of these, all but Midland are also among the heaviest grain and corn producers. The only major grain and corn counties where Wickes is not directly represented are Allegan, Eaton, Ingham, Calhoun, Washtenaw, Hillsdale, and Lenawee.

10. Gormley Bean was acquired for 150,000 Wickes shares, then quoted at around $20. The pretax earnings of Gormley's 1974 pinto bean shipments of 1.2 million hundredweight were about $2.7 million.

11. The division bought its first Nebraska elevator at Gering in September 1974.

12. Clemens O. Putz was born in 1918 in Bay City, Michigan, where he later attended parochial schools and junior college. His major wartime assignment was to supervise shipments of supplies along a 400-mile section of the Alcan Highway.

13. The 6,000-square-foot Caro store, for example, which opened in September 1973, chalked up $60,000 of business that December. The average daily customer count was 330, and the average purchase came to $8.50. Brighton was added in 1974.

14. Country elevator sales of fertilizer, seed, feed, and chemicals are expected to total about $15 million in fiscal 1976.

15. At the annual Wickes Management Conference at John's Island, Florida, in January 1975, Bob Dodge had this to say about the future of Wickes Agriculture:

> Every day the world population increase is equal to the city of Des Moines, Iowa. In the next ten years, at the present birthrate, there will be one million more mouths to feed. The experts say it will take a half-billion bushels more grain each year just to feed the new people in the world a subsistence diet . . . it will take twice that amount—a billion bushels—to provide an adequate diet. . . .
>
> Increased food production is needed to reduce rapidly accelerating food prices here at home [and] to provide a continuation of our favorable balance of trade, a point particularly important when we are paying quadruple prices for oil. We need additional food production to meet the humanitarian commitments our government has made, along with governments of other developed nations. . . .
>
> While dry beans are not readily accepted in all of the underdeveloped countries, nevertheless, this crop will play a leading role as a source of protein, particularly to supplement inadequate supplies of meat and soybeans. We see indications of increased domestic consumption of beans, particularly as the economic crunch pinches down on family incomes.
>
> While dry bean acreage may vary from year to year depending upon market conditions, we are convinced that farmers will continue to plant beans. Dry beans traditionally have been part of the farmers' crop rotation program.
>
> If we are able to find more adequate ways of distribution around the world— perhaps in the form of bean powder or as a blended protein supplement—we should see even greater demand for beans in the coming years.
>
> All things being equal, we see a favorable outlook for dry bean production, handling, and distribution in the United States. It follows then that we anticipate continued expansion of Wickes Agriculture in the dry bean business in this country. At the same time, we are exploring the possibility of participation in this area in other countries of the world, and particularly in South America. . . . If the economies of some of these countries show some stability, we see opportunities for Wickes.

Chapter 10

1. Dan Fitz-Gerald estimated that the average volume of the lumberyard retail business at the Wolohan elevators totaled about a half-million dollars a year. These five lumberyards were in Birch Run, Davison, Freeland, Hemlock, and Merrill, and shortly after the Wickes acquisition of Wolohan, they were run as a

separate department, which remained under the auspices of the Charles Wolohan, Inc., Division through fiscal 1953.

The Wickes-Wolohan merger on June 9, 1950, involved an exchange of stock at the rate of twenty-seven shares of Wickes for each share of Wolohan, representing an acquisition price of about $1 million at the then-quoted market value of approximately $9 per common share of Wickes. The acquisition reduced the Wickes family's interest in The Wickes Corporation from 57.3 to 48.5 percent.

The consolidation gave The Wickes Corporation total assets of $9,497,000, with current assets exceeding current liabilities at the rate of nearly three to one. Working capital and surplus totaled $6,998,000. The merger brought the total of Wickes shares outstanding to 888,074 out of an authorized 2 million shares.

With the merger, Charles Wolohan, Inc., became a division of the corporation. Richard V. Wolohan, then thirty-four years old, who had been treasurer of the Wolohan firm, became general manager of the division and a vice president and director of the corporation. His brother, Robert E. Wolohan, formerly vice president and general manager of the Wolohan firm, then thirty-eight years old, assumed the office of general manager of the Saginaw Grain Company, which was a wholly owned Wickes subsidiary at that time. Robert Wolohan also was named a vice president and director of The Wickes Corporation. The oldest Wolohan brother, Thomas, who had been president of the family firm, was in ill health and retired to Gladwin, where he died in 1958 at the age of fifty-four. Charles Wolohan, the founder of the Wolohan firm, had died in 1943 at seventy-seven years of age.

2. The 1952 board had practically the same composition as that cited in Note 17 of Chapter 8 for 1955, except that F. B. Godard, sales representative of the U.S. Graphite Company Division, was still a member, as was R. J. Stormont, general manager of Wickes Boiler; and that James M. Shackleton, of the Michigan National Bank, had not yet been elected to a directorship.

3. Joe McMullin was especially expert at judging bean crops. He'd visit the farms in his area long before harvest time, inspect the fields, and if something looked good he'd say, "I want that field for this fall," and proceed to get it. He never dickered. He named his price and that was it. But then, no matter what happened, he held to the price he said he'd pay. Few indeed are the processors who can take such risks. Of course, market factors are involved here too, and Michigan Bean today will never "buy blossoms" as McMullin did.

You had to get to know Joe quite well to find out that inside that rough husk of a hard-nosed businessman there were kernels of compassion. As is often the case with feisty types like that, he was more likely to show his human side to the people who were working for him and with him than to those he was working for. Arriving at the office in the morning, he almost always stormed in, looking neither right nor left, and slammed his door behind him without so much as wishing anyone a good day. But when he wasn't pressed by business matters, he often engaged in personal conversations with his staff, and his usually serious— you might even say grim—face lit up whenever the conversation turned to family matters, especially children. Roland Pretzer (see text), who as a young man went to work for McMullin, was the son of one of the farmers in McMullin's bailiwick.

"There were eight children in our family," Pretzer recalls, "and of course being on a farm, money wasn't flowing very frequently, and it was very common for Joe to say, 'Whatever you need, just come up and get it, seed or feed or anything, and you can pay me back when you sell your crops.' This is how Joe operated and built his reputation around Hemlock."

He was no less respected at the lumber mills on the West Coast, where he was considered one of the sharpest buyers in the business—possibly because he never took their word for anything. Although a Michigander, he was strictly from Missouri: he had to see everything for himself before he made any kind of deal.

Joseph S. McMullin, who was born in 1891, retired in 1961 as purchasing director of what by then had become the Wickes Lumber Division. He still makes his home in Hemlock and spends his winters in Phoenix, Arizona.

4. The value of the initial inventory was somewhere between $40,000 and $50,000.

5. The first manager of the Bay City Cash Way was Raymond Piggott, McMullin's son-in-law. In the 1960s (see later text) when Richard V. Wolohan left Wickes to start his own similar lumber retail chain, Ray Piggott also went on his own. He joined with McMullin's son Edward and another man by the name of William Carter, who had been assistant purchasing director of the Wickes Lumber Division after McMullin's retirement, to establish the MPC Lumber Company in Lansing, Michigan, a single outlet also based on the McMullin cash-and-carry principles of low cost, low markup, and large volume.

6. Another out-of-state lumberyard was opened in Springfield, Ohio, at about the same time. Its first manager was Gordon Meyers, who is still with the Wickes Lumber Division. Springfield did about $6.5 million in its peak year.

7. If a customer showed up who asked the pertinent question of why prices were so low, he was referred to Pretzer, who would say something like this: "The typical lumberyard is charging you for delivery, for any credit losses it might have, and for the overhead of its millwork and its estimating. All of that adds up. Now, we don't make price estimates, and we don't sit down and draw blueprints for you. You can do all this yourself. So we're passing all these savings along to you. Now it's up to you to take advantage of them."

8. The other locations weren't doing poorly either. Bay City's volume for that year was about $2 million and Kalamazoo about $3.5 million.

9. The total volume for the area is now well above that of Rootstown's banner year. On the average, Norwalk and Saegertown do close to $3 million each, and Newcomerstown around $2 million. With Rootstown's $4 million, that adds up to about $12 million.

10. Carter Lumber Company is an offspring of Carter-Jones, a partnership that operated a number of independent lumberyards in northern Ohio. Shortly after Wickes moved into Rootstown, Warren E. Carter purchased the property directly across from the Wickes yard, apparently with the intention of opening a competitive outlet. According to Pretzer, Dick Wolohan convinced Carter that such an effort would benefit neither organization, and Carter then opened a cash-and-carry yard right in Akron instead. Since then, the Carter Lumber Company has expanded considerably and competes with Wickes not only in Ohio but in some other parts of the Midwest as well.

11. The first Wickes lumber centers outside the Midwest were opened in Selkirk, New York (November 1959); Swedesboro, New Jersey (September 1961); Frederick, Maryland (September 1961); Georgetown, Texas (March 1962); Windsor Locks, Connecticut (March 1962); Petersburg, Virginia (March 1962); Alvin, Grapevine, and Tyler, Texas (all April 1962); New Braunfels, Texas (May 1962); Ontario, California (May 1962); and Fowler and Modesto, California (June 1962).

12. In 1954, the Wickes Lumber Division became a separate profit center. Here are its sales figures for its first ten years through 1963, shown in relation to the total sales of the corporation (see respective annual reports and financial statements):

Fiscal year	Lumber Division sales	Total corporate sales	Net corporate income after taxes
1954	$ 5,395,952	$ 39,717,612	$1,531,188
1955	8,736,179	33,928,279	1,407,664
1956	14,491,849	56,995,621	1,250,303
1957	26,225,610	78,401,576	1,970,165
1958	34,429,357	82,831,609	2,027,552
1959	37,857,343	94,346,274	2,245,459
1960	47,923,257	103,852,701	2,965,865
1961	60,424,241	113,892,527	3,844,844
1962	73,423,918	134,423,099	4,228,199
1963	107,005,886	166,200,937	4,661,075

Since then, the growth of both Lumber Division and corporate sales have been even more phenomenal.

Fiscal year	Lumber Division sales	Total corporate sales	Net corporate income after taxes
1964	$130,879,000	$ 198,820,622	$ 5,756,897
1965	176,791,000	248,452,551	8,123,681
1966	201,713,000	278,091,769	9,171,521
1967	200,072,000	268,428,654	9,710,039
1968	223,194,310	284,417,657	8,341,669
1969	267,295,000	375,731,043	11,198,779
1970	292,283,000	489,031,784	11,514,950
1971	309,528,000	515,346,842	7,539,322
1972	358,686,000	614,803,000	12,184,000
1973	403,609,000	873,373,000	16,925,000
1974	499,202,000	1,132,825,000	21,348,000
1975	483,000,000	1,120,781,000	11,906,000

You'll note that, after a certain point, the last three digits show up as zeros. That's what happens when a company gets big. Figures on financial statements are then generally given in thousands.

Chapter 11

1. At that time, Wickes was organized into divisions as follows: Wickes Boiler Co., under George A. Kendall; Wickes Machine Tool, also under Kendall; Wickes Marine Terminal Company (which operated as a separate entity for overseas shipments), under Otto C. Krohn; Wickes Lumber Co., under Richard V. Wolohan; Wickes Plumbing, Heating & Electrical Co., also under Richard Wolohan; Michigan Bean Company, under Albert L. Riedel; Saginaw Grain Co., under Robert E. Wolohan as divisional president; The United States Graphite Company, under Ralph J. Zemanek, who replaced Smith Bolton on his promotion to corporate vice president of operations; Compañía Minera de San José, S.A. de C.V. (the Mexican subsidiary that owned the graphite mine), also under Zemanek; and Wickes International N.V., the export corporation registered in the Netherlands under Cornelis van Bergeijk.

Corporate officers were Randall Wickes, president; Daniel M. Fitz-Gerald, executive vice president; Smith Bolton, vice president—operations; Robert E. Wolohan, vice president; Melvin J. Zahnow, vice president—finance; Thomas W. Cline, secretary; and Arthur E. Pufford, treasurer.

All these men, except Cline and Pufford, also served as directors, as did four outsiders, Albert G. Rounds, James M. Shackleton, R. Dewey Stearns, and J. W. Symons, Jr. (see *Annual Report To Stockholders* for the fiscal year ending June 30, 1962).

2. Interview with Smith Bolton, November 1973.
3. Interview with Roland Pretzer, January 1974.
4. This was the situation in 1961, prior to Smith Bolton's promotion. Robert Wolohan then relinquished Saginaw Grain, becoming a corporate vice president instead. He remained, however, on the Wickes board of directors (see Note 1, above).
5. Bolton interview, op. cit. (see Note 2, above).
6. Wolohan Lumber opened five yards in the first year. As this is written, there are twenty-five yards in Michigan, Ohio, Indiana, Illinois, and Wisconsin. Only one of these outlets—in Saginaw—is in exactly the same community where Wickes has one of its centers. Some of the others are perhaps 20 or so miles down the road. Wolohan Lumber is still headquartered in Saginaw, and Richard V. Wolohan is still its president.
7. This does not mean cheating the customers. It merely induces them to buy everything at your store since elsewhere they'd have to pay just as much for the other items they buy, as well as full price on your special.

Chapter 12

1. T. E. Rulison was born and raised in Saginaw, then attended an Episcopal boarding school in Sycamore, Illinois, on a football scholarship. There, in addition to graduating at the top of his class, he received the honor of being the only player from a private school in that state who earned an honorable mention for All-State as a halfback. His first full-time job at the age of eighteen was that of a collector for Household Finance in Chicago—a difficult and unpleasant assignment in the depression year of 1937. When a lady he was trying to collect from hit him on the head with a broomstick (it was precisely because of such emergencies that Household's dunners were uniformed with hard straw hats), he quit and returned to Saginaw where he managed to get a job with a burglar alarm monitoring company. This position also didn't last overly long: He responded to an alarm, entered the building before the police arrived, and found himself shot at.

It was then that, thanks to a church connection with Eugene Bierlein, the traffic manager at Wickes Bros., Tom Rulison obtained employment in the company's sales and traffic department as a combination office boy and shipping clerk. When the traffic departments of Wickes Bros. and Wickes Boiler were combined into one, he became its assistant manager.

Next he was preempted by Carl Bintz, general manager of Wickes Bros., to become a salesman, first of machining time to clients like Chevrolet, and later of blueprint machines. He was involved in the development of a white-print machine with which Wickes Bros. attempted to compete with Ozalid Corp. After this part of the business collapsed (see Chapter 4), and after he was rejected by the armed services because of a deaf ear, Rulison was asked by Bintz to take on some personnel functions. This field really struck Rulison's fancy. He enrolled in correspondence courses in personnel management, but when he tried to apply what he had learned, Bintz asked Rulison to quit. At this point Ran Wickes interceded, made Rulison personnel manager, and as his first assignment told him to fire his predecessor.

With Dan Fitz-Gerald's advent, credit and insurance functions were added to Rulison's domain, and he was named personnel director in 1961 and a vice president in 1965. He developed the corporation's extensive employee benefit programs, which are among the best in the retail industry. In December 1973 he became the vice president of field operations of the Lumber Division.

2. This happened at The Golf Club, an exclusive eighteen-holer near Columbus, Ohio. McNeely's opponent was Air Force General Lauris Norstad, the former commander of NATO. McNeely overdrove the eighteenth hole on his second shot and Norstad congratulated him on being out-of-bounds. As McNeely tells it, "There was a pro standing there and he said, 'It isn't out-of-bounds, you can play it.' But the ball was under an automobile. So eventually they moved the car and gave me a drop back a ways. I hit the ball over a flock of trees and landed it reasonably close to a pin and sunk it for a par. And took my money. It aged the General a little bit." McNeely's explanation: "I've played a lot of baseball in my life and I attack the golf ball the same way. I can get myself out of situations once in awhile which I get myself into because I swing a little wild." His handicap is 11.

3. This happened in the Philippines during a leap-frog landing of the First Cavalry Division on the west coast of Leyte in December 1944. McNeely's ship, acting as a radar picket, was attacked by five Zekes and nine Betty bombers. Air Corps ace Major Dick Bong and his wingman shot down all the Zekes, which flew at a higher altitude, but couldn't get close to the low-flying Japanese bombers because the limited maneuverability of the American P-38 fighter planes prevented their operating between the mountains of this jagged coast. Navy antiaircraft fire downed four of the Betty bombers. The other four dove into McNeely's ship. If they had still carried their bombs, the end would have come right there, but even so, they did set the ship on fire, and when the number one magazine exploded, the complement had to abandon ship.

4. E. L. McNeely, son of a well-to-do northern Missouri farmer, graduated from high school in 1934 when he was sixteen, then attended Central Business College in Kansas City before transferring first to the University of Missouri and from there to Northeast Missouri State University at Kirksville, which had counted his mother among its 1913 alumnae.

With Montgomery Ward's management training behind him, he was promoted to mail-order merchandiser in the firm's Chicago office after his discharge from the Navy as a lieutenant in 1946. He then made a lateral move to become an assistant buyer of lamps and other accessories in the furniture department, became a buyer nine months later, then joined the staff of the vice president of merchandising, Ted Platt. Here he worked with the McKinsey Company, an outside consulting concern, and others on Platt's team on developing a new merchandising system. Upon completion of this task, he was promoted to the post of West Coast merchandise manager out of Oakland, California, in the hard lines of home furnishings, like hardware, electrical goods, and automobile accessories. After two years on the West Coast, he returned to Chicago from where he ran all Ward's hardware and electrical departments until his recruitment by Wickes.

McNeely took over the Lumber and Building Supply Division from Smith

Bolton in 1965 as senior vice president and general manager. He was named president and chief operating officer in May 1969, and two years later also inherited the post of chief executive officer from Dan Fitz-Gerald. He succeeded Fitz-Gerald as chairman of the board in May 1975.

McNeely has been married since 1948 to Alice Hall, daughter of a former president of the Central Soya Co. of Fort Wayne, Indiana. They have four grown children, a daughter and three sons, and live in La Jolla, California.

5. John Drum was born in Lyons, Ohio, in 1920. His grandfather had been president of the Murray Body Company and of Hayes Manufacturing Co. (the predecessor of Kelsey-Hayes), and has been credited with the origination of the progressive assembly line. John Drum moved with his parents to Grosse Pointe, Michigan, when Walter Chrysler left Willys Overland in 1925 and started the Chrysler Corporation, taking John Drum's father, who had been chief inspector at Willys, along to become the new corporation's manufacturing manager.

With the Depression, the Drum family lost all its money and John Drum's father his job, and they moved back to Toledo, where John Drum graduated from high school at sixteen. He then attended Michigan State, and while still studying agriculture, started working an 80-acre farm. He kept expanding until he farmed nearly 800 acres. While taking special courses in animal husbandry at Kansas State, he met his future wife and they were married in 1941.

After his temporary health problem forced him to leave farming in 1945, he joined Graham Paige Motors as a project engineer, soon was promoted to assistant sales manager, later sales manager, and at age twenty-five was named vice president in charge of the farm implement division at Graham Paige. Almost at the same time, Graham Paige was absorbed by the Kaiser Frazer Corporation, and Drum "being young and impetuous," as he puts it, "didn't think that was right and resigned." Drum then established his own consulting firm in Detroit to build up sales organizations for client firms. During this time he designed a gadget that made it easier to handle heavy tractor and truck wheels when tires had to be changed and bearings or brakes repaired. With the royalties and his other, not insubstantial, income from consulting, he bought another farm in 1950 where, on his 220 acres, he and his wife raised Herefords.

In 1956, he liquidated all his holdings and went to work as general manager of the Brass and Malleable Co. in Detroit. Interestingly enough, that company's owner was a gentleman by the name of Ralph Geddes, who had worked at one time at Lybrand's for Dan Fitz-Gerald's father—a connection that was not discovered until after McNeely had recruited Drum. Drum ran that foundry business for three years, then decided he wanted experience with a big company and went to work for U.S. Rubber as marketing manager in the Mechanical Goods Division. This division, whose products included V-belts and automotive molded rubber, counted Montgomery Ward among its largest customers. Drum handled this account himself, and in 1960 switched smoothly to Ward's as merchandise manager of lawn, garden, and farming equipment.

Drum joined Wickes in 1966 as vice president and general merchandise manager of the Lumber Division. Two years later he was moved laterally to become the division's marketing manager, an arabesque he did not appreciate until he found out in 1969 that McNeely had arranged it in order to broaden Drum and get him ready to take over the Lumber Division as general manager and, shortly thereafter, as senior vice president. Drum continued to run the division until he was named executive vice president in charge of operations in

1971. The administrative functions, including planning, research, and data processing, were assigned to G. W. O'Dair, who was brought in from the Celanese Corp. at that time. Later, some of the operations were assigned to O'Dair, and Drum in turn got some of the administrative departments. O'Dair's title was also executive vice president—a post that had been unfilled since Dan Fitz-Gerald's nomination to the presidency in 1964. Until O'Dair's resignation in late 1974, Wickes had the unusual corporate structure of possessing two executive vice presidents.

John Drum assumed the office of president and chief operating officer in May 1975. He and his wife, Lois, make their home in San Diego. They have two grown children, a son and a daughter.

6. The mistaken hunch that housing starts would soon go up again prompted one Wickes executive in 1974 to go long on lumber contracts. This speculation cost the corporation dearly when those futures went through the floor. Needless to say, the gentleman was asked to resign. He would have been no more of a hero, however, had he made a profit. His fate, in any case, would have been exactly the same as that of several commodity traders in Wickes Agriculture who, sometimes successfully and sometimes not, have been tempted over the years to play futures on behalf of the corporation. None of them is any longer with the company. Futures trading is undertaken at Wickes only for the purposes of hedging and obtaining favorable spreads.

7. The goal of "Project Twenty-First Century" is the formulation of action plans in thirty-five areas, ranging from expansion strategies to coping with inflation and government regulations. A number of Wickes corporate officers have been in charge of the project at various times.

8. Richard W. Fruechtenicht, a native of Fort Wayne, Indiana, graduated with a bachelor of science degree in business administration from Butler University. He served for nearly three years overseas as a fighter pilot and squadron operations officer in the Army Air Corps. After a brief stint as trainee at General Electric, he joined Montgomery Ward's financial department in April 1946. He remained with the company until May 1965, filling a variety of financial posts that culminated in his position as corporate controller—accounting. He then joined the Allied Radio Corp. as financial vice president and treasurer for three years, and from May 1968 to February 1974 served as vice president for administration and finance of the Beacon Manufacturing Co., a division of National Distillers.

Fruechtenicht then joined Wickes as vice president and controller, recruited by McNeely who remembered him from Ward's. He is married and the father of two grown children.

9. Richard G. Cotton was born in Detroit in 1925, graduated from high school in Port Huron, Michigan, and then served in the U.S. Army as a forward observer in the Field Artillery. After his return from the service, he attended Michigan State University and graduated with a major in speech and a minor in business administration in 1948.

He then joined the Telephone Directory Advertising Company in Saginaw. He continued with Directory Advertising when this company was absorbed by Michigan Bell in November 1950, handling various assignments as salesman and sales supervisor in Flint, Lansing, and Detroit. In August 1958, while serving as general sales manager in Detroit, Cotton was loaned to the American Telephone and Telegraph Company for four months. Upon his return to Michigan Bell, he was appointed general commercial personnel supervisor at Detroit. In December

1959, he was transferred to Saginaw as commercial manager of Michigan Bell's Central Division.

Cotton joined Wickes on July 1, 1964, as director of operations for the Lumber and Building Supply Division, and was later promoted to vice president of operations. In 1966, he was appointed vice president of personnel and public relations, and in 1969 named a senior vice president.

He was general chairman of the 1963–1964 United Fund Campaign for Saginaw County, has served on the executive council of the United Funds of America, and is a former member of the boards of directors of the Saginaw Chamber of Commerce, the YMCA Industrial Executives Club, the Rotary Club, and the Greater Saginaw Safety Council.

Cotton was transferred from Saginaw to San Diego in 1974. He and his wife, Evelyn, have three sons and two daughters.

10. T. W. Cline, a native of Birch Run, Michigan, first did business with Wickes while still in his early teens: he was the paperboy whose route included the corporate offices on North Washington in Saginaw. Tom's mother, Helen, was the oldest daughter of Charles Wolohan (see Chapter 7). His father, Leo, after working for the Wolohans, left the firm just before World War II to run his own bean and grain business, taking over the two Brand & Hardin Milling Co. facilities in Saginaw, one of which was the oldest steam-operated flour mill in Michigan. After Leo Cline's death, both plants were leased to the Frutchey Bean Company, and both burned down in the mid-1950s within one year of each other.

Tom Cline, who had worked for his father at the Brand & Hardin elevators as a boy, first intended to go into agriculture and move to the West. Eventually, however, he took a combined degree in commerce and law at the University of Detroit, graduated with a degree in accounting in 1954, completed his law training in 1956, and was admitted to the Michigan State Bar in 1957 at the age of twenty-five. While attending college he had applied for a summer job at Lybrand, Ross Bros. & Montgomery, and so impressed John McCullough that the latter offered him a full-time job. The University of Detroit, however, would not permit Cline to take on a heavy course schedule on a part-time basis, so he never did go to work for Lybrand's. McCullough then recommended him to Dan Fitz-Gerald, and Tom Cline started working for the Wickes accounting department a few months after his graduation.

One month later, in October 1956, he was drafted and did not return to Wickes until the fall of 1958, still in the accounting department but drifting ever more into the area of taxation, and thereby into law, until he became, in effect, the corporation's then one-man legal department. He almost immediately got involved in setting up Wickes International with Corky van Bergeijk (see Chapter 9). Later, as the corporation's top lawyer, he handled most of the acquisitions of the 1960s. He was elected a director in January 1975.

Apart from all his other accomplishments, Tom Cline enjoys the distinction of having been fired from Wickes more often than anyone else. Fitz-Gerald, driven to distraction by division managers who were not used to legal interference from the corporate level, kept on losing his temper with Tom almost on a monthly schedule. He used to can Tom one day, then rehire him the next morning. Cline finally informed Fitz-Gerald that from now on he'd insist on severance pay every time he was given his walking papers. Fitz-Gerald burst into laughter, and that was the end of the Cline firings.

Chapter 13

1. By the summer of 1964, when McNeely joined the company, Wickes building supply centers had been established sequentially in the following states: Michigan, Ohio, New York, Indiana, Wisconsin, Pennsylvania, Illinois, New Jersey, Maryland, Minnesota, Texas, Connecticut, Virginia, Kentucky, California, and Massachusetts. In 1964, new centers were built in Grand Rapids and Mason, Michigan, and in Bartlett, Illinois.

2. The Varina stores were located in Fuquay-Varina, Farmville, Rockingham, Raleigh, Clinton, and Greensboro, North Carolina; Timmonsville, Orangeburg, Conway, and Goldsboro, South Carolina; Danville, Virginia; Winchester, Louisville, Owensboro, and Bowling Green, Kentucky; Huntsville, Alabama; Tupelo and Jackson, Mississippi; and Murfreesboro, Tennessee.

3. Robert Douglas Powell, short, stocky, and built like a prizefighter, was one of fourteen children of a Fuquay Springs, North Carolina, farmer. His five brothers who had survived into adulthood, every one of them highly successful in his own line of business, also were involved in the Varina Builders Supply Company, but R. Douglas Powell did all the work. He continued to run Varina-Wickes for some time after the merger as the Lumber and Building Supply Division's director of operations for the Southeast. He is now president and chairman of the board of Products International, Ltd., a worldwide marketing service based in Fuquay-Varina.

4. Ross Builders Supplies had outlets in Greenville, Anderson, Seneca, Rock Hill, Columbia, Spartanburg, North Charleston, and Greenwood, South Carolina; Shelby, Salisbury, and Statesville, North Carolina; and Augusta, Doraville, Columbus, Forest Park, Mableton, Macon, and Athens, Georgia. The one under construction, completed in March 1965 shortly after the acquisition, was at West Charleston, South Carolina.

5. Wade H. Stephens, Jr., had joined Ross Builders Supplies shortly after its founding as vice president and general manager, reporting to George Ross, the company's first president and chief executive. Stephens is now vice chairman of Builder Marts of America, Inc., an outgrowth of the Daniel Construction Company of Greenville, South Carolina, whose founder, Charles E. Daniel, had been one of the original investors in Ross Builders Supplies.

6. Among the successful home supply stores are those in Owosso, Bay City, Jackson, Port Huron, and Adrian, all in Michigan. The first store that was opened was the one in Jackson, and what happened there made Wickes think that the concept would work everywhere else too. But in most cases there was not enough business to sustain the stores. If one of them did a half-million dollars a year on thirty points of margin, that meant $150,000, which wasn't enough to keep the store open six days a week. Moreover, from a management point of view, it took as much effort to supervise three home supply stores as it did ten lumber and building supply centers.

7. The Timberline yards were in Waterloo, Canadaigua, Phoenix, Endicott, and Horseheads, New York, and Southington, Connecticut.

8. Newly built in 1965 were centers at Walden, New York; Hillsboro and Logansport, Indiana; Des Moines and Iowa City, Iowa; Tolono, Illinois; Succasunna and Phillipsburg, New Jersey; Traverse City, Michigan; Beloit, Wisconsin; Jackson, Tennessee; Crossett, Arkansas; Springfield, Missouri; and Paducah, Kentucky. The new installations in Tennessee, Arkansas, and Kentucky were at that point integrated into the Ross-Varina network.

9. This constituted a tremendous change in the purchasing policy. Drum says that prior to his guidelines, the Lumber Division's buyers "worked mostly with a hammer. They beat what they could out of a source, with no concern for his profits." Under the new policy, any buyer who breaks his source is out of a job, "because we can't exist without strong, growing, loyal sources of supply that can match our growth."

10. Controlling the merchandising out of Saginaw also added efficiency to sales promotion. Much of the advertising could now be broadsided into a whole state or region instead of only to the market areas of specific centers.

11. Surprisingly enough, Wickes is still the only company in the lumber business to use the retail system.

12. Thus no store manager is ever tempted to brag about low costs: he doesn't know what they are. This is not an attempt, however, to hide special prices from authorities. The Wickes purchasing guidelines specifically demand that all laws, from local to federal, must be strictly followed by the buyers.

13. Within two years the Lumber Division saw an increase of 3 percent in the gross margin, a dramatic improvement indeed.

14. The Turpin building supply centers were located in Bastrop, Monroe, Alexandria, Shreveport, Baton Rouge, Lafayette, and Houma, Louisiana; Greenville, Mississippi; El Dorado, Crossett, and Springdale, Arkansas; and Tulsa, Oklahoma. The outlet at Alexandria, Louisiana, included a door-unit assembly plant.

15. A. T. Turpin, Sr.'s original associates in the Bastrop Supply Company were Charles Snyder and A. G. McBride. They were eventually bought out by Turpin, who mortgaged his home for that purpose in 1936. With money short and the company in receivership, all but one of the employees of the firm were then members of the Turpin family. Lucille, A.T.'s wife, served as bookkeeper, secretary, and salesperson of decorative materials. The two elder sons, Alan, Jr. and Corbin, who had dropped out of college in 1934 to help stock the family purse, did double duty as salesmen and warehousemen and at the same time moonlighted at outside jobs to ease the strain on the Turpin business. In 1938, the only Turpin daughter, Dorothy, also was old enough to lend a hand, and she assisted in all the duties assigned to her mother.

At last the nation's economy turned around and the firm gradually began to prosper, so much so that the Turpins were able to pay off the old obligations in half the expected time. Ownership of what was now a family partnership was distributed in equal 20 percent shares to each of the four children, including the youngest son, Carl, who completed his college education in 1947 after his discharge from the Army. With Alan Turpin, Sr.'s death in 1948, the fifth 20 percent came into the hands of his widow, and these shares of ownership were held until Wickes acquired the Turpin enterprise.

Carl and Corbin ran merchandise and personnel; Alan, Jr., was in charge of systems; and Dorothy, after being out of the business for some years as a housewife, came back in to handle advertising. When the family partnership was incorporated in 1961, Dorothy agreed to serve as vice president, and the remaining offices were assigned to her three brothers by drawing lots. Thus Carl became president, Alan, Jr., a vice president, and Corbin, secretary-treasurer. In actuality, all major decisions continued to be made on a unanimous basis, with all officers holding equal authority in the management.

Interestingly enough, when first approached by Wickes, the Turpins weren't cagey. They told Smith Bolton outright that they would be ready to sell after another year or two of growth. When they did, each of them joined the ranks of Wickes-made millionaires.

16. At the end of 1968, Wickes had centers in the following states: Alabama, Arkansas, California, Connecticut, Georgia, Illinois, Indiana, Iowa, Kansas, Kentucky, Louisiana, Maryland, Massachusetts, Michigan, Minnesota, Mississippi, Missouri, New Jersey, New York, North Carolina, Ohio, Oklahoma, Pennsylvania, South Carolina, Tennessee, Texas, Virginia, and Wisconsin.

Opened by Wickes between January 1966 and November 1968 were outlets in the following towns, in this order:

Dubuque, Iowa; Lawrence, Kansas; Mosby, Missouri; Eau Claire, Wisconsin; Copley, Ohio; Florence, South Carolina; Grand Blanc, Michigan; Petaluma, California; Jackson, Michigan; Lostant, Illinois; Mishawaka, Indiana; and Waterloo, Iowa (all in 1966).

Findlay and Columbus, Ohio; Wilkes-Barre, Pennsylvania; another in Columbus, Ohio; Port Huron, Michigan; Alpha, Ohio; and Orchard Park, New York (in 1967).

Lexington, Kentucky; Owosso, Michigan; Essexville, Michigan; Davenport, Iowa; Midland, Michigan; Kokomo, Indiana; Reading, Pennsylvania; Ellettsville, Indiana; Green Bay, Wisconsin; and Anderson, Indiana (in 1968).

The four Ohio outlets acquired from Home Materials in April 1968 included two in Mansfield. The other two stores were in Galion and Shelby.

17. Building supply outlets established by Wickes between January 1969 and December 1972 were as follows:

Appleton, Wisconsin; Exton, Pennsylvania; Indianapolis, Indiana; Sandusky, Ohio; yet a third in Columbus, Ohio; Kewanee, Illinois; Marion, Indiana; Newark, Ohio; Holland, Michigan; Quincy, Illinois; Chicopee, Massachusetts; Rochester, Michigan; Austin, Texas; Bakersfield, California; Monroe, Michigan; Holland, Ohio; Petoskey, Michigan; Omaha, Nebraska; Skandia, Michigan; Adrian, Michigan; Decatur, Illinois; Niles, Michigan; Alpena, Michigan; Harlingen, Texas; Kentwood, Michigan; Schererville, Indiana; Oklahoma City, Oklahoma; Watertown, New York; Russellville, Arkansas; Jonesboro, Arkansas; Stevensville, Michigan; and Amarillo, Texas (all in 1969).

Salinas, California; Hammond, Louisiana; New Iberia, Louisiana; Richardson, Texas; Elyria, Ohio; Danbury, Connecticut; Allentown, Pennsylvania; yet a fourth in Columbus, Ohio; and Dover, Delaware (all in 1970).

Corpus Christi, Texas; Portland, Maine; Bangor, Maine; and Gurnee, Illinois (in 1971).

Rhinelander, Wisconsin; Beaumont, Texas; Greenville, North Carolina; Tulare, California; Houghton Lake, Michigan; Wichita, Kansas; Roanoke Rapids, North Carolina; Ponca City, Oklahoma; Ruston, Louisiana; Fairfield, Maine; Chattanooga, Tennessee; and Freeland, Michigan (in 1972).

18. The Lewis Lumber Company merger involved 12,372 shares of Wickes stock, valued at $559,833.

19. The Bond-Howell acquisition involved four additional Florida locations, which, however, were discontinued.

20. This number of outlets at the end of 1972 includes only those which are still in operation at the time of this writing. Actually, at any given time there were still a few more which have since closed, and are therefore not reflected in current company statistics.

21. The Harvey Randall Wickes Foundation (for its origins see Chapter 6) has long ceased to be involved in Wickes corporate affairs. Conversely, the Wickes Corp.

no longer contributes any part of its 5 percent tax-free charitable deduction to the Foundation, as it had in the early days in order to give it a good start. Wickes now donates directly to various charities and community programs.

The Wickes Foundation's prime purpose is to provide the "brick and mortar" rather than operating expenses for projects in the Saginaw Valley area, as, for example, the initial $1 million that helped start the four-year Saginaw Valley College. Of the $6 million required to build the school, another million was contributed by The Dow Foundation, and the rest raised through a public fund drive. More recent projects have included Wickes Park, additions to hospitals, new community centers, and a junior high school gymnasium.

The director of the Foundation is Melvin J. Zahnow, a former Wickes Corporation executive and director, who had joined Wickes in 1935 as a cost clerk at the Wickes Boiler Company. He eventually became controller of Wickes Bros. and Wickes Boiler, and was the first secretary when Wickes was incorporated. His succeeding posts included those of secretary-treasurer, vice president for finance, and senior vice president. Zahnow was probably Dan Fitz-Gerald's leading competitor for the top position until a nervous collapse following an automobile accident in the mid-1950s put an end to his ambitions. Zahnow was born in Saginaw in 1911, attended Saginaw public schools, and graduated from Albion College. He has been deeply involved in civic and educational affairs most of his adult life, including service on the board of trustees of both Delta and Saginaw Valley Colleges, and his assumption of the Harvey Randall Wickes Foundation leadership was a logical thing for him to do upon recovery. Assets of the Foundation now total around $8 million, yielding an annual income after expenses in the neighborhood of $425,000. All donations are made from this income.

22. Dr. Samuel Marble served as a director of The Wickes Corporation from 1970 to 1973.

23. The regional offices of Wickes lumber and building supply centers are in Allentown, Pennsylvania; Greenville, South Carolina, Orange Park, Florida; Copley, Ohio; Saginaw, Michigan; Indianapolis, Indiana; Bartlett, Illinois; Richardson, Texas; and Santa Clara, California.

24. Where Wickes Lumber was once strictly cash-and-carry, more than 60 percent of its business today is on a credit basis. Trade credit to builders was particularly important for Wickes to stay ahead of its major competitors—Grossman's and Moore's (both owned by Evans Products) and Lowe's—as well as regional building supply retail chains such as Wolohan's (see Chapter 11), Scotty's in Florida, and Diamond National in New England and California.

Of Wickes's more than 70,000 contractor-customers in the last two years, slightly in excess of 40,000 have been carried on the books one time or another.

No less vital was expansion of the consumer credit program by means of credit cards. In addition to its general convenience, this program enabled individual customers to come to Wickes for big-ticket items like appliances and carpeting jobs, which they'd otherwise be buying somewhere else. There is no additional cost if the customer pays within ten days of billing; after that, there is the usual service charge of 1.5 percent per month on the unpaid balance.

25. As the term implies, the cash-and-carry customers took their purchases away with them. Eventually, as business with bulk buyers grew, there was an increasing demand for delivery. Wickes then hooked up with local "contract haulers" and provided their names as a convenience to its customers. Of course, the customer had to pay the hauler. Now flip the calendar forward a few years—until

a builder walked in who said, "I've been buying from you all this time but this guy down the street wants my business and says he'll deliver. What are you going to do about it?" A smart manager naturally agreed to provide the same service and then paid the hauler to drop the merchandise off at the job site and raised his price to compensate.

However, in many cases, in order to keep the steady customer happy, the manager then often cut the price by the amount of the delivery fee. Over a period of time the situation deteriorated to such a degree that Wickes found itself giving away free trucking. The expenses soon got out of line. On top of that, the Interstate Commerce Commission at that time started to tighten up on contract haulers and forced them to file their tariffs if they crossed state lines. If a trucker then lowered his rates in order to drum up business, he was in trouble. Then the Teamsters Union also got involved. The net result was that a lot of common carriers went out of business, and Wickes figured it could lick both problems—those of offering free trucking and of having fewer haulers available—by buying its own trucks. But now the situation grew worse than ever before. Not only did the trucks constitute a heavy investment, but they were not used to their full advantage at many centers. When a builder called saying he had made a mistake and needed, say, four more windows, some center managers would throw them on a truck and make a special trip of 20 miles or more. This service added to the already high overhead of owning the vehicles.

To correct the situation, Johnson first instituted a training program on how to bulk-load trucks, and at the time of the Arab oil embargo, issued strict orders, which have stayed in effect, that only full loads are ever to be dispatched.

26. International development is now under Vice President Paul Hylbert (see Chapter 14). Both he and Tony Swies of Wickes Europe report directly to John Drum. Johnson, in turn, has the additional responsibility of supervising the Wickes Recreational Vehicle and Yorktowne Divisions. For more on Johnson, see Chapter 17.

27. The Tustin and Fremont, California, outlets were purchased from Lumbermen's Mercantile Company for $1,197,560 in September 1973. Centers in Mammoth Lakes, California, and Reno, Nevada, were purchased from Home Lumber for $3,288,201 in March 1974. Single outlets, one in Burlington, North Carolina, and another in Lafayette, Indiana, were acquired from Zimmerman Lumber Company and Best Bilt Cash & Carry Lumber Company respectively for a combined cost of just over $1 million.

28. The Home Mart stores were in College Park, Rome, Dalton, Cedartown, Douglasville, Tallapoosa, and Carrollton, Georgia. The Tallapoosa store was sold off on March 8, 1975, less than two months after the acquisition.

29. Hagen's executive staff at Wickes Lumber at the time of this writing consists of Richard G. Passaglia, vice president of merchandising; Robert H. Welsh, vice president of marketing; Thomas E. Rulison, vice president of operations; and William A. Hensler, vice president of administration. All are based in Saginaw.

William A. Hensler, forty-six, is a native of Saginaw. He attended Bay City Junior College and earned his bachelor's degree in business from Ferris State College, Big Rapids, Michigan. In 1960, after seven years with General Motors, he came to Wickes, where he served in a number of corporate financial and accounting positions before being assigned in 1969 as controller of the Lumber Division. He was promoted to his present post in 1974.

For more on Tom Rulison, see Chapter 12; on Bob Welsh, Chapter 16; and on Dick Passaglia, Note 11, Chapter 20.

For the story of Oregon-Pacific and Leslie Hagen's part in it, see Chapter 17.

30. Opened in 1973 were building supply centers in Columbus, Indiana; Hooksett, New Hampshire; Rudyard, Michigan; Fort Myers, Florida; Vincennes, Indiana; Coldwater, Michigan; Cartersville, Georgia; Alma, Michigan; Wilmington, North Carolina; Scottville, Michigan; Menands, New York; Melbourne Beach, Florida; Albany, Georgia; Stockton, California; Victoria, Texas; and Columbia, South Carolina.

Added in 1974 were the Home Lumber outlets cited in the main text plus the following: Fort Pierce, Florida; College Station, Texas; San Marcos, California; Lufkin, Texas; Hampton, New Hampshire; Harrisburg, Pennsylvania; Lancaster, California; Napa, California; Fort Collins, Colorado; Ontario, Ohio; and Hardeeville, South Carolina.

Aside from the Home Mart stores, the only new center opened in 1975 is in Burlington, Vermont.

31. Wickes's participation in the production of residential housing is the subject of Chapter 16.

Chapter 14

1. Up to the present, all the Wickes stores in Belgium are in bilingual areas, where Flemish either predominates or is at least understood by most people. Since, in its written form, Flemish is virtually the same as Dutch, the *VOOR BOUWEN EN WONEN* signs are used at Wickes's Belgian outlets too.

2. Arthur E. Pufford probably knew and understood the early Wickes Corporation better than anyone else with the exception of Dan Fitz-Gerald, and in some areas may well have been more expert than even the latter. Shortly after Fitz-Gerald's recruitment by Ran Wickes, Pufford had joined Lybrand's where he was soon put in charge of the Wickes account, and he became intimately involved in the preparations for incorporation. At the same time, he handled Lybrand's auditing of the Michigan Bean Company and Charles Wolohan, Inc., which gave him great insight into these firms that were later to be the Wickes Corp.'s first acquisitions.

After the Wolohan merger and Wickes's subsequent growth into building material retailing, Fitz-Gerald brought the then twenty-eight-year-old Pufford into the organization in 1953. At Wickes, Pufford held a variety of corporate executive positions, including controller, treasurer, and vice president. One of his major contributions was his wholehearted support of E. L. McNeely's push to establish a structured corporate planning program after Wickes's billion-dollar goal was set in 1965. At the same time, Pufford developed the corporation's new management information system, which embraced the installation of John Drum's retail inventory system (see Chapter 13). Pufford, assisted by Robert McLean, also set up the original credit and collection policies and procedures of the Lumber Division; and with James E. Morton (see below), he put in place a security program against pilferage and customer collusion which has saved Wickes millions of dollars over the years. He was, moreover, one of the key Wickes people involved in the acquisitions of Michigan Bean, Wolohan, Inc., Kux Machine, Varina, Ross Builders, Farmaster, Timberline, Bond-Howell, and Turpin.

Pufford, a native of Detroit, had attended the Detroit High School of Commerce and later studied business administration and finance at Wayne University (now Wayne State) and the University of Detroit. He left Wickes in 1972 to become executive vice president, treasurer, and a member of the board of

American Forest Products, a subsidiary of the Bendix Corp. He now lives in San Rafael, California.

James E. Morton, who worked with Pufford on the Wickes security program, is now senior director of insurance and corporate protection for Wickes, reporting to W. W. Boyle, the treasurer. Morton, a native of Dallas, studied law at the University of Houston and is a member of the State Bar of Texas. He is headquartered at the main office of Wickes in San Diego.

3. The original Wickes N.V. is now called Wickes B.V., reflecting a legalistic difference in government requirements for disclosure of corporate statistics.

4. A. J. ("Tony") Swies was born in 1926 in Shenandoah, Pennsylvania, deep in the anthracite country. After his World War II stint in the Army, he majored in English at St. Francis College and taught for a year. He then joined Armour & Co. in a clerical capacity while attending Akron University three nights a week for three years until he was able to add a business administration degree to his liberal arts credentials. He rapidly advanced to the post of operating sales manager at Armour, later switched into merchandising with Montgomery Ward, handling hardware products. He joined Wickes in 1965, where he reported to George Kelch, who served the Lumber Division as vice president of merchandising until John Drum's arrival on the scene the following year.

It was then that merchandising became organized into product areas. Swies took over hardware and electrical; John O'Connor, lumber; Del Mear, plywood and paneling; Robert McIntosh, building materials; and Charles Mayer, plumbing.

After Swies returned from Europe in 1972, he took charge of Wickes Lumber's California and Colorado operations, and was headquartered in Santa Clara, California. In early 1975 he was reassigned to Wickes Europe (see later text).

5. Raymond F. Roeser, born in Saginaw in 1918, was hired when Dan Fitz-Gerald started an auditing department at Wickes in 1951. Fitz-Gerald's initial instructions to Roeser are revealing. "He told me that I was going to be auditing figures, not people," Roeser recalls. "He said that this company, without people, was just bricks and mortar, and that people were what made it live. Therefore, he didn't want any inquisitions going on or anything like that. What he was telling me was that as an auditor, it wasn't my job to judge whether people were doing right or wrong. It was my job to get up the figures, and let them tell their own story."

Roeser, who had previously been accounting supervisor for the Standard Oil Company of Indiana in Saginaw, held a number of positions with Wickes. Before he was sent to Holland as financial director of Wickes Europe in late 1972, he served successively as supervisor of general books, controller of the agricultural divisions, manager of data processing, and manager of systems and programming.

6. Most of the merchandise sold by Wickes Europe is produced in Western Europe, but some, especially construction timber, is shipped in from Scandinavia and even Russia. Much paneling and plywood is imported from South America, the Far East, and Africa.

7. Paul Hylbert was born in Washington, D.C., in 1944, moved to Chicago at an early age, and lived there until enrolling at Denison University. At that time, his father, a Culligan vice president, was assigned to Brussels, and Paul went over on vacations. One of these college summers, Paul and a pal went to Switzerland and worked on construction projects. He speaks fluent Dutch, some German, and a little French.

Hylbert's wife, Nancy, from Oak Park, Illinois, whom he married during his last year at Denison, is a semiprofessional soprano of considerable promise, and has performed on the Netherlands broadcasting system during their tour of duty abroad. They have two children, and now live in San Diego.

8. Wickes Europe is now under Clark A. Johnson (see Chapters 13 and 17). In the quick shuffle of executives that's a specialty at Wickes, Arthur J. Nasso, one of the corporation's young troubleshooters (see Chapter 19), was boss for an interim period in 1974.

9. With land much more expensive in Europe, 20,000 square feet of showroom and warehouse space (combined in one building), plus another 20,000 square feet of parking (which allows room for slightly in excess of 100 cars), are about average. The short-lived Helmond store was an exception—it encompassed only about 2,000 square feet.

10. R. E. T. Clark was born in Marlborough, attended school in Canterbury, and later lived in England's Midlands where his father was a banker. Clark's merchandise manager for the United Kingdom operation is Peter Dale.

Their big challenge today is to spruce up trade sales—the retail end already is doing very well. The effort to establish the position of Wickes Building Supplies Ltd., as the U.K. operation is called, with the individual consumer has put Clark in the somewhat ironic situation of resenting the fact that, during a paint promotion, one single customer bought 200 pounds of it—about 10 percent of the inventory—when Clark would much rather have had 200 walk-ins buying one pound each, in order to spread the good word on Wickes.

Interestingly enough, the market approach in the United Kingdom is far more "proletarian" than many Americans, who envision Britain as a cultural center, would expect. Practically all the advertising is done in newspapers and broadsheet flyers whose tabloidy circus makeup would make Madison Avenue shudder—a jumble of primitive drawings, catchwords, and prices designed to show the vast quantity of merchandise Wickes carries here. The stores themselves reinforce this impression of overwhelming plenitude by draping their fronts with banners that tell you that you can get "all you need for your house under one roof." Store openings are equally flamboyant. At Nottingham, for example, a hot-air balloon floated over the complex. Gail Craig, who held the number two rating in British telly shows appealing to housewives, presided; lion cubs cavorted on the parking lot; and there were all sorts of giveaways and discounts available that day. But the approach seems to work. One customer per 100 broadsides shows up at the stores—an unusually high response ratio for that type of advertising. Clark's sales volume has risen from a prorated £200,000 a year to well over £500,000 in less than thirty months.

11. The Heerlen opening in September 1973, while entrenching Wickes in one of the most promising border areas of Europe, marked—as fate would have it—the turning point of Dan Fitz-Gerald's life. Accommodations for the hierarchical entourage from Wickes headquarters had been arranged at the exquisite Chateau Neubourgh, a castle turned exclusive hotel, off the highway between Maastricht, the Netherlands, and Aachen, Germany.

This hostelry's drawing cards are its cuisine and wine cellar, features that a healthy Dan Fitz-Gerald would not have been likely to neglect, but Dan was suffering an attack of phlebitis and feeling so miserable that he was put off by the Chateau's old-fashioned arrangement of accommodations. He insisted that Ray Roeser drive him back to the Hilton Hotel in Rotterdam—a ride of more than three hours—that very same night. Dan's phlebitis, which recurred time and again, predated the diagnosis of his cancer by only a few months. Despite the show of good spirits

Dan Fitz-Gerald was inclined to put on, it's doubtful that he enjoyed so much as a day of true well-being after the Heerlen opening.

12. The Enschede store was purchased in April 1974 from Fijnfix, a Dutch home supply store firm that went out of business.

13. The Wickes Europe lineup at the end of 1975 was as follows:

United Kingdom—Manchester (Whitefield), Nottingham (Kirkby-in-Ashfield), Hull, and London (Harrow)

Netherlands—Utrecht, Breda, Apeldoorn, The Hague (two stores), Eindhoven, Heerlen, and Enschede

Belgium—Antwerp (Wilrijk), Gent (Gentbrugge), Brussels (Machelen), and Kortrijk

Germany—Frankfurt

Of the new stores to be opened in 1976, three are projected for the United Kingdom and two each for the Netherlands and Belgium. Tentative plans also call for opening at least one additional outlet in Germany, and it's highly likely that more will be launched.

Although, superficially, the life styles of Western Europeans may seem very much alike today, there is a considerable difference between the markets Wickes is carving out for itself in these countries. This difference is manifest not only in the spending power of the respective audiences but also in their affinity for different goods. Thus, while central management control is vital to success, Wickes Europe must be decentralized enough to function efficiently within each of its market areas. To this end, the organization is now being restructured on a regional setup similar to that of Wickes Lumber. Every country will have an experienced general manager, a national of that country, supported by administrative and merchandise managers, who are also nationals.

As for the relative degree of affluence of the different markets, it is interesting to note that the consumers in all Western European countries still lag far behind those in the United States. Where the average purchase in a domestic Wickes building supply center comes to about $55, it totals only about $18 in the Netherlands, less than $15 in Belgium, and only $12 in Britain. And this despite the fact that, by and large, the retail price is higher abroad in almost all product lines. The first German statistics are not in yet, but presumably the average sale here will come to a bigger total than in any of the other European countries where Wickes is currently in business.

The sales mix is also quite different from that at home. In the American building supply centers, lumber and plywood traditionally account for about 45 percent of all sales. On the Continent and in Britain, they make up only about 30 percent of the overall volume. On the other hand, while decorating materials sell only marginally in the United States centers, such products account for about 8 percent in Europe. Similarly, hardware is only of marginal consideration stateside, but sales abroad of such items (called "ironmongery" in Britain) account for 10 percent. All in all, the European merchandise mix and the per-sale transaction totals indicate that there are many more people over there doing small jobs, improving their homes bit by bit.

Chapter 15

1. George W. Kelch, a Pennsylvanian, joined Wickes in 1965 at the age of forty-nine as merchandising manager of all nonlumber items sold through the building supply centers. His earlier career had included the posts of vice president and

general manager of the Pittsburgh plant of the Fisher Scientific Company, executive vice president of Humphreys Manufacturing Company, Mansfield, Ohio, and president of the Ingersoll-Humphreys Division of Borg-Warner Corp. after the latter purchased Humphreys in 1956.

At Wickes, Kelch held a variety of top positions with the Lumber Division, later became a senior vice president and a director of the corporation, and served as Wickes's chief financial officer for two years. He left Wickes in early 1972 while recuperating from serious spinal surgery that took him out of action for the better part of a year. Since recovered, he serves as a consultant to several big corporations.

2. Walter Dietrich Behlen and his brothers Gilbert ("Gib") and Herbert ("Mike") were born on a small farm 10 miles south of Columbus, Nebraska. Altogether, there were nine children: another son (Adolph), and five daughters (Selma, Norma, Ruth, Ruby, and Frances). Their parents, Fred Arthur and Ella Sarah Benthack Behlen, who was the local parson's daughter, were both of German extraction, and German was still spoken in this second-generation family—a circumstance that later accrued to Walt's advantage, since in the first half of this century the bulk of scientific and technological literature was published in that language. The family never had any money to speak of and the Behlen children enjoyed a minimum of formal education, but life in this household was far from primitive. Father Behlen made it a point to teach the boys astronomy out of a German *Sternenbuch*, and frequently interrupted work to take them on excursions that he thought would be educational, as, for example, to see the remains of a mastodon found in an excavation not far from Columbus.

For a detailed account of Walt Behlen's life and the growth of his business, see William H. McDaniel, *Walt Behlen's Universe* (Lincoln: University of Nebraska Press, 1973).

3. Here is Walt Behlen's explanation of this experiment: "Instead of the brim of the hat section spreading out at the center and collapsing to the floor, the section actually became ¼ inch narrower, and therefore also deeper, when the rods were stacked on top. This narrowing was caused by the stretching of the inner edges of the brims, causing them to curve inward at the center, with greater force than the outward pressure of the hat sides." (Ibid., p. 62.)

4. "The walls and the gable roof were made of deeply formed 16-gauge sheet metal panels, bolted together at the eaves and roof ridge to form complete arches or rigid frames. The sheet metal arches were in turn bolted to each other to form a complete monolithic weather shell. Originally the rigid frame strength of the individual arches in the monocoque structure was counted on to carry the entire vertical and horizontal loads. If the entire strength of the building had derived from this feature alone, then only narrow spans would have been possible without the use of tie rods at the eave line. As a safety measure, we provided tie rods in the original construction. Fortunately a slight error was made in laying out the footings for our experimental building. The footings were out of square about an inch on the diagonals. By the time one end wall and 175 feet of the building had been erected, it was discovered that the sidewalls were about three inches out of plumb at the open end of the building. Both sidewalls leaned in the same direction and would have been straightened up if the open end of the roof could have been shifted horizontally a distance of three inches. It was when this light sheet metal roof shell defied any and all attempts to right it by means of heavy loads applied to the wayward eave lines with winches and hydraulic jacks that we realized that the entire roof was behaving as a monolithic unit or a huge

beam. So we discovered, quite by accident, the 'roof beam effect' in our monocoque sheet metal buildings. Subsequent tests showed that this effect accounted for even more of the structural strength of Behlen buildings than the rigid frame strength originally anticipated. All attempts to straighten our 200-foot experimental building by use of physical force failed." (Ibid., pp. 62–63.)

5. Harold E. Joiner was born in Mill Spring, Missouri, in 1925, served as a petty officer in the U.S. Navy in World War II, and in 1947 went to work as a foreman at Douglas & Lomason Company, a major supplier of seating and decorative trim to the automotive industry. In the ensuing twenty-two years he rose to manager of that company's plant in Columbus, Nebraska.

Joiner's accomplishments at Douglas & Lomason did not go unnoticed by Walt Behlen: Joiner had started the plant in 1965, and by 1969 it employed a work force of 850—more than Behlen Manufacturing had at the time. He was recognized as a comer, and Mike Behlen introduced him to McNeely when it became evident that, with the retirement of the Behlen brothers, the division required leadership that Wickes could not supply from within.

Joiner's staff currently includes R. W. Theilen, general sales manager; Douglas Hofeldt, controller; R. E. Apthorpe, director of mechanical engineering, research, and development; Jack Lasley, director of structural engineering; T. E. McKinnon, director of personnel and employee relations; Warren Rood, director of manufacturing; and I. J. Schaecher, director of purchasing.

H. J. Rempel, general manager of Behlen-Wickes Company, Ltd., the Canadian subsidiary, also reports to Harold Joiner.

Behlen now employs about 1,200 in Columbus, 180 in Canada, and 175 at Farmaster.

6. Farmaster has its own rather involved history. Shortly after World War II, Hugh Wolf and Carl Kessler, two young fliers who had become friends (and brothers-in-law) at James Connally Air Base in Waco, Texas, conceived the idea of making farm gates out of surplus aircraft aluminum and for this purpose formed the Aluminum Products Company of Stephenville, Texas. One of the franchisees for the assembly and distribution of the gates was Henry Field's Seed & Nursery Company in Shenandoah, Iowa, whose objective in getting into this totally unrelated activity was to keep its labor force busy during the slack winter months.

In 1950, the erstwhile sideline evolved into the Henry Field Aluminum Products Company. Eight years later, it was purchased from Henry Field by George Rose, who had been its general manager, and several minority stockholders. At this point, the name was changed to Farmaster Products, Inc.

The company prospered and in 1967 acquired the Alprodco Gate Manufacturing Company of Dublin, Georgia, its former franchise manufacturer for the southeastern states. In 1970, Met-Form, Inc., of Nebraska City, Nebraska, a small tubing manufacturer, was added. George Rose, then sixty-five, decided to retire in 1971, whereupon Farmaster Products merged with Wickes, retaining Rex Whitehill, who had been with the company since 1950, as its general manager. Farmaster was integrated into the Behlen operation after the latter's status was changed from subsidiary to division in 1973.

Farmaster makes about 300 different sizes, models, and types of gates of steel and aluminum wire and tubing. Many of the sales are for unique applications— for example, to confine geese used to pick the boll weevils from cotton plants in the South. One gate made for the confinement of antelope was of such height that special transportation equipment was needed for shipping it. Other applications include gates for hogs, sheep, cattle, all types of small animals, wildlife pens in forest reserves, and for fencing of assorted residential, commercial, industrial, and government properties. Farmaster also manufactures "earth anchors," which are used to hold mobile homes in place. This product promises to tie in with yet another of Wickes's operations, which is covered in Chapter 16.

7. Behlen Manufacturing's foreign sales, other than Canadian, account for only about $4 million of its volume, very little of which derives presently from stressed-skin steel buildings. Europe, especially, is still inclined to build monuments of brick and mortar. Behlen's biggest export is in stitching presses that stitch large coils of steel together for processing in steel mills. These presses are sold mostly in England, Germany, Yugoslavia, France, and Japan.

With Ceres International, Inc., a sales organization based in Denver, Behlen recently launched a pilot project of supplying agricultural equipment to Russia, which could develop into a profitable sideline without taxing Behlen's already stretched production facilities, since the Soviet Union is primarily interested in obtaining manufacturing expertise, and would erect its own Behlen plant. If such a deal is made, Behlen will receive royalties.

The Canadian sales in fiscal 1975 approached $10 million.

8. Two of these men are still with Wickes Buildings: Bud Bowell, fifty, director of operations; and Jack Warner, forty-three, district manager for Michigan and a part of Ohio, whose office is in Hastings, Michigan.

Bud Bowell's experience with pole buildings dates back to 1954, when he went to work for the Palmer Construction Company of Plymouth, Indiana, which built pole barns for the Farm Bureaus of Indiana and Michigan. Bud then returned to his hometown of nearby Argos to become Moriarty's sales manager for Indiana, Ohio, and Michigan. In 1963 he bought into the Moriarty-controlled Farm Building Construction Company of Argos. Shortly after the acquisition of the corporation by Wickes, he became district manager and, later, area manager. He was promoted to his present position in 1974.

Jack Warner—like The Wickes Corporation itself—has devoted most of his efforts to man's basic needs for food and shelter. Until 1958, he ran Harvey's Café, a local eatery near the Moriarty headquarters in Argos, then switched careers to sell pole buildings out of Cassopolis, Michigan. He later transferred to Hastings, Michigan, where he bought into the Moriarty-owned company in 1966.

9. Moriarty offices were located in Argos, Angola, and Rushville, Indiana; Kenton, Ohio; and Hastings, Michigan. The Moriarty lumberyards were in Argos and St. Johns, Michigan. All are still operating.

10. Otto C. Krohn was born in New York City in 1922, earned his B.A. in economics from Hofstra College in Hempstead, Long Island, and later attended Cornell University (on a Navy program) and the New York University School of Business Administration. For several years he worked in public accounting in New York City, then joined U.S. Radiator in Detroit as cost supervisor in 1951, and later became controller and secretary of another Detroit firm, H. W. Rickel & Company, a supplier of malt to the brewery industry. He came with Wickes International in 1960, working as purchasing agent for Corky van Bergeijk's beans, and eventually managed the Wickes Marine Terminal at Bay City. His subsequent Michigan Bean Division posts were administrative. He joined Moriarty as director of safety and market research, then became director of administration.

11. Wickes pole buildings are currently sold out of Macon, Georgia; Galesburg, Mendota, Mount Vernon and Taylorville, Illinois; Angola, Argos, Crawfords-

ville, Fairmount, and Rushville, Indiana; Creston, Dubuque, North Liberty, and Webster City, Iowa; Concordia and Lawrence, Kansas; Franklin and Winchester, Kentucky; Frederick, Maryland; Hastings, Kingston, McBain, St. Louis, and Stockbridge, Michigan; Moberly, Missouri; Waterville, New York; Salisbury, North Carolina; Ashland, Circleville, Kenton, Lebanon, and Napoleon, Ohio; Ephrata, Northumberland, Saegertown, and Stroudsburg, Pennsylvania; Florence, South Carolina; Jackson, Tennessee; and Elkhorn, Wisconsin.

12. Wickes Buildings, which employs a work force of 500 to 650 depending on the season, sold about 3,200 buildings in fiscal 1975. The average structure costs about $6,500, which comes out to about $2.50 to $3 per square foot for the shell, including metal siding. The specially treated wooden skeleton has a life expectancy of forty years. Bigger shelters are also marketed, as, for example, a 200- by 120-foot dairy building that sold for $87,000.

Wickes Buildings erects only the shell, and at this point is not involved with interior partitions, plumbing, heating, and electrical. These fixtures, however, or anything else that's required, can be added by buyers and the total cost still will be well below that of traditional frame construction. Wickes-Behlen steel-frame buildings are sold by Wickes Buildings in Indiana, Michigan, and Ohio, out of sales offices located respectively in Argos, Stockbridge, and Columbus.

13. Harold R. Pearson, until then vice president of operations of the Lee L. Woodward Sons subsidiary of Wickes, was appointed general manager of Yorktowne in January 1976. He succeeded Leigh R. Bench, who had been in charge since ill health forced Charles Pechenik, Yorktowne's founder, to retire shortly after his company's acquisition by Wickes.

Pearson, a native of Michigan, is a graduate of Spencerian College, Milwaukee, Wisconsin. Before he joined Wickes in April 1973, he was president of The Mulkey Company of Kansas City, a division of Symons Corporation. Earlier he had held management posts with American Motors, and Babcock and Wilcox.

Leigh R. Bench, Pearson's predecessor, was a self-made man of independent means when Wickes recruited him to run Yorktowne, which was then still known as Colonial Products Company. Bench had founded I-XL Furniture of Goshen, Indiana, another successful manufacturing company of kitchen cabinets and bathroom vanities, and sold it to Westinghouse in 1965.

14. When Wickes acquired Colonial, the latter had nine small plants, all in central Pennsylvania: in Dallastown, Meads, Mifflinburg, Milton, Pottsville, Red Lion, and Stewartstown. The Pottsville factory was sold in 1972. The headquarters of the division are at Red Lion.

15. After the passing of Lyman E. Woodard I, the original Woodard Furniture Company was split into two divisions, Woodard Furniture and the Owosso Casket Company. Their demise was due not only to the Depression and the depletion of Michigan's forests but also to the advent of the automobile industry, with whose high wages furniture makers could not compete. Some converted to making other products or moved to southern states where lumber was plentiful and operating costs were lower. Woodard Furniture and Owosso Casket—then in the hands of Lyman's sons, Fred, Frank, and Lee, and a son-in-law, Joe Osburn—held out several years longer than most others of their kind.

The new Woodard firm interrupted its metal-furniture making during World War II, producing components for trucks, tanks, ships, and aircraft. The demand for efficiency in defense production led to the installation of a conveyer system and other advanced devices in the plant. This stood Woodard in good stead in the years that followed.

Lee L. Woodard, of the second generation, was the first designer of the new company's products. His styling was an immediate success and the furniture found its way into the homes and gardens of celebrities (like the Duke and Duchess of Windsor), the White House, the Congressional Club, and embassies around the world. A number of pieces are in the collections of the Metropolitan Museum of Art and other museums. Upholstery was an important early feature of Lee L. Woodard's designs. Clients could send in their own material and many decorators did.

The third-generation Woodard brothers were blessed with an extremely harmonious relationship in private life as well as in business. It was their custom to rotate the company's presidency, and no action was ever taken unless all three agreed. Joe was in charge of engineering and production, Russell of administration and accounting, and Lyman of design, sales, and advertising.

The picturesque old Owosso plant is still in operation. The Salisbury factory was built in 1959, the Maxton installation in 1967.

16. Scotsmen are reputed to be extremely conscious of money, and this has certainly been true of George G. Valentine, who has devoted his entire career to date to keeping track of it. Valentine, born in Dumbarton, Scotland, in 1919, emigrated with his parents to Detroit at the age of eight, attended Albion College, served in the U.S. Army Infantry during World War II, and then, as an ex-first lieutenant, graduated with a B.A. in business administration from the University of Michigan. Whereupon he joined Lybrand, Ross Bros. & Montgomery in 1947.

What happened next is predictable for anyone who has read this far. Valentine was assigned to John McCullough's Wickes audit the very first year of the merger, and stayed with it off and on until, like Dan Fitz-Gerald and Art Pufford before him, he was recruited by the client corporation. He became its general controller (as opposed to divisional controller) in 1961.

Since then he has been responsible for the consolidation of the corporation's financial statements and the internal and external reporting of results. He prepares monthly summaries for top management, quarterly and annual reports for shareholders, and all filings to the Securities and Exchange Commission. When acquisitions are being considered, he handles the financial reviews of these companies. Wickes's accounting being decentralized, Valentine also sets accounting policies for the divisions to keep their procedures in line with the corporate approach.

Valentine's title today is assistant controller, and as such, he is responsible for his areas to Richard L. Barker, who joined Wickes in the spring of 1975 as vice president and controller. Barker succeeded Richard W. Fruechtenicht after the latter was temporarily assigned to work with Richard G. Cotton on Project 21st Century, the corporation's long-range planning arm for external as well as internal policies.

Barker, forty-one, came to Wickes from Hart, Schaffner & Marx, of Chicago, where he had been vice president and controller since December 1969. His first position after graduating from the University of Oregon in 1956 as a bachelor of business administration with a degree in accounting was as audit manager with Price Waterhouse & Company. In 1966 he became assistant controller of the Household Finance Corporation.

Reporting to Barker, besides George Valentine, are John Rice, director of corporate financial planning and analysis; John Wagner, director of internal audit; and Don Zwanzig, director of financial controls.

The responsibility of Rice's department is to establish financial guidelines for the various divisions, budget their operations, and assemble that information into the corporate budget. The Wickes planning cycle starts with the definition of five-year sales and income objectives and the projection of the general strategies required to achieve these goals. This part of the planning is now supervised by Paul Hylbert, who works on it with the general managers and group officers. In the process, the divisions are asked to identify specific programs, and it is at this point that the plans are translated into the more detailed budgeting process which then is in John Rice's domain. His department, however, does not establish budgets per se. These are generated within the divisions following the guidelines set up by Rice, and the budgets then become division commitments. In effect, Rice coordinates the aims and capabilities of the corporation with the plans of the individual divisions. The divisions don't always get what they want, but their managers are asked to forecast the results of the allotments, and are expected to live up to their projections.

John F. Rice was born in Cincinnati, Ohio, in 1928, earned his M.B.A. at Indiana University in 1954, and later went back to school at Loyola University to obtain his law doctorate in 1965. Prior to joining Wickes at corporate headquarters in San Diego in 1974, he served as staff assistant to the comptroller of Chrysler Corp. in Highland Park, Michigan (1954–1958), and then rose from business analysis manager and director of research and development to assistant treasurer of Montgomery Ward in Chicago (1959–1969). He then became group vice president for corporate planning and development of Ramada Inns in Phoenix, Arizona (1969–1971), and executive vice president of Investment Leasing Service, Inc., also in Phoenix (1972–1974).

17. John H. Hekman was born in Grand Rapids in 1921, the same year his father started the Hekman Furniture Company, which made a line of fine tables. Hekman attended parochial schools in Grand Rapids, graduated from Calvin College in the same city, subsequently earned his M.B.A. in banking at the University of Wisconsin. Rather than join the family furniture company or his uncle's Hekman Biscuit Company, he went to work for the William Iselin Division of CIT, whose Grand Rapids business was largely concerned with the furniture industry.

In 1952, he went into the import/export business, establishing a firm called Hekman & Meeter, which was engaged chiefly in importing fine foods from Europe. He was finally persuaded to go into the family's biscuit business, one of the founding firms of the United Biscuit Company, which is today known as Keebler. A stint in banking with the Old Kent Bank & Trust Company of Grand Rapids and in management consulting with Science Management followed. It was during this period in early 1970 that Hekman's work brought him in contact with The Wickes Corporation and to the attention of its executives.

Chapter 16

1. The list of firms that went along with HUD's Operation Breakthrough reads like a veritable *Who's Who*, including, in addition to the companies cited in the text, the following: Aluminum Company of America, General Electric, Hercules, Republic Steel, Tappan, Borg-Warner, Grumman, Portland Cement, Celanese, 3M, American Standard. For the giants among them, the investments were small relative to the companies' sizes. The outfits that really got hurt were those that put all, or most of, their eggs in the modular basket.

2. Shortly after its acquisition by Wickes as a wholly owned subsidiary, Monitor Coach Company, Inc., of Wakarusa, Indiana, purchased the assets of Ace of

Alfred, Maine, for $562,000. One year later, in August 1970, the Monitor subsidiary under President Robert E. Stump merged with Action Industries of Elkhart, Indiana, the maker of the Swinger line. This merger involved 27,572 shares of Wickes, then worth $754,783. In January 1973, along with almost all other Wickes subsidiaries, Monitor was totally integrated into the corporation and became part of the Wickes Homes Division.

3. Douglas P. Crane is now with AMF Corp. He is its vice president and group executive for industrial products and is headquartered in Richmond, Virginia.

4. At 9:30 A.M. on August 31, 1972, at the same time Wickes announced its retreat from modular housing, Welsh held a meeting of his staff at his Mason office with loudspeakers hooked up to Shamokin. The terrible human part of retrenchment had only begun. The discontinuance of modular operations meant laying off nearly 400 people. The Shamokin plant was to be closed entirely. The production line in Mason would stop when the last remaining orders were filled, and the labor force would be cut to the bone until the sale of the components justified a bigger payroll. "I wouldn't like to go through that again," says Bob Welsh. "After the announcement I went down to Shamokin. They had about 180 people working there in that 80,000-square-foot plant, and I was met at the gate by Don Ogrum, the manager, and he said to me, 'Bob, I think you'd better not go down into the plant. There is a great deal of animosity down there and I think they want to hurt somebody.'" Welsh told him that it was important to explain to the employees why this was happening. "That's your decision," Ogrum said, "I'm not going with you." Welsh went to the office, took off his jacket, and walked into the plant.

It is likely that only his audacity saved him from physical assault, for he faced down an angry knot of workers the same way Ran Wickes, many years earlier, had marched through the strikers to throw the power switch back on again at the old Wickes companies. As Welsh, scared to his marrow but not showing it, approached the group head-on, the workers dispersed. Only one of them stood his ground. "He used some pretty profane language," Welsh says, "and I couldn't blame him. He said there was another worker there who had a child lame with polio and another whose wife was in the hospital, and how I was putting them all in the poorhouse. I tried to explain to him that we couldn't find ways to make the product profitable. But of course when you're out of work none of this means anything."

In Mason, Michigan, it was no easier, although every effort was made to find jobs for the many employees who had to be dismissed. Welsh would spend all day talking to the individual employees about their jobs and prospects, and when he left late in the evening, there were almost always families lining the sidewalk outside the plant. Some people would stop him and ask, "Have you met my children?" Others would spit. One night when Welsh opened his car door, there was a snake on the driver's seat. He poked it out with a stick, climbed in, then saw another snake on the floor. His family got threatening phone calls, and Welsh grew so worried about his wife and five children that he finally moved them to a motel.

Putting aside the ugliness of this particular situation, the question remains of whether employees discharged for the sake of cutting losses have a just grievance. Who has prior claim to a company's resources—its employees or its owners? Society has been arguing that point for years, which is puzzling since the facts seem so clear. People buy into a business to get a return. A family, say, in Atlanta, Georgia, does not invest in Wickes in order to finance what would be, in effect, a welfare program for Shamokin, Pennsylvania. For all you know, that

Atlanta family may need the dividends to help pay therapy bills for its own polio-stricken child.

To support the employees of an unsuccessful venture is not part of the investment contract. If it were, nobody would put money into anything—including banks, pension funds, whole life insurance, mutual funds, all of which depend on investment. Social programs are the responsibility not of the private sector but of government, to be supported by taxes of which business pays its share. Asking any one company, just because it stumbled into an unprofitable line, to keep on supporting the resultant losses is to penalize that company's owners by forcing them to carry more than their proportionate social load as stipulated by the tax laws.

5. This was the income of the new component operation. The Manufactured Housing Division, now discontinued as an operating entity, still left its mark on the books of fiscal 1973 with a pretax loss of $3,762,000, and of fiscal 1974 with one of $729,000. These losses included inventory write-offs.

6. The Shamokin plant was sold at a pretax profit of $56,000.

7. The original truss plants were in Sarasota, Bradenton, Englewood, and Ormond Beach, Florida; Flint, Michigan; Mansfield, Ohio; and Ephrata, Pennsylvania.

   Since then, Mansfield and Ephrata have been expanded, the Flint operation has been merged into Mason, Ormond Beach closed down, and the Bradenton and Sarasota facilities have been united in a new installation. Added were plants in Jacksonville, Fort Myers, and Edgewater, Florida; Columbia, South Carolina; and Kinston, North Carolina. Englewood, Florida, is the door plant.

8. HaiCo Manufacturing, Ltd., was the creation of J. T. C. ("Todd") Haibeck, who started in business in 1942, when he was twenty-four, by founding a firm in Lethbridge, Alberta, called General Farm Supplies, which sold farm machinery. Three years later he branched out into the automotive field by establishing a Reo dealership in Calgary, which grew into United Machine Distributors, Ltd., with branches in Edmonton and Lethbridge. Later the Edmonton and Calgary offices were closed and Haibeck concentrated his efforts in southern Alberta.

   He began manufacturing recreational vehicles in 1964 under the name of Holiday Trailers. In 1968, his three companies were amalgamated under the name HaiCo. Among HaiCo's activities was the sale of Behlen farm buildings, and soon Haibeck and Behlen agreed that the tariff picture would be more favorable if the Behlen structures were built in Canada instead of shipped across the border from Nebraska. After HaiCo's acquisition in November 1969 for 38,917 Wickes shares, which then had a market value of about $1.5 million, a 48,000-square-foot Behlen-Wickes plant was built in Brandon, Manitoba. Todd Haibeck retired in 1972, and HaiCo became Wickes Canada, Ltd., the following year. Henry Camp is general manager. Wickes Canada, Ltd., has been a highly successful contributor to the corporate earnings. Its travel trailer and motor home sales held up even during the oil embargo, since petroleum-rich western Canada was not affected by the fuel shortage.

9. Since Indian "bands," as they're called in Canada, are not considered legal entities, the Blood Indian tribe formed a holding company, Red Crow Developments, to represent the 4,500 people living on its reservation, Canada's largest. Red Crow Developments obtained loans from the Department of Regional Economic Expansion and the Department of Indian Affairs and Northern Development to help finance the ownership of the fixed assets of Kainai Industries at Standoff, Alberta. July 18, 1971, was a big day in Standoff's history. Because of Kainai, the settlement now had water, sewers, power, natural gas,

and a few telephones, and hundreds of enthusiastic Blood people, including their chief, Jim Shot Both Sides, showed up for the dedication ceremonies. Among the official guests were Prime Minister Pierre Elliott Trudeau and Alberta's Premier Harry Strom. Wickes was represented by Dan Fitz-Gerald and Douglas Crane.

10. At the time of the Ritz-Craft acquisition, John Ritzenthaler was chairman of the board of Ritz-Craft, and his eldest son, Larry J., president and chief executive officer. The latter remained with Wickes as vice president of operations of the Mobile Homes Division until 1974, when he went into business for himself, starting a new mobile home company in Louisiana. Another Ritzenthaler son, Donald, also stayed with Wickes temporarily as a plant manager. John Ritzenthaler is a member of the corporation's board of directors.

11. Pinpoint 1973 as the pivotal year when the cost of conventional housing went through the roof. According to a study by the Congressional Joint Economic Committee, the median price in 1973 of a new conventional home was $37,100, resulting in an average monthly outlay of $397. The minimum annual family income required to sustain this expense was $19,060. High enough—but at that point 21.5 percent of American families still qualified. A few months later, in 1974, the median price of a new house had jumped to $41,300, with a monthly cost of $486, which required a minimum income of $23,330. The potential market plummeted to 15 percent of the population.

   As for older housing, the committee report cited the average 1973 price as $31,200, with a monthly upkeep cost of $348, and thus requiring a minimum income of $16,700. In that year, this figure applied to 29.6 percent of American families. In 1974, the median price jumped to $35,600, its monthly cost to $441, and the required minimum income to $21,170, thereby reducing the potential market to 20 percent of households. ("The Ivy-Covered Cottage, Nearly an Impossible Dream," *The New York Times*, May 11, 1975, sec. E, page 9.)

12. Ron Woods was born in Buffalo, the son of a cab driver who died when the boy was two years old. His mother, a beautician, could not both work and take care of him at the same time until she remarried six years later, and he was raised by his grandparents and his uncles, who were all plumbers. Most young men in the same circumstances might well have ended up living in a mobile home (old style)—not manufacturing them (new style).

   In 1951, Ron graduated from Buffalo Technical High School as a tool designer, intending to work his way through the University of Buffalo. Instead, he was persuaded to try out for the football team of Michigan State University, then Michigan State College at East Lansing, and although he didn't make it, he found out in the process that Michigan State, at $550 a year including his dorm, was $75 cheaper than Buffalo. So that's where he went to study mechanical engineering, working part-time and in the summer. He dug ditches, delivered furniture, waited on tables, carried United Parcels, and made out all right until, between his junior and senior years, ROTC required him to spend six weeks at Fort Campbell, Kentucky, and there was no money to continue to graduation. But he knew about the GI Bill, and that was worth going into the Army for. Thanks to a snafu when his orders were cut for Korea, he ended up in the U.S. Occupation Forces in Austria and Germany, and when he came back he had lost his itch to go to school. Although he had no degree, he did manage to get a job as engineer for Bell Aircraft Corp. in Niagara Falls, New York, working on inertial guidance systems. His supervisor finally persuaded him to go back to Michigan State. When he did, he found that he had lost so much time that he couldn't graduate in his chosen field in the reasonable future. So he switched to production management and graduated from business school the following spring.

It was the custom of Lybrand's to take interns in their final year and Ron Woods had been among them, earning credits as well as being paid for his work. But when Lybrand's did not hire him on graduation, he stayed with the GI Bill and took advanced courses in accounting. In June 1959, he was accepted in the controller's training program of Chevrolet in Flint, Michigan, starting off in the accounts payable section, only to be constantly frustrated by General Motors' highly structured practices. He eventually managed to arrange his working hours so that he could take some more accounting courses, and then once again applied at Lybrand's and joined the firm in January 1960, being assigned almost immediately to the new management consulting department. One of his consulting jobs involved reorganizing the Wickes corporate structure in general and its Lumber Division in particular. As a result, Ron Woods was offered three different jobs at Wickes, one to become manager of personnel under Tom Rulison, another to take over the management information service department under Mel Zahnow, and a third to start a profit-planning section under Art Pufford. Although an offer from Xerox came along at about the same time, Woods opted for the Wickes profit-planning job.

It's interesting to note that John McCullough who, as managing partner at the Detroit office of Lybrand's, was so high up that Woods didn't even meet him as an intern, was later one of Woods's close associates. McCullough, after his retirement, became a Wickes consultant at the time Woods headed the Office of the President. Their biggest joint project was an analysis of fifty-two industries to determine whether they were businesses that Wickes should be in.

13. The mobile home plants Woods closed at that time were located at Aberdeen, North Carolina; Elkhart, Indiana; Jefferson, Georgia; Lewisburg, Tennessee; Thomasville, Georgia; and Stephenville, Texas. But, since the Texas market was remarkably strong under the circumstances, he opened a new, more efficient plant, the division's sixteenth mobile home facility, in Stephenville. Other plants he kept in operation were those in Jordan, Minnesota; Maxton, North Carolina; Mifflinburg, Pennsylvania; Neligh, Nebraska; Riverside, California; Sarasota, Florida; Snyder, Texas; and Vivian, Louisiana.

14. It's astounding to what degree the dealers' perception of the market varied from their customers' actual attitude. In a Woods survey, dealers and consumers were asked if their opinions were "favorable" or "unfavorable" when it came to carpeting throughout the home in a cost range of $75 to $125. The dealer response was 27 percent unfavorable, 35 percent favorable. The consumer response was 23 percent unfavorable, 50 percent favorable. Almost exactly the same percentages—except in reverse—held for exterior styling at a cost of $200 to $300. Dealers were still trim-happy rather than living-oriented, whereas consumers knew they'd spend more time inside their houses than looking at them.

15. Universal Mobile Services Corp. was acquired in a November 1973 exchange of stock that involved 735,000 shares of Wickes, then worth $11,116,875.

16. Western Diversified's exchange of stock with Wickes took place in January 1974. The pooling involved 87,500 Wickes shares, then worth $1,192,187.

17. American Homes Industries, along with a metal stampings manufacturing subsidiary, Maron Products, was acquired in January 1974. The pooling involved 330,000 Wickes shares, whose market value at that time was $4,826,250.

AHI's principal was an enterprising Sicilian-born American by the name of Mariano ("Mario") Randazzo, whose success story is worth telling, not only for its own interest but because it illustrates the complex entrepreneurial maneuvers that gave birth to mobile home service companies in their heyday.

In 1954, at the age of twenty-two Randazzo went to work for the Exchange National Bank in Chicago as a check filer. He rose quickly and the following year went to the Mutual National Bank of Chicago as manager of its proof and transit department. About a year later, he was promoted to assistant cashier and assistant personnel director. In 1956, when Jacques Mosler purchased control of the bank, Mario Randazzo was assigned to supervise the installment loan department.

Mosler also controlled some other banks, including the American National Bank and Trust Company of South Bend, Indiana. Randazzo was named a vice president of this bank in 1961 and put in charge of its loan division. In short order, this became the largest such department of any bank in Indiana. In 1962, at Mosler's suggestion, Randazzo organized a mobile home dealership in Kokomo, Indiana. This dealership was also owned by Mosler, and its primary purpose was to generate additional sales contracts for the bank as well as insurance premiums for the Allen-Parker Company, a credit life and casualty insurance company also owned by Mr. Mosler. Eventually, Mosler met an untimely end at knife-point in his Key Biscayne apartment, a murder case that kept tabloid headline writers busy for months.

In 1965, Lex Wilkinson and Mario Randazzo organized a local group and purchased control of the American National Bank from the Mosler estate through a holding company, American Affiliates, Inc. By now there were three locations that sold mobile homes, and American Affiliates acquired these as well, naming them Price Mobile Home Centers. In January 1966, American Affiliates became American Homes Industries.

At the time of Wickes's acquisition of the firm, Price Mobile Homes had thirty-five sales locations in Ohio, Indiana, Kentucky, and Florida. American Affiliates Life Insurance Company was chartered as a subsidiary of American Homes Industries in 1969 to reinsure credit policies generated on conditional sales contracts sold by Price Mobile Home Centers to American Homes Industries.

Wickes did not acquire the American National Bank, which was spun off separately at the time of the merger.

18. You may well ask why Wickes does not build labor contracts for key personnel into acquisition agreements. The answer is really very simple: You can't force people to do good work if they don't want to. They might just come in for the specified number of years merely to collect their paychecks. Too, there is always the possibility that Wickes might not be satisfied with them after the acquisition. As a general practice, Wickes does not believe in labor contracts, anyway.

19. Three of Hyman Lee's grandparents had been born in China; one grandmother, in San Francisco. He was born in San Diego, where his parents ran a grocery store, in 1942. In high school he was active in school politics. At San Diego State he first was a pre-med with hopes of becoming a psychiatrist, and after several switches settled on a major in political science with a strong backup in statistics, since his interest had changed from psychiatry to a field not totally unrelated to to it, behavioral politics. He graduated from San Diego State in 1964 with a straight A average, attended Yale for a year on a Woodrow Wilson Fellowship and took his master's in political science, then went to Harvard Law. In 1968, he joined a San Diego firm of about thirty lawyers, jumped the fence in 1970 to the attorney general's office, then returned to private practice for a year before he got tired of divorces and "piddly" criminal cases, and went to Wickes on the basis of an ad in *The Wall Street Journal*. That's when most of the piddle stopped,

although not all of it, since a corporate legal department often gets dragged into the private affairs of employees, such as the problem of a divorced wife who wants a lien on her ex-husband's salary. But most of Lee's work has been in the acquisition area. Among the mergers he handled were Hogsett Lumber; Zimmerman Lumber; Coast Millwork; Best-Bilt Cash & Carry Lumber, of Lafayette, Indiana; Home Lumber and Supply, of Reno; Gormley Bean; and Celebrity Homes Corp., of Athens, Georgia. (Celebrity Homes was a small mobile homes manufacturer acquired by purchase in March 1974. All the other acquisitions cited here have been dealt with in previous chapters, except Coast Millwork.)

Like E. L. McNeely, Lee is a jogging addict, but one suspects that he runs farther. He is now up to 10 miles a morning. But then, unlike McNeely, Lee still has quite a way to go.

20. In acquisitions, it is general practice for the acquiring company to hold the shares it tenders in escrow, so as to be protected against prior liabilities of the acquired company that may not have been disclosed by the latter's management or were unknown to it. When it comes to pooling, the merger process by which Universal Mobile Services was acquired, this safeguard is possible only for six months, since holding the shares in escrow for a longer period imposes accounting penalties. For instance, the earnings shown by the acquired firm during the part of the acquisition year that preceded the pooling then can't be carried to the acquiring firm's bottom line. This makes the operation look a lot less profitable than it really was. Why this is so and how it works is too complex to go into here; suffice it to say that a longer escrow period is not practical if pooling rather than purchasing is to be the acquisition mode. In Universal's case, Hyman J. Lee was worried about the six-month escrow limitation, and devised the liability agreement in order to protect Wickes over the long haul.

21. David J. Primuth's story is told in Chapter 19.

22. Arthur J. Nasso's story is told in Chapter 19.

23. The $7,608,000 represented the after-tax loss from operations of the discontinued businesses during the first thirty-nine weeks of the calendar year. In the third quarter alone, these businesses had dropped $4,074,000. On the other hand, the earnings of the continued operations—i.e., all the other Wickes interests—came to $6,523,000 for the thirty-nine weeks (or 66 cents per share), of which $2,779,000 (or 28 cents a share) arose out of the third quarter. After deducting the operating losses from the discontinued operations and the $17,400,000 provision for after-tax loss on disposal of the discontinued properties, the net loss totalled $18,492,000 for the thirty-nine weeks, or $1.86 per share.

Chapter 17

1. Thomas Jefferson Hedrick was born in Kansas City, Missouri, in 1912, attended high school in his hometown, and then went on to Central College at Fayette, Missouri, to study engineering. His first job was with the Texas Pipeline Co., which pumped crude oil from Oklahoma to Chicago. Eight years later, T. J. Hedrick left Texas Pipeline as senior engineer in charge of operation and construction, and joined Du Pont as superintendent of maintenance and transportation at the Kankakee Ordnance Works at Joliet, Illinois.

It was only after his service in the Navy, which culminated in his being operations officer for the Seventh Fleet in the South Pacific, that T.J. became involved—at first indirectly—in the lumber business. Teaming up with his father at Grants Pass, Oregon, he went to work installing electrical equipment in sawmills. The following year, T.J. joined Engler Huson Co., which was involved in most phases of the lumber business with the exception of residue product manufacturing. Here he worked his way up to executive vice president and general manager, a position he held until he was brought in by the Luellwitz organization to liquidate Continental Moulding. He eventually became vice president and general manager of this operation, and remained in that position until 1972 when he took over as boss of Wickes Forest Industries.

T.J. is a tinkerer and hobbyist from way back. The Dinuba house he lives in during the week (between spending weekends with his family in Los Angeles) is filled with professional recording and photographic equipment, and it is where he himself puts together the excellent documentary movies distributed by Wickes Forest Industries. Much of the film footage, in fact, is his own.

2. One of the newest and most successful types of Bark Humus composts produced by Wickes Forest Industries is Turf-N-Tee, which is used as a soil conditioner on golf courses and athletic fields, in parks, and by commercial growers. It is also marketed to homeowners as seed covering for new lawns. Bark Humus possesses several highly desirable qualities formerly found, though to a lesser degree, in peat moss and leaf mold. It supplies rich organic matter, locks moisture and fertilizer into the soil, counteracts alkalinity, and aerates the soil to encourage root development.

3. Decorative Barks are screened into three basic sizes: Pea, ¼ to ½ inch; Acorn, ½ to 1½ inch; and Jumbo, 1½ to 2½ inch. Practically all the bark processing is done at the Dinuba plant.

4. Other annual residue sales by Wickes Forest Industries are as follows: wood flour, 2,000 tons; grape-packing sawdust, 1,500 tons; industrial sawdust, 1,200 tons; lath, 1 million pieces; processed shavings, 150,000 bales plus 75,000 cubic yards of bulk; screened sawdust (#6 and #12), 400,000 cubic feet.

5. The 8-foot particleboard panels delivered by Chowchilla are true to $\frac{1}{16}$ inch in lateral dimension, and $\frac{1}{8}$ inch in square. A Kimwood sander controls panel thickness to $\frac{1}{5000}$ inch.

The residue material—pine and white fir—first passes through huge surge bins (one for wet material, the other for dry) before being put through shredders. Later, a dryer removes all but 2 percent of the moisture. The material then passes through an oscillator, which separates the big and small wood particles, the former becoming core material; combined with glue in a mat-forming unit, the mash is conveyed into the press, which can turn out one 8'6" × 45'1" sheet every four to five minutes. Three saws handle increment sizes up to 8 × 24 feet.

To support Chowchilla's gigantic 750-ton press, 120 yards of concrete foundation had to be poured when the plant was built.

6. Of the present Forest Industries key management, only four executives besides Hedrick were with Sequoia when it was acquired: Bertil H. Dennis, who has been sales director since 1959; T. T. Connolly, who joined Ivory Pine in 1952 as secretary-treasurer, and who has been controller of the Wickes division since 1973; Roger S. Marsh, forty-nine, the general manager of Continental Moulding, who came aboard as assistant sales manager of lumber in 1963; and David J. Johnston, operations manager of the Emmert sawmill, who started as a cut-up plant supervisor in 1966.

Bert Dennis, fifty-five years old in 1975, attended high school in Washington and Oregon, and graduated from Washington State University at Pullman in 1942 with a B.A. in business administration and accounting. After service in World War II, he held various sales and managerial positions with the lumber division of Ohio

Match Co., Spangler-Lorenz Lumber Co., and Builders Supply Co. before joining Ivory Pine.

Tom Connolly, a fifty-three-year-old Minnesotan, graduated from the St. Paul College of Accounting, and later took postgraduate work at St. Thomas College and the University of Minnesota. He was with Weyerhaeuser from 1942 to 1952 as internal auditor and office manager.

Roger Marsh, a forty-nine-year-old Oregonian, attended McMinville High School, studied prelaw and law at the University of Oregon, served in the Navy in World War II, and worked for the Willamina Lumber Co., the Riddle Manufacturing Co., and North Pacific Lumber Co. in positions that ranged from production foreman to log-purchasing agent and wholesale lumber trader. He has been general manager of Continental Moulding since November 1972, when he succeeded T. J. Hedrick.

Dave Johnston, forty-eight, is a forest management graduate of Oregon State University at Corvallis. Prior to joining Sequoia he had worked for American Forest Products and the State of California Division of Forestry.

Wickes Forest Industries' management team now includes Roy E. Ashbrook, operations manager in Dinuba (see Chapter 20, Note 13); George M. Hughes, operations manager at Chowchilla; Arthur C. Hall, manager of all Idaho operations; Jim Weeks, operations manager of the reel and wood specialties unit; Richard Schmautz, Idapines operations manager; Robert Cleveland, stud division manager; and H. O. Tipton, operations manager of the King River sawmill. At Lindsay, Don MacLean is in charge. J. R. Leach runs Lodi.

7. The original Idapine acquisition included sawmills previously owned by the Prairie Lumber Co. and Haener Planing Mills, Inc., that had been consolidated by lumberman John Casey.

8. Wickes Forest Industries operations are now composed of three sawmills each in Idaho and California (at Auberry, Clovis, and Dinuba), two "Cal Reel" plants (in Lindsay and Lodi), a cut-up plant (in Dinuba), the Sequoiaboard plant (at Chowchilla), and Continental (in Orange). Logging runs to about 40 percent pine, 50 percent white fir, and 10 percent cedar. In California practically all the timber comes off leased government lands, and in Idaho, about 85 percent.

9. For more detailed accounts of Johnson's and Hagen's careers, see Chapter 13.

Darrell Robinson was born in Eugene, Oregon, in 1927, and, after brief service as a college student in the Navy's V-5 air program in the closing days of World War II, entered the University of Oregon School of Business on a football scholarship that took him into the 1949 Cotton Bowl. In his last year he broke the pass-receiving record in the Pacific Conference, and his teammates, besides Les Hagen, included Norm Van Brocklin, later a pro quarterback and NFL coach, and John McKay, now coach at the University of Southern California. After graduation, Robinson stayed with the University of Oregon as public relations and ticket manager of the athletic department until he decided to learn the lumber business in late 1951. He started as personnel manager at the Western Division of Edward Hines at Westfir, Oregon, then moved into the sales training program in 1955. After two years as a sales representative in Dallas, Texas, he joined Oregon-Pacific in 1957, was made sales manager in 1960, and at that point hired Les Hagen. Robinson, who held the title of president of Oregon-Pacific although he and Hagen operated much like a partnership, remained in charge of the operation until mid-1974, when he left the corporation.

10. The original Evans Products was an old company that, among other things, manufactured bicycles in Michigan and made equipment for railroad freight cars

to keep loads from shifting. Decades thus passed and then Monford A. Orloff and Norton Simon made it the vehicle for an entirely different type of enterprise. Here is more or less how this happened.

Orloff, after he finished at Harvard Law School, moved to Bellingham, Washington, to start a practice. One of his clients was a worker-owned plywood mill which wasn't doing well. Orloff became interested and decided to manage it although he knew nothing about that business. That's precisely why he succeeded in turning it around: He did things that the industry said couldn't be done. Emboldened by his success, he got together a group of investors and bought a large plywood plant in Aberdeen, Washington, that had failed and was shut down. Orloff started it rolling again and called it the Aberdeen Plywood Company.

At about the same time, Norton Simon, a gentleman of far-flung interests, became familiar with Harbor Plywood Co. in Aberdeen, Washington, which owned about ten warehouses and a specialty plywood mill. In addition, Harbor had its hands on about $25 million worth of timber it had bought at a very low price and which had since appreciated. Simon found out that a controlling interest in that company could be picked up for very little money on the open market. This he did, then liquidated the timber and took a significant gain. At that point he had Harbor Plywood and didn't know quite what to do with it. So he arranged with Orloff to merge Aberdeen Plywood into Harbor Plywood, and Harbor Plywood was eventually merged into the old Evans Products, of which, a couple of years later, in, the early 1960s, Orloff became president.

By the time Johnson worked for Evans Products, the original Harbor Plywood chain of some ten warehouses had grown to nineteen, and they formed the core of the Wickes acquisition of 1975.

11. The actual price of the Sequoia Supply, Inc., warehouses purchase, aside from the carried-over receivables, was $15,559,316, of which about half was cash and the balance on a note. The financing was arranged through the Continental Illinois National Bank by David Primuth, Wickes chief financial officer (see Chapter 19).

12. But brokerage by telephone—where you never see the goods you sell—is not what Wickes is really all about. As of this book's final deadline (June 1976), a preliminary agreement has just been reached to sell Oregon-Pacific and parts of Steel City Lumber to Merrill Lynch & Co., Inc.

13. The Sequoia Supply, Inc., acquisition included one warehouse in Roodhouse, Illinois, and one under construction at Council Bluffs, Iowa. The Roodhouse facility was closed and the Council Bluffs building put up for sale.

Sequoia Inc.'s locations, including Oregon-Pacific's warehouse properties, are as follows: Birmingham, Decatur, Mobile, and Montgomery, Alabama; Phoenix, Arizona; Fairfield and San Francisco, California; Jacksonville and Orlando, Florida; Atlanta, Georgia; Mundelein (north of Chicago) and Peoria, Illinois; Indianapolis and Fort Wayne, Indiana; New Orleans, Louisiana; Minneapolis, Minnesota; Jackson, Mississippi; North Kansas City and St. Louis, Missouri; Greensboro, North Carolina; Cincinnati, Columbus, and Dayton, Ohio; Oklahoma City and Tulsa, Oklahoma; Wilsonville, Oregon; Pittsburgh, Pennsylvania; Memphis and Nashville, Tennessee; Houston and San Antonio, Texas; Tacoma, Washington; Huntington, West Virginia; and Wausau, Wisconsin.

The warehouses, totaling approximately 2,300,000 square feet of floor space, range anywhere from 32,000 square feet to over 100,000. Headquarters of the chain, as well as of Oregon-Pacific, remain at Wilsonville. The Andersen Windowall facility at Santa Ana, California, is part of Sequoia Supply.

Ernest Warns, formerly head of operations of the Evans warehouses, is general manager of Sequoia Supply. Reporting to him are three regional managers. They are Jack Walker, Birmingham, Alabama; George Thompson, Chicago; and Harold Huff, Wilsonville. Also reporting to Warns is Al Hanson, formerly administrative manager of the Evans warehouses, who retains the same position with Sequoia Supply.

Glenn A. Hart, who was operations manager for the three Oregon-Pacific warehouses, is now in charge of Wickes Wholesale and is responsible directly to Clark Johnson.

14. That's precisely why Johnson did not recommend purchase of several mills of which Evans Products was divesting itself at the same time. Being forced to act as a sales arm for these mills would have detracted from the flexibility of the Sequoia warehouses.

Chapter 18

1. Pete Willox, then still with Parker, Willox, Fairchild & Campbell, was informed in April 1972 of the anticipated move to San Diego later that year, and it was his job to prepare the public announcements—a ticklish assignment, for it was predictable that Saginaw would not take kindly to the exodus of Wickes executives (see Chapter 20). At the time, Willox thought he was "writing [his] own obituary." He reasoned that, once in San Diego, Wickes would hire a San Diego agency to run its corporate public relations.

Still, when Fitz-Gerald asked Willox to join Wickes and build a department from scratch, as it were, on the West Coast, his first reaction was, "No way." Willox was the partner in a prosperous business, had lived in the same Saginaw house for twenty-six years, raised four kids in it, and was encumbered by a lifetime collection of odds and ends and numerous dogs. But Dan always had been a great salesman, and he finally talked Pete around. Pete and his wife, Barbara, now live in a hilltop condominium up in the Mission Valley, inland from San Diego. It's interesting to note that the Midwestern grass-roots Wickes executives, like Willox, John Drum, and Tom Cline, tend to buy places inland, while the newer, less tradition-oriented crowd generally opts for La Jolla and other oceanside locations.

Peter W. Willox was born in 1917 in Saginaw, went to high school there, graduated from Bay City Junior College, and then took his degree at Northwestern University's Medill School of Journalism. He put in a stint at the *Waukegan* (Illinois) *News-Sun* and two years as editor of a weekly in Wisconsin, *The Jefferson County Union* (which earlier in its history had given birth to *Hoard's Dairyman*, the bible of the dairy industry). Willox then returned to his home town and became an advertising man with the *Saginaw News*. Equipped with the pilot's license he had obtained under the wartime Civilian Pilot Training Program, he joined the Navy as an aviator in 1942, and after some time as an instructor, was transferred to a ferry squadron of the Naval Air Transport Service based at Floyd Bennett Field, New York. As it happened, San Diego was almost regularly on his flying schedule.

In 1945, he turned down the Navy's invitation to stay on as a full lieutenant and returned to Saginaw to join Seemann & Peters, a printing and advertising firm, since defunct, that had started its existence in the late 1800s as stationers and publishers of a German-language newspaper. The advertising arm of the firm became separated a few years later and went into business as Price, Hedrick

& Tanner. Willox later bought out Hedrick, and the agency was then called Price, Tanner & Willox. Robert F. Price eventually sold out to E. A. Fairchild, making the agency Tanner, Willox & Fairchild. Martin Tanner retired before the partnership finally merged with Parker Associates and Campbell & Stark, the other two Saginaw agencies. Robert F. Price, of the original firm, had handled the U.S. Graphite account even before Willox came aboard, and this piece of business was turned over to young Pete almost immediately, as were the annual reports, starting with Wickes's first at the end of fiscal 1947.

In turn, Jack Parker, another old Saginaw hand, was sitting on the other Wickes accounts. When the Lumber Division suddenly blossomed in the mid-1950s, Parker first suggested to Fitz-Gerald that he should set up his own public relations department. At that time, Fitz-Gerald offered Parker the job, but Parker felt he could not abandon his going business. The merger of the three agencies came about some ten years later, and from that time on the newly formed firm of Parker, Willox, Fairchild & Campbell was for all practical purposes the corporate as well as the divisional public relations and advertising branch of Wickes.

This organization is still Saginaw's leading agency and still handles the advertising of several Wickes divisions, including Lumber, whose annual budget runs around $10 million.

At the San Diego office, Willox's right-hand man is Karl Dahlem, who was brought into the organization by McNeely in June 1973 from a public information director's post in New York Governor Nelson E. Rockefeller's executive department. Dahlem, whose title is associate director of corporate communications, was born in Burlington, Iowa, in 1912, attended Central Wesleyan College, and then worked as reporter and editor for weekly newspapers in Missouri for nine years. From 1941 to 1944, he was the secretary to the Governor of Missouri, then joined American Airlines, which he served as public relations director of the Boston and Chicago regions and finally of the corporation. He was named vice president of American Airlines in 1965, and was recruited by Rockefeller forces in 1971. Dahlem is a member of the Public Relations Society of America, the Overseas Press Club, the Wings Club of New York, and the Public Relations Club of San Diego.

2. In order of their openings, the Wickes furniture warehouse-showrooms so far in operation are: Minneapolis, Minnesota (Fridley), July 1971; Cincinnati, Ohio (Sharonville), and St. Louis, Missouri (Maryland Heights), September 1971; Chicago, Illinois (Itasca and Harvey), and Milwaukee, Wisconsin (West Allis), November 1971; San Diego, California (El Cajon), May 1972; Los Angeles, California (Anaheim), Chicago, Illinois (Wheeling), and Detroit, Michigan (Warren), June 1972; Norfolk, Virginia (Virginia Beach), July 1972; Pittsburgh, Pennsylvania (Coraopolis), September 1972; Minneapolis, Minnesota (Edina), October 1972; Rochester, New York (Henrietta), November 1972; Chicago, Illinois (Willowbrook), and Los Angeles, California (West Covina and Woodland Hills), February 1973; Charlotte, North Carolina, May 1973; Pittsburgh, Pennsylvania (Monroeville), October 1973; Detroit, Michigan (Livonia), November 1973; Detroit, Michigan (Riverview), and Chicago (Woodfield Mall in Schaumburg), January 1974; and Merrillville, Indiana, March 1974.

The store in Schaumburg is serviced by the warehouse of the Itasca, Illinois, complex.

3. Among Wickes Furniture's major suppliers are many of the best-known firms in their lines: Thomasville, American of Martinsville, Broyhill, Burlington House,

Bassett, U.S. Bedding, Simmons, Kingsley, Berkline, Howard, Shannon, Montclair, Singer, and, on the West Coast, L. A. Period and Gillespie. Case goods are usually purchased on a national basis. Bedroom, dining, occasional, and upholstered furniture is merchandised regionally to satisfy varying regional tastes.

4. The Levitz warehouse-showroom in Tucson, however, never was part of the Levitz chain. Sam Levitz, one of the three Levitz brothers, had moved to Arizona from their native Pennsylvania for reasons of health, and had opened a conventional furniture store in Tucson. The store did not do too well, so the other two brothers, Ralph and Leon, went down to help out. They arranged for a discount sale out of Sam's warehouse and were so impressed by this strategem's success that a few years later, in 1963, they launched warehouse-showrooms in Allentown, Pennsylvania, and in Phoenix, the first two of the sixty in operation at the time of this writing. The chain's administrative offices are in Pottstown, Pennsylvania. Executive headquarters are located in Miami.

5. Eugene N. Gordon was born in Memphis, Tennessee, in 1926, grew up in Chicago, and while in high school got a menial job at the University of Chicago's Alonzo Stagg Field piling lead bricks around a little building, and when this job was done, he delivered bottles of distilled water to people whose tags bore strange names like Oppenheimer and Fermi. As circumstance would have it, this was the same atomic laboratory for which U.S. Graphite was providing shielding materials at the time. Gordon didn't hear of the atomic bomb until years later, and of U.S. Graphite even later than that. Meanwhile, he was fortunate to graduate from high school at seventeen, because that way he managed to put in some time at Northwestern University before being drafted into the Army, and upon his discharge was immediately able to resume his schooling while other veterans had to wait for their turn, sometimes as long as a year, to get into institutions overcrowded by the GI Bill.

Gordon studied business administration and liberal arts, and right after graduation went to work for Montgomery Ward as assistant buyer for juvenile furniture. So far as he was concerned, the major advantage of that job was that at parties he attended as a young bachelor, he ended up talking cribs and carriages with the girls while the guys talked baseball in the other corner. From there he moved into bedding, and ended up as a buyer of "dual sleep." That, however, has no romantic connotation. It means convertibles. Running this department, he was instrumental in developing a vibrating recliner with a heating pad in the back produced by Berkline Manufacturing. Ward's sold 35,000 of them in the first year they were out. It was during this period that Gordon first met McNeely, who was at that point still assistant buyer in Ward's furniture division.

After nine years, in 1959, Gordon left Ward's to work briefly in semipartnership with a furniture designer in Chicago and then rejoined Ward's to put together its Salem Square program, an early-American promotion that involved coordination of case goods, drapery, carpeting, accessories, etc. As a division-straddling effort, Salem Square became a project in its own right and Gordon remained in charge of it for two years. He then joined Sidney Ladin & Associates, an independent manufacturer's representative headquartered in Houston, and eventually became vice president of marketing and sales of Sprague & Carleton in Keene, New Hampshire, in which Ladin had a substantial interest. That's where Gordon learned about furniture manufacturing. He was recruited by McNeely into Wickes in 1965 as manager of the Midwestern region of Wickes Lumber, and was soon thereafter named division vice president of marketing.

6. Under a plan developed by John Drum, roughly 25 percent of the Wickes Furniture advertising budget goes for image advertising, about 40 percent for assortment broadsides, and the rest for impact, usually in newspapers.

7. Robert Weinstein left Wickes in 1972 to buy into Bauman Weitz, a manufacturer of occasional furniture and case goods in Sylmar, California. In 1975 that firm was acquired by the Rowe Furniture Corp., of which Weinstein is now vice president.

8. Wickes Furniture's volume was $12.7 million in fiscal 1972, the first year of its operation. By 1973, it had jumped to $52.9 million. For fiscal 1974 and fiscal 1975, the figures were $82.7 million and $91.4 million respectively.

9. Paul H. Tatz studied law at Drake University in his native Des Moines, and was admitted to the Iowa bar in 1962 after service in Korea. Since the best employment offer he had at that moment was as a $400-a-month assistant attorney general for the state of Iowa, he figured that for that kind of money, he could starve on his own, and hung out a shingle. His law partnership, later merged into the larger Des Moines firm of Williams and Hart, engaged in a good deal of securities work, i.e., stock offerings, debentures, Securities and Exchange Commission problems, etc. In 1968, he accepted a political appointment to work for the Iowa State Highway Commission on bridge and bond financing, and then decided to try to get into corporate law. Through the American Bar Association, he was introduced to Inland Steel of Chicago, which gave him the opportunity during his training to become acquainted with the Kepner-Tregoe system of "rational management" that later greatly influenced his approach to Wickes Furniture.

Tatz's first position with Wickes, after he joined the corporation in Saginaw in 1970, was that of a general attorney in the law department under Tom Cline. During this early period he was primarily involved in changing the company's domicile of incorporation from Michigan to Delaware. After the shareholders' approval at the 1971 annual meeting, this change became effective at the end of fiscal 1972, giving Wickes greater flexibility in its acquisition program.

Under Michigan regulations (since changed) it had been impossible to acquire a small company and merge it directly into Wickes unless two-thirds of the corporation's shareholders voted for it. It had thus been necessary to create tiers of subsidiaries, a situation that caused nothing but administrative headaches, among them filing individual state tax returns for all of them—and that meant every state they were incorporated in. At one point, Wickes was obliged to prepare more than 1,500 tax returns for its subsidiaries, an average of between three and four a day for every working day of the year.

Another important consideration in switching to Delaware was that its laws permitted board meetings by conference telephone, a useful tool in a company that moves as fast as Wickes. (The Michigan law, finally recognizing Alexander Graham Bell, has since been changed also in this respect.)

Largely as a result of this work, Tatz came to the attention of the right people at Wickes. He was elected secretary of the corporation in March 1971, and general counsel and vice president in November of that year. In July 1972 he was named senior vice president while still in charge of the law and tax departments, and in March 1973 succeeded Ron Woods as head of the Office of the President. At that point, the Office of the President was in charge of the legal department, planning and marketing, acquisitions, and Wickes Europe. Tatz then served briefly as chief personnel officer until his appointment to Wickes Furniture.

The Office of the President has since been at least temporarily abandoned; the tax department was spun off the legal department into the financial group under Dave Primuth (see Chapter 19); and Wickes Europe now reports directly to Wickes President John Drum.

10. Other Wickes Furniture officers are Eugene Davis, vice president of operations, who was recruited from Gamble Skogmo in the fall of 1974; Robert Thele, vice president of administration and the division's chief financial officer (see Chapter 20); and G. J. Yager, vice president of personnel, B. L. ("Lou") Blair, Furniture's former vice president of administration, is now at Yorktowne.

Chapter 19

1. The fact that the stock went up so much during and after the offering was especially surprising since the originally announced intention had been to issue only 1 million shares. This was then upped to 1.2 million, and should have increased the dilution effect. It turned out to be the sixteenth largest common stock offering in the United States in ten years.

   Had Nixon not imposed Phase 1, Wickes would probably·have made a similar offering fairly soon anyway. The history of the corporation indicated that the Wickes multiple was at a comfortable level somewhere around 15 to 16 times earnings. But with the PE at twenty-four, Primuth saw little prospect of improving it. The downside risk was great in any case.

2. Bill Boyle is anything but hard-boiled. Warm and charming, he gives the lie to the public's image of what money men are like. He was born in 1934 in a small Pennsylvania town on the fringe of the Poconos, was raised in Jersey City, and took his degree in economics at St. Peter's College there. Two years in Army Intelligence at an unbeatable peacetime billet followed: he was stationed in Verona, Italy. Then Bill joined Dun & Bradstreet in New York City as a credit reporter, and a year later, in 1959, he went to work in the treasury department of Remington Rand. From 1962 to 1968, he was manager of the banking and financing department of American Tobacco (now American Brands) in New York, and during that period, attended night school at Rutgers University to obtain his M.B.A. His next step up was as consultant to the treasurer of General Electric, a position he held for a year before moving to Los Angeles as assistant treasurer of Occidental Petroleum Corp. He was wooed into Wickes in November of 1972 as treasurer, and elected vice president six months later.

3. Arthur E. Kirchheimer, born in 1931 in New York City, graduated from Bayside High School on Long Island and earned his law degree at Syracuse University. Eighteen years of private law practice in that city followed, the last two of which he also served as counsel of the Norwich Pharmacal Company, of Norwich, New York, Kirchheimer joined Wickes as a senior attorney in June 1972, became director of the corporation's law department that November, and simultaneously served as assistant secretary of the corporation. He was elected general counsel in August 1973 and vice president in April 1974. He is a member of the state bars of New York and California, and has been admitted to practice before the U.S. Supreme Court.

4. The three foreign banks involved are the Algemene Bank Nederland N.V., of Amsterdam; Williams & Glyn's Bank, Ltd., of London; and the Bank of Nova Scotia. Warburg Paribas Becker, Inc., assisted in the arrangement of the agreements. Negotiations had also been conducted with the Banque de Bruxelles, the Dresdner Bank and Kreditbank of Germany, and Barclays Bank of London.

In connection with this financing effort, and to update the European financial community in general on the Wickes story, McNeely and Primuth held a series of luncheons in June 1974 in Zurich, London, Paris, Frankfurt, and Brussels, which were mostly arranged by the European offices of Merrill Lynch.

5. The Boyle plan for the private placement of preferred stock was kept in abeyance, and it is still pending. The furniture stores were sold and leased as scheduled, and the Eurodollar financing and the domestic $50 million revolving credit agreements were arranged the same year. The senior debenture issue was delayed, as was the lease-back of the planned factory in the Midwest—the additional productive capacity was not needed at that time. The repositioning of the bank credit lines presented no undue problems; the debenture exchange was accomplished, and it added $28 million to the corporation's coffers, half as debt reduction, half as gain.

   Such an exchange offer involves a tremendous amount of legal preparation, which in this case was handled by Wickes's in-house authority on SEC matters, Navarre T. Perry.

6. How Dave Primuth managed the transition from public accouting (with Leo G. Lauzen & Company in Aurora, Illinois) to an officer's post in industry makes an interesting story in itself. During his college years, he had come to admire Frank Kaple, a successful businessman who was donating his time to Wheaton in his semiretirement years to teach a few courses. The admiration was mutual and Kaple and Primuth became friends, as often happens between charismatic mentors and their promising students. Kaple first gave Primuth a leg up at the accounting firm by persuading fellow directors at Mid-America Water Refining to make that Chicago company a Primuth client, but seeing the young man's eagerness to get into decision making, he advised him to take the seemingly humdrum job of business secretary of the local YMCA in Racine, Wisconsin, on a six-month contract.

   The Y was just moving into a new $3.5 million facility, and it was Primuth's responsibility not only to handle the fund drive but to set up new systems for accounting that would for the first time include food services, a full-time YMCA program, and dormitories. Kaple guessed correctly that Primuth's performance would impress a whole lot of important people. Dave had four offers to go with local companies and decided on Foundry Allied, a diversified company that did a lot of international business and whose treasury was therefore deeply involved in international finance, dealing with such organizations as Ford Motor Company, Chrysler International, and GM Overseas Corp.—experiences that would eventually accrue to Wickes's credit.

   As for Fitz-Gerald's courtship of Primuth, that's not too surprising. Apart from ever-reliable George Valentine, who was, moreover, used to the Wickes ways, the corporation hadn't been satisfied with its choices in the financial area, and Primuth was the fourth controller to be hired in a twelve-month period. This clutched him a little at the beginning, but it needn't have. Three months after his arrival, he was promoted to senior vice president of finance.

7. At Sears, about 45 percent of net earnings derive from Sears Credit Corp. and Allstate. J. C. Penney runs at around 25 percent. At Ward's, it's about 15 percent. In all cases, the percentage was growing in 1974, and seems to continue to do so.

8. In 1974, Wickes was thirty-second in terms of volume, and twenty-fourth in earnings, on *Fortune*'s list of fifty top retailers.

9. At this point, only about 5 percent of the Lumber Division's sales to individual customers are on installments. Of course, individual purchases are much

smaller. Even so, the ratio of time payments is going up. Contractor-builders are on a thirty-day cycle.

10. Richard H. ("Rick") Chambers, a third-generation Californian, was born in Whittier in 1935. He graduated from University High School in West Los Angeles and earned his bachelor's in business administration at the University of Southern California. From 1958 to 1967, he served as credit manager of Gulf Oil Corp. in Los Angeles. He then joined Powerine Oil Co. of Santa Fe Springs, California, in a similar capacity, and the following year became corporate credit manager of Occidental Petroleum, Los Angeles. He came to Wickes in March 1973 as credit and finance manager, reporting to William W. Boyle. He was appointed vice president and general manager of Wickes Credit in late 1974.

11. Ralph E. Pfaff, a native of Rochester, New York, did his undergraduate work in physics at Wheaton College (several years before Primuth) and received his M.B.A. from the University of Chicago in 1966. While earning the advanced degree as a part-time student, he first worked as administrative assistant to the vice president of engineering at Seeburg Corp., Chicago, and later as systems engineer for IBM in Evanston, Illinois.

12. Richard J. Ainslie, then thirty-eight, was recruited by Wickes in December 1974. Prior to that time, he had been corporate tax manager of Rohr Industries, and had held supervisory and management posts in the tax departments of several other U.S. manufacturing companies. He is a graduate of Seattle University and holds an M.B.A. from the City College of New York.

13. Nasso was born in 1938, attended public schools in New York City, majored in accounting at New York University, and took his law degree from Brooklyn Law School. While attending night classes at New York University in order to earn his master's degree in taxation law, he worked in the tax departments of several CPA firms, including Arthur Andersen & Company. He dropped his studies in 1968 when the chance came up to go with Chrysler Corporation in Detroit as manager of its international tax department. Doing tax work exclusively soon began to bore him, and although the first job he took at Wickes was in the same field, it was obvious to him that time would fix that. Six months later, it did.

14. If it hadn't been for his older brother, Ed Edelstein would not be the successful man he is today. On his release from the Air Corps in 1945 after three years as a fighter pilot, he really didn't have much on his mind except flying, and he joined his brother Milton, who was in the life insurance business in Chicago, mainly because it was a convenient thing to do. His brother had acted very much as a parent to Ed since their father died, and finally got him to attend Northwestern University at night. They remained general agents for Connecticut Mutual and other companies for a number of years and then founded a life insurance company of their own, which they called the Funded Security Corporation. This firm was based on the then still novel concept of binding life insurance and mutual funds into a single sale. Even at this date no one has been successful with this combination. The Edelsteins weren't either. Overexpanded, they were in trouble when the stock market suffered its severe setback in 1962. It was then that they went into credit insurance—life, accident, and health insurance that covers the payments of installment debtors. In 1969, together with Fred Wollock, they organized Ram Life.

15. Transamerica Corp. performs a variety of services for Wickes. Among them is the profitable job of moving Wickes executives from assignment to assignment. Example: In less than two years, senior vice president Tom Cline was transferred

from Saginaw to San Diego, shipped back to Saginaw, and then sent to San Diego once again. Realtors also benefit from this wives' nightmare: in that period, Tom sold and bought three houses.

Chapter 20

1. E. L. McNeely, who is Scotch-Irish and therefore not of the true green, used to have a lot of fun with Fitz-Gerald's Irish predilections. There was the time when the two men, accompanied by George O'Dair, then executive vice president, visited Goldman, Sachs in New York about some equity offering. McNeely walked up to the receptionist and said, "I'm McNeely, and they're Fitz-Gerald and O'Dair, and we've come to get money for the church." The young lady was flustered at first, then caught on and broke up. She laughed so hard that she could hardly make herself understood when she announced their arrival on the intercom.

2. At the same directors meeting on May 22, 1975, Walt Behlen retired from the board, and C. E. Hartnack did not stand for reelection because of the press of business at the Security Pacific National Bank, where he is president. Newly elected to the board were Preston Martin, president and chief executive officer of P.M.I. Mortgage Insurance Co., San Francisco; and Ray A. Watt, chairman and chief executive officer of Watt Industries, Santa Monica.

3. To start with, in the autumn of 1973, it was just "that stupid leg" which gave Fitz-Gerald trouble. Not until he couldn't cut it on the golf course one afternoon because of the pain did he seek help, and then the doctors didn't catch on immediately that it was phlebitis, but had him come in to have a spinal disk removed. The leg improved, then got worse again, and all the time he felt a lump growing in his left cheek but preferred not to think about it. In early 1974, his leg got so bad that he went to a physician-friend in Boca Raton, Florida, where Dan spent his winters. This doctor, formerly associated with Henry Ford Hospital in Detroit, was something of an authority on cancer. He saw Dan's face and instantly bundled him off to St. Joseph's Hospital in Houston. But before the growth could be operated on, further complications developed.

   Diagnostic tests showed that Dan had been living on borrowed time for quite a while. Both his carotid arteries were clogged, and a stroke might kill him at any moment. To fix that was even more urgent than removal of the malignancy. The right carotid was reamed out the very next morning. As soon as he'd recovered from the operation, he returned to the hospital (at the time of the billion-dollar dinner of Chapter 1), and that's when most of the cancer was removed and the artery next to it cleaned out. This radical operation severed nerves that controlled movement on the left side of his face.

   Apart from the shock of knowing that he was potentially a goner, the surgery must have been a tremendous blow to his ego, for Dan had always been a good-looking man and extremely proud of his appearance. After an initial period of depression, however, he pulled out of it with remarkable vigor. He made no attempt to hide his disfigured face, and was as roguishly if paternally flirtatious as ever with the ladies he chanced to meet.

   From then on Dan Fitz-Gerald commuted, depending on the time of year, between Saginaw, Boca Raton, and Houston, as the physicians of St. Joseph's tried in vain to eradicate with chemotherapy and cobalt radiation the cancer cells that had invaded his lymphatic system.

4. The new Wickes Building at the corner of Saginaw's Washington Avenue and Carroll Street, on the original Wickes companies' acreage, adjoins the old Wickes Building and the corporation's Machine Tool Division. Four stories of the new building rose in 1962. James A. Spence, of Saginaw, was the architect, and Calvin Smith, also of Saginaw, the designer, of the $850,000 structure, whose east and west walls are a combination of glass, white baked enamel insulated panels, and aluminum framing. The south facade is covered with natural green Vermont slate. As the corporation grew, three floors were added later. The general contractor was Spence Brothers. Other prime contractors were Hugh Laundra Electric, Inc; John E. Green Plumbing & Heating Co. of Saginaw; and the Otis Elevator Co.

5. Deloris Menthen, who had been born and raised in Saginaw, came to work for Wickes in the fall of 1942, just a few months after Dan Fitz-Gerald. For the first four years, however, she had nothing to do with him: she was assigned to the traffic department.

   On a tape of personal memoirs recorded by Dan Fitz-Gerald for this book shortly before his death, he had this to say about Deloris:

   > She saved me from many, many mistakes. When she first came with me, she didn't know how to make up a tax return. I take pride in the fact that she is pretty competent at it today. I think the relationship—well, I like to feel it was mutually advantageous. The one thing I always had at my side was my gal Friday. Nobody was permitted to say anything about me. I am sure there were times when she didn't like me very much at all. I was probably impatient. I was thoughtless. I didn't give proper consideration to her, but I think as I've become more mellow, why, I began to realize that she should be classified as my office wife. Nothing gets by her ears that's derogatory about Fitz-Gerald. She's absolutely loyal—and by loyal, I mean loyal to me!

   Deloris Menthen still sits at her old desk. She is now secretary to Bob Dodge, who, as the corporation's most senior officer in the Saginaw executive suite, occupies Dan Fitz-Gerald's former office.

6. William A. Hensler was born in Saginaw in 1929. He went to Bay City Junior College and later to the Ferris Institute (now Ferris State College) in Big Rapids, Michigan, where he earned his degree in business administration with a major in accounting. After working for Chevrolet, he joined Wickes in July 1960. He served in various corporate auditing and controller functions until 1964, when he went to the Lumber Division as supervisor of merchandising accounting. Four years later, he was named controller of the division, and since February 1974 has been its vice president of administration.

7. Tom Cline is now stationed in San Diego (see Note 20 of Chapter 19), but by the time he was permanently transferred, Fitz-Gerald had been taken ill and spent very little time in Saginaw.

8. When the corporation's headquarters removed from Saginaw to San Diego, Wickes employed approximately 1,500 persons in the Saginaw area. The local payroll was $17 million, about the same as the total sales volume of the corporation had been in 1950.

   In late 1975, the number of Wickes employees in Saginaw was around 1,000 after some cutbacks because of the general economic conditions. And, although corporate headquarters had moved to San Diego, there were almost as many corporate people in Saginaw as in that California city: seventy-five in Saginaw, ninety-nine in San Diego. Another eighty-one corporate staffers were located in Wheeling, Illinois.

Other head-count figures as of March 1975 were: Wickes Lumber (total) 4,446; Behlen Manufacturing, 1,324; Wickes Furniture, 927; Wickes Forest Industries, 878; Wickes Homes, 860; Yorktowne, 783; Wickes Buildings, 584; Wickes Engineered Materials, 511; Wickes Financial Services, 402; Wickes Agriculture—Michigan, 374; Lee L. Woodard Sons, 284; Wickes Europe, 227; Oregon-Pacific, 209; Wickes Machine Tool, 123; Kux Machine, 106; Saginaw Machine and Tool, 96; Wickes Agriculture—West, 29, the employment figures totaled 12,418 (including corporate staff), a reduction of some 2,500 since March 1974.

Staff cuts are rare at Wickes, but other budget conservation methods are constantly in progress. Here we have room to cite only a couple of examples.

Before Dick Cotton, now corporate sales manager, was assigned to co-manage Project Twenty-first Century together with Vice President and former Controller Dick Fruechtenicht, his responsibilities as corporate senior vice president of operations included sales (including intracompany sales), marketing, and corporate purchasing. In this position, he didn't boss the respective divisional vice presidents, but worked with them whenever a problem arose, or where he could see the possibility of greater efficiencies.

Take adhesives, a material purchased by many of the Wickes divisions for their own manufacturing uses or for resale. Customarily, adhesives had been bought by the divisions individually. To Drum, this didn't make sense. Why not take advantage of the total purchasing power of the corporation? So Cotton was assigned to see how this might be handled. He went to the three top adhesive companies, told them all about Wickes, and asked if they were interested in the Wickes business. Then he invited their representatives to San Diego to make presentations. The H. B. Fuller Co., of St. Paul, Minnesota, walked off with the business. This little effort saves Wickes more than $120,000 a year—a plus that translates directly to the pretax bottom line.

Economies could also be effected by means of intracompany sales. Although goods as such cannot be sold within an organization at lower prices than those charged to outside customers, there was nothing to stop the corporation from having divisions share the use of their equipment. T. J. Hedrick noted that the trucks of his Wickes Forest Industries fleet would frequently run down to Los Angeles with loads of particleboard, say, and then drive back empty. Meanwhile, the Lumber Division was hiring a private carrier to pick up merchandise at a San Pedro dock and haul it to various California building supply centers. It was evident to Hedrick that this was a waste of money. With Cotton's help, a coordinating unit was established at Wickes Forest Industries headquarters in Dinuba, California, to match up all truck hauls in the state.

9. In Saginaw, it was a big month when a half-dozen applicants for high-level positions showed up. In San Diego, McNeely gets as many as fifteen or twenty executive candidates a week.

As for himself, McNeely was somewhat reluctant to leave Michigan, where he owned a highly unusual and "extremely livable" house at 1445 West Delta Drive. It had been built by an architect, Dan Toshach, a pupil of Alden Dow, for himself. Toshach had sold it after a divorce, and McNeely happened to be there at the right time. Not only was the house very modern, with most of the furniture built in, but it had a large yard on the site of a long-since demolished brewery whose excavation had left the ground bumpy, almost hilly, a rarity in that part of

Michigan. McNeely found it a great place to bring up his children. One thing that the Toshach house didn't have was a panorama of the Pacific Ocean, and McNeely has that now. His new place sits against the side of a ridge between La Jolla and Mission Bay, with a sweeping view over both. McNeely walked into that deal, too. He bought it from a bank that had taken it over when the original owner, a broker, went broke. The house is still wired for ticker tape.

The airline statistics cited in the text are based on the May 1975 arrival and departure schedules of the airports serving Saginaw and San Diego.

10. Douglas E. Hofeldt, born in 1945, graduated from Coleridge (Nebraska) High School in 1963 and from the University of Nebraska in 1967. With his degree in accounting and finance, he went to work as tax auditor for the State of Nebraska in Lincoln, and remained there until 1969 when he joined Behlen as a management trainee. After three years in the tax and cost accounting department, he was named manager of accounting in 1972. He was promoted to the post of controller in May 1975.

11. Richard D. Passaglia, born in Chicago in 1939, graduated from De Paul University as a bachelor of science in 1962 and then attended the University of Chicago Graduate School of Business. After five years as a buyer for Montgomery Ward & Co., he joined Wickes Lumber in 1967 as a senior buyer, was promoted to merchandise manager of commodity products the following year, and to regional manager in 1972. He has been vice president of merchandising since December 1974.

12. Robert B. Thele, born in 1940, is a native of Montgomery, Alabama. He went to high school in Richfield, Utah, and then attended first the College of Southern Utah and later Utah State University, where he graduated with an industrial management degree in June 1963. After a variety of jobs in California with, successively, the Metropolitan Life Insurance Company, Moore Business Forms, and Montgomery Ward, he joined Wickes Furniture in 1972 as general sales and display manager in training. He was named the division's administrative vice president and controller in 1975.

13. Roy E. Ashbrook came up fast, even though his education was interrupted by a two-year service in Viet Nam. He was born in Riverside, California, in 1940, attended the local high school, then took his B.S. at Humboldt State at Arcata, California, and earned his M.B.A. at the University of Oregon in 1969. He joined Wickes Forest Industries that June, and has been the Dinuba operations manager since January 1973.

14. Fred Arthur ("Art") Simmons was born in 1943 at Herrin, Illinois, attended high school there, and graduated from the University of Missouri at Rolla in 1966 with a degree in mechanical engineering. Before joining Wickes in 1968, he was an engineer with the Saginaw Steering Gear Division of General Motors Corporation. Simmons was named general manager of Saginaw Machine and Tool in October 1974.

15. Jonathan ("Jon") Fish was born in Brooklyn, New York, in 1944, and, amazingly enough, got his start as a financial man by being treasurer of various extracurricular organizations at Middlebury College, Vermont, where he studied European and African history. At one time he held four different treasurerships, including those of the school's winter carnival, his fraternity, and the Mountain Climbing and Ski Clubs. In the process, he became so intrigued by figures that he went on to Harvard Business School, and after a stint in the Navy, mostly as chief engineer on a cargo ship in Viet Nam, decided he wanted to join a firm that was active in the shelter industry. At that time Wickes had just gone into manufac-

tured housing (see Chapter 16), and Fish applied for a job. Dick Cotton, then senior vice president of personnel, put him into a new and since-discontinued training program for M.B.A.'s in June 1972, and after two months, Fish was offered a position as corporate financial analyst for the Lumber and Furniture Divisions, Oregon-Pacific Industries, and Wickes Europe. In 1973, he was named director of corporate financial planning and analysis, and in 1975 assigned as controller to Wickes Homes.

16. The highest average monthly sales volume for the ten stores combined in the preceding six months had been $270,000. In the belief that the consumer sales were there, a goal of $1 million in sales was set for the two weeks of the "grand openings." This proved to be conservative. The final total was $1.25 million.

Appendix A

Officers and Directors
(From October 3, 1947)

Chairman of the Board

H. Randall Wickes	1947–1953
	1965–1969
Daniel M. Fitz-Gerald	1969–1975
E. L. McNeely	1975–

President

H. Randall Wickes	1947–1964
Daniel M. Fitz-Gerald	1964–1969
E. L. McNeely	1969–1975
John V. Drum	1975-

Chief Executive Officer

Daniel M. Fitz-Gerald	1964–1971
E. L. McNeely	1971–

Chief Operating Officer

E. L. McNeely	1969–1971
John V. Drum	1975–

Executive Vice President

Daniel M. Fitz-Gerald	1956-1964
John V. Drum	1971-1975
George W. O'Dair	1971-1974
David J. Primuth	1975-

Senior Vice President

Smith Bolton	1965-1966
George A. Kendall	1965-1972
E. L. McNeely	1965-1969
Melvin J. Zahnow	1965-1967
George W. Kelch	1966-1972
George C. Deecken	1968-1970
Thomas W. Cline	1969-
Richard G. Cotton	1969-
John V. Drum	1969-1971
Douglas P. Crane	1970-1972
Eugene N. Gordon	1970-1974
Clark A. Johnson	1971-
Grant B. Potter	1971-October 24, 1972*
David J. Primuth	1971-1975
Ronald J. Woods	1971-
Robert G. Dodge	1972-
Laurence E. Mullen	1972-1973
Paul H. Tatz	1972-1975
Ralph J. Zemanek	1974-
Leslie L. Hagen	1975-
T. J. Hedrick	1976-

Vice President

Carl Bintz	1947-1955
Smith Bolton	1947-1955
	1962-1964
William E. Stone	1947-February 7, 1959*
Robert J. Stormont	1947-1954
Robert E. Wolohan	1950-1955
	1962-1963
Richard V. Wolohan	1952-1955
Melvin J. Zahnow	1961-1965
	1967-1968
George A. Kendall	1963-1965
B. Louis Blair	1965-1968
Robert G. Dodge	1965-1972
E. P. Garwood	1965-1966
George W. Kelch	1965-1966
J. A. Oeming	1965-1968
Arthur E. Pufford	1965-1972

*Date of death.

Thomas E. Rulison	1965–1968
Wade H. Stephens, Jr.	1965–1968
Ralph J. Zemanek	1965–1968
	1973–1974
Richard G. Cotton	1966–1969
John V. Drum	1966–1969
Eugene N. Gordon	1966–1970
Robert A. Heym	1966–1968
Douglas P. Crane	1969–1970
John B. Weium	1969–1970
Ronald J. Woods	1970–1971
David J. Primuth	1971
Paul H. Tatz	1971–1972
Thomas J. Hedrick	1972–
Peter W. Willox	1972–
Leigh R. Bench	1973–1976
William W. Boyle	1973–
Robert J. Jacobs	1973–
Harold E. Joiner	1973–
Clemens O. Putz	1973–1975
Larry J. Ritzenthaler	1973
Darrell L. Robinson	1973–1974
Mark W. Schiedinger	1973
Robert E. Stump	1973
Richard W. Fruechtenicht	1974–
Arthur E. Kirchheimer	1974–
Arthur J. Nasso	1974–1976
Roland R. Pretzer	1974–
Richard L. Barker	1975–
John H. Hekman	1975–
Paul W. Hylbert, Jr.	1975–
Ralph E. Pfaff	1975–
Anthony J. Swies	1975–
E. F. Warns	1976–

Secretary

Melvin J. Zahnow	1947–1961
Thomas W. Cline	1961–1969
Homer R. Sessions	1969–1970
Paul H. Tatz	1971–1974
Thomas W. Cline	1975–

Treasurer

Charles G. Morrell	1947–1948
Daniel M. Fitz-Gerald	1949–1956
Melvin J. Zahnow	1956–1961
Arthur E. Pufford	1961–1965
Homer R. Sessions	1965–1972
William W. Boyle	1972–

General Counsel

Thomas W. Cline	1965–1971
Paul H. Tatz	1971–1973
Arthur E. Kirchheimer	1973–

Comptroller

| Daniel M. Fitz-Gerald | 1947–1948 |

Controller

John B. Weium	1969–1970
David J. Primuth	1971
George G. Valentine	1971–1973
Mark W. Schiedinger	1973
Richard W. Fruechtenicht	1974–1975
Richard L. Barker	1975–

General Controller

| Arthur E. Pufford | 1958–1961 |
| George G. Valentine | 1961–1969 |

Divisional Presidents and General Managers

Wickes Boiler Co.
| Donald H. Barnes | 1956–1960 |
| George A. Kendall | 1961–1963 |
Wickes Machine Tool Division
| Carl Bintz | 1956–1957 |
| George A. Kendall | 1958–1963 |
The United States Graphite Company
| Smith Bolton | 1956–1961 |
Michigan Bean Company
| Albert L. Riedel | 1956–1961 |
Wickes Export–Import Division
| Cornelis van Bergeijk | 1956–1960 |
Wickes International N. V.
| Cornelis van Bergeijk | 1960–1961 |
Charles Wolohan Incorporated
| Richard V. Wolohan | 1956–1958 |
Wickes Lumber Co.
| Richard V. Wolohan | 1958–1961 |
Saginaw Grain Co.
| Robert E. Wolohan | 1956–1961 |

Former Directors

Carl Bintz	October 1947–October 1956
Smith Bolton	October 1947–October 1956
	August 1962–June 1972

Daniel M. Fitz-Gerald	October 1947–July 24, 1975*
Frank B. Godard	October 1947–October 1956
Walter J. Harris	October 1947–October 1948
Charles G. Morrell	October 1947–June 1950
William E. Stone	October 1947–February 7, 1959*
Robert J. Stormont	October 1947–October 1954
H. Randall Wickes	October 1947–May 1970
Melvin J. Zahnow	October 1947–May 1969
Elbert G. Rounds	December 1947–May 1967
Herbert F. Russell	December 1947–October 1961
Richard V. Wolohan	June 1950–October 1956
Robert E. Wolohan	June 1950–October 1956
	August 1962–October 1964
James M. Shackleton	October 1952–June 4, 1968*
R. Dewey Stearns	October 1961–April 17, 1970*
John W. Symons, Jr.	October 1961–June 1966
Robert H. Blanford	August 1963–May 1967
George A. Kendall	August 1963–January 1972
Thomas W. Cline	July 1964–June 1972
Robert P. Gerholz	June 1966–June 1972
Howard J. Stoddard	June 1966–June 15, 1971*
George W. Kelch	August 1966–January 1972
George C. Deecken	August 1968–June 1970
Walter D. Behlen	May 1969–May 1975
Samuel D. Marble	April 1970–June 1973
Kemmons Wilson	March 1971–June 1972
George W. O'Dair	August 1971–November 1974
Carl E. Hartnack	June 1973–May 1975

Current Directors

Thomas W. Cline	January 1975–
John V. Drum	August 1971–
Thomas C. Harvey	August 1963–
E. L. McNeely	June 1966–
Preston Martin	May 1975–
David J. Primuth	August 1975–
John A. Ritzenthaler	March 1972–
Paul C. Souder	March 1972–
Ray A. Watt	May 1975–

*Date of death.

Appendix B

Index

The
Wide World
of Wickes

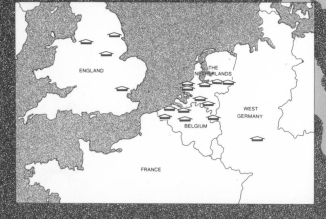